Riding Two Horses
Labour in Europe

Glyn Ford

SPOKESMAN

Typeset using Industria for headings and Utopia for body to a design by Cicely Spence.

Industria is designed by Neville Brody, who also created the anti-racist logo used for SOS Racism (featured on the cover of the Socialist Group's *Against Racism and Fascism in Europe* booklet), of which a homage is used as the icon for chapter 8 of this book.

Published in 2022 by
Spokesman
5 Churchill Park, Nottingham, NG4 2HF, England
spokesmanbooks.org
Spokesman is the publishing imprint of the
Bertrand Russell Peace Foundation Ltd.

A catalogue record is available from the British Library.

Printed and bound in Britain.

ISBN 978 0 85124 907 0

To Wendy Elizabeth†, ultimately responsible for the cast in order of appearance Elise, Dando, Ida and Eme.

Contents

A comment on nomenclature . . . . *v*
A note on Asian names . . . . *v*
Abbreviations . . . . *vi*
Acknowledgements . . . . *xi*
Preface . . . . *xiii*

1 Capture 16

2 From Gloucester to Reading 45

3 Tameside to Tokyo 75

4 European Parliamentary Labour Party . . . 103

5 Ranging Asia 153

6 Science Politics 189

7 Hard Power, Soft Power and Trade 216

8 Racism and Fascism 255

9 Vignettes and Curiosities 303

10 Turbulent Resolution? 342

Appendix *380*
Select bibliography *381*
Index *385*

A comment on nomenclature

With regards to capitalisation, when written as a single word, Parliament with a capital P refers to Westminster, and parliament with a lowercase p refers to the European Parliament. Certain entities are referred to by different names, colloquially, geographically, and historically. As a matter of reference, please use this as a guide.

The European Union through its evolution has gone through various name changes. First the European Economic Community (1957-1993), then the European Community (1993-2009), and since the ratification in 2009 of the Lisbon Treaty, it has been the European Union.

The European Parliamentary Labour Party was previously the British Labour Group.

A note on Asian names

For Korean names, I follow the DPRK style for North Koreans, with the family names followed by first names, capitalised and unhyphenated. Thus: Kim Il Sung, Kim Jong Il, and Kim Jong Un. For South Koreans, I follow their style, with a hyphen and a lowercased last particle. Thus: Kim Dae-jung, and Park Geun-hye. This creates a problem for the period up to the end of the Korean War, but this has been resolved by selecting the style to reflect political identification.

Some names are given in a different form or order if they are already established in common usage, such as Syngman Rhee. For the Chinese names, the standardised pinyin transliteration is used: Mao Zedong rather than Mao Tse-tung, Beijing instead of Peking. Japanese names invert the name order (eg. Junichiro Koizumi, Tomiichi Murayama, and Tsutomu Hata).

Abbreviations

AAPL	Afro-American Patrolmen's League (Chicago)
ACP	African, Caribbean and Pacific Group of States
ACTA	Anti-Counterfeiting Trade Agreement
AFET	Foreign Affairs Committee (EP)
ALDE	Alliance of Liberals and Democrats for Europe Party (EP)
AMM	Aceh Monitoring Mission
ANC	African National Congress
ANL	Anti-Nazi League
ASEAN	Association of Southeast Asian Nations
AUEW	Amalgamated Engineering Union (1920-1992)
AWRE	Atomic Weapons Research Establishment
B&ICO	British and Irish Communist Organisation
BAC	British Aircraft Corporation
BBFC	British Board of Film Classification
BLG	British Labour Group (later the EPLP)
BNP	British National Party
BSSRS	British Society for Social Responsibility in Science
CDU	Christian Democratic Union of Germany
CEDRI	Comite Europeen de Defense des Refugees and Immigres
CFSP	Common Foreign and Security Policy
CLASS	Centre for Labour and Social Studies
CLP	Constituency Labour Party
CND	Campaign for Nuclear Disarmament
CPGB	Communist Party of Great Britain
CPP	Cambodian People's Party
CSP	Confederation of the Socialist Parties of the European Community (later the PES)
CSU	Christian Social Union (Germany)
DLP	District Labour Party (Labour Party)
DPD	Dewan Perwakilan Daerah (Indonesia): Regional Representative Council
DPJ	Democratic Party of Japan
DPR	Dewan Perwakilan Rakyat (Indonesia): People's Representative Council

DPRK	Democratic People's Republic of Korea
DR	Droit European: Group of the European Right
EC	Executive Committee
ECJ	European Court of Justice
EDA	European Defence Agency
EEC	European Economic Community (later EU)
EIAS	European Institute for Asian Studies
EMAC	Economic and Monetary Affairs Committee (EP)
EMU	Economic and Monetary Union
END	European Nuclear Disarmament
EP	European Parliament
EPA	Economic Partnership Agreement
EPEN	Ethniki Politiki Enosis (Greece): National Political Union
EPLP	European Parliamentary Labour Party (previously BLG)
EPP	European People's Party – Christian Democrats (EP)
ERC	European Research Council
ERT	Energy, Research and Technology Committee (EP)
ESPRIT	European Strategic Programme on Research in Information Technology
EUEOM	European Union Election Observation Mission
EUMC	European Monitoring Centre on Racism and Xenophobia (later the FRA)
FCO	Foreign Common Office
FN	Front National (France), later Rassemblement National
FP	Framework Programme
FPÖ	Freiheitliche Partei Österreichs: Freedom Party of Austria
FRA	European Union Agency for Fundamental Rights (previously the EUMC)
FTA	Free Trade Agreement
GAM	Gerakan Aceh Merdeka (Indonesia): Free Aceh Movement
GMC	General Management Committee (Labour Party)
Golkar	Partai Golongan Karya (Indonesia): Party of the Functional Groups

GRECE	Groupement de recherche et d'études pour la civilisation européenne (France): Research and Study Group for European Civilization
GSLP	Gibraltar Socialist Labour Party
HFO	Heavy Fuel Oil
HFSP	Human Frontier Science Programme (Japan)
HSE	Health and Safety Executive
iEPA	Interim Economic Partnership Agreement
IGC	Intergovernmental Conference
ILP	Independent Labour Party
IMF	International Monetary Fund
INTA	International Trade Committee (EP-previously REX)
IOC	International Olympic Committee
IPCAA	Inter-Parliamentary Council Against Antisemitism
ISK	International Socialist Struggle League
IWC	Institute of Workers Control
JCP	Japanese Communist Party
JCPOA	Joint Comprehensive Plan of Action (Iran nuclear deal)
JKLF	Jammu-Kashmir Liberation Front
JSP	Japan Socialist Party (later DPJ)
KEDO	Korean Peninsula Energy Development Organization
KPU	Komisi Pemilihan Umum (Indonesia): General Elections Commission
LDP	Liberal Democratic Party, Jiminto (Japan)
LEA	Local Education Authority
LHASC	Labour History Archives and Study Centre
LIBE	Civil Liberties and Internal Affairs Committee (EP)
LME	Labour Movement for Europe
MFA	Ministry of Foreign Affairs (DPRK)
MITI	Ministry of International Trade and Industry (Japan)
MOU	Memorandum of Understanding
MRP	Marine Resources Project
MSI	Movimento Sociale Italiano: Italian Social Movement
NAC	National Administrative Council (ILP)

NCB	National Coal Board
NEAEF	North East Asia Economic Forum
NEC	National Executive Committee (Labour Party)
NLP	National Labour Press
NSB	National Society of Brushmakers
NSK	Nippon Seiko Kabushiki-gaisha
NU	Nahdlatul Ulama
NUM	National Union of Mineworkers
NUPES	Nouvelle Union Populaire Écologique et Sociale
OECD	Organisation for Economic Co-operation and Development
OSCE	Organization for Security and Co-operation in Europe
OTA	Office of Technology Assessment (USA)
ÖVP	Österreichische Volkspartei: Austrian People's Party
PASOK	Panhellenic Socialist Movement (Greece)
PCI	Partito Comunista Italiano: Italian Communist Party
PD	Partai Demokrat (Indonesia): Democratic Party
PDI-P	Partai Demokrasi Indonesia – Perjuangan: Indonesian Democratic Party – Struggle
PDS	Partido Democratico della Sinistra (Italy): Democratic Party of the Left
PDUP	Partito di Unita Proletaria per il Comunismo (Italy): Proletarian Union Party for Communism
PES	Party of European Socialists (previously the CSP)
PKI	Partai Komunis Indonesia: Communist Party of Indonesia
PLA	People's Liberation Army (China)
PLP	Parliamentary Labour Party
PNFP	French and European Nationalist Party
POUM	Partido Obrero de Unificación Marxista (Spain): Workers' Party of Marxist Unity
PR	Proportional Representation
PSOE	Partido Socialista Obrero Español: Spanish Socialist Workers' Party Unification
QMV	Qualified Majority Voting
RAXEN	Racism and Xenophobia Network (part of EUMC)
R&D	Research and Development
RD&D	Research, Development and Demonstration

RDC	Rapid Deployment Capacity
REX	External Economic Relations Committee (EP- later INTA)
RN/FN	Rassemblement National (France), formerly Front National
ROK	Republic of Korea (South Korea)
S&D	Progressive Alliance of Socialists and Democrats (previously the Socialist Group)
SBY	Susilo Bambang Yudhoyono, former President of Indonesia
SDI	Strategic Defense Initiative ("Star Wars")
SDLP	Social Democratic and Labour Party (Northern Ireland)
SDP	Social Democratic Party (UK)
SERA	Socialist Environmental and Resources Association
SISCON	Science in a Social Context
SPD	Social Democratic Party of Germany
SPES	Stimulation Plan for Economic Science
SPÖ	Sozialdemokratische Partei Österreichs: Social Democratic Party of Austria
STOA	Science and Technology Options Assessment (EP)
TUC	Trades Union Congress
UCL	University College London
UKIP	United Kingdom Independence Party
UMIST	University of Manchester Institute of Science and Technology
UNCLOS	UN Conference on the Law of the Sea
WMD	Weapons of Mass Destruction
WPK	Workers' Party of Korea (DPRK)
WTO	World Trade Organisation

Acknowledgements

My first acknowledgement must be to all my loyal staff over the years for their help and support. It's impossible to list them all but some have provided outstanding service. Marialaura De Angelis, Sarah Chilton, Stuart Emmerson, Oona King, Kamila Kingstone, Arlene McCarthy, Elodie Sellar, Chiara Zannini In Brussels, Cherry Burrow in the Forest of Dean and a peripatetic Irina Kalashnikova.

In Beijing Nick Bonner, Simon Cockerell, Zhang Lijia and Zhang Zhijun.

In Brussels and the EU Institutions Mary Bannotti, Alison Birkett, Elmar Brok, Luigi Colajanni, Nick Costello, Patrick Costello, Jean-Pierre Cot, Harlem Desir, Alexandra Dobolyi, Morag Donaldson, Padraig Flynn, Jas Gawronski, Peter Guilford, Dick Gupwell and his EIAS, Geoff Harris, Sophie Heitz, David Martin, David O'Sullivan, Christos Papoutsis, Luis Planas, Julian Priestley †, Francesca Ratti, Arielle Rouby, Fode Sylla, Marijke Van Hemeldonck, Michael Wood.

In England Weymand Bennett and all at the Anti-Nazi League and Unite Against Fascism, Mike Davis and Chartist, Keir Dhillon, Tony Dubbins and the GPMU, Alf Dubs, Enke Enhjargal, Bill Evans, Ian Freestone, Richard and Zerbanoo Gifford, David Hanman, Fariah Khan, Eddie Lopez, Mark Seddon and the staff of 'old' Tribune.

In Gibraltar Joe Bossano, Carlos Perez † and Albert Poggio.

The Indonesian and Aceh 'core teams' and in particular Risa Amrikasari.

At Manchester University and in the Science Policy Community, Michael Gibbons, Ken Green †, Gordon Lake †, Erik Millstone, Steven Rose, and Ziauddin Sardar.

The 'North Korean team' of Choe Il, Kent Harstedt, Hyon Hak Bong, Kang Suk Ju †, Tereza Novotna, Jonathan Powell, Ri Su Yong, Ri Ung Gil, Bill Ury.

In Seoul the staff of the EU Delegation and Kang Hyeyeon, Kim Dae-jung †, Kwon Soyoung, Moon Chung-in, Chad O'Carroll and John Sagar.

In Tameside my fellow Labour councillors and officials in the Education Department, and in particular Cheryl Eastwood, Phil Tomlinson, Alan Whitehead and Geoff Mayall †.

In Tokyo and Japan the staff of the EU Delegation across the years, the Diet members of all parties who served on their EU Friendship Group, especially Fujita Yukihisa, Hata Tsutomu †, and Nakayama Taro, Kina Shoukichi and Champloose, Takagi Hiroko and Takahashi Hajime.

In the US Sonja Bachman, Bob Carlin, Lee Jay Cho †, Keith Luse, Sam Martell, Stephen Noerper, Alice Palmer, Buzz Palmer †, Jenny Town, Terry Walz.

I must also thank Tony Simpson at Spokesman Books, Joe Haining my editor, Simon Liddiard for photography, and Cicely Spence whose indefatigable work made it all happen.

Finally my mother and father, Matilda and Ernest, and my long suffering family with Elise and Alessandro at the fore, but also Hazel and Daniela, Ida and Emelyn.

Preface

Small beer

The pattern my political life took came from chance and necessity. The warp was a belief in socialism, democracy and equality that provided the long threads. There was no didactic education within the narrow or extended family, rather it was a lived experience from start to finish. It was political osmosis.

The weft reflected life's contingencies with the 'white heat of the technological revolution' pushing me in a direction that both served me well and yet one I spent decades gently unpicking as performance moved to policy, while in parallel my travels drove my anti-racism and my love of the far abroad in all its facets.

For all their lack of formal education – maybe because of it – both my parents, unlike so many of their contemporaries, were prepared to sacrifice in order to deliver what they saw as a key to success – education in the widest sense of the term. They gave me a long leash and I ran. Yet the greatest sacrifice was made by my sister Wendy Elizabeth whose death after scarcely twenty-four hours allowed me life. Born on 9 December 1948 she died the following day. I dedicate this book to her and the cascading family that followed my birth.

My childhood, for my environment, was far from deprived yet nevertheless choices had to be made. I was denied many wishes and whims, sometimes to my enormous annoyance and frustration. The one thing that I was never denied was books. It gave me a love of reading that has endured throughout my life and I've passed on to both daughter and son. I've been lucky in my education, a working-class refugee in the middle-class milieu of the grammar school and then university, an undreamt of passage for my childhood peers living along the streets of Stonehouse's Park Estate or in the clusters of the Forest's council houses. The union of home and education, nature and nurture, made me who I became.

A thick slice of that is contained in the following pages. As one of my best-loved political predecessors, ILP MP Jimmy Maxton, said in 1935, 'If you can't ride two horses at the same time you shouldn't be in a bloody circus.' I've spent much of my life with a travelling company of political acrobats, clowns and other entertainers as we've performed home and away for the public. Here I've juggled internationalism and a fidelity to the European project with the English left's socialist chauvinism. I've survived, but that is not to say that at times it wasn't a bumpy ride.

Many will disagree with my version of history particularly with respect to the passage to Europe. I would encourage them to write their own stories. The danger is that like in 1984, the uncomfortable and inconvenient is being written out of an increasingly mutable British history. It's clear why Boris Johnson and the European Research Group xenophobes desire to eradicate those 47 years when we were of Europe, but less obvious why Labour is complicit in helping history stop, for it was on the platform of the European Union that the party played out a string of successes on a second front in the long opposition to Thatcher and Major. Those achievements – and lessons – deserve to be preserved and this will be best done by those who played the part. For, to paraphrase Jamaican Prime Minister Michael Manley, if there is one thing worse than contested history it is no history at all.

E. H. Carr's *What is History?* judged the historical status of the fact that during Stalybridge Wakes in 1850 a gingerbread salesman, as the result of a 'petty dispute', was kicked to death by an angry mob. They story's status and durability as a 'fact' depended on what questions it could help answer. As someone who for 15 years and more represented Stalybridge I have compassion for that hapless hawker, the victim of a drunken rabble. We currently face the same problem – Labour's European history is on probation. It can become a foundation from which to launch our future re-engagement with Europe's Union or become relegated first to footnote then limbo, before being lost entirely. The best we can hope for is structural change, but for the moment situational adjustment might be all that is on offer.

In Labour's European camp there were both saboteurs – more solipsists than semi-detached – and their fellow travellers that knew no better. The former were unpleasant, but not bright enough to be evil, and the latter painted their politics in fifty shades of grey. Nevertheless, collectively across a short half century Labour in Europe has much to be proud of, whether in the front lines of the parliament amongst the hundred plus MEPs or Commission, in the back offices of members, the Socialist Group and the Party of European Socialists, EU Institutions or via the Labour Party in exile – the Brussels Labour Group. But, with rare exceptions, these achievements were less because of the party back home than despite it. Interestingly the trade union wing of the movement has been more acute in its perceptions than the politicians lost in Westminster's jungle of European illiteracy.

Maybe, here's the rub. British self-absorption strands all our politics on the further shores of an inchoate nationalism. Arthur Scargill lost the Socialist Group in Strasbourg on one infamous occasion when he opened his remarks proclaiming his delight to be over here in Europe, while his bookend at the other end of the left's shelf, Gordon Brown, was to cast the xenophobe spell, 'British jobs for British workers'. The old divisions between domestic and international policy have long been washed away by economic and industrial globalisation. We have to create the means of control. The levers we need no longer have a fulcrum – if they ever did – in small and medium nation states. On the continent there is a, sometimes albeit reluctantly, recognition of that reality. Only England denies it thrice!

1 Capture

A frightful hobgoblin stalks throughout Europe.

From Helen MacFarlane's translation of The Communist Manifesto (1850)

Looking back from past my allotted three score years and ten, I realise I was deeply shaped by my working-class family – whose roots were in the rural mining communities of the Forest of Dean – and milieu and by the waves of history that broke over and around. The post-war Attlee government had pushed wide open the door of opportunity – now long closed to a narrow crack – and with the support of my parents I was able to barge through. My intellectual formation was founded on the disparate twin pillars of radical politics, and science and technology. They provided early scaffolding for the paradigm within which I have lived and acted. This was more serendipity than preordination. You can only throw the dice you are given.

It was a long and winding road. Born English, I'll die European, a citizen of a Union from which the land of my birth has absconded. To see the possibility of socialism in one country – the United Kingdom – would make the wish father to the thought. Late capitalism is organised in increasingly large agglomerations as the forward march of technology continues unabated, but never forced to pass the gateway to modernity England is left adrift in history. Europe is the field of battle. But we have removed ourselves in a gesture as futile as repealing Newton's law of gravity, leaving the country in political limbo and economic purgatory. How did

Britain choose to drive itself off this economic and political cliff? There is no simple answer. It's a potent brew of history and hubris, genealogy and geography that we have stirred and concocted together to justify setting ourselves apart from our neighbours in a form of hopeful apartheid. Self-worth is a useful trait to avoid being disabled by doubt, but when it slipped across to closed minds and narcissism, alarm bells should have rung. If they did, nobody was listening. Either way, there is no refuge in a contested past in constant flux.

In late Victorian England, after the 1867 Reform Act, one front where class antagonism was fought out was in the city halls of Britain's conurbations. But capital concentration and the 'nationalisation' of industrial organisation stripped towns and cities of their bourgeoisie and the labour movement of its levers. By the Great War this process was well advanced. The jockeying for position among the victorious imperial nations climaxed after the beating of Berlin. London was overtaken on the inside by Washington; John Maclean's *The Coming War with America* identified the challenge, but missed the hidden off-ramp.[1] The British Empire side-stepped Thucydides' Trap, warm in the proffered comfort blanket of a 'special relationship' where London was submissive first ally, and subaltern, to Washington.[2] This was more about race than righteousness; the coming passage of arms between China and the US will not have the same amicable out-turn. This first was sibling rivalry, the second will be race war hidden under the rubric of a 'clash of civilisations'.[3] Running down the Union Jack in favour of the Stars and Stripes is one thing; hoisting the five-starred red flag another.

After the world wars, save for late skirmishes, the game was to be played on a global pitch. Industry and economy burst the constraints of nation. Economic and political boundaries were no longer congruent. The mismatch saw one economic corral forming in Western Europe. The question was how to put back in kilter the political with the economic, and there was some hunting before the European path to reunification was found. It was a long march that after industrial union moved along a preordained path through Economic and Monetary Union (EMU) to Common Foreign and Security Policy (CFSP) and defence union. The passage was far from smooth for, like evolution, integration jumps. Crises drive saltation where rapid advance punctuates long episodes of stasis and backsliding. The pace was contingent, but the passage prescribed with Immanuel Wallerstein the orienteer, laying it out in his *The Modern-World System* (1974–2011). Missteps were many; the 1952 European Defence Community Treaty, for example, was born decades before its due time. Its rejection in 1954 by the French National Assembly had a logic, even if obscured by the miasma of squalid domestic politics. It was playing the finale before the prelude.

Changing states

To craft the future, you must go with the grain of history. The destination is far from predetermined, yet the broad direction of travel is set by the deeper currents of history and technology. As I wrote in *Changing States* – our counterpoint to Will Hutton's very modish British-focused *The State We're In* (1993) –

> *The European Union is not primarily the product of politicians. The single European Market was neither invented by Jacques Delors, nor built in his image ... What drove integration forward again were not political imperatives but economic ones. By the early eighties a single market was being formed sector by sector within the bounds of the European Economic Community, as thousands of businessmen and women, managers, scientists and entrepreneurs recognized that the only way to compete with Japan and the United States was through the enlargement of the home market to a truly continental scale. By design or accident, leading European companies, from ICL to BMW, from British Aerospace to ENI, Europeanized their operations. Industrial Union was built piece by piece, far away from the hands of politicians.*[4]

European nation states were both too small to deal with global issues and – often – too large for the local and regional. The

future was European union and the European Community the stage on which it would be acted out. The challenges, contradictions and uncertainties facing us demanded shared policies and politics, and the pooling of our resources and sovereignty in the interests of mutual cooperation and mutual benefit. Late capitalist industry rests most securely on the firm foundations of a large domestic market.

It was both the process and resulting product that made it all worth fighting for. The European system offered three modes of governance: technocracy, aristocracy or democracy. Immediate post-war high politics was played out in the leached-out landscape of expertise. As the decades ticked by, intergovernmentalism sprouted, as proficiency bent to power and invasive elites took root and grew. The heading was right, but still short of democracy. Those with whom the power rests are leery of its surrender; it is rarely, if ever, given away, but rather taken. The European Council's oligarchs, in acting to protect their interests, have been undertaking a secret war to frustrate and subvert the people's passage to power. They have their clairvoyants. One artful theorist and ideologue peddling that the intergovernmental way station is manifest destiny is the eloquent right-wing liberal Luuk van Middelaar.[5] His alter ego issuing the democratic challenge was Julian Priestley.[6]

Van Middelaar lauds the serial covert *coups d'état* that step by step have expropriated power from member states to Europe's centre. The end faultless, the manner flawed. Global decisions require global players, but built on the democratic foundations of popular assent and not the shifting sands of privilege and position codified as twenty-first century *noblesse oblige*. It was this – in an inchoate way – that was the root of Britain's voters' rejection of the European Union (EU) in the 2016 referendum. Both major parties were at fault. At best, the Union was foreign policy; at worst, a convenient whipping boy taking the punishment for domestic malfeasance. For van Middelaar, the pinnacle of power is the Lisbon Treaty's five-card trick that adds a president of Council to that of the Commission selected by the same shabby peer consensus.

Parliamentary power

Priestley, in contrast, was wedded to parliament. He had served successively as the general secretary of the Socialist Group, the chef de cabinet of Klaus Haensch – the German Social Democratic Party (SPD) president of parliament (1994–97) – and as secretary general of the parliament (1997–2007). He, as a European Parliament (EP) staff member, had turned legislative creep into an art form, taking what had been grudgingly given to parliament and stretching it to near breaking point.[7] Alongside was a roadmap to design and bring into being the institutional architecture and apparatus required for a fully democratic governance and polity at EU level. Priestley's knowledge and appreciation of American political history was reflected in the blueprint. European citizens, parties, politicians and programmes were accessories before the fact, whether institutional reform with a statute for members of the European Parliament (MEPs) harmonising their rights and duties across member states to build a European political class, or the creation, growth and development of European political parties.[8] But mere existence was not sufficient. They needed to be lived.

In autumn 2010 I wrote, with this caution in mind, 'Many in the Labour Party may be unaware that the Party of European Socialists [PES] even exists, let alone that they are members of it. But the PES is no mere paper organisation conjured temporarily into existence to satisfy some whim of the left's wilder federalists. Rather, this is a fully-functioning body with offices, officers and staff – and even a parallel political foundation.'[9] Yet the PES, like the other European political parties, was born a bureaucratic body that still needed to be animated as an organic part of the labour movement. To achieve that, I endorsed three demands of the Delors Foundation, *Notre Europe*: 'First, European Parties should allow individual membership. Second, the party membership as a whole should approve by secret ballot the programme and manifesto of the PES for European Elections. Third, the parties should designate a candidate for President of the European Commission on the basis of primaries.' This would represent a clear gain for Labour. I continued:

> *In 2009, despite a PES congress – yes, the PES has those as well – agreeing to have a 'socialist' candidate for President of the Commission, and the Lisbon Treaty requiring the European Council to 'take account of the European election results in proposing to the European Parliament a nominee for the presidency of the Commission,' we saw Gordon Brown, together with his Spanish and Portuguese counterparts, also supposedly on the centre-left, endorse the right-wing Christian Democrat candidate José Manuel Barroso. It's as if the leaders of the Welsh and Scottish Labour parties had endorsed David Cameron before May's elections.*[10]

Politically, Priestley repurposed the EP as an analogue of the US Electoral College.[11] Post Lisbon, each new parliament's first task was to elect the president of the Commission. Its representation weighted towards smaller member states offered a political contract and legitimacy. Combined with the newly minted European political parties, democracy was to march in through the front door.

It was an unintended consequence of the Lisbon Treaty that allowed democracy to be driven forward against the resistance of the Council. Now, confirmation of the Commission's president required a qualified majority vote (QMV) in the parliament. The Socialist Group led the way. If confirmation of the Commission's president was to be the domain of the EP, why should parliament allow itself to be marginalised in the role of rubber stamp? Why not select as well as elect, commandeer and pre-empt the Council's lowest common denominator selection with the alternative of a European-wide public clash of personalities wedded to political platforms? The PES lead saw a more diffident European People's Party (EPP) follow with what was termed the *Spitzenkandidat* process. The EU's political parties, the PES, the EPP, and Alliance of Liberals and Democrats for Europe Party (ALDE) and others would select lead candidates and adopt political platforms at their party congresses in the run-up to the 2014 elections. These candidates would traverse the continent, criss-crossing countries with a medley of rallies, debates and mass campaigns.

When the dust had settled, the PES selected Martin Schulz and the EPP Jean-Claude Juncker. Unhappily, Schulz had been the unanimous choice of those PES member parties who engaged. Labour stood in the corner, face to the wall. All that was missing was the dunce's cap. They were hiding, but it was also bad behaviour. The luckless unanimity meant the spectacle of selection went missing. This was not the case on the right. The very notion of a *Spitzenkandidat* was an anathema for Angela Merkel and Herman Van Rompuy, but they acquiesced in the pageant, blinded to the hard reality beneath. Gordon Brown had been equally apoplectic.[12] The EPP, in contrast to the PES, saw a contest at their Dublin Congress, with 2200 delegates representing 73 parties from 39 countries. The three candidates were Juncker, Michel Barnier (France) and Valdis Dombrovskis (Latvia).[13] Dombrovskis pulled out on the eve of the vote, throwing his support behind Juncker, who went on to beat Barnier 382–245. After the procession of the PES convention, Dublin looked like a dog, barked like a dog and answered to the name of 'Fido'. It was a presidential convention in all but name.

Juncker's 2014 campaign bus. (European People's Party/Flickr)

The making of a president

Schulz appointed Priestley as his campaign manager, while Juncker chose Martin Selmayr (to become Juncker's chief of staff and then secretary general of the European Commission). The two candidates did the deal that whoever's group delivered the most seats would take the presidency. This first

time was rehearsal and precedent setting. More important than the winner was the institutionalisation of the process, which needed to be kept simple. Both agreed to rally behind the candidate whose party delivered most MEPs. The two campaign teams then choreographed their European tour and roadshow. This passed British voters by entirely. The Tories had fled the EPP in 2009 to nest with a gaggle of right-wing Eurosceptics, while Labour's Ed Miliband was so feared of the toxic taint of Europe he refused to countenance Schulz's presence anywhere Labour's writ ran. Schulz visited all twenty-eight member states, campaigning in Belfast under the auspices of the North's Social Democratic and Labour Party with its leader, Mark Durkan. Labour's safety-first approach saw support slip to less than one in four UK voters, while across the Union as a whole, the EPP and Juncker beat the PES and Schulz 221–191.

Merkel dropped the ball. She didn't want Juncker and said so, and was immediately taken to task by Germany's media. It all looked a little too East German. After all, one element of the centre-right's campaign had been posters urging 'Juncker for President' – rather than the SPD's Schulz – and the media thought the public were entitled to get who they had voted for rather than watch bemused as Merkel's sleight of hand pulled yet another recycled former PM out of her hat. While she was bent by the press, David Cameron snapped. Cameron – in concert with Hungary – tried to veto the deal, seemingly ignorant that he had been disarmed by the ratification of the Lisbon Treaty, thus compounding his helplessness after his estrangement from the EPP. He ludicrously claimed that this first engagement with democracy at a European level was a squalid 'backroom deal.'[14]

There were hard negotiations over the Commission's work programme. The promises demanded by the progressives included €315 million in job creation, increased transparency over trade negotiations, a thoroughgoing budget review in 2016 switching more resources to social and infrastructure spending and pushback against fiscal dumping.[15] Deal done, Juncker was elected by secret ballot, with the EP in Electoral College formation as specified by Rule 124 (2), namely, 'In accordance with Article 17(7) of the Treaty on European Union, Parliament shall elect the President of the Commission by a majority of its component Members'. Ostensibly, he won by 422–250 with 47 abstentions, but that was disingenuous. The rules specify a 'majority of its component members', thus requiring at minimum an absolute majority of 376 out of 751. Juncker's margin of victory was thus a respectable 47, rather than the landslide 172 commonly reported.

Juncker was far from a perfect candidate – even for the EPP – but to set principle and precedence, it was a price worth paying. Choose carefully the fight before engagement. Here the important fight was interinstitutional with the Council, not the EPP. It was parliament against the oligarchs, and my enemy's enemy is my friend. Juncker was that friend and temporary partner. For two and a half years, with Schulz serving his second term as EP president and Juncker in the Berlaymont, it was a virtual diarchy as the two phoned each other a dozen times a day.

In this battle for power between parliament and Europe's political oligarchs, the EP's secret weapon is Rule 124 (4): 'If the candidate does not obtain the required majority, the President shall invite the European Council to propose a new candidate within one month for election in accordance with the same procedure'. For the election of the president of parliament after three rounds, the top two candidates run off against each other by simple majority. Here, in contrast, with the president of the Commission, there is no emergency exit after three rolls of the dice. The self-same process recycles in perpetual motion. Any European Council attempt to browbeat the EP risks triggering a constitutional crisis. Once one candidate is rejected, the chances of each subsequent candidate declines. If the EP keeps its nerve, there can only be one winner.

In the run-up to the 2019 elections the EPP leader in the European Parliament, Manfred Weber, overwhelmed the former Finnish prime minister Alexander Stubb 492–127 at their Helsinki Congress in November 2018. Dutch Socialist Frans Timmermans followed from the PES Madrid Conference in February. This time there was no pre-cooked deal between the two main parties. The results saw both suffer to the benefit of the Liberals and Greens, with the EPP holding its lead over the PES 182–154, but with a clear centre-left win at the expense of the right.

For Merkel there was more than one way of skinning a cat. Initially encouraging Timmermans to sideline Weber, she then stabbed the Dutchman in the front, using opposition from Hungary and Poland to suggest the necessity for a more 'consensual' nominee, despite the fact Timmermans still had a guaranteed win in the Council with QMV. Using Germany and gender to subvert the forces of democracy, she proposed a favourite daughter in Ursula von der Leyen. Then she coyly abstained in the vote in Council, because of opposition from her Grand Coalition partners the SPD. Some claim she was a reluctant assassin, but that seems somewhat implausible. In wielding the knife she was twice blessed: she sabotaged a system she feared and simultaneously jettisoned a Dutch Socialist in favour of one of her Christlich Demokratische Union Deutschlands (Christian Democratic Union of Germany) acolytes.

In the EP, von der Leyen was dragged across the line with a mix of generosity and intimidation, pleading and duress. This time the vote was 383–327 with 22 abstentions. The threshold was 374 (out of 747) – a majority of 10.[16] Merkel's machinations had been a dangerous gamble, threatening to throw the Union into crisis and chaos. Hopefully, the run-up to 2024 may, in consequence, see Europe's political families choose to drive rather than subvert the process a second time. There is a limit to how many times you can play double or quits and expect to win. It will be the best of three, and parliament has nothing to lose. The runes read well. Germany's Coalition Agreement in November 2021 endorsed both the *Spitzenkandidat* process and the introduction of the system for future EP elections where a proportion of MEPs are elected on trans-European lists. Macron is sympathetic and the EP again endorsed the detail in May 2022. On that basis, von der Leyen's hope for a second term may prove wishful thinking. All of this was the political backdrop to my bit part in the play whose theme was the future of Europe.

Back in Britain

Empire, past and place shaped a British state of mind, unconscious of the irony of that apocryphal *Times* headline 'Fog in Channel, Continent Cut Off'. Winston Churchill in the late 1940s, offering support for a Franco-German 'kind of United States of Europe', encapsulated his view in a catchphrase that identified the UK as voyeur not performer: 'we are with Europe, but not of it'.[17] He was, perhaps unconsciously, speaking collectively for Britain's political class. There was vanishingly little counter to Churchill on the left. For the Communist Party of Great Britain (CPGB) the forward march of Europe had halted, after stumbling ahead a few steps, thirty years earlier. Lenin reversed course after earlier support, deciding in 1915 that 'the slogan for a United States of Europe was an erroneous one'. The subsequent Stalin–Trotsky schism in the Soviet Union, which saw 'socialism in one country' facing off against 'permanent revolution',[18] left Stalin intoning Lenin's mantra to close down debate, with the gramophone minds of the CPGB replaying that old 78. *The British Road to Socialism* (1951) was a CPGB retrospective on national communism.[19]

Labour was barely better, although it took decades for me to see through the rhetoric of internationalism to reality. The Tories bought nationalism wholesale and Labour retail. Labour is described by sections of the left as never a socialist party, but rather a party with socialists in it. The most interesting of the three Milibands is the father, Ralph, rather than either Ed or David. Ralph was the author of *Parliamentary Socialism* (1964), in which he concludes the book's title is a contradiction in terms. The same is equally true of Labour's internationalism. Labour is a chauvinist party with internationalists in it. Its essence is social-democratic nationalism. The socialists and internationalists have been more often than not – but far from always – one and the same. Reformism in one country might be an apt conspectus.

Some believe Labour's xenophobia is craven expediency. Gordon Brown's promise of 'British jobs for British workers' in January 2009 was a sickening sound bite that I took personally. Targeted by Brown were Italian and Portuguese contract labourers. My son is Italian![20] Yet maybe Gordon's churlish intervention was a reflection of his upbringing. History rhymed

to older harmonies. Back before the first Labour government in 1924, Labour's deputy leader J. R. Clynes had gone on record claiming, 'Labour will not be influenced, should it be trusted with the power of Government, by any consideration other than that of the national well-being.'[21]

If Jean-Marie Le Pen had said of France what Brown said of Britain there would have been a wellspring of revulsion. Yet Unite's general secretary Derek Simpson was photographed with the right-wing *Daily Star* next to a 'British jobs for British workers' banner. To paraphrase, 'Labour doth protest too much.' Loud protestations of internationalism were not entirely successful in drowning out the sounds of creaking nationalism at the core. The self-same worship at the pernicious altar of English exceptionalism bedevils most of the rest of the British left.

Dummy dawns

It was civil society's resistance to Hitler before and during the Second World War that kindled the federalist flame across the political spectrum in continental Europe. The Italian Resistance led the way, followed by the French, yet the German contribution must not be forgotten. The *Europäische Union* (European Union) resistance group, formed in Berlin in 1939, saw the future in a new unified, socialist Europe.[22] The group was broken in 1942 when, under torture, the Gestapo extracted names from a member captured meeting incoming parachutists. Fifteen were sentenced to death and thirteen executed. The only two survivors were Annaliese Groscurth and Robert Havemann. The latter was freed by the arriving Red Army. Havemann, a professor of physical chemistry, had the singular distinction of being dismissed from academic posts by the Nazis, the Americans and the Stasi. But that was over there, not over here.

In Britain the moment of war sparked interest, but it wasn't to catch. The incendiaries were political refugees, Labour radicals and the left. Labour's – temporary absentee – Kim Mackay made the case that socialism would be the product of unification rather than its author.[23] He challenged head on the (then) Independent Labour Party (ILP) chair C. A. Smith. Smith was rerunning the anti-Stalinist left's gambit in Spain, 'Workers' Power FIRST: then Socialism: then Federal Union will follow'.[24] Mackay, an Australian, had fought Frome for Labour in 1935, but had resigned in 1940 over Labour's uncritical stance towards the government. He joined the rebel Common Wealth Party and spent time as its chair before re-defecting back to Labour in 1945 just in time for selection and election in Hull North West.

In 1943 Hilda Monte (pseud., actually the German political refugee Hilde Meisel), published with the Left Book Club *The Unity of Europe*. She had been part of the split from the German SPD that formed the International Socialist Struggle League (ISK), teetotal and vegetarian, anti-Stalinist and pro-European federalism. The British section of the ISK was the cultish Socialist Vanguard whose anti-communism had by the mid-1950s driven them hard, along with their journal *Socialist Commentary*, into Labour's right-wing fringe. Hilde herself was shot and killed in Germany in April 1944 while on an intelligence mission.

The United Socialist States of Europe

The only sustained campaign in favour of federalism came late on in the war from the ILP. They fought the Bilston by-election in September 1944 and got within 349 votes of ousting the Tories, running on F. A. Ridley and Bob Edwards's *The United Socialist States of Europe* – Bob was to end up representing the constituency on behalf of the Labour Party from 1955 to 1987.[25] The argument was that 'the revolt of the economic productive basis of society against its political and social superstructure' meant politics and economics now had no option but to come into line with culture and geography. German wartime industrial integration of Europe – the proto single market – needed political matching. They were spot on. Yet what was mainstream in resistant Europe proved to be the political tip of the spear among Britons. It explains a lot about where we are today. Nietzsche was right: Britain was the 'bad' European. The ILP continued to run

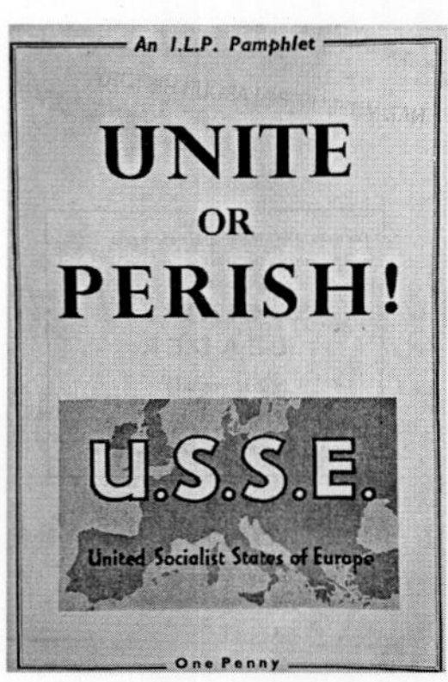

the campaign, and themselves, into the ground in the 1950s as they faded from history waiting for the workers who never came.

They were joined in the wake of war by some of the flotsam and jetsam of left politics: the etiolated Common Wealth Party, plus that small group of Labour MPs – Fenner Brockway, Mackay and Will Warbey included – comprising the Socialist Europe group in the House of Commons.[26] Together they were the British Centre of the Socialist Movement for the United States of Europe. These usual suspects were present in Paris for the Movement's Third International Congress in November 1949. They were unsung, but in illustrious company. From France there were two prominent resistance leaders, Andre Denis MP and state councillor Leo Hamon, and from Germany future federal chancellor Helmut Schmidt. From Italy, meanwhile, there were Ignazio Silone, Altiero Spinelli and Giacomo Matteotti (whose father had been assassinated by Mussolini's fascists in 1924, precipitating the leap by 'Il Duce' into dictatorship). Another of the Italians was Mario Zagari, who I served alongside for five years (1984–89) in the Socialist Group. Spinelli was also there in the EP's Communist Group until his death in 1986.

One of England's most prominent federalists was George Orwell, a righteous European spelling out that, in a post-colonial world, Europe's nations had no choice but to unite. It had been their failure to adapt as the world moved under them that was the root cause of the thirty-year civil war of 1914–45. His voice was stifled as his manifesto for an English socialism was ignored.[27] He made his case in 'Towards European unity' for America's *Partisan Review* (July/August 1947), sandwiched between *Animal Farm* and *1984*: 'A Socialist United States of Europe' is the 'only worthwhile political object today'. The road to recovery lay *within* the new community of European states. Orwell accepted it was an almost impossible task. Sabotage was certain from the Soviet Union and its franchised Communist parties, the United States and its corporations, all abetted by a 'fifth column' of opposition from the Catholic Church and neatly wrapped in imperial delusion. Orwell warned: 'The Russians cannot but be hostile to any European union not under their own control,' and that, hostage as Britain was to Washington, 'there is always the danger that the United States will break up any European coalition by drawing Britain out of it.' A dog that barked seventy years later. Orwell was clearly influenced by Ripley and Edwards – an avid reader and collector of left-wing pamphlets and former member of the ILP who remained sympathetic to their anti-Stalinism – he would have read *The United Socialist States of Europe*.[28] Orwell's same polemic aimed at a British audience was almost certainly the only one of his pieces *Tribune* failed to publish.

The case for the United Socialist States of Europe was lost in abeyance. Labour's soft-centre leadership looked across the Atlantic, not the Channel, when it looked up from trying to pull itself up with its own bootstraps. The Tories were the party of empire and free enterprise, and Labour that of national capitalism forward-leaning in the direction of industry rather than finance under the influence of the UK and Labour's powerful trade unions. Labour's fellow-travelling left were no less attached to the map of empire. The pro-European left, which Orwell epitomised, ended crushed between the jaws of that Soviet–American political vice that left neither space nor purchase for an independent, non-Stalinist left. It was either Washington or Moscow. Britain failed to realise that in winning the war we lost the peace. There was to be no post-war snapback to the *status quo ante*. Labour, unlike Churchill, understood part of that conundrum, but remained unconscious of its full import. The war, in destroying a global empire and imagination, drew forth a commonplace nation.

Thus, the creation of the European Coal and Steel Community and the Treaty of Rome passed Britain by. The Suez invasion tested to breaking point Washington's tolerance for English adventurism, while back home in the 1960s new economic forces saw Europe replace empire and beyond as the mainstay of the UK marketplace, as the American challenge cast its shadow over the continent. The failure of both Labour and Conservative governments to arrest or even slow the UK's post-war comparative decline left few options. Britain

wrestled with the idea of Europe from 1961 to 1973. The 1963 and 1967 vetoes by de Gaulle – who some would argue first recognised Britain's ingrained 'deep hostility' to the European project – delayed the inevitable until 1973 when the Tories chased influence and power over formal sovereignty.

If the Conservatives put class before nation, Labour stood that on its head and played the national game. Labour leader Hugh Gaitskell had earlier claimed that membership of the 'Common Market' would mean 'the end of a thousand years of history'. Which parts of the dark ages, feudalism, absolute monarchy and proto-capitalism he favoured preserving were unclear. Others in the party argued membership would prove a barrier to socialism in the UK. It would have been a truly impressive impediment to be more effective in that regard than Gaitskell's own leadership. His death in early 1963 opened the door to Harold Wilson and Europe.

Wilson was a visionary technocratic nationalist cut with social democracy. Looking backwards, he was the last best hope of an economic and political transformation of Britain. His radical programme equated socialism with efficiency and technology. It was not Lenin's 'communism is socialism plus electricity' but it rhymed. Its promise was as radical as Thatcher. There was social liberalisation, education reform, slum clearance and house building, but the economy was strangled by austerity. But the numbers were not there in the House of Commons from 1964 to 1966, with a Labour majority of four, and by the time of the victory in 1966 the energy was spent.

Even with its prime minister in favour, Labour divisions on Europe remained. It was political: the right pragmatically in favour and the left ideologically against. For the former it was the least-worst option. The extra-parliamentary left saw the CPGB still intoning Stalin. Britain's fissiparous Trotskyists, divided into four parts – the International Socialists, the International Marxist Group, the Workers Revolutionary Party and Militant – sang with different cadence from the same hymn sheet. Unlike the Communists, their faith in the infallibility of their founder was fickle. Immediately battle was joined, with Heath – and Wilson – knocking for a third time on Brussels' door, they rearranged their political clothes to all neatly line up on the left with the CPGB and its 'national' socialist inflection inside the Labour Party and trade unions. All that was left outside were minuscule Maoist groups. The only 'organic intellectual' arguing Giorgio Amendola's case that 'international integration is a reality with which one will have to come to terms', was Tom Nairn.[29] At Labour's Special Conference in 1971, the only left voice in favour of membership was Edwards, the leader of the ILP contingent of the Partido Obrero de Unificación Marxista (POUM) with George Orwell and one of the British representatives at the Paris Congress of 1949. He was the last survivor of that war-time political tontine backing the United Socialist States of Europe, but he was not to inherit.

Sitting on the suitcases

The Tony Benn-inspired 1975 referendum confirmed membership of the European Economic Community (EEC) by more than two to one, but the Labour Party's predilection was to change public rather than policy. Labour's line had 'nation' stamped through it like 'Blackpool' through rock. The 1983 manifesto promised that the next Labour government would jab the ejector button and depart post haste. I was elected a Labour MEP in 1984 to sit on my bags in Brussels' departures to await a majority Labour government. This was to change as Michael Foot made way for Neil Kinnock after the 1983 general election. In fact, some first footings were in place, prepared by the reanimation of transnational politics across Western Europe via the emergent peace campaigns fired up by Washington's nuclear adventurism. There were even stirrings behind the Iron Curtain. The 1980 European Nuclear Disarmament (END) movement – which opposed the actions and escalations of both Washington and Moscow – was led by Ken Coates from the Bertrand Russell Peace Foundation. Ken was to be elected to the European Parliament in 1989, bringing a left pro-European voice into the European Parliamentary Labour Party (EPLP). I claim no credit here: I was a follower, not a leader.

Labour has had twelve leaders since Clement Attlee was elected in 1935. Some cursorily genuflected in the direction

of Europe like John Smith and Tony Blair, others like Brown and Miliband were 'rice' Europeans, in it only for what they got out.[30] Blair was the shiftless European. The only one that had a European bone in his body was Neil Kinnock. It was Neil that turned the party to face Europe after he was elected leader in 1983 and was the only one who engaged in Europe's politics as a contestant rather than spectator. He lived Europe, while the others were just visiting. He listened while the others talked. He wanted to reset Europe's politics on the left, bringing into the fold those Euro-communists whom the collapse of the Soviet Empire had freed from history. It made an enormous difference to the perception and reception of Labour in Brussels.

Poster for 1975 Referendum.

After Labour's defeat in 1992 there was a real prospect at the European Socialist Leaders Meeting in June in Lisbon that Kinnock would be endorsed as leader of the PES for November's congress in The Hague. It looked like a done deal. If the colour of the office curtains hadn't been chosen, the furniture had. At the last minute, Kinnock withdrew, concerned that he would be forced to end up politically at odds with Labour's next leader. A decade later, Robin Cook was to occupy the post from 2001 to 2004.

Conference call

2016 Referendum sticker.

After my election as EPLP leader in 1989 (see Chapter 4), I had a speaking slot at party conference. It was definitely not peak viewing time. One memorable preamble had the party chair telling delegates there would be no more votes before lunch and to try and make their way out quietly as the European Report was up next. Attacking the Tories was easy. In 1990 at Blackpool I asked, 'What is the Tory vision? The government are alone, aloof and adrift from Europe. Led by Mrs Thatcher, they have sat on, blocked and thwarted many European measures to improve the quality of life for ordinary people. Under this government, Britain has become the sick man of Europe, the thick man of Europe, the dirty man of Europe. The Conservative government have opposed each of the measures put forward under Europe's social action programme. They have vetoed countless measures that would guarantee the rights of workers.' I contended Labour's counter should be: 'Britain is our country and we are proud of our identity, but we are Europeans too, and we know that the new Europe is our future. Let us seize it.'[31]

The following year in Brighton saw my support for the euro. The paradigm was the American lurch down the same path in the nineteenth century, when the National Banking Act in 1863 – during the Civil War – legislated parallel currencies out of existence, leaving the dollar alone and supreme. The British argument is that one size doesn't fit all, but I argued it works in the EU and also the US. Not all British Eurosceptics oppose a single currency, however. The Tory MEP Roger Helmer – who was to defect to the UK Independence Party (UKIP) in 2012 – claimed the right single currency for the UK was the dollar, rather than the euro. As I urged, 'We need a single currency to help our exporters, our workers, to produce and sell goods in the rest of Europe. Our people are more concerned that their money keeps its value, rather than its design or designation. I must tell conference: we need that single currency.'

The conference was back in Blackpool in 1992, and now it was a plea to ignore the vocal siren songs wanting to go back to the future: 'Those who most want a referendum want to vote against the irreversible shift that took place in 1975. I voted and campaigned for a no then, but you cannot turn back the clock of history. Now our choice is to be European or a sickly, declining economy, isolated, alone and adrift.' Instead, I felt we should go forward. 'We need Maastricht to bring into force political authority to counterbalance rampant free market capitalism.' As I said at the time, a referendum on Europe would be our Pearl Harbour.

Snatching defeat from the jaws of victory

This is not a book about Brexit, but the elephant cannot be wished away. It was a long quarter century, but the writing was on the wall from the late 1980s as the Tories pivoted from uncompromising actuality to wistful nostalgia. Their Jesuitical tendency took John Major hostage and ransomed the country to Tony Blair, who cut and ran from his European responsibilities under the watchful eye of Rupert Murdoch, while Gordon Brown subsequently denied he had any. David Cameron gave up his country for his ambition, selling principles for position and then, ignoring the lessons of the Scottish independence referendum, ran a campaign Hillary Clinton would have been proud of.

Brexit's roots lie deeper yet in the sweet spot of labour and capital, the process innovation that was Fordism. Mass production of goods and a mass labour force saw vaulting productivity gains that for a third of a century, stretching from the 1940s to the late 1970s, produced cornucopian capitalism. The requisite massed workforces drove trade union power, while productivity furnished the economic gains that provided capital with the coinage to buy off the demands this working-class leverage and self-confidence generated. Living standards and profits rose together and the resultant social-democratic compromise in its variant mixes put in place mirrored welfare capitalisms. But among nations it only worked for the few and not the many, the West not the rest. It was the quiet at the eye of the storm. By the late 1970s it was passing, with technology and development hurrying its departure.[32]

The lack of tension between labour and capital in the UK and US during this period could not continue if rates of return were not to be eroded. The challenge for capital was to take on and beat skilled workforces possessed of strength and the ability to withdraw cooperation and consent. That strength was sapped at home with the increasing elimination within the production process of the need for skilled intervention. The new technologies adopted favoured unskilled or, at worst, semi-skilled labour. Where deskilling had little or no purchase, the answer was to offshore to countries where the writ of social contract between domestic labour and capital did not run and where consequently skilled labour was to be bought on the cheap. One key was containerisation.

There were two escape routes for the West. To save what could be saved by moving manufacturing upstream using increased specialisation to enhance added value was the triage of choice for Germany and, to a lesser extent, the US. The callous alternative was to abandon ship and watch manufacturing wither, while re-gearing the country to finance and alongside a minimum wage zero-hours service economy. The gig economy was the path Britain walked and the start of the journey to Brexit. It was not fated, but it proved the consequence of Tory hands on the tiller rather than Labour; of Wilson's failure to forestall and Thatcher's pyrrhic victory for the people of Britain. The choice of focus on low wages rather than high skills shattered private-sector unions and working-class solidarity. Labour became the party that was defensive of industrial capital and the Tories offensively favouring finance. Manufacture failed to recognise which side Labour was on. The same was not true of the banks, hedge funds and the financial grey market. Tory donors cascaded cash from that financial cancer in the heart of the British economy the City of London. Johnson put it most eloquently during the referendum campaign with his reported *sotto voce* comment 'fuck business',[33] widely misconstrued as irritation rather than manifesto in sound bite.

For all the Tory Eurosceptic jeremiads about the need to take back control and save our sovereignty, the Brexit debate

was rather about a different dependence, not independence. In terms of serving the interests of their paymasters, Brexit was right. Eurosceptics were marching to the beat of a different drum. Long disconnected from concerns over the health of Britain's industrial economy, but entwined deep in the nexus of finance and speculation's darkening web, they were increasingly at odds with Brussels. Both the EU's thrust in terms of the direction of economic and industrial policy, and its parallel attempts to discipline tax-havens, offshore banking and corporate spivs were an anathema to the new Tories. 'One Nation' Tories favoured sitting on the fence, but the problem was that that seat disappeared as fences moved. With the Lisbon Treaty, Brussels recognised that to maintain position vis-à-vis Washington and Beijing it needed to look increasingly to its own interests and started giving itself the means to do exactly that. The EU drive was underway for industrial and economic consolidation and centralisation, alongside a foreign policy and security capacity capable of expressing and defending those interests.

As Europe's embrace threatened to bite back in Britain, it was time to abandon a central role in Europe for fresh subordination to casino economics on the other side of the Atlantic. The referendum rode the broken working class's alienation from a political system, best exemplified by the austerity visited on Britain's 'left behind', to keep bankers in bonuses and to satisfy those very same interests funding the campaign and the Conservatives. The Leave vote corralled over two-thirds of the Tory vote (68%) but less than a third of Labour's (32%). Yet it was enough.

My contribution was a second edition of *Our Europe, Not Theirs* at the urging of Lawrence and Wishart, a series of public events across South West England on behalf of the Labour Movement for Europe (LME) and street campaigning and door-knocking with the Labour Party. Local campaigning was desultory and depressing with no leadership and no message. Yet it was clear that the national Leave campaign was reaching parts of the electorate other campaigns had not. This time there were no safe seats. In the pubs, streets and council estates of the Forest of Dean the apolitical found politics, and both disdain and distaste a vehicle. Those who'd brought the public austerity, and themselves the expenses scandal, couldn't see the cold revenge and retribution looming. Those who hadn't voted in decades and those who'd never found the ballot box in the first place turned out to show their contempt for the establishment that Labour had yoked itself to. Labour's campaign was a marriage of smug bipartisanship.[34] Brexiteers gave intellectual dishonesty a bad name. All it reminded me of was the deranged rationality and logic of mid-Victorian Britain, where someone injuring themselves in an unsuccessful suicide could be indicted for wounding with intent to kill, an offence for which Parliament had carelessly provided the death penalty.[35]

The LME executive had been told by Baroness Royall, Labour's former leader in the House of Lords, to laud and applaud Cameron's triumph when his Chamberlain moment arrived and he came down those metaphorical aircraft steps waving that piece of paper with his deal brought back from Brussels to help keep Britain in the Union. It was political gibberish. Cameron came back with more power for the Houses of Lords and Commons to block EU legislation and interfere on eurozone monetary policy, a downgrading of EU aspirations on future integration, and the creation of second-class workers in Britain's factories and services as EU citizens were stripped of in-work benefits. I argued we should be saying that, when Labour won its next election, we would tear the deal up. But this was no democracy, we were there to obey orders.

Labour had failed to heed the lessons of the Scottish referendum when it branded itself 'red Tories,' with Miliband shepherding Labour's sheep into the maw of Tory and Liberal wolves as part and parcel of a paternal establishment telling the 'naughty' Scots what was best for them. We destroyed in months a tartan wall of Labour support that had taken a century and more to build. The lesson burnt into Labour should have been 'never again.' If Labour wanted to save anything, it needed to reject Cameron rather than embrace him. As I wrote in *Tribune*:

> *There is a third way – to coin a phrase. It is absolutely in the interests of Labour supporters to remain in the EU, despite Cameron's concessions rather than because of them. The message should be: 'We stay to*

> *create our Europe, not theirs.' Labour should pledge that those opt-outs with an adverse impact on the labour market will be torn up the next time Labour is in power, in the same way that Tony Blair did on entering office in 1997 when he dispensed with John Major's precious Social Chapter opt out. If we want to marshal our voters into the In camp, this has to be our message. The 'red Tory' gambit wrecked Labour in Scotland. This time it threatens the breakup of Britain, as Brexit would be followed by Sentry – with Scotland entering the EU after a second independence referendum.*[36]

My position wasn't new, it was common sense. But no idea is too stupid for a politician to adopt it. I'd gone – seemingly slightly incoherently – on the record a year earlier, suggesting it would be better Britain leave than scuttle the whole enterprise: 'If we were being asked to vote to stay in by destroying social rights in Britain with the threat this would set a precedent in future for right-wing governments in other EU countries to demand the same the left should adopt the same selfless heroism Captain "Titus" Oates did, say "I am just going outside and may take some time" and vote to quit Europe rather than infect it with this toxic Tory virus.'[37]

I carried on in that same vein as the referendum put normal politics in the shade. In an article titled 'Not for Cameron, but despite him!', I argued that another Europe was possible:

> *In an increasingly global economy the future lies together not separately. The EU is currently bigger and richer than the US. The EU can set global standards – whether social or political – on trade and the environment, human rights and equality, in a way no medium sized nation state could ever contemplate. We want to stay inside Europe to change it, but in entirely the opposite direction from where Cameron wants to take us.*

> *We need a European Economic Strategy that rejects the neo-liberal austerity programme, a commitment*

to fighting climate change and a rapid drive towards a 'green economy,' a trade policy that puts people first, paralleled by a foreign policy underpinned by multilateralism, human rights and democracy accompanied by security and defence policy that has the EU prepared to tackle today's – and tomorrow's – threats rather than yesterday's.

Today's Europe wears its social-democratic cloth all too lightly, all progressives would agree. Yet while it would be wonderful if we could build Socialism in one country, if it was ever possible it isn't any more. What miracle of English exceptionalism, what fantasy, allows us to think we can go it alone when our Socialist sister parties across Europe whether in Italy or Germany or France, all believe their future is inside the Union? The Greek Left, despite all the harsh indignities visited upon it by the World and Europe's Bankers know that their best future is in Europe – and the Euro – not outside.

The Marx and Spencer of the 'Leave' campaign – Groucho and Frank, that is – Boris and Farage – offer nothing that we want. These 'Del Boys' of politics are selling xenophobic right-wing populism wrapped up in a flag of St. George and a nostalgia for a past that never was for Britain's poor and needy. Another Europe is possible but the only way to get there is to vote to 'remain' on June 23rd – despite Cameron not because of him – and go on from there.[38]

During the referendum campaign my 'stump' speech opened as follows: 'The reality is that the costs and benefits of leaving are massively exaggerated by the Leave campaign, but almost equally exaggerated in their mirror image by Remain. The choice we face is not economic, but social, political and historical.' Tempered, it went on, 'We can only build "castles in the air" if we have our feet on the ground – and foundations deep in everyday reality.' The era of globalisation I illustrated

through a story involving a friend in Belgium, booking on her mobile phone in France a UK train with a Chinese credit card via a call centre in India. Then I reprised Wallerstein and the 'red Tory' trap. The finale was that the concessions granted Cameron were either trivial or dangerous. The most dangerous of which was the compromising of free movement with condoning of discrimination against EU citizens in Britain, and the axiomatic reciprocity, producing second-class workers on both sides of the Channel to be exploited by unscrupulous employers and used to undermine workers' rights and conditions. The ultimate choice was: which side of history did we want to be on?

The English chose yesterday over tomorrow by 53.4 to 46.6%. The fact that a majority of English voters disliked the EU was no surprise. It had long been one-way traffic. The last best hope was to take on and challenge the Cameronite centre-right's pro-European agenda that offered nothing to Labour voters, and to refuse to consort with the business-led duller-than-royalty Remain campaign. The failure to do so was the ultimate sin of commission that concluded forty years of dereliction of duty. In Britain's other nations it was more complicated. Scotland overwhelmingly chose Brussels over Westminster, Northern Ireland's Catholics chose Dublin over London with the Protestants the reverse, while the indigenous Welsh only lost to Leave with the weight of votes from England's migrants added to the scales. It was rage against the dying of hope, the fury of a class betrayed as much as by their dislike of the EU. Absent Brexit, any other excuse would have served. They were grasping for a straw of empowerment and found it there.

The claim that Labour's defeat in December 2019, and the referendum, was the party being broken on the wheel of Brexit needs to be put to the question. The careless and convenient assumption that the 'red wall' fell because of Labour's studied ambiguity of Brexit – coupled with the media's demonisation of Corbyn – needs testing. Brexit was as much pretext as cause. Labour's heartlands, ignored and marginalised for a quarter of a century, had reasons plenty to revolt: public services crippled by austerity, wages stagnant, or falling, as the rich shook the money tree leaving the poor the pain.[39]

There was no Brexit in the United States. 'Their' Boris came early. Look around Europe as the populists and xenophobes grow in Hungary and Poland, and socialist and social-democratic parties threaten either to disappear down political sinkholes of their own making in France, Italy and Greece, or to remodel themselves like the Danish Socialists – even in an era of slack definitions – to no longer warrant the name.

What is to be done? As the Scotsman said to an enquiring traveller: 'I wouldn't start from here'. But this is where history, culture and politics have cast us away. Our point of departure is set, but where we go is our destiny. Left high and dry, stranded in mediocracy, irrelevance and inequality, our escape depends on our ability to break with a past that has coffled us in line to serve privilege, patriotism and prerogative. Whether together within the United Kingdom or by our separate nations is far from clear, but concurrently or consecutively it must be done.

Endnotes

[1] John Maclean (1919), *The Coming War with America.* [2] Graham Allison (2017), *Destined for War: Can America and China Escape Thucydides's Trap*, New York: Houghton Mifflin Harcourt. [3] Samuel P. Huntington (1996), *The Clash of Civilizations and the Remaking of World Order*, New York: Simon & Schuster. [4] Glyn Ford, Glenys Kinnock and Arlene McCarthy (eds) (1996), *Changing States: A Labour Agenda for Europe*, London: Mandarin. Written today, Beijing would elbow Tokyo aside. [5] Luuk van Middelaar (2013), *The Passage to Europe: How a Continent Became a Union*, New Haven: Yale University Press; and (2019), *Alarums and Excursions: Improvising Politics on the European Stage*, Newcastle upon Tyne: Agenda Publishing. [6] Nereo Penalver Garcia and Julian Priestley (2015), *The Making of a European President*, London: Palgrave. [7] Julian Priestley (2008), *Six Battles that Shaped the European Parliament*, London: John Harper. [8] Julian Priestley (2010), *European Political Parties: The Missing Link*, Paris: Notre Europe. [9] 'The missing political link and how to find it', *Tribune*, 29 October 2010. [10] 'The missing political link and how to find it', *Tribune*, 29 October 2010. [11] Until 2020 and Trump's 'contested' defeat, this would have required no comment. Today, two points need to be made. First, it would be a massive step forward from where the Union currently stands democratically, and second, all MEPs would vote individually as opposed to in a bloc. [12] Denis MacShane (2021), *Must Labour Always Lose?*, London: Claret Press, p. 187. [13] While Juncker won, Barnier went on to become the Commission's chief Brexit negotiator and Dombrovskis, former Latvian prime minister, the chief of financial services and later trade commissioner. [14] Nicholas Watt and Ian Traynor (2014), 'David Cameron loses Jean-Claude Juncker vote', *Guardian*, 27 June. [15] Julian Priestley and Glyn Ford (2016), 'Introduction to the second edition', *Our Europe, Not Theirs*, London: Lawrence and Wishart. [16] The Spanish Government had refused to certify the election of four Basque nationalists, reducing the EP's effective membership from 751 to 747. [17] *Saturday Evening Post*, 15 February 1930. [18] Trotsky was in favour; see Leon Trotsky (1929), 'Disarmament and the United States of Europe', *Bulletin of the Russian Opposition*, October. [19] Communist Party of Great Britain (1951), *The British Road to Socialism*. [20] My response in the ensuing European election campaign was to demand 'Proper jobs for workers in Britain' and table a resolution demanding that

the next parliament reject the incoming Commission unless it would change European legislation to stop the export inside the Union of low wages and inferior conditions. Even one Tory MEP signed – Neil Parish. [21] Quoted in Jonas Marvin (2021), 'Brexit from below: nation, race and class,' *Salvage*, 19 November, https://salvage.zone/articles/brexit-from-below-nation-race-and-class/ (accessed 12 February 2022). [22] Merilyn Moos and Steve Cushion (2020), *Anti-Nazi Germans*, Community Languages in association with the Socialist History Society. [23] R. W. G. Mackay (1940), *Federal Europe: The Case for European Federation*, London: M. Joseph. [24] *Left*, December 1939. [25] F. A. Ridley and Bob Edwards (1944), *The United Socialist States of Europe*, National Labour Press. [26] Brockway left the ILP in the late 1940s and was elected as Labour MP for Eton and Slough in the 1950 general election. [27] George Orwell (1941), *The Lion and the Unicorn: Socialism and the English Genius*, London: Secker & Warburg. [28] George Orwell and Reginald Reynolds (1948), *British Pamphleteers*, vol. 1, London: Allan Wingate. [29] Tom Nairn (1972), 'The left against Europe,' *New Left Review* 75, September/October. [30] Rather like 'rice Christians' whose faith is based on material benefit. [31] Conference proceedings accessed through the Labour History Archive & Study Centre at the People's History Museum, Manchester. [32] All summed up in Harry Braverman (1974), *Labor and Monopoly Capital: The Degradation of Work in the Twentieth Century*, New York: Monthly Review Press. [33] Tim Ross (2021), 'Boris Johnson's "f*** business" approach to the supply chain crisis is a risk for Brexit Britain,' *New Statesman*, 5 October. [34] During the 'terror' of the French Revolution, a republican marriage saw naked men and women tied together and thrown into sea or river to drown. [35] This comes courtesy of Stephen Sedley (2021), 'A decent death,' *London Review of Books*, 21 October. [36] 'How Corbyn can confront Cameron's Chamberlain moment,' *Tribune*, 5 February 2016. [37] Denis MacShane (2015), *Brexit: How Britain Will Leave Europe*, London: I. B. Tauris. [38] 'The EU – In or Out? Not for Cameron, but despite him!,' *Forest of Dean & Wye Clarion*, June 2016. [39] See Mike Makin-Waite (2021), *On Burnley Road: Class, Race and Politics in a Northern English Town*, London: Lawrence Wishart. See my review 'None so blind ...,' *Chartist* 313, November/December 2021.

2 From Gloucester to Reading

If you don't know where you're going any path will get you there.

The Cheshire Cat, Alice in Wonderland

The Second World War was not one conflict, but several. It was two imperialist wars setting London against Berlin and Washington against Tokyo, interlaced with an anti-fascist crusade against Hitler and Mussolini and serial national liberation struggles across Eurasia. The choreography saw sharp changes of tempo and tone with partnerships made and broken. Its long tail stretched to 1989 in the West and beyond in the East. For Britain it was a pyrrhic victory hidden in the euphoria of American and Soviet military sacrifice. We'd put our fingers in the dyke, but repair and restoration fell to Washington, Moscow and Beijing.

At the start of the war we were an imperial power, at its end one of Europe's nations. In 1945 Britain was the bankrupt ruler of a collapsing empire. For all Japan's atrocities, they had smashed the myth of European invincibility and had gifted self-confidence to Asians and Africans that liberation was both possible and nigh. We traded on our reputation as we shrivelled in a generation from superpower to mediocrity masked behind the trappings of history and authority. The global economic boom meant Harold MacMillan soon claimed we'd never had it so good, but others were having it better. We'd beaten the Germans - and Japanese - in 1945, but struggled in 1956 at Suez with the Egyptians. Within a quarter of a century even the victories over Berlin and Tokyo looked less clear cut. Early Trumpian-style deniers of Japan's defeat among their diaspora in South America claimed vindication when they finally returned to Japanese wealth and opulence in the 1980s.

The institutional architecture of Britain with the monarchy and House of Lords is trapped in history, worse so is society. For close to two hundred years, Britain's advantage of 'first mover' in terms of power, position and pocket protected its pole position. Its erosion was evident by 1914–18. By 1945 Britain was running on empty. Two decades on, it was self-evident the education system was not fit for purpose, and Britain's industries were struggling to compete with emerging industrial powers unburdened by levels of military spending requisite for those nursing global pretensions. Britain's Industrial Revolution was the first. It told as we suffered the punishment of priority. We were never required to complete that total economic and political transformation necessary for those who followed in our wake. In the twenty-first century we're still waiting. It's capitalism with feudal characteristics.

This British – or rather English – question has been the one within whose answers I've lived throughout my whole life. How do we find a new place in the world where we can restore ourselves to something like a constructive role? None of the sequence of answers to date has taken us anywhere near that promised land. Some have moved us in the right direction, some sideways and a few backwards. Labour governments gained yardage, but nothing close to the scale of advance needed, while the Conservatives, with limited exceptions, either preferred form over substance or subcontracted the search to the market.

Juvenation and family

I was born in Gloucester Royal Infirmary on 28 January 1950, a week after the death of George Orwell. My existence I owe to my sister Wendy. In 1948 my mother, Mathilda Alberta James, had had a difficult pregnancy and Wendy Elizabeth was months premature.[1] She came into the world on 9 De-

cember and left the following day. Dr O'Dowd advised my mother it would be dangerous to try again. But she did. With the help of the good doctor and the newly minted NHS – she was hospitalised for more than six weeks before my birth – I also arrived early, but this time not too early.

My maternal grandfather, Tom James, married Lucy – born on Christmas Day 1874, the year Camille Saint-Saëns's *Danse macabre* premiered – when she was twenty. Five daughters – my mother was the youngest – and one son survived him. Family lore had my mother the last of thirteen, which sounds implausible while Lucy was birthing between the ages of twenty-one and thirty-six, but there were still-births and early deaths.

My great-grandmother standing in the doorway (far right) with Lucy, Tom and the children.

My mother was from Bream in the heart of the Forest of Dean, wedged in that forgotten corner of England north of the Severn's loop and east of Wales. The inhabitants were branded on the tongue. At the offer of a cigarette handed round most take a 'dofer' – do for later – and stick it above an ear. The local burr was strong, more patois than accent. The male welcome was a hearty 'ow bist ould butt'. It just went downhill from there. The local archetype was the fictional Jolter: ''Im used ta be butty wi' owls Charlie Goode at pit. Thay run the zame stall together. Jolter worked nights an' Charlie days. One night when Jolter got inta stall 'im zin a broken shovel stuck up agen the zide an' chalked across the blade was, "Take these out Zurry, I vorgot un." Next marnin' when Charlie come in that 'ad bin rubbed off an' chalked on there instead were, "thou take un out theezelf, I 'a'n't zid un".[2]

A skilled pianist, my mother would provide the accompaniment to carols at Christmas. She was bright. At eleven, she achieved a 'half-pass' to the grammar school. The 50 per cent reduction in fees was as much use as a chocolate watch. The family's half simply was not there, and she was unable to stay on. After leaving school she went into 'service' in London for a couple of years and then ended up working for Great Western Railways in the buffet at Reading station. Until her death we still had the odd knife stamped 'GWR' in the kitchen drawer, and the family aversion to curry was prompted by her railway stories that when the meat was on the turn, curry was on the menu. She never reported finding T. E. Lawrence's *Seven Pillars of Wisdom*, lost on the station at the time.

My mother with grandparents Lucy and Tom and sister Elsie (far right).

The men and boys of my mother's extended family were all colliers. This was not atypical: in 1945, 50 per cent of men in the Forest were miners. The family remembrance had my grandfather Tom victimised for his role in the 1926 General Strike, and bitter about the Miners' Lockout five years earlier.[3] I've no reason to doubt it, but he would have been just one of many. A key player back then had been the Forest's MP Albert Purcell, who served from July 1925 – when he won a by-election – until May 1929. Purcell was the most influential Labour MP to represent the constituency. He served on the General Council of the Trades Union Congress (TUC) (1919–28) and in 1924 led a TUC fact-finding mission to the Soviet Union.

The facts found were far too pro-Soviet for both the *Daily Mail* and Hergé, who caricatured him in the bilious *The Adventures of Tintin in the Land of the Soviets* (1929). Purcell was an early European Federalist. His preface to Edo Fimmen's *Labour's Alternative: The United States of Europe or Europe Limited* (1924) comes down firmly in favour of a muscular version of the first. Purcell was central to the TUC stance in the 1926 strike. A hardline syndicalist, he believed the industrial struggle took precedence over Parliament. His future was crushed by the miners' fate and theirs by the owners.

Forest memories were long: in Bream in the late 1950s there was a family shunned because the father had been a scab more than a quarter of a century earlier. It had been a long, hard and bitter struggle following on from the Miners' Lockout. Grandfather Tom died on 14 April 1949, aged seventy-seven, and one of my uncles bled to death after a mining accident when the ambulance taking him to hospital ran out of petrol. He was not the unluckiest. Others were crippled by pneumoconiosis; years of sucking in coal dust left them shuffling and gasping to garden gate and grave, locked in breathless bodies. The report of Tom's funeral had him dying 'after a long illness' – one can only suspect it was related to 'serving over 40 years at the New Fancy Colliery'. Bream Labour Party sent a wreath.

The inevitable closures that faced the Forest's pits, due to depleting reserves and narrow seams, came early. The National Coal Board's (NCB) South West Division held a larger deficit than the NCB as a whole, and despite attempts to keep pits open, they became inevitable victims. While the Forest's 'free miners' avoided nationalisation of their assets, relentless cost-cutting efforts saw pit closures through Labour and Tory governments alike.[4] It was Labour that oversaw the last pit closure in 1965; for too many, absent coal it was dole.

My father, Ernest, was orphaned at twelve when his mother, Mrs J. H. Ford (women were designated by their husband's initials in those days), died 6 April 1918. His father, John H. Ford, had been an alcoholic, the reason he signed the pledge and never allowed a drop of alcohol to pass his lips. Ernest was the third and youngest son according to the report of the wedding in the Forest newspaper fifteen years later. Yet the 'family Bible' seemingly lists three brothers, Arthur, Charles and Robert, and one sister, Elizabeth. Two brothers died in the trenches. According to the inscription, this Bible – an illustrated King James version – was awarded to my father at Union Street Elementary School from the 'Prize Fund for Proficiency in Biblical Knowledge' by the Religious Tract Society. Ernest ended up employed as a bellboy at The Grand on Plymouth Hoe, aged thirteen. He escaped by three months the extra education the raising of the school leaving age to fourteen would have provided. There, in an oft-told tale, he reported his mortification when one of the hotel's Grand Dames, living semi-permanently in the hotel, dispensed all the way down Christmas gifts that turned out to be Bibles. That anticlimactic present is very definitely not still in the family.

My father was finally rescued by a cousin who brought him and second cousin Jean up to the Forest. While Dad married Mum, Jean married Mum's nephew Garnet. My father was the exception to the mining rule, employed as he was at Richard Thomas and Company's tin works in Lydney. He was a keen footballer, playing in goal for Aylburton, where he lodged before my mother's attraction poached him away to Bream AFC. When the Second World War came, he was too old for conscription and was instead directed to Hoffman's in Stonehouse, the other side of the Severn and at the bottom of the Cotswold escarpment, producing ball-bearings for Britain's Spitfires. He stuck there as a toolmaker and internal grinder and was rewarded in 1953 with one of those 'homes fit for heroes' on the village's massive new council estate, built for the company's convenience. In the mid-1960s he was presented with a tie for twenty-five years' service, and his redundancy notice. He'd been an Amalgamated Union of Engineering Workers shop-steward and was, at one time, considered for being made up to foreman, but it was decided he was too good a worker to lose. Outside of work, roses were his hobby. There was a set of *The Rose Growers Annual* going back a decade or more on the bookshelves, and he'd go off into the local copse looking for wild rose standards to bring home and then graft a 'bud', a skill he taught me along with pruning. His favourite was Harry Wheatcroft's 'Peace' with its ILP and pacifist connections. Beautiful as the roses were, my mother's paper-hanging skills proved more useful.

I recall, at three, crying on the edge of the kitchen sink with soap in my eyes while my mother washed me. My first fixed point of reference was my fourth birthday when I fell down on the garden path, cutting my knee. We lived less than ten miles from the Forest as the crow flies, but over thirty when forced to loop east through Gloucester by road or west on the train via Sharpness and the Severn Bridge to Lydney. That latter route was closed off in October 1960 when two tanker barges hit one of the piers, collapsing two spans. The broken bridge lingered toothless and stricken for a decade, allowing the passage of time to dim memories of all those easy promises of repair. We were lucky: the ball-bearings were booming, although this meant I scarcely saw my father. He was working twelve-hour shifts four, sometimes five, days a week plus Saturday mornings and all day Sundays. The years were punctuated with television (installed in the front room, where you went to watch your programme before retiring back to the kitchen), holidays and – following the Severn Bridge 'disaster' – a Morris Minor ROH 362, as the train no longer took the strain.

We went at least every other weekend to the Forest and stayed with my grandmother in a semi-detached cottage surrounded by oak forest. There were no mod cons. Cooking was coal. There was neither an indoor toilet, nor bathroom. A potty under the bed served at night, though Granny merited a commode. Washing was porcelain jug and basin, with a kettle of hot water for the soft and the winter. There was running water, but for choice well water was preferred. There was no septic tank at the bottom of the garden; rather, hung beneath the privy was a large, flanged, iron basin whose contents were dosed with disinfectant. One task, for an unlucky victim every fortnight or so, was deep digging in the extensive garden to drain the contents and back-fill. Granny's yellow gages from the tree beside the privy were luscious. Next door in the same shed were dolly-tub and mangle for the sheets and blankets.

Wakened by the cock's crow, further sleep was a fight easier won in June than December. The smell of Granny's house was leaf mould, mildew and coal dust. The taste was home-grown, from the garden which served England's vegetables to the table. I never felt deprived. Spam featured regularly for tea, as did sugar sandwiches. The extended family all kept chickens for breakfast eggs and Sunday lunch (although we called it dinner). Generation upon generation the hens ran faster. Darwin gave nature history. On the Sabbath morning the 'duty' butcher would case the coop. The slowest of the battery was strangled, plucked, dressed, cooked and eaten within three hours. Some of the leftovers were transported home to hang in the pantry safe for later in the week.

Late one autumn, I must have been ten or eleven, I recall going off with my cousin Jean, who was twenty-five years my senior, and her four kids to the local Princess Royal slag heap as the conveyor hovering over the apex drizzled a stream of fresh spoil. We'd taken an old pram and spent a couple of hours scrabbling through the waste for the small fragments of coal that screening had missed. A lump the size of a walnut was a lucky find. The pram full, home we went, with the day's haul providing the evening's warmth. My recollection is this was during a local miners' strike, possibly over the planned closures.

Twice a year the family gathered. The family congregated at Granny's for Christmas – Christmas Day was her birthday, of course – when twenty-five or more sat down with the adults in one room and the children sequestered next door. The large Christmas tree was forest forage. Over-eating was followed by carol singing. The family were non-practising chapel, rather than church. I still can't hear 'The Holly and the Ivy' or 'Once in Royal David's City' without being transported back into that past. It's not a journey I make often. Those medieval carols have fallen far from the tree.

In the summer we played away. A thirty-nine-seater coach would transport the whole family off to the seaside. Margate, Blackpool and Plymouth were favoured destinations. We'd block book a couple of bed and breakfasts next door to each other and transpose family from forest to foreshore. The children swam and played under adult eyes until the sun went down. Then men headed for the public bars, and the women to the B&Bs to feed and bed the children before – absent that night's duty roster – joining the men several rounds in arrears.

False promises

It was Harold Wilson's fault. It was his 'white heat of technology' speech at the Labour Party Conference in Scarborough in 1963 that set my course. My mother was one of the last members of the National Society of Brushmakers, whose origins dated back to 1757. Her job was taking small clumps of Chinese bristle, dipping it into molten pitch and then screwing it into wooden stocks. Her hands were constantly burnt and blistered. Modernisation and technology had a timbre, and jobs like my mother's were soon to become a thing of the past. A 'new Britain' would be forged in the 'heat' of 'scientific revolution'. I wanted to play my part. Of that more below.

NSB badge. Courtesy of the Working Class Movement Library, Salford.

My first school was Stonehouse County Primary on the periphery of our estate. It had two forms with just shy of forty in each class. The Stroud area had two grammar and two technical schools (segregated by sex) and half a dozen mixed secondary moderns. This was before the coming of the comprehensive school. The eleven-plus saw two from my year at Stonehouse get passes for the grammar schools and twice that number for the techs. A pass rate that would have led to riots in the honey-stoned villages of the upper Cotswolds, was a success for the factory's dormitory estate.

I passed the eleven-plus and went to Marling School from 1961. I was a good all-rounder, in the top set of five for all my subjects, save French in which I languished in the fourth set. Languages were my *bête noire* and still are. I blamed the fact I was tone-deaf, but teacher intimidation didn't help. My limitations were catered for when it mattered to the school, but not when it mattered to me. The school day started with morning service with homilies and announcements, sports results – at least when Marling had won – and hymns. The reward for failure to sing was detention after school. Yet my lusty vocal contributions were stilled. Uniquely, I was given amnesty for dissonant singing. Silence on my part was golden.

The school had a system where you were sent to the headmaster's study at the end of the day for conspicuously 'good' or 'bad' work, where you then signed the relevant book. My French and myself were repeat offenders, yet this was more than balanced by my other subjects. One particular evening I enjoyed presenting simultaneously my bad French work with my good geography. The head was impassive on that occasion, but seemed decidedly more ambivalent some months later in responding to good work on human reproduction in biology. The 'sister' high school regularly lost pupils consequent to the union of theory and practice. Needless to say, contraception did not figure on the syllabus in either school back then.

At school I was a natural organiser. Weekly or fortnightly tests were the stepping stones of progress, but ten or twenty questions swapped with your next-door neighbour for marking led to easy collusion. However, one member of staff either cared or was a social psychologist, and attempted to impose more integrity upon the process. He decided we would now pass our papers to the desk behind with the pupil in the rear bringing his paper up to the front. I negotiated with my row that during marking everyone would leave the papers blank and pass them back unsullied by any dangerous crosses to allow their owner to fill in the blanks to their own satisfaction. What was a lesson was the power of expectation and the consequent self-imposed limits of grade inflation. Those with 'real' nines or nine and a halfs announced tens, while those overshadowed with the prospect of crime and punishment with 'real' threes and fours muttered 'five' and lived to cheat another day.

In September 1965 the school forced choices in the run-up to O-levels. C. P. Snow's *The Two Cultures* remained unread and unwelcome by the head: it was arts or science. Giving up Latin was more relief than hardship, but choosing between history and biology was a wrench. In the last exams I'd been top in history and second in biology. In January Churchill died, and the whole school was to sanctify the event with prize essays. It turned out to be a partisan rather than prime-ministerial affair: there would be no putting pen to paper with the death of Attlee in October 1967. The main thrust of my contribution was 'Remember Tonypandy', recalling the occasion in November 1910 when Churchill, as Home Secretary, had ordered the army to break a miners' strike against

the Cambrian Combine, after the police lost control of the Rhondda. Local miners' folklore saw two killed, but history now says the deaths may have occurred with Winston's earlier strike-breaking in Newcastle. My history teacher gave a wan smile when he handed my effort back. Neither he nor I were surprised when I failed to make the shortlist, let alone win a prize.

It was clear to me that Britain's future was set to follow Wilson's 'white heat', with the past abandoned for the future. The path was clear: biology bested history. My history teacher enquired after my decision, and we were never to speak again. Entering the sixth form it was to be A-levels in maths, physics and chemistry, although I did grab a crumb from history's table with a subsidiary O-level in 'World Affairs since 1945'. The road proved harder than anticipated. Fluent mental arithmetic stuttered and crashed on the rocks of trigonometry and quadratic equations. Try as I might, it remained almost as much a mystery at the end as at the beginning. My early yearning towards astronomy was unrequited by higher maths. Reality spoke. If I was to be the first of my family to go to university, it would be chemistry rather than the universe calling.

Cotswold Capers

The Stroud Valley was a good place to grow up. The Subscription Rooms hosted Saturday night bands and discos for the fourteen-to-twenty age group. The Beatles had played there to no audience and no acclaim in 1962. I don't remember how but 'Jack' Hill (a friend from school) and I became cloakroom attendants before being promoted turn and turn about to 'DJs'. Heavily spun, it actually meant we played half a dozen singles 'sans patter' between the band's two evening sets. The grammar/secondary modern divide in the area was deep, and in such social hubs the hundreds of adolescents pre-stoked with illicit scrumpy were not welcoming of my grammar school peers. One night one of the local hooligans burst in boasting he'd just sorted out one of the grammar school 'ponces'. It turned out to be a classmate who'd ventured into the wrong area at the wrong time.

A consequence of Jack's and my rising through the Subscription Rooms ranks was, after a little argy-bargy, we came to be accepted by the regulars who formed the town's physical force cohort. One Friday Jack and I were engaged in the adolescent sport of underage drinking in a Stroud pub, likely the Swan Inn, when we were invited to join eight or ten of the group to gatecrash a party a few miles away. Off we went, packed into the back of a couple of old vans, eventually arriving at a large house with music, which was promptly invaded with the two of us trailing the vanguard. As we pushed our way in, I was shocked to come face to face with the head of school, vainly trying to staunch the flood. Jack and I quickly made our excuses and left, abandoning the posse. We were expecting serious recriminations on Monday morning. Nothing was ever said.

Our favourite pub became the Imperial, situated adjacent to Stroud station, where we drank 'Forest top' – a bottle of Forest Brown topped up to a pint with draught bitter. Earlier, I'd been at the Rolling Stones' 1965 concert in the Cheltenham Odeon. Despite being in one of the front half a dozen rows and even standing on top of the seats, the band were a staccato sight as those further forward were doing the same. The girls screamed throughout, with the group's set lost behind the wailing wall. Brian Jones may have come home, but he spent the night at the Imperial. Another regular was Slad poet and writer Laurie Lee, finding in the Imperial a convenient stopping-off point after a train down from London. *Cider with Rosie* was a school text, but there in the pub was its author happy to talk. He favoured at one point a turquoise corduroy suit. One evening, around the time he was finishing *As I Walked Out One Midsummer Morning*, we cajoled him into an overfull car and off to a teenage party where he disappeared in the throng.

Early peregrinations

Before becoming fully embroiled in higher education, my summers had been devoted to travelling. Between lower and upper sixth I'd gone off hitch-hiking with Jack. After a train to

Milan we'd hitched to Naples, taken a ferry to Sicily and then a boat to Tunis. From there we'd crossed the Maghreb. Annaba, Constantine, Setif, Algiers, Oran and Tclemcen, Oujda, Fes, Meknes, Casablanca, Rabat, Tetouan and Tangier, before crossing to Algeciras and Gibraltar. It was in that interregnum – after the Gibraltar sovereignty referendum in September 1967 in which 99.6 per cent of voters on a 96.5 per cent turnout had voted to stay British – when, although Franco had closed the land border, the small passenger ferry between Algeciras and Gibraltar still ran. In Algeria the shadow of the Arab–Israeli Six-Day War was still there and Britain and the British were less than popular with walls papered with pictures of our 'atrocities'. We claimed to be Swiss. Worse, two young men travelling together were seen as gay and thus fair game. After a week sleeping on the Bahía Little beach, it was up through Spain and France to home.

The next year it was Turkey: this time a train to Istanbul and then the slow boat *Ege* bouncing along the Turkish Black Sea coast, Sinop, Samsun, Ordu, Giresun, Trabazon, Rize and Hopa before overland to Artvin, Ardehan, Kars, Igdir, Dogubeyazit, ferry over Lake Van, Iskenderun, Izmir and back. We had served our time in Istanbul's famous Pudding Shop, and after seeing Mount Ararat and Persia from Dogubeyazit, the third voyage could only be India, target Taj Mahal.[5]

My future was locked in my exam results, which were due to be released while I was in Turkey. Well prior to the invention of the mobile phone, my parents lacked even a landline. Thus, any idea of phoning never crossed my mind. Juggling itinerary, publication and post, the earliest coordinating conjunction looked to be Istanbul. Hence, before leaving I'd arranged with my parents that they would send the results c/o poste restante, Istanbul Main Post Office. The letter failed to arrive before I had to leave, however, so instructions were left to forward it to Thessaloniki. Thwarted a second time, the last best hope was Ostend. Here, finally, in a well-travelled envelope, I found my future the day before my return to the UK. I was off to Reading to become a chemist, with a detour via Bristol.

Building harmony

In an attempt to draw university and industry together there were experiments with thick and thin sandwich courses from the late 1950s onwards. The first was one-three-one, with a year in industry, three years in university and a year back in industry, while the second was a six-year alternation of half-yearly spells between company and campus. I applied and was accepted for the first as a chemist at what was then the British Aircraft Corporation (BAC) at Filton, where Anthony Wedgwood Benn (later rebranding himself Tony Benn), the local MP, Minister of Technology and the left's techno-nationalist, seemed determined to build the Anglo-French Concorde himself if necessary. I was in the BAC laboratory, which was shared between aircraft manufacturing and the guided weapons division. My job was a weekly analysis of the dozen or so plating solutions in use. I'd report the results to two decimal places and hear the foreman shout 'A couple of shovelfuls, mate' to an underling.

The British aircraft industry after the war was seemingly incapable of making a right choice, as it juggled load and speed, technology and price. First in the aftermath of Europe's civil war was the Brabazon. Underwritten by soft government money, it was an enormous, propeller-driven plane, bigger than an Airbus A300, designed to carry a hundred passengers in luxury. It flew in 1949, but by 1953, absent a single order, it was cancelled. Airlines were buying the narrow-bodied Comet jet from de Havilland. That failed in a different way. It was too revolutionary, and early accidents that were the result of over-innovation nevertheless demonstrated that speed beat luxury: lessons well learnt by the competition at Boeing and Douglas.

The BAC1-11 threatened to break the chain of failure, but it was a design by Hunting Aircraft that was almost accidentally swept up in the forced amalgamation of the UK aircraft manufacturers into BAC in 1960. Despite these hints of promise, BAC snatched defeat from the jaws of victory with the cancelled 2-11 and 3-11. Next was the TSR-2, a tactical strike and reconnaissance aircraft intended as a low-altitude interdictor and a high-altitude reconnoitring platform, designed to fly at speeds of up to Mach 2.3. The TSR-2 was cancelled by the

new Labour government in 1965, officially on cost grounds. The UK's batch production was being crucified by US mass production. By comparison, General Dynamics' F-111 was a financial bargain and a stake in the heart of Britain's aircraft industry.

The TSR-2's failure was financial and technological. In the Rolls-Royce Technical College during my apprenticeship, we had one of the Bristol Siddeley Olympus engines from the TSR-2 to dismantle and reassemble. The word in the workshop was that the TSR-2 could certainly have flown at Mach 2.3, but only at the expense of replacing the engines on landing. Concorde, meanwhile, was the Brabazon writ large. A luxury aircraft in the dawning era of mass travel, it was conceived in the time of cheap oil, but commercial operation (1976) dawned post the 1973 oil shock. It only survived for so long on Anglo-French government life support. Technologically sweet, it beat the rest because Washington and Moscow pulled their runners from the race. That in itself was a message. I flew in it three times, and was one of a handful of individuals on the edge of the Filton runway thirty-four years apart for its first take-off (2 March 1969) and last landing (26 November 2003). Pigs don't fly, but white elephants do. Brabazon and Concorde were the best – but far from only – examples of Labour's technological trailblazing, with the many manufacturing for the few.

Indian summers

The following year, after twelve months with BAC and prior to going up to Reading, it was, as promised, off to India. To the Iranian border the itinerary was a recapitulation of twelve months earlier, then followed Tabriz, Tehran and Mashhad on into Afghanistan with Herat, Kandahar and Kabul, and finally Peshawar in Pakistan. I was more impressed with the Kabul Gorge than the Khyber Pass. For target Taj Mahal, it was necessary to pass the Pakistan–India border. By now there were four of us travelling together: three Brits and a Frenchman, meaning there was – we thought – no need for visas; however, the last leg of the journey to the actual border in Pakistan required a 'Road Travel Permit.' We went to the police station in Lahore and for some small consideration received an official looking paper with names, dates of birth and passport numbers neatly typed at the top.

En route we discovered many fellow travellers about to fall into the bureaucratic trap that ignorance of that law was no excuse. To rectify the omission involved backtracking hundreds of kilometres. There was another option with the *tabula rasa* of space under the shortlist of names on our document. We rapidly shipped stowaways as names were added under ours. Demand was high and space at a premium. Soon the sheet was covered on both sides with semi-legible names, dates and numbers in a blue-black continuum. My memory is that about twenty-six of us arrived at the border and nervously presented the, by then, dog-eared document. The Pakistani official didn't bat an eyelid, and pleased to be rid of us, cheerfully waved us on through to the queue for India. Here there were dragons. It turned out the descendants of Britain's imperialists were welcome unannounced, but the French needed notice. Our Frenchman – with whom we'd travelled together in a loose group from Teḥran to the Indian border – was cast asunder and dispatched back to Rawalpindi for a visa at the Indian Consulate there.

The next barrier was customs control. A Sergeant Major type took about eight or ten of us aside. He explained that the drug laws in India were exceptionally draconian for foreigners, and that he was aware that we had all transited Afghanistan where drugs were freely available. He said that this was a final opportunity to surrender any drugs before we and our backpacks were searched. He scanned the circle. Most were fascinated by their feet. A quiet voice from a sheepish face said he'd 'bought some herbs in Kabul.' The putative miscreant then presented an inch thick slab of hash the size of a sandal sole. The Sergeant Major growled, 'Any more?' There was a long silence, broken at last by our inquisitor. Snapping the piece in half he returned the smaller portion to the guilty party saying, 'Half for you, half for me! Off you all go.'

Delhi came and went as we headed for Agra and the shrine. Like a swimmer on the turn, mission accomplished, we headed back. Half a dozen of us were catching a Lahore–Rawalpindi train. Buying tickets was the easy part. More

difficult we knew would be finding a seat or even space to stand. The trains were rammed with people clinging to the doors and windows and sitting on the roof. When the train arrived on the platform there would be an impromptu brawl as hundreds struggled to lay claim to dozens of seats. There were solutions for sale, however. Slip some money to those in the marshalling yard who knew which carriages would make up the train and they would allow you to scurry on board in advance. It worked, but required patience. Safely entrained, we sat bored for several hours. Finally, we felt and heard the jolts and clanking as train and carriages coupled.

Well before the scheduled departure time the train pulled out of the yard and alongside a platform as the tide of passengers washed over it. We sat with nowhere to go – at least yet. One of my compulsions has long been news and newspapers. Later in life, a forty- or fifty-mile round trip to buy a day-old copy of the *Guardian* was unexceptional. In Pakistan there probably wasn't a *Guardian* for sale within a thousand miles, but there was the next best thing, the *Pakistan Times*. The kiosk was just twenty paces away. With a 'back in five minutes' I was off, leaving everything behind. With the paper secured I was waylaid by loitering passengers with the standard catechism of 'What is your name? Where do you come from? Do you like Pakistan?' I finally glanced towards my train. It was pulling out at pace with the last carriages passing in front of my eyes. The decision was instantaneous. I ran and leapt onto the running boards beneath the last door of the final carriage. The door was locked and I was on the outside looking in. I perched there for a good hour with the train making speed. Eventually it found a station it liked, where it slowed to a halt and the doors opened. With some relief I got myself back inside and, as we pulled away, I went looking for my friends. They weren't there.

I was on the wrong train – an express train – with no luggage, passport or ticket and the equivalent of 2p in small change. The ticket inspector when he found me was sceptical. But he could hardly throw me off. We weren't due to stop again for a couple of hours and he thought my original slow train should pass through about five hours behind. In the meantime, I was sent to stand in the corridor outside the second-class compartments. We finally arrived at the next stop and I was cast adrift, my pacing of the platform punctuated by compulsive checking and rechecking of the timetable. It refused to change. I had my doubts. Was this going to be the right train? Were my friends still on it? What had they done when I disappeared? Had they left my luggage, passport and money behind somewhere? Worse, I was now getting tired, and with neither money nor ticket the restaurants and waiting rooms were out of bounds. My 2p bought me a small bottle of water.

Finally, late into the night, 'my' train pulled in. I scurried on. It was the right train, friends, luggage, passport and money were back together again. It was such a relief that I failed to chide my companions for their spectacular lack of imagination over my fate, an indifference cut with somnolence. They fatalistically assumed it would all turn out for the best, which thankfully it did. In retrospect, maybe their languor was fortuitous. After all, if they had proactively offloaded luggage and passport in Lahore, my situation would have been far worse.

The next major hurdle was crossing from Afghanistan back into Iran. There had been some incidences of cholera in the former and, although we had the relevant vaccination certificates, the Iranians were concerned we might be carriers. All those crossing the border were shepherded into a tented encampment, tested daily and treated. We were fed and watered better than we treated ourselves; not an unpleasant furlough. The tests went off – presumably to Mashhad – and forty-eight hours later a list was read of who was free to leave. It was rather like waiting for luggage at the baggage carousel. Yours always seems to be invariably last, but from time to time it doesn't come at all. The interminable roll call ended absent my name. Everyone else from my cohort was free to go, but I was stuck there until the day I was listed. I can recall exactly when that was. Someone in quarantine had a radio one day – 31 August, the day Bob Dylan played the Isle of White Festival. Next day, my name set me free. Back in Istanbul later it felt like home, even if we did resort to selling blood to stretch the financial envelope.

My pilgrimages continued during university as I filled in the missing parts of my European jigsaw. Steve Harriman, an equally eclectic traveller among my friends, and I chose Albania in 1970. We flew to Dubrovnik to be picked up as part

of a group of around fifteen by Progressive Tours, who specialised in the Communist bloc. From there we were whisked off by coach to Cetinje – now in Montenegro – where we overnighted before crossing the border the following lunchtime. The crossing was pedantically smooth. The sting was in the tail. A small group of younger males were pulled aside and told that to conform with Albanian cultural mores we would need haircuts. The long hair of university and revolt might have been knocking on Tirana's door, but it wasn't coming in. It was Hobson's choice: be left marooned on the Yugoslav border or shorn. Our bus stopped at the first small town and the five/six of us were queued for a short back and sides. Suitably cropped, we were driven on to Durres to reside in a small hotel on the beach, where we passed the evening with okra, local beer and Italian TV.

We had ten days of the country's national communism. We visited Tirana and travelled down as far as Ohrid and its lake, through countryside whose fields were cornered with pillboxes and slopes tagged with slogans. An attempt to row out on the lake and around the buoy marking the boundary with Yugoslavia saw us met with a speedboat crewed by unsmiling and armed border police, firmly indicating that was not the way to go. All this was punctuated with visits to a series of eponymous 'Mao Tse Tung' farms, factories and workshops. The only freighter in the port of Durres hailed from Shanghai. The Mao rash was only matched by Skanderbeg, Albania's fifteenth-century nobleman who led the successful rebellion against Ottoman rule in Northern Albania. He was commemorated in the gaps between Maos. Tirana's isolation was validated with touchstones half a world and half a millennium away.

Not that they didn't have a scattering of friends. The group's English guide had volunteered two years running to help with railway construction. In the meantime, he was engaged in some serious missionary activity as he expounded the virtues of the British and Irish Communist Organisation (B&ICO), a semi-Maoist group whose political claim to fame was their Two Nations Theory, which claimed Ulster Protestants were or had the potential to become a nation in their own right. Our guide claimed that B&ICO members in Ulster were supporting Protestants in their armed struggle against the IRA with the vocal backing of the Party of Labour of Albania (PLA). We were urged to tune into Radio Tirana's English-language broadcasts. That call I resisted, but I did subsequently end up with an extensive collection of B&ICO pamphlets. I then lost track of them for a couple of years before they resurfaced around the 1975 European Referendum as the backbone of 'Communists for Europe' and later published *The EEC: The Economic Case For!* (1979).

Our flock in Albania was a mix of pilgrims and completists. The B&ICO clique put their latest theological thinking to the question by subjecting the officials ministering to our varied visits to cross-examination on the use and merits of machine tractor stations and the like. That aspect of Stalinist liturgy had clearly passed even the PLA cadres by. A more rewarding companion was the Tyneside communist 'Spike' Robson, who by then was well into his seventies. He had been a stoker on a ship that had transported seven hundred British soldiers to Murmansk in 1920. There the local Red Guards converted him, and back in Britain he became active in the 'Hands off Russia' campaign and was responsible for 'blacking' ships taking munitions and supplies to the intervention forces fighting the Bolsheviks. Later he did the same in the US and South Africa for shipments to Franco's forces in the Spanish Civil War and to Japan's military leaders after the invasion of Manchuria. In the Second World War he was delivering weapons to Yugoslav partisans. Yet my most enduring capture was discovering Ismail Kadare and his *General of the Dead Army* and later *Broken April* and *Palace of Dreams.*

Reading readings

Reading was an unusual university. Not only was it the only university incorporated in Britain between the wars, but the first year had students studying three subjects until first university exams after the Easter break, before – within limits – choosing which to pursue for a degree. When I signed up, chemistry and maths were givens; I could then opt for physics or geology as my third. I knew nothing about geology, but novelty and a judicious inclination to steer away from higher

maths made my choice. Chemistry was the stale rote learning of normal science; maths was, as Churchill said of Russia, a riddle wrapped in a mystery inside an enigma; while geology was a revolution. Plate tectonics was imposing Schumpeter's 'creative destruction' on the subject. As one paradigm was dying, another was being born in thrice-weekly instalments. The majority of the geology department staff were card-carrying scientific revolutionaries - some Mensheviks, some Bolsheviks - save a small minority stranded in history and seeking sanctuary while the clock ticked down to the release of early retirement. Not alone, I was intellectually seduced. Geology was stimulating and intoxicating. It was what university was supposed to be. Between tedium, incomprehension and metamorphosis, there was only going to be one winner. In retrospect, we providentially lived the confirmation of Thomas Kuhn's *The Structure of Scientific Revolutions* (1962).

My favourite lecturer, apart from Beverly Halstead, was the sedimentologist J. R. L. Allen. He had a droll sense of humour. On a local field trip accompanied by some visiting American geologists I took a whistle. At 12.30 p.m. I blew loudly and the whole group promptly downed hammers and clinometers, nibbled on snacks, produced a ball and had a kickabout. Exactly an hour later I blew again and the whole party returned to the rock face to the bemusement of the transatlantic visitors, but with no comment from Allen. That summer three of us were with him doing field mapping on Mynydd Eglwyseg to the north-east of Llangollen. We were all expecting to end up for a late lunch at the Ponderosa Cafe perched at the top of Horseshoe Pass. But promptly at 1 p.m. he stopped, extracted sandwiches, flask and apple from his rucksack and took a lunch hour as we watched in hunger.

BAC required few chemists. They needed even fewer geologists. Despite my parents telling me I was abandoning a career with prospects, the corporation and I parted company amicably; probably as much to their relief as mine. In my slash and burn approach in the second year, I surrendered my subsidiary in chemistry for soil science, a subject still awaiting its Newton, Darwin or Einstein. When the lecturer repeated the same lecture two weeks running, we failed to protest, despite this being the era of student sit-ins. Reading certainly had its share of demonstrations and I was a participant. My two memories were a vote to burn down the admin block that failed by one – I didn't favour the arsonists – and a friend struggling to explain in a subsequent job interview how come she was a skilled telephone switchboard operator without formal training.

Before and during university I had summer and sometimes winter jobs. I was a warehouseman at the Co-op Depot in Cainscross and a tent erector based near Eastington – no mere two-man canvases, these were the big marquees for gymkhanas, fetes and point-to-points. I also did the Christmas post several years running. In this employ my best gig was at Stalybridge railway station, loading and unloading mailbags from two trains an hour. They conveniently arrived from opposite directions within five minutes of each other. So, ten minutes of frantic activity was broken by three-quarters of an hour's reading. I remember getting through Michael Foot's *Aneurin Bevan 1897–1945* in a couple of days thanks to Royal Mail.

Atomic kittens

My best 'holiday' job by far was Soil Mechanics. In the summer of my first year at Reading I was at a bit of a loss and was casting around rather desperately for inspiration when I saw a post advertised in Cheltenham for site investigation. Why not? A friend drove me over and within twenty minutes I had a job. I was sent off the following morning to Connah's Quay as a site geologist, on the basis of the equivalent of ten weeks training. My job was to find a patch of land suitable for a nuclear power station, more specifically the reactor building. I did the core logging from three or four drill teams to map the underground stratigraphy. What was wanted was unbroken rock beds. The threat of differential compaction, either side of fault lines, was not a good foundation for reactor buildings.

I was also in charge of keeping the timesheets and calculating the weekly bonuses. My own weekly wages were higher than my father had ever earned in his life, and I was by far the lowest-paid person on site. Soil Mechanics liked me. If nothing else I was cheap. I worked for them every vacation

for the next couple of years, helping ensure the stability of the Aberfan spoil heaps, three years on from the disaster that had killed 116 children and 28 adults, and plotting the line for the extension of the M4 motorway deep into Wales. I was most grateful for the dog that didn't bark: the proposed Connah's Quay nuclear power station, the first in a zone 3 population area, was never built.

After three years of Reading, I wanted more. I ended up with a master's in Marine Earth Science at University College London (UCL). I thought I'd like living in London. I didn't. Without money, London is like swimming in treacle. Public transport took forever. I ended up living above a Turkish Deli in Stoke Newington with two fellow students on my course. Our vehicle was the infamous 73 bus. Going was not too bad, with an intermediate terminus along the road where a waiting bus was almost inevitably perched. It was coming back that was more of an issue. They may have been timetabled for one every ten minutes, but inevitably they arrived, like condoms in packs of three, every half hour.

It was during my stint at UCL that I met, for the first and only time, Harold Wilson. He gave a presidential address to the Royal Statistical Society in November 1972 and I was invited along by a statistician friend and party member from Reading University. The lecture was dull and boring for those not in love with big data's history.[6] I got to shake the hand at the end. There were few disciples, and even fewer with the imagination to see him back in 10 Downing Street in barely more than a year.

After a taster of a day down the Thames on the *Sir John Cass*, we went big with a five-day 'field trip' to the Bay of Biscay in January 1973 on the *Sir John Murray*, where we practised our micropalaeontology in a force seven gale. At night you had no option but to strap yourself into your bunk. Meals were not taken by most. It did wonders for my 'sea legs', less for my acquaintance with foraminifera. My thesis was 'The Seismicity of the Mid-Atlantic Ridge from 12 Degrees North to 2 Degrees South.' What was required was large quantities of earthquake data. The only source was the Atomic Weapons Research Establishment (AWRE), which monitored seismic events around the globe, looking for clandestine Soviet Bloc underground nuclear tests.

To be allowed into AWRE I had to be vetted and sign the Official Secrets Act. I'd signed it before back at BAC. This time it was more serious, with atomic weapons trumping guided missiles. I faced interrogation. Had I ever been to the Soviet Union? Had I been to China? No and no. They never asked about Albania, yet seismic activity in the Western Balkans triggered all the whistles and bells that featured for the rest of the Soviet Empire. The likelihood of Enver Hoxha having a secret nuclear weapons programme, however, was remote. Tirana was at complete odds with Moscow after the latter's failure to intervene in Hungary early enough in 1956. Interestingly, AWRE did get background data on France's atmospheric nuclear tests in the Pacific that the British government was busy protesting, overnight. Clearly not all of the British Establishment were on the same page. Six weeks later I had thousands of data points and several hundred pages of maps, seven thousand words and one more brick in the wall confirming seafloor spreading and plate tectonics.

Partisan politics

Politically, I'd joined the Stroud Constituency Labour Party in the late 1960s, but even before then I'd been a weekly collector of party dues up and down Severn Road in Stonehouse where we lived. When I went off to university, I took a subscription to *Labour Weekly* with me. In the first days at Reading, I joined a march from the university to the town centre demanding the release of Nelson Mandela. There were scarcely a dozen of us, flanked by an equal number of bored policemen. None of us expected that Mandela and we would wait more than twenty years.

Like all of Britain's universities, a thousand political flowers were blooming at Reading, although many proved to be weeds. Labour was definitely not *à la mode,* with the International Socialists, the International Marxist Group and the Spartacus League, among others, vying for who was ruling the university's left-wing roost. Some went on to greatness, others became Labour Party bureaucrats. One became a Business Journalist of the Year award winner, while another

Maxims for Members

1. Pay your subscriptions promptly.

2. Don't leave the whole of the Branch work to be carried on by the Branch officers, but in the comradeship of the Cause and for its success in your district undertake your full share of the work.

3. Always be on hand at the public propaganda meetings of the Branch, so that their effectiveness may not be impaired by lack of helpers.

4. Always be on the look-out for new members of the Branch—especially amongst workmates.

5. Keep some I.L.P. leaflets by you to distribute, and circulate the I.L.P. pamphlets.

READ THE

Socialist Leader

EVERY WEEK

and get others to do so !

MEMBERSHIP CARD
OF THE

Independent Labour Party

Head Office:
197 KING'S CROSS ROAD
LONDON, W.C.1

SUBSCRIPTIONS do not count for membership UNLESS this card is receipted for every month's subscription paid.

BRANCH: MANCHESTER

MEMBER'S NAME J. G. Ford

ADDRESS: 299, Whiteacre Road, Ashton-under-Lyne.

BRANCH MEETS AT 34, Temple Road, Bolton or 6, Gee Street, Stockport.

SECRETARY Denis Pye
34, Temple Rd., Bolton. Tel. 0204 42869

ROLL NO.	MONTHLY SUBSCRIPTION	CARD ISSUED
—	25p.	January 1974.

Branches have the right to fix their own membership subscriptions, but the minimum amount to be sent to Head Office is 1s. per full member per month. From this affiliation fee, the National Administrative Council will remit ½ to the Divisional Council.

Power Fund, a form of Socialist Income Tax, is paid by individual members. Up to and including £10 per week income is exempted from payment, and for each £1 per week in excess of £10, one penny per week should be paid.

MONTH	CONTRIB. £ p	Signed	POWER FUND £ p	Signed
January ..	25p	JD		
February ..	25	JD		
March ..	25	JD		
April ..	25	JD		
May ..	25	JD		
June ..	25	BSD		
July ..	25	BSD		
August ..	25	BSD		
September	25	BSD		
October ..	25	JD		
November	25	JD		
December	25	BSD		
January ..	25	JD		
February ..	25	JD		
March ..	25	BSD		
April ..	30	BSD		
May ..	30	BSD		
June ..	30	BSD		
July ..	30	BSD		
August ..	30	BSD		
September	30	BSD		
October ..	30	BSD		
November	30	BSD		
December	30	BSD		

was Nick Sigler, who worked for forty years in the labour movement with a year's secondment as National Liaison Officer in the EP's Socialist Group. I did my duty and voted in the interminable student elections. Additionally, a small group of us did its utmost to improve the calibre of the Conservative Party. At weekends of inclement weather with nothing else pressing we'd send off postal orders for two and six to sequentially sign up the university's leading Tory activists to the CPGB. We assumed MI5 would do the rest. Certainly, none made it to Westminster.

It was my enthusiasm for George Orwell that led me astray. *Homage to Catalonia* has Orwell fighting in the Spanish Civil War in 1936 with POUM, whose sister party in Britain was the ILP. The ILP still lived. It was to re-badge itself at its Easter 1975 Conference as Independent Labour Publications, confirming its abandonment of electoral failure for entrism. The battle was between the 'old guard' and the reformers based around the ILP HQ in Leeds. The ILP's two full-timers in the Leeds head office were Barry Winter and Pauline Bryan. It was Pauline who had earlier informed me that local government reorganisation in 1973 had made Leeds unwinnable for Labour – mercifully, she was quickly proved wrong – which meant they could now develop a proper Labour Party. The reformers operated with a more amorphous group of radicals who wanted to take the ILP further and faster into late 1960s politics than Leeds was prepared to travel. The 'red smoke' of victory for the Leeds faction (see below) at Conference saw the fortnightly *Socialist Leader* transformed in June into a monthly *Labour Leader*, reverting to Keir Hardie's original title that had been abandoned in 1946.

While I was at UCL I was writing for *Socialist Leader* and selling it amongst friends and acquaintances. In 1974 I wrote on 'Science and the future of man' (5 January) and a report on a visit to revolutionary Portugal (12 October), while early the following year I tackled 'The Spokesman Conference on Socialism and the Environment' organised by Ken Coates (1 February). I'd been there at the founding conference of the Socialist Environmental and Resources Association (SERA) in 1973 and subsequently served for several years on the executive.

So when I arrived in Manchester in August 1973 to begin my second master's and PhD, I searched out the ILP. There was a functioning 'old guard' branch in Stockport led by Brian Dean, the man behind 'Winston's Soccer Column'; Brian lived within earshot of Stockport County's ground, although as a fan was more City than County. Shortly after I arrived in Manchester, a new set of members emerged around Geoff Hodgson (who was to be Labour's unsuccessful candidate for Manchester Withington in the 1979 general election), Peter Jenkins and Antony Easthope. They, as vanguard rather than rearguard, wanted their own branch. The Manchester Branch became the centre and we, as the Greater Manchester Branch, the doughnut. We did – to the fury of the ILP National Administrative Council (NAC), who decided they had better things to do with our money – publish John McNair's *Spanish Diary* (1979) with a forward by Don Bateman, an ILP stalwart from the 1940s, and we continued, along with the rest of the ILP, to collect money to smuggle into Franco's Spain to aid POUM veterans.

The ILP was a political ghost town. The institutional architecture was there with branches, divisions and a head office. Annual conferences and summer schools marched on. It was all made possible with the financial underpinning that came from the ownership of National Labour Press (NLP) and the profits accrued from its *Used Car Guide*. I was instantly a delegate to the North West Divisional Council and almost as quickly elected to the NAC. The first order of business for the NAC was my appointment to the Board of Directors of NLP, and the second signing an undated letter of resignation to be held by head office.

There was a desert blooming, watered by a search for solutions rooted neither in sectarianism nor social democracy. During this brief rejuvenation, ghosts emerged from the mist before disappearing. There was both an internal bulletin, *Between Ourselves*, and a series of magazines driven by locale and/or doctrine. If there was an opportunity for the ILP to really achieve something, it was well and truly spurned. The ILP proved no better than the rest – when the workers finally came, they were turned away.[7] There were eight issues of *Labour Leader* (February 1974–75). Its first issue proclaimed it to be *The Voice of the West Riding ILP*, though that part of the masthead subsequently vanished as it sailed on under the direction of Eric Preston and Mollie Temple as a substantial bimonthly fighting the battle that was to return the ILP paper to Keir Hardie. The Lancaster branch that summer produced at least two issues of a thin *Socialist Leader*. Later, from early 1977 until April 1979, *Calder Voice* spoke for the local ILP over twenty-five and more issues.[8] The January 1979 issue published the policy statement of the Labour Common Market Safeguards Committee, stating, 'We should seek to support EEC candidates who share these views – AND AT ALL COST REJECT PRO-EEC CANDIDATES AS BEING BEYOND THE PALE' (emphasis in original). In parallel were a minimum of six issues of the *Greater Manchester Labour Leader* between April 1977 and December 1978 – renamed *Socialist Citizen* from issue 5 under pressure from Leeds.

I reported in *Greater Manchester Labour Leader* issue 2 on June's 'Towards Socialism' conference in Manchester, which was sponsored by 'Clause 4', the ILP, the Institute of Workers Control (IWC) and SERA. The highlight was Mike Prior and Dave Purdy from the Euro-communist wing of the CPGB revisiting the 1930s Popular Front with a demand for 'all progressive forces on the centre-left to counter' the rising right. Geoff Hodgson urged rather a return to extra-parliamentary action. Immediately after, Hodgson published an open letter to Prior and Purdy, demonstrating the barren impotence on both sides of the argument: 'It is perfectly proper to outline the problems and limitations of the slogan for import controls, or expose some chauvinism behind opposition to the EEC, but when battle commences one has to fight with one's side, to support import controls, to oppose EEC entry. Analysis on its own is not Marxist politics, and silence on 'active' questions can lead theory into misuse' (emphasis in original).[9] The tail was wagging the dog. March 1979 saw Southampton ILP bring out the first issue of a quarterly *Labour Independent* that called for Southampton Football Club to be brought under municipal control. It was the last swallow.

After the incident with McNair's *Spanish Diary*, I was no longer favoured by the now dominant Leeds faction of the NAC. The process was democratic centralism in miniature. I was singled out both for failing to seek permission to publish

in the Socialist Workers Party's *Socialist Review* ('Science in society: even the truth is relative'), and for allowing my name to go forward on the panel of European candidates. For the first, I was informed by the NAC that they were 'not happy', while the second warranted a vote of censure because I had treated the NAC 'very shabbily' as *Between Ourselves* reported.[10] There was history, but I turned out not to be the past. The enduring ILP position was that 'we must oppose direct elections at all costs. For all their seeming democratisation they are, in fact, the opposite. For they will result in more power being wrested from Westminster, so making it even more difficult for the labour movement and indeed the people of Britain as a whole, to control the economic and political development of their community'.[11] This approach left the ILP alone defending Eurosceptic battlelines long abandoned by the keepers of the left's anti-European flame in the Labour Common Market Safeguards Committee. Doctrinal purity trumped political presence and activity. Someone had clearly lost the plot. To be fair, I should have known better.

Some go with a bang, others a whimper. Hodgson – who had defended me – left the following February and Harry Barnes in September, both with letters of resignation in *Between Ourselves*. My valediction was a critical review of Tom Nairn's *The Breakup of Britain* in the February 1978 issue of *Labour Leader*, in which I thought he confused ends and means, and in the June 1979 issue a recognition of the perspicacity of director James Bridges for *The China Syndrome*, which previewed the Three Mile Island nuclear accident twelve days before it happened. It was a slow goodbye as the clock ran down on my NAC membership and I changed horses to *Tribune*. Yet that NAC proved fertile political ground. Apart from myself as an MEP, two ended as Labour MPs – Barnes (North East Derbyshire, 1987-2005) and Jon Trickett (Hemsworth, 1996-) – while Pauline Bryan was elevated to the House of Lords in 2018 on Jeremy Corbyn's recommendation.

Endnotes

[1] My father was Ernest Benjamin Snell Ford, born in Stoke, Devonport, 20 May 1905, while my mother was born in West Dean in Monmouth District, 8 July 1910. They were, for the time, 'old parents' at forty-four and thirty-nine, respectively. Snell – which my father never used – was a Cornish name. [2] Harry Beddington (1977), *Forest Humour*, Forest of Dean Newspapers. [3] Ian Wright (2020), *God's Beautiful Sunshine: The 1921 Miners' Lockout in the Forest of Dean*, Bristol: Bristol Radical History Group; and (2017) *Coal on the One Hand, Men on the Other: The Forest of Dean Miners' Association and the First World War 1910–1922*, 2nd edn, Bristol: Bristol Radical History Group. [4] William Ashworth and Mark Pegg (1986), *The History of the British Coal Industry, vol. 5, 1946–1982: The Nationalized Industry*, Oxford: Clarendon. [5] This was written up in *Stroud News & Journal* on 2 October 1969 under the headline: 'To India and back for £52 per head; ex-Marling boys' trip to the Taj Mahal.' [6] The Rt. Hon. J. Harold Wilson (1972), *Statistics and Decision Making in Government – Bradshaw Revisited*, Presidential Address, 15 November. [7] Peter Thwaites (2020), *Waiting for the Workers; A History of the Independent Labour Party 1938–1950*, Gloucester: Choir Press. [8] This was principally the work of Alistair Graham, who has continued to plough with colleagues his independent socialist furrow. His *Forest of Dean & Wye Valley Clarion*, as of September 2021, was on issue 151. [9] Geoff Hodgson (1977), 'Open letter to Purdy & Prior', *Between Ourselves*, September. [10] See Eric Preston, *Between Ourselves*, December 1979. [11] See *Labour Leader*, March 1976.

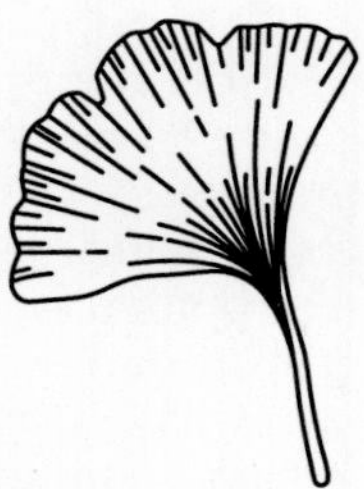

3 Tameside to Tokyo

> I was a victim of a series of accidents.
>
> Kurt Vonnegut, The Sirens of Titan (1959)

Back in 1973, the Constituency Labour Party (CLP) in Ashton-under-Lyne was a genuine working-class organisation, just a very small one. The 1975 AGM heard the chair announce that the CLP membership had gone up to a dizzy 166. The membership was limited to a self-selected class cohort in their fifties and sixties, which orbited around a series of family clusters: the Easons, Travises, and Pettits, the McEnaneys, Davises and Marsdens, all headed by patriarchs recently elected as councillors for the new Tameside Metropolitan Borough that had been created by the Tory reorganisation of local government in 1973. They were factory workers – some active, some retired – and small businessmen. Some were linked to the local Freemason lodges. Socially deeply conservative, they were yet to be touched by the feminist movement, let alone gay rights. Some members of the General Management Committee (GMC) had signed 'the pledge' and resigned rather than cross the threshold of a public house when the GMC was forced to abandon the Pleasant Sunday Afternoon Society (Brotherhood) Building for the Albion local next door.

The 1973 reorganisation in Greater Manchester had stitched together the towns on the eastern penumbra to form Tameside, named after its all-too-forgettable eponymous river. The locals weren't alone in their confusion. Job applicants who waxed lyrical about their enthusiasm for London and the Thames didn't make their way onto shortlists, let alone merit selection. The 1973 election had delivered a Labour council with a good majority and the local party was complacent. During the campaign for the February 1974 general election, volunteers expressing an interest in joining the party were told it was full. I was persistent and more difficult to block as I was transferring membership from Stroud CLP. That coupled with a year of endless campaigning with two general elections plus a series of local by-elections made it impossible to keep me out.

In the 1975 European Referendum I campaigned for Leave. This was the left Labour position. I remember being over in Leeds with a group from the ILP, running a street stall where the call was, 'What do workers get on the Common Market stall?', and the response, 'Fuck all!' The campaign made lacklustre look lively. The public were furiously uninterested. In Ashton-under-Lyne, we organised a 'NO' event. There were six on the platform – from somewhere we'd even managed to find a Liberal against the Common Market – and five in the audience. When the meeting's chair announced he was a member of the Communist Party, 40 per cent of the audience stood up and left.

When the referendum results came in, 'YES' had got 67.2 per cent and we got slaughtered. Yet there was no agonising reappraisal after a two-to-one defeat. Repudiating reality, we reverted to the 'one more heave' theory of political change. Even 1979's ousting of Jim Callaghan by Margaret Thatcher – the first Labour prime minister never to win a general election, a feat that remained unmatched until Gordon Brown – changed little. Callaghan's belated retirement as Labour leader eighteen months later saw Michael Foot take charge and dig the European hole deeper.

Counselling victory

In 1976 I was a candidate for the council in Hurst East, a Tory ward that Labour could win. I lost and so did the party on a heavy swing against the government. For the first time since

local government reorganisation in 1973, the council went, narrowly, Tory. They were reborn zealots, reversing Labour's long-term plans to introduce comprehensive education with less than four months' notice and instead retaining the borough's grammar schools. It was chaos, with teaching unions refusing cooperation, and selections being determined in local solicitors' offices. At least there were no algorithms. Two years later I ran again – the 1977 interim election was for the Greater Manchester Council, which didn't excite me – and this time I crept over the threshold by 103.

Those whom the gods wish to destroy they first make mad. The comprehensive debacle was bad enough, but then in 1978 the Tories took a leaf out of Kim Jong Il's playbook. Every school in the borough was to have a picture of the Queen hung in its entrance hall after a presentation by a member of the Education Committee. I was by then one of four Labour councillors the Tories had allowed onto the committee and was the most left-wing, though the competition was far from fierce. The result was a series of invitations from heads restrained by the letter of the law but keen to tease its substance. I did my duty on four or five occasions, sending myself into the breach with a loud rendering of the Sex Pistols' 'God Save the Queen' and returning after a short, sharp and low-key speech.[1] After Labour took control, the portraits discreetly disappeared. Years later while canvassing, a voter opened his front door and there was one of those Queen's pictures hanging in the hallway. He wasn't voting Labour.

Canvassing had its droll side. The Palace Road estate in Hurst was then a solid bank of Labour votes that needed to be massaged during the campaign and got out on the day, so it was frequently canvassed. There was always an attempt to ensure a fledgling activist ended up door-knocking one particular house at the end of Leech Avenue. The curmudgeonly man of the house, on being asked if he was voting Labour, would in a tirade first demand the restoration of the death penalty and the bombing of Belfast. He was a bitter sort, who had trained as a hangman and received his licence shortly before the abolition of the death penalty in Britain. There was a, possibly apocryphal, story in the party that he'd attended a public meeting in Ashton-under-Lyne when Sydney Silverman, responsible in the 1960s for successfully leading the abolition campaign, spoke on a platform with Robert Sheldon, who was running for re-election in 1966. During questions the man demanded the return of the death penalty. Sheldon rather dismissively said that was all well and good, but expressed doubt that the man would be prepared to do it himself. When the man passed up his hangman's licence, Sheldon was forced into an apology.

In 1979 with Callaghan ousted by Thatcher, the meagre silver lining saw the Tories swept from control of Tameside Council. After an ephemeral three years, the Conservatives were still waiting for a return forty-five years later. The electorate had been well and truly immunised. With Labour back in control, I was elected chair of the Environmental Health and Control Committee. It had a dog's dinner of responsibilities ranging from refuse collection to cemeteries, Sunday trading, taxi licensing to film censorship. On the Sunday I was elected by the Labour Group, the department had chosen to send out officers on a sting operation to a number of local corner shops to buy a newspaper, allowed under the 1950 Shops Act, along with some forbidden item such as a ball or – God forbid – a Bible. Few of my local corner shops would have had the latter on the premises, let alone for sale. Those found to be vending prohibited goods were issued a final warning. Monday saw my first meeting with the Director of Environmental Health, during which I indicated that such zeal indicated a degree of over-staffing that would safely allow cuts in the department budget at the next review. No further Sunday trading violations were discovered during my term of office.

Sanitation

Labour had its puritans. The Environmental Health and Control Committee met monthly and one fixed item on the agenda was reviewing a list of new films and a synopsis of their plots from *Screen International*. On this flimsy basis the committee decided whether they required our pre-approval before they could be shown in local cinemas. It was Pat McEnaney's *raison d'être* for being a councillor. He claimed he hadn't been canvassing since *Coronation Street* started

–1960 – and attended the committee to impose his particular Catholic fundamentalist views on the wider public for that item and scarcely anything else. He would pick three or four films he thought unsavoury and propose to add them to the pre-approval list and the committee would meekly comply. The result in the majority of cases was that the local cinemas would just not show them. They could justify neither the time nor expense of shipping the film up from London and putting on a special private showing for the committee with no guarantee of the outcome. It was an invidious form of hidden censorship, and one I was not inclined to support. I had a different view. Cinema attendance was even less compulsory than watching TV. First, I tried subterfuge, bouncing the item around the agenda – one month first, then last, then in the middle. But it was like taking a bone from a hungry dog. I rarely managed to break his grip.

The first film I had to actually watch in the role of censor was – the subsequent cult gang film – *The Warriors*, a modern take on Xenophon's *Anabasis.* Despite the recurrent violence it narrowly passed. Next was Monty Python's *Life of Brian*. I was nervous. In the cinema there were two groups of three plus one councillor sat alone. My gang of three were in hysterics, the other four stoically silent. Tameside's public was given permission to view by 5–2. Last was Joan Collins's sleek and sleazy *The Bitch*, which was a breast too far. The committee banned it. There were front-page tabloid headlines and queues outside Manchester's cinemas. It was a truly dreadful film, rescued only by Tameside's ban. It made Joan Collins millions and helped get her the part of Alexis Carrington in *Dynasty*. *The Sun* sent a team of reporters up to find who among the councillors had been paid off. The answer was no one; it was simply a case of parochial Catholicism and working-class puritanism belatedly meeting the 1960s. One Labour woman councillor – who voted for the ban – said, 'It's not the violence I object to, that's all around us, it's the sex. It's not like that, it's once on a Saturday night'.

The British Board of Film Classification (BBFC) rated all new films. Yet the U, A, AA and X were only advisory. I invited James Ferman, the BBFC's secretary, to speak to the committee. He was captivating, yet unconvincing. Richard Gere and Vanessa Redgrave saved the day. They had starred together in the mediocre *Yanks*, fortuitously shot in and around Stalybridge, in Tameside, with a plot based around a series of relationships between American GIs and local women in the run-up to D-Day. It appeared on the list for the committee's approval rated AA, meaning it could only be seen by children over fourteen accompanied by an adult. I proposed we rated it U ('Universal') to allow all those youngsters who had stalked the sets the previous year to see the film. This, as intended, threatened a whole new imbroglio. When the decision came to the Labour Group for ratification, they on my proposal abolished film censorship. James Ferman was no longer our concern. The committee agenda was one item shorter, and when McEnaney was next up for election, the CLP and District Labour Party (DLP) deselected him. He stood, unsuccessfully, first as 'Independent Labour' and then Liberal/SDP.

The department's other responsibilities were easier to handle. I spent, unannounced and unreported, a day as a casual bin man, testing the merits of 'task and finish,' and learnt that for post-nuclear planning purposes, the cemeteries section was responsible for the provision of 'mass graves.' On the basis of my involvement in the radical science movement (see below and Chapter 5) that saw science more weapon than handmaiden, I co-opted onto the committee Dave Eva, a left-wing environmental scientist based in my department at Manchester. We organised a day-trip by coach to visit the local nuisances. We called in on Smith Brothers, a bone-rendering plant whose answer to complaints about the cloying miasma enveloping the neighbouring houses, was to raise their stack higher and become a more equal-opportunity polluter, spreading the stench across an ever-widening borough footprint. One evening I caught the unforgettable smell three miles away in Ashton. The argument hinged over 'best practical means': did it mean – as the company argued – that it was what they were willing to afford or rather what was available in the marketplace? That smell lasted for over twenty years, before the plant closed in 1997.

Smith's did at least let us in. Chemstar in Carrbrook refused point blank, leaving the committee and its charabanc locked outside with the members left to peer at the plant through rusty wire netting. Their demise was quicker than

Smith's. The company had opened in 1975 in an abandoned textile works adjacent to housing that, as the *Sunday Times* admiringly put it a year later, catered to 'the dirty end of the market – soups of waste which no one else would touch.'[2] After one hundred and fifty inconclusive visits from Tameside's environmental health officers and thirteen from Health and Safety Executive (HSE) inspectors, the plant caught fire and blew up in September 1981. The HSE report a year later concluded that the mix of ingredients that caused the accident had been in place throughout its operation – it was only a question of when, not if. No 'improvement notices' had ever been issued to the company. Years later, dioxins were detected on the site.

The Environmental Health and Control Committee also opened up the whole borough for hackney carriage hire, breaking the old town boundaries, and helped eliminate the tension between taxis and private hire drivers by moving to a common licence for both. The private hire operators lobbied hard for visibility, parading the threat to customers of getting into unmarked cars if they were not allowed to have clear identification. There was a point mixed in with a heavy dollop of self-interest. The Hackney Carriage Licensing Sub-Committee recommended 'Private Hire – ADVANCED BOOKING ONLY' on the doors. Since then, that label has been cloned across Greater Manchester and far beyond, and has more recently made it onto Ubers.

In parallel, I was active in the Labour Party in the Ashton-under-Lyne CLP and Tameside DLP. For a number of years in the late 1970s and early 1980s, I chaired the DLP. The meetings were Monday nights in Stalybridge Labour Club starting at 8 p.m. This clashed first with *The Water Margin* and then *Blake's 7* that both ran from seven to eight, although after Blake was written out of the latter at the end of series 2 my interest waned. So, although I almost certainly broke the speed limit, I was notorious for being late. There were worse problems. It was not unknown for delegates to turn up much the worse for wear. On one occasion, my deputy-chair, annoyed by a ruling, invited me outside when he was so drunk he could barely stand.

Environment to enlightenment

Both in 1978 and 1979 I had supported Roy Oldham for group leader. It had been a three-way fight between him and two others, George Newton and Percy Travis. Each time, Roy had been ahead on the first ballot with George second and Percy narrowly third. Yet when Percy was eliminated, the large majority of his votes switched to George, delivering victory to the latter. It was as much parochial as personal. This was still a comparatively new authority and Percy's voters from Ashton-under-Lyne knew George from neighbouring Hyde, while Roy was from the most remote corner of the new borough in Longdendale. In contrast, George's voters knew Roy from sharing the Stalybridge and Hyde CLP and a majority would be partial to him over Percy were there to be any run-off.

The question was how to deliver. With some careful calculation, secrecy and luck, three of us voted Travis in the first round. It worked like a charm, the result was Travis 16, Oldham 15 and Newton 14. In the run-off it was 26–19 in favour of Oldham, with a bemused Travis trying to understand what had happened. Roy remained the leader of the council for over thirty years. The by-product of his victory was a vacancy for chair of education. Despite my limited experience, I was elected unopposed. I'd benefited from being one of only four Labour members on the Education Committee during that last year of Tory control and the reality that many Labour councillors were intimidated by the teachers, their unions, and the local education establishment. Early on, I was the only Labour councillor with a degree.

Within three days of my taking the post, the Conservative government caved in and gave permission for Tameside to go comprehensive. This was not my doing. When Labour took back control of the council in 1979, we immediately reinstituted the comprehensive education plans ripped up by the Tameside Tories at four months' notice in 1975. Their compatriots in Whitehall played for time. But the cavalry failed to arrive. The 1980 local elections were another wipeout for the Tories, with Labour's majority swelling to over thirty. There was nowhere left to hide.

Education v. administration

The danger was to let oneself be engulfed by education administration at the expense of education. At that time, local authorities still controlled the curriculum, and I thought it was time to bring it up to date. But that required resources. Yet with education absorbing close to half the overall budget on a falling financial tide, this would not be easy. Early on I discovered that on some educational measures, Tameside was the second-worst authority in England and Wales. I immediately leaked the story to the *Ashton-under-Lyne Reporter* and *Tameside Advertiser*, and ruthlessly quoted it back in Labour Group meetings whenever attempts were made to shave my budget.

Tameside School visit as chair of the Education Committee with Cllrs Alan Stelfox (to my left) and Harry Stachini (right).

The two key areas that I tried to tackle over my five years in post were science and languages. For science, the first priority was to set a rolling programme to refurbish and modernise science laboratories to provide a better platform. Second was to improve performance. That meant more and better teaching. Science teachers were in short supply, but there was strong resistance from the unions when I wanted to advertise a block of science posts with recruitment starting at scale 2. It never happened. More easily, there was growing evidence of girls' under-achievement in science in the early years in secondary schools with mixed classes. One answer was the introduction of single-sex science teaching. Third, coming from my own background at Manchester University, was a proposal for an O-level course in Social Aspects of Science. I was recruited to be part of a panel to devise a syllabus for one of the examining boards, and I ensured the authority recruited at least one teacher capable of teaching the subject. I also tried to start a programme for exceptionally gifted children; the local party signed off on it, but it never went anywhere in the education department. This was one of the 'chairman's funnies' – as Director of Education Geoff Mayall used to refer to them – that proved no laughing matter.

On the languages side, without actually intervening, my enthusiasm for 'the classics' in particular in the ex-grammar schools was limited. Instead, we advertised for teachers of Russian, Japanese and Arabic to be targeted at the fifth and six forms. The other innovation was trickier: I wanted to introduce foreign languages into primary schools. Talking to the education advisors, I was told that earlier attempts had all floundered at the transition from primary to secondary, with early progress squandered because in the new classes not all pupils had previously studied the languages and teachers were unsure of what level those that had taken languages were at. The answer – when we finally found it – was that it had to be one foreign language across all schools and that we needed to smooth the transition. Primary French was born, with new teachers based in secondary schools going out to the 'feeder' primaries and teaching the same pupils both there and for the first years after they made the passage to secondary education. I summed up this enthusiasm for wider and deeper modern language teaching in my Keynote Address to the Joint Council of Language Associations Annual Conference in March 1986.[3]

The results of these initiatives were mixed. On a positive note, Tameside moved off of the bottom of the educational ladder. Russian took off to the extent that, a few years later, I was told we had the highest number of applicants from any local education authority (LEA) to study Russian at university. After I stood down in 1986, the Japan Foundation offered financial support for teaching of their language, but the new chair of education had no interest. Science teaching improved, but science teachers remained scarce. The door of *ijtihad* (innovation) closed with Thatcher's imposition under

the 1988 Education Act of a National Curriculum. It left little space and even less money for adventure.

Schools or learning

The biggest problem facing the education department was dealing with falling school rolls. After the UK's second baby boom in the 1960s – peaking in 1964 – it was a long, not-so-slow decline. In 1980 the peak cohort was passing into the sixth form or out of the LEA system altogether. The coming decade would see rolls falling by a quarter and more, first with an intensification of the already ongoing contraction in primary schools and then into the secondaries.

There was threat and opportunity. Tameside is an urban area with some dormitory suburbs. There were few small primaries to worry about, but there were too many old, run-down schools in the wrong places. The inner-urban wards of 'back-to-back' housing had undergone slum clearance and white flight to the crescent of private-build estates of semi-detached houses that were eating into the green belt at the rural edge of the borough's towns. This left behind inadequate voluntary-controlled and voluntary-aided Church schools catering for the children and grandchildren of the Pakistani migrants who had been recruited – often from Mirpur – to spin in the cotton mills of Ashton-under-Lyne and neighbouring towns in the 1950s and 1960s. New technology in the mills required a three-shift system, but women were not allowed to work nights and local men were deterred by low wages. With competition from the Indian subcontinent already threatening, the coping device was to on-shore cheap Kashmiri labour.

The LEA was responsible in the voluntary-controlled Church schools for providing everything, while in the voluntary-aided, the Church retained some responsibility for capital costs. A great deal if you could get it. The piper is prepaid and you get to call the tune. So we had Church authorities with significant input to the education and ethos of schools whose pupil cohort was 90% Muslim and teachers 90% Christian – and white. In the case of the aided schools, they also had the responsibility – but no interest – in finding money towards the capital costs of school improvements while there were church spires and roofs to be saved. The plan was to close the worst schools – one had a classroom with no windows – in the depopulated urban cores to manage the trough and then build anew, where the population now lived, as rising rolls allowed.

That worked for the primaries, but the secondaries were a different problem. Here the danger was that today's parents would fixate on saving buildings and brands to the cost of tomorrow's pupils. Instead of educational triage, cutting the least efficient sites for delivering education and enhancing – or at least retaining – the standards of those remaining, the choice would be an equality of misery as the refusal to close left educational standards bereft. With falling entry, teacher numbers would follow, options would narrow and the curriculum would collapse back to basics. Any prospect of preparing pupils for their futures in the new century with more and better science and languages would vanish.

Months of meetings, seminars and working groups finally came up with an overall plan that involved closing a number of primary and secondary schools. We went out to public consultation that included fiery and near kinetic confrontations with parents at the earmarked schools. I would arrive early and park my car near to and facing the exit with the podium set up by the doors of the school hall. I, and the education officers accompanying me, survived. My deputy chairman at the time, Ron Foster, wanted to be involved and do one of the meetings. He didn't do two, fleeing the scene of the first, chased off the premises by marauding parents, bereft of his coat with which he was never reunited.

After all this, the proposal required the endorsement of the Labour Group at one of its Sunday morning meetings. Each of the schools under threat had its partisan supporters among the parents and had consequently captured a clique of local Labour councillors. I knew it would be a close vote. Anticipating I could lose, I prepared a statement in advance announcing my resignation as chair of education. After heated argument in the group, my proposal narrowly lost. I immediately stood up, announced my resignation and walked out assuming that was that. I was startled to be doorstepped

that afternoon by a delegation of senior councillors asking me to reconsider. They offered a gently tweaked version of the plan – to save some faces – that would be endorsed by a special meeting of the group before the full council meeting on Tuesday. It was.

Belling the cat?

Why was it so simple? My threat of resignation may have changed one or two minds, but at root I judge it was more cock-up than conspiracy. The groups of partisans had not conspired together as one to stop the plan, in fact the very opposite. The months of meetings with officers, going through the demographics and the threat to education, had worked their magic. They were convinced it all needed to be done, just not by them. They wanted the cheap political cover of being able to affirm to parent-voters 'I voted no'. They hadn't wanted or expected to win. It was like the dog catching the car. Winning was a mischance that forced enough to face their responsibilities that meant the day was won at the second time of asking.

The long aftermath saw some tricky manoeuvring to maximise the council's benefits. The land of one school listed for closure had been gifted to a predecessor authority when Victoria was in her prime. It came with conditions. The land could only be sold for the authority's benefit while the school was still functioning, otherwise the ownership reverted back to the benefactor's estate. When the sale was delayed, a 'stay-behind' class was left in place to bridge the gap.

There were, of course, parental protests over the closure decisions. That I could appreciate. What was more difficult to understand was, in the same vein, Ashton's local MP Robert Sheldon taking a delegation to meet Education Secretary Sir Keith Joseph to urge him to refuse permission for the closures. When I tackled Sheldon, he said he had no option but to comply with a request from constituents, giving spinelessness a merit I failed to comprehend. I wondered if there were any limits. Taking the man at his word, I then demanded, as a constituent, that he arrange for me to see Sir Keith and make the case for closure. To be fair he did, and when we met the education secretary he seemed more interested that I was both an MEP and chair of education than the details of the case. Tameside got its permission to close.

Parental choices

One annual nightmare was secondary school allocations. Parents could apply to any school in the borough, but without any guarantee of a place. The results were all issued on one day in May. It was pandemonium, at least for me. Well over 90 per cent of parents were happy, or at least accepting, of the place offered, but that still left hundreds who were not. I would have them knocking on my front door, back door and the telephone would ring incessantly. As the phone was put down it would ring again. I steadfastly refused to intervene. Discretionary power is a dangerous remedy that slips all too easily into nepotism and then corruption.

There was a single exception. I had a mother on the phone complaining that her daughter had failed to be allocated her school of choice. I explained for the twentieth time or more that when a school was oversubscribed, proximity was the key allocation criteria, although that was tempered with the sibling rule (if there was a brother or sister already in the school then an exception would be made). She responded, her voice breaking, that her son had been at the school, but that he'd died the previous year. I phoned the education department and spoke to the officer dealing with school allocations. I said there would now be a new additional rule. If you would have had a sibling in the school if they hadn't died then you could exceptionally be allocated a place. I was told this would set a precedent. My response was, 'Yes, and so?'

I was in a privileged position with inside knowledge. Yet I was shocked by the fight parents put up to place their children into substandard schools. The quality of education depends on a multitude of factors. One of the most significant is the head teacher. An incoming head can invigorate a school and transform its reputation, but there is a life cycle: the same head a decade on coasting into retirement slackens

engagement and the school stagnates. Reputation is the past, not the future, and that was what parents chose.

We were confrontational at times and evasive at others. One of the first actions was to restore free milk in primary schools. Thatcher, as Secretary of State for Education, in 1971 had abolished the provision of free school milk for seven- to eleven-year-olds. I had a poster in my window in my Reading hall of residence: 'Margaret Thatcher Milk Snatcher.' In 1980, when I was chair of education, the advice from our legal department was that we couldn't do it and we could be sued if we did. They were sent away to make the best case possible and respond to any threats of legal action by the Tories with 'Please!' We did and they didn't.

The borough had its problems with the National Front and racism (see below). The Muslim community was starting to get organised and I was asked as chair of education both to introduce halal meat in school dinners and to allow Muslim girls to wear trousers. It seemed to me that both were battles best avoided. With no reference to the Muslim community whatsoever, we introduced a new school uniform regulation that provided an option of skirt or trousers for all. I was asked if boys were allowed to wear skirts. The answer was yes, but seemingly none took the option. As for dietary requirements, I responded to a then-imaginary concern – the same would not be true today – about the growing number of vegetarians in schools and, therefore, a daily vegetarian option was mandated in all school canteens without the slightest breath of controversy.

Unschooled ventures

Tameside was, on 31 March 1981, one of the first authorities to declare itself a Nuclear Free Zone, with the minor roads – major roads were not ours to command – entering the borough labelled 'You are now entering a Nuclear Free Zone.' A running battle ensued between right-wing vandals who defaced the signs and the council's cleansing department. My view of the urgency of the situation increased five months prior on 4 November 1980, the day Ronald Reagan beat Democratic incumbent Jimmy Carter for the US presidency, and the day I put my cheque in the post to join the Campaign for Nuclear Disarmament (CND). I would not have imagined at the time facing off with Reagan in Strasbourg five years later. On another battlefield, Tameside also led the way, with helpful pressure from the Society of Teachers Opposed to Physical Punishment, in abolishing corporal punishment, becoming in late 1980 the first LEA in the country to do so.

As well as puritans, Labour also had its killjoys. The threat of a motorbike rally in Hyde had the local Labour councillors demanding a ban. I stuck up publicly for the bikers. The rally went ahead untroubled. Consequently, I was later invited as the MEP to meet the Stockport Hell's Angels to discuss Commission proposals on controls on motorbike noise. It was the only political meeting I recall that ended with 'three cheers' for the speaker. Subsequently, approaches by bunches of leather-jacketed youth while street campaigning, which made Labour's flock of canvassers huddle nervously, was generally a bit of banter and no more. On one occasion queuing for a City match, I was loudly greeted by a friendly, 'It's our fucking Euro MP!'

National affront

I learnt from experience that there are more ways of killing a dog than by hanging. There had been a spate of break ins and arson attacks in our schools. There was no money for sophisticated alarms, but there was for simple red metal boxes labelled 'Alarm.' The problem subsided.

Not everything was so easy. As chair of education, I had oversight of school speech days, including the appropriateness or otherwise of guest speakers. One controversial local figure was James Anderton, the Chief Constable of Greater Manchester, a bombastic, uncompromising 'blue' caricature of Mary Whitehouse running the force as a paramilitary operation, importing best practice from Northern Ireland's Royal Ulster Constabulary. Fantasising over left-wing conspiracies threatening democracy, his priorities matched his prejudices. There were campaigns against pornography in

local newsagents, late-night drinking and homosexuality. Later, after the first easing of discrimination against gay men, he went on record: 'sodomy between males is condemned by the word of God and ought to be against criminal law'.

In January 1978 he'd spent tens of thousands of ratepayers' money ensuring that the National Front could meet in Hyde Town Hall. That May, the Labour Party manifesto for the local elections promised under no circumstances to allow council premises to be used by extreme-right and fascist groups. On one occasion during my tenure as chair of education, a secondary school headmaster decided to invite Anderton to be the guest of honour at his school's speech day. I vetoed the invitation and paid the price in protest, denunciation and attack. Some months later another head, acting as agent provocateur, reprised the invitation. It turned out the education department not only approved speakers, but also set the date. Anderton's office was phoned for his availability. This time he was not banned, the date just happened to be when he was unavailable.

Some years later I flew into Manchester from Dublin after a Socialist Group meeting. At border control the police demanded to know where I had been staying, but I refused to tell. I had been with Mary Banotti, a Fine Gael MEP descended from Irish Republican hero Michael Collins, who was subsequently to be her party's candidate in the 1997 presidential election, in which she finished second to Fianna Fáil's Mary McAleese. At the time it would not have helped either of us for it to have been known publicly. The police recorded my passport details and I was told that Anderton would be informed. One of the reasons I was in Manchester, however, was for a civic dinner where Anderton was to be present. I responded saying I'd be happy to tell him that evening myself.

Falklands fallout

In 1981 I was re-elected chair of education unopposed at the group AGM. It was in late 1981/early 1982 that I ran in the Manchester Gorton seat against the sitting MP Gerald Kaufman. Mandatory reselection had been passed by the

Labour Conference in 1979 and those of us in the Greater Manchester Labour Coordinating Committee wanted to prove the system. One of our targets was Kaufman, who was famously to describe Labour's 1983 manifesto as 'the longest suicide note in history'. The obvious local candidate was Peter Hildrew, a *Guardian* journalist, who had fought and narrowly lost Manchester Withington in October 1974. However, Peter wouldn't run because of the difficult position it would put him in locally. We agreed on a job swap: I would tackle Gerald and he would challenge Robert Sheldon in Ashton-under-Lyne. Neither of us got anywhere near winning. I do remember being with Gerald in the back room of a social club on Kirkmanshulme Lane waiting our turn to address the GMC. He never said a word. He was barely friendlier when I was later EPLP leader and he was on Labour's National Executive Committee (NEC).

Things were trickier in 1982 as we ran up to the local elections on 5 May. Margaret Thatcher had sent a task force to tackle the Argentinian invasion of the Falkland Islands. Patriotism fed popularity. My ward, Hurst, had long been the most marginal in the borough. By then Hurst had three Labour councillors, but we didn't have a majority of three hundred between us. There had been my 103, then 14 in 1979 and 159 in 1980. Under the shadow of the Falklands War, the group – with various degrees of enthusiasm – concluded I was destined to lose and pre-selected Percy Travis to replace me. I was lucky to have some stalwart and innovative campaigners in Phil Tomlinson and Cheryl Eastwood. Phil was an outstanding agent, but his maths was dire. When I arrived at the count on the night, he told me the early samples from the ballot boxes had me running third. In the end I put my majority up by more than five times; the final tally was Labour 1845, Conservative 1298, Liberal/SDP 941. Nationwide, the Tories held their ground and Labour slumped at the expense of the newly formed SDP–Liberal Alliance.

Things only went from bad to worse: twelve months on, Thatcher called a general election and Labour lost 45 seats to give the Tories a majority of 144 and Labour its worst result since 1935.

Science in society

Underpinning the political was the academic. I had bills to pay, initially from a grant, then from salary. Back then, attendance allowance for councillors was not much above nominal. I'd arrived in Manchester for a PhD in 'Labour Party Energy Policy 1945–1974'. It will not be a surprise that it is, as yet, uncompleted. As a foundation I followed the MSc on 'The Structure and Organisation of Science and Technology' in the then Department of Liberal Studies in Science that, as Thatcher's thought bit, later became the Department of Science and Technology Policy. When my grant finished, I found work in and around the universities. I ran the gamut up the academic ladder, moving from research assistant to research associate, a sidestep to temporary lecturer and then back on track to research fellow and, ultimately, senior research fellow. My longest contract was eighteen months.

The department's intellectual base was a kaleidoscopic mix of Marx, market and Methodism. I favoured the first. Early on, Ken Green, senior lecturer in the department, organised an early evening Marxist reading group, where we gamely tackled the writings of Frederick Engels, who had lived down the road from the university. *Anti-Dühring* and *Dialectics of Nature* remain largely impenetrable. The only real gleam of understanding and appreciation came with Engels's *The Part Played by Labour in the Transition from Ape to Man*, resounding with the vertebrate palaeontology of Reading's Beverly Halstead, who reputedly had moonlighted with 'Nature Notes' for the *Daily Worker*. I went on to reference *Tidal Friction – Kant to Thompson-Tait* in my attempt to use the authority of geology to resolve debates in astrophysics by looking in the sedimentary record for evidence to prove any early close lunar approach. It was my obscure and only contribution to geology's corpus.[4]

Ken was under the influence of the International Marxist Group along with Rod Coombs. In contrast, Harry Rothman, whose *Murderous Providence: A Study of Pollution in Industrial Societies* was an early environmental admonition, was closer to the further shores of politics inhabited by the cultish Workers Revolutionary Party. Harry's father, Benny, was famous for being one of the leaders of the 1932 Kinder Trespass and served time as a result.

In the middle were those flirting with the Manchester Business School across Oxford Road. At far remove were Michael Gibbons and Geoff Price who both wore their religion well. Geoff was trying to integrate modern Christian thinking into understanding the philosophy of science. As part of this, I helped prepare with Bill Mathews and Geoff an experimental undergraduate course, under the auspices of Science in a Social Context (SISCON): 'The Nature of Scientific Discovery.'

At one point I was a two-thirds-time lecturer in the Department of Management at the University of Manchester Institute of Science and Technology (UMIST), a half-time research fellow at the Science Policy Research Unit at Sussex, working for SISCON, and an Open University course tutor in Oceanography. When I was elected to Tameside Council, something had to give and Oceanography went, before I picked up teaching a third-year option, 'Social Aspects of Geology,' in the geology department at Manchester University. After all this, I considered a fixed five-year contract as an MEP stability.

Theory and practice were symbiotic. My self-understanding of science, technology and society shaped my politics and vice versa. This had practical consequences: the co-option of Dave Eva onto the Environmental Health and Control Committee, the refurbishment programme for the Secondary Sector's science labs, and the experiments with 'Girls' Science' with single-sex teaching and a teacher for science in society (see above). Under my urging, the council commissioned a study of the impact of new technology on jobs. The project 'was to provide an assessment of the likely extent of penetration of microelectronic technologies in Tameside industry over the next ten years; and of the employment consequences for those who live or work in the district.'[5] It forecast that 3.5–9.5 per cent of jobs within Tameside would be at risk in the 1990s as a result of the diffusion of microelectronic equipment and products. It recommended that council strategy should seek to attract to the area 'new' industries made possible by microelectronics, and lead in a large-scale public education programme about the development and application of microelectronics. The forecast, if anything, was

conservative. Tameside tried, with some limited success, to look attractive, but failed to educate.

Arabic interlude

I discovered by chance that Manchester University's academic staff could attend any course in the university for free. In 1975 I signed up for first-year Modern Literary Arabic, taught by Catherine Cobham. I learnt enough of the language (now long lost) to prove useful for trips to Maghreb and Mashreq, but it gave me a lifetime's love for the literature. Catherine was a fan of Yusuf Idris and Naguib Mahfouz. The latter was more prolific; his twenty-volume Centennial Library became available in 2011. My other favourite was *Alf Laylah wa-Laylah* (A Thousand and One Nights) in its multiple editions and variations, although there are few rivals to Richard Burton's translation.

It was while in Cairo on a trip across northern Egypt, Libya and Syria that I first met my long-term American friend Terry Walz in the Pension Anglo-Swiss, as he researched mid-nineteenth-century Egypt–Sudan trade. He was later director of the American Research Center in Egypt. We have kept in touch across close to fifty years, and he provides the solid foundation for my limited knowledge of the politics of the Dar al-Islam. It was probably on that trip that my amateur Arabic proved most fruitful. Crossing the land border between Libya and Tunisia was a nightmare, with hundreds milling and sitting about around frontier control and little sign of any passage. At one point, bags had to be searched and the Libyans discovered in my rucksack a small collection of Arabic children's books. I explained I was trying to learn the language. I was asked to demonstrate. My rendition of the Arabic version of 'The Cat Sat on the Mat' saw my group immediately fast-tracked through the frontier.

All at sea

Much of my later research work was funded by the Marine Technology Directorate of the Science Research Council. They provided core funding for the department's interdisciplinary Marine Resources Project (MRP) that interlocked science and technology, economics and international law into the policy process. I swiftly ended up leading a growing team. We assessed emerging technologies, one being manganese nodule mining. This took us around the world, across the US from New York, via Washington DC and Los Angeles to Hawai'i and on to Japan. The third UN Conference on the Law of the Sea (UNCLOS) was closing on the final wording of its convention making the deep oceans the Common Heritage of Mankind, and we talked with Bernardo Zuleta, the UN Secretary-General's Special Representative to UNCLOS.[6] I also spent time with the International Ocean Institute in Malta and its founder Elizabeth Mann Borgese. The only female founding member of the Club of Rome, she organised the first major law of the sea conference. I remember a feisty lecture in Valletta on 'Thomas Mann and the Sea.' He was her father.

The MRP also looked at disposal of nuclear waste at sea – if that was the question, the answer was mid-plate, mid-gyre – and ocean thermal energy conversion, which took us back to the US and Japan with the addition of India's Andaman and Nicobar Islands, and the opportunity there to see the statue of the Indian nationalist Subhas Chandra Bose on Port Blair's seafront. Bose founded and led the Indian National Army that fought with the Japanese against the British during the Second World War. The islands being an 'Inner Line Zone', alcohol was banned, consequently we were billed for as many as half a dozen 'omelettes' of an evening. All this was the gateway to a more sustained engagement with Japan.[7]

In 1982 I applied to the British Council to sponsor a trip to present papers at a marine technology conference in Bhavnagar, India. The response was positive, but conditional. They had been unsuccessfully hunting for an academic to undertake a short tour of Japan. If I was willing and available, they offered to fund both as a package. After negotiating travel back via the US, it was all settled. I learnt two things in India. Gandhi's 1930 Salt March had terminated in Dandi across the

estuary from Bhavnagar. I think not a solitary speaker in the conference's three days missed referencing the event. More usefully, the food was far superior in the vegetarian tent.

At Todai, sinking Nakasone

In Tokyo I was lucky enough to encounter one of Japan's pre-eminent historians of science, Nakayama Shigeru, who worked with both Thomas Kuhn and Joseph Needham. It was Nakayama who had written the introduction to the first edition of Kuhn's masterful *The Structure of Scientific Revolutions* (1962). Clearly, something clicked, and he arranged for me to be invited back the following year. Tokyo – and Japan more generally – back in 1983 was a different world from today. The facades masked jerry-built interiors dating back to reconstruction after Japan's defeat in the Pacific War. I was to be a visiting professor employed by Monbusho (Ministry of Education) at Tokyo Daigaku (Tokyo University), or Todai as it is commonly known, and would be located in the Department of System Sciences on the subsidiary Komaba campus. I was a Japanese civil servant. In postgrad student accommodation between Meguro railway station on the Yamanote line and Hiro-o metro station on the Hibiya line, my morning commute was a twenty-minute walk to Meguro, two stops to Shibuya and a switch to the Inokashira line for another two stops to Komaba-todaimae before another ten minutes on foot to my office.

My work was to give a series of lectures in English to postgraduates in the department. I spent long hours preparing these fifty-minute presentations. I would almost certainly have been better off learning some serious Japanese. At the end of each presentation, I asked the class for questions. I never had a single one. Later it was explained that two competing tensions guaranteed silence: to ask a question either demonstrated your ignorance in failing to understand what had been said or, to the contrary, implied that you thought the lecturer's exposition had been inept. Even as a postgraduate student, neither of these were attractive options.

Japan's parliamentary politics were frozen. A ceaseless Liberal Democratic Party (LDP) government faced the interminable opposition of the Japan Socialist Party (JSP). The political system in Japan is known as the '1955 System', in reference to the year when the two wings of the JSP reunited after their split four years earlier over the San Francisco peace treaty. More importantly, the reunification immediately provoked the merger of the two right-wing parties, the Japan Democratic Party and the Liberal Party, to form the LDP. The LDP got the better part of the reorganisation, as Japanese politics ossified into a one-and-a-half-party system, with the right in perpetual power and the left in perpetual opposition. With Japan's idiosyncratic electoral system – multi-member constituencies with single non-transferable votes – by the 1970s the JSP was failing to stand sufficient candidates to deliver a majority in the Diet even if, by some miracle, they all won (see Chapter 5). Opposition was driven onto the streets.

After the Soviet Union's Twentieth Party Congress in 1956 – notable for Khrushchev's denunciation of Stalin – and the Hungarian Uprising, the Japanese Communist Party went through a period of constant abrasion as fragments and slivers flaked off to the left. It produced a series of waves as demonstrations, riots and violence swept the cities, seemingly oblivious of the booming economy. In retrospect, the last ripples of these waves were dying during my time in Tokyo. Early in 1983, Prime Minister Yasuhiro Nakasone had promised to make Japan an 'unsinkable aircraft carrier in the Pacific' as Washington's ally against Moscow. Shortly after my arrival I was whisked off to Yoyogi Park to join a 'Sink Nakasone' rally.

I'd been in some of the tougher demos in the UK when the left in 1976 had marched in Blackburn to protest the election of two members of Kingsley Reed's neo-fascist National Party, a Strasserite split from the National Front, where public and police hostility was blatant. You marched in rows with linked arms to stop snatch-squads grabbing individual marchers – a tactic learnt from the policing of the Troubles in Northern Ireland – with the vanguard and rearguard wearing crash helmets and not a motorbike or scooter in sight. In Tokyo it was intimidating in a different way. The whole march was enveloped by riot police who – at their chosen pace – walked

the protestors through the streets masked behind their mass ranks – an early form of mobile 'kettling'.

Violent protest in Japan was franchised out.[8] In the early 1980s, Senki-ha (Mainstream Battleflag) monopolised attacks on US bases, while Chukaka-ha (Middle Core Faction) affiliated with the Sanrizuka protest over the construction of Narita airport and focused on attacking and destroying the airport's infrastructure for decades after its opening. At one point, they attempted to send in a remote-controlled petrol tanker with a bomb onboard. The result was levels of security not far off Israel's 'gold standard'. Chukaka-ha's last attack came in 2001.

Waterwheels

One friend, Satofuka Fumihiro (see Chapter 4), invited me to join him on a field trip with the West Japan Waterwheel Association. By then I'd been joined by my first wife, Hazel, and our daughter, Elise. A group of about thirty set off on the overnight train – no Shinkansen for us – from Tokyo to Kyushu where we ended up bunched on a coach to tour the villages clustered around the foot of Japan's most active volcano, Mount Aso. The activity there offered a stark contrast of old and new technology. Venerable wooden wheels, seen through a yellow brume down the declines of narrow streets, were creaking and grinding as one-man operations in succession crushed sulphur ores produced centuries, if not millennia, earlier as a by-product of volcanic activity. This sight was counterposed by the small, modern, steel wheels spinning away on the plains across the narrow channels of the irrigation ditches delineating the greening rice paddies.

In the evening we retired to a *ryokan* – a Japanese-style hotel. As reputedly the first *gaijin* to visit, my family and I were segregated in a separate sleeping room. Everyone else was sharing. The whole coach disrobed and dressed in *yukatas* and, after washing, went to single-sex bath houses to soak up the benefits of the natural hot springs. Returning to the group room, we sat on the tatami with low tables arranged around three sides as an elaborate meal rang the changes of Japan's cuisine. Miso soup, sushi, sashimi, tempura and yakitori followed one another at speed. Equally rapidly, so did beer and saki, shochu and whisky. It was a moveable feast as people chased down preferences and passed on aversions.

In Europe we mix our drinks consecutively and get drunk without haste. In Japan it's concurrent and brisk. As the evening progressed, a voluntary and involuntary wave of prone bodies crept up from the bottom of the room: those who knew they'd had too much to drink and those who didn't. The first retired to a futon and the second was carried – or dragged – there. As the bodies encroached closer, tables were removed and the flotsam and jetsam of dinner and drink congregated on the shrinking space left. When the company was down to low single figures and I saw my host being dragged past me to a futon, I chose discretion over valour and retired to my haven. The next morning, the majority were clearly suffering from acute dehydration.

Revelations

My time in Tokyo was a transformation. It changed my stance on the EU. Inside the goldfish bowl of the UK, London loomed large. It was only when viewed from the other side of the world, from a Japan with soaring growth rates and technology transforming the country and resetting global markets, that Britain could be seen as the declining power it was, at the end of its era and not the beginning. If the countries of Europe were to march in step with Japan, it would be together, not separately. I can't claim the change was overnight but the seeds were sown deep and germinated.

Distance helped, but so did science. Within weeks of my return, alongside my branch nominations for MEP I had a weekend trip to Imperial College for the Joint European Association for the Study of Science and Technology and Science Technology and Society Association's 'Choice in Science and Technology' conference. There were nearly fifty papers. My Japanese champion, Nakayama Shigeru, was there looking at America's search for the secret of Japan's innovative success, having eschewed both big and pure science. The US answer

was American scientific illiteracy, but the real answer was hidden in plain sight in the question.

In retrospect, the paper with most effect was Ken Green's 'Choices in the direction of science and technology in Europe: reconstructing a radical programme'. The argument was twofold. First, the world was going through a period of international economic restructuring, watched over by centre-right governments. The economies had traded the production of goods for individual consumption at the expense of the degradation of work. Second, a mix of new social movements – anti-war, women, environment and alternative trade unionism – was changing the game. Recycling was not the solution. New aims and answers, qualitatively and quantitatively, were required to old questions; alternative processes should produce alternative products. 'The very scale of the international economic crisis precludes simple "national" solutions to economic and political problems ... There is some sense in trying to develop new programmes and policies at a *European* level' (emphasis in the original).[9] Today the argument of the need to operate at a European level of aggregation would be trite and unexceptional; back then and coming from the tough left it was both startling and liberating. Politics – or at least science politics – had to break beyond the curtilage of the national state.

Endnotes

[1] This was my karaoke song of choice in Tokyo. I entertained future prime minister Hata with it during several 'performances'. In Pyongyang the catalogue of most karaoke machines was more restricted and my default was 'I Will Survive'. [2] Quoted in Tom Craig (1983), 'Who inspects the factory inspectors?', *New Scientist*, 30 June. [3] Glyn Ford (1986), 'Languages on the Move', pp104-111, *The British Journal of Language Teaching*, Vol. 24 (2). [4] Glyn Ford (1975), 'The earth, the moon and tidal sediments: an analytical review', *Mercian Geologist* 5:3, September. [5] Kenneth Green, Rod Coombs and Keith Holroyd (1980), *The Effects of Microelectronic Technologies on Employment Prospects: A Case Study of Tameside*, Aldershot: Gower. [6] In October 1984, as the deadline ticked down, I was urging the EU to ignore Britain and Reagan and sign and ratify the Law of the Sea Treaty (see EP, *Debates*, 25 October 1984). The EU signed on 7 December after Luxembourg's signature two days earlier made the EU majority. [7] All summed up in Glyn Ford, Chris Niblett and Lindsay Walker (1987), *The Future for Ocean Technology*, London: Pinter Publishers. [8] The political history and cartography of Japan's extra-parliamentary left is to be found in Muto Ichiyo and Inoue Reiko (1985), 'Beyond the New Left: in search of a radical base in Japan', *AMPO – Japanese-Asia Quarterly Review* 17:2 (Part 1), 17:3 (Part 2,1) and 17:4 (Part 2,2). The promised Part 3 never appeared. [9] Joint EASST/STSA 'Choice in Science and Technology' Conference Papers, Imperial College, University of London, 16–18 September 1983.

4 European Parliamentary Labour Party

Madness is something rare in individuals – but in groups, parties, and ages, it is the rule.

Friedrich Nietzsche, Beyond Good and Evil [1886]

Early in the morning of 18 June 1984, rather to my surprise, I was elected as the MEP for Greater Manchester East. The party was in transition. In the previous decade there had been two Labour prime ministers, Harold Wilson and James Callaghan, and a Labour leader, Michael Foot. All three had been born before the end of the First World War and all had been elected as MPs in 1945, with Wilson and Callaghan serving as ministers in the Attlee government. In contrast, Labour's new leader Neil Kinnock – elected in October 1983 – had been three years old when the Labour landslide swept Churchill away.

Kinnock was a frustrated moderniser, forestalled and held hostage by the biggest industrial conflict since the 1926 General Strike. The year-long miners' strike from March 1983 to March 1984 cost twenty-six million lost days of work. It was class war, counterposing Margaret Thatcher and Arthur Scargill. Having beaten the enemy without in the South Atlantic, now she turned on the enemy within, determined to wreak Tory retribution for the humiliation of 1974. We knew what side we were on, even if Scargill's obdurate refusal to call a national ballot of National Union of Mineworkers (NUM) members made George Custer look an astute tactician.

Thatcher won; the miners, their communities and the country lost. The conflict made early Labour renovation impossible. Rather, Labour went forward to imagined futures already past as Scargill brought with him history's heavy baggage. It was back to the future with nationalisation and nationalism.

DAILY HERALD

Attlee Accepts Premiership: Now Forming Government

LABOUR IN POWER

Night Climax To The Great Landslide

LATEST ELECTION FIGURES AT A GLANCE

FOR TORIES - - 210 AGAINST - - - - 416

ATTLEE SPEAKS: A New Era Dawns

PALACE DRAMA

Vast Amount Of Talent

World Acclaims The New Regime

JAPS TOLD TERMS

ATTLEE'S TRIUMPH

STOP PRESS

Churchill: I Lay Down My Charge

27 July 1945.

Yet despite Labour being in limbo, the paltry seventeen seats won in 1979's first direct elections to the EP had been all but doubled to thirty-two. When I'd been selected back in January from a shortlist of six – I finally won on the fourth ballot at the selection meeting in Denton Labour Club – there was little expectation of Labour winning the seat. Firstly, we were lagging in the polls as Thatcher basked in the blood-red afterglow of the Falklands War, and secondly, Labour just couldn't add up – the message from the regional office was that the constituency was thirty-sixth on Labour's list of winnable seats. Later, 'alternative maths' sprung the seat up to a still daunting thirtieth. In the end, Labour had a majority of 8686 with 42.7 per cent of the vote.

I nearly missed the selection. I'd returned from my spell as a visiting professor at Tokyo University in late August. Almost as I landed, a Japanese colleague, Satofuka Fumihiko, arrived in Manchester for a brief stop-over on a wider British tour. We

had worked together on radical science and he was close to the JSP, having been one of their list candidates in the Upper House elections in June. He wanted to see the Labour Party in action and so I took him to a ward meeting in Mossley as my own branch, Hurst East, wasn't meeting that week. Quite how exciting he found minutes, matters arising and any other business was unclear. In Tokyo he had been more entertaining, having had me address the semi-Trotskyist *Rentai* (Solidarity) on workers control and march at a 'Sink Nakasone' rally and experience kettling by Japan's riot police (see Chapter 3).

At the end of the evening, in correspondence, nominations for Labour's candidate for the EP elections came up. Seeing me sitting there, someone – I don't remember who – said, 'You do a lot of travelling abroad, why don't you stand?' I had actually been on the list of possible candidates in 1979, but here I had the first of what was to end as three branch nominations out of a possible fifty plus. I'd later added my own ward, plus a ward in the Hazel Grove constituency. This subsequently translated into two CLP nominations out of a possible eight, with six other candidates claiming one each. One was former cabinet minister Barbara Castle. She'd been elected in 1979 for Greater Manchester North, on a promise of only serving one term. As we'll see later, Barbara's self-imposed term limits were elastic. With boundary changes, the bulk of her old constituency was in the new Greater Manchester West and a minority in the East. She kept the East as a fallback, but was selected for the safest of the Greater Manchester seats early and pulled out. I'd been in the right place at the right time. With both the other Greater Manchester seats listed as safe Labour after boundary changes, and with Barbara initially hovering over both East and West, interest had focused on Greater Manchester Central, an open seat with no sitting Labour MEP.

This was the heyday of Labour's anti-Europeanism. The party's manifesto for the 1983 general election had a no-nonsense commitment of immediate withdrawal once a Labour government was elected:

> *The European Economic Community, which does not even include the whole of Western Europe, was*

> *never devised to suit us. The next Labour government, committed to radical socialist policies for reviving the British economy, is bound to find continued membership a most serious obstacle to fulfilment of those policies. British withdrawal from the Community is the right policy for Britain – to be completed well within the lifetime of the parliament.*

I was there with the party in body, but semi-detached in spirit. A number of those who had voted for me at the selection meeting subsequently said that I got their support as the least anti-European of the six candidates. The reality was that I was beginning to have doubts, driven by my work on science and technology policy catalysed by Ken Green, a colleague in the Department of Science and Technology Policy at Manchester University, and a belated epiphany after my Japanese pilgrimage (see chapters 3 and 6). From the inside looking out, blinkered by English exceptionalism, going it alone seemed possible, but with the fetch of Tokyo, the future for solitary medium-sized nation states looked bleak. As Huxley said of Darwin's *On the Origin of Species*, 'how extremely stupid not to have thought of that!'[1]

In the run-up to the elections, I saw that with the miners' strike in full swing the *Manchester Evening News* was discretely advertising for scabs. I made the call and applied along with Paul Stonier, one of my campaign volunteers. We had a cursory interview and were offered jobs. We phoned the NUM and arranged to meet a couple of officials from Wigan in a lay-by just off what's now the M60, where we gave them all the details and that was that. A few days later, a sympathetic daily reported how prospective MEP Eddie Newman had helped the miners to expose scabbing. I later asked Eddie why he'd never corrected it. The response was, 'Someday, someone will vote for me because of that.'

Fractious factions

The factions inside the British Labour Group (BLG) were armoured for battle. I was tagged on the left with my *Tribune*

connections. A month or so before the election I was phoned by Janey Buchan MEP, a visceral anti-Marketeer, and put to the question. I passed, I suspect much to her subsequent chagrin, and was invited – on election – for induction into the BLG 'left' caucus. On the Tuesday after the Sunday night count, Labour's winners were summoned to London for the group's AGM. Prior, those who had passed muster were shepherded to a pre-meeting of the caucus, who promptly voted a full slate of candidates. It was done with a celerity and prowess that suggested this might not have been the first meeting of the day. It was puppet theatre and the strings showed. With twenty-three MEPs sworn in, the left was in control and this dress rehearsal was replayed on the larger stage at Queen Anne's Gate. Barbara Castle, the group leader since 1979, escaped the push by promising to jump the following year. She was placed under the baleful watch of her new deputy, the veteran left-winger Alf Lomas, with all other positions filled by 'boys in the band.' Alf was a lovely man, but his politics were from Straight Left, the fellow-travelling 'tankies' parked on the lawn in the CPGB's faction fight with *Marxism Today's* Euro-communists. Alf laid on trips for Labour MEPs to meet with the sister parties allied to the Bulgarian Communist Party in the Fatherland Front coalition.[2]

Faction-fighting continued as the enlarged BLG engaged with the EP's Socialist Group. Labour was the group's largest national delegation, subsequent to hanging on, as the UK did, to the political 'double or quits' that was 'first past the post.' Delivery required discipline. As a block, the BLG could be decisive, or riven irrelevant. This was achievable either by accommodation or intimidation. Coercion was determined. The BLG's majority would vote to mandate the minority for positions within group and parliament. Group elections were by secret ballot, but that was easily side-stepped; completed ballot papers were to be checked and verified by a BLG officer before being deposited in the ballot box.

As much by good luck as good judgement, the BLG chose the right candidate more often than not. The previous Socialist Group leader, the clement francophone Belgian Ernest Glinne, was standing for re-election against Germany's Rudi Arndt from the SPD. In 1979 the BLG had backed Glinne, but this time – seemingly out of sheer bloody-mindedness – we picked the robust Arndt, who won and was grateful. It wasn't always reciprocated. Arndt could be impatient and rode roughshod over protest. He didn't suffer fools gladly and we had fools aplenty. Forced into voting a long series of amendments at one group meeting, three or four BLG members, incensed by Arndt's authoritarianism, protested by voting with straight-arm salutes until it was pointed out – not that there was any excuse – that Arndt's father, Konrad, a trade union organiser and Jewish anti-fascist, had been held in Sachsenhausen concentration camp and subsequently murdered by the SS.[3] Ken Stewart had earlier remarked, 'last time I saw a German it was at the point of a gun.'[4]

Once the EP was up and running, the caucus separated into semi-miscible factions. There was a disciplined Campaign Group, a more wilful Tribune Group and an umbrella Broad Left spanning the two, where I became convenor. By February 1985 the Campaign Group was grooming the Broad Left into adopting its 'Twenty-one Conditions.'[5] To remain a member, it was necessary to sign up to unilateral nuclear disarmament, the nationalisation of major industries and industrial democracy. All unproblematic. But battle was joined over the demand by Bob Cryer to add 'Maintain the principle of withdrawal from the Common Market.' Cryer's catechism was a last desperate attempt to hang on to a politics pickled in the past. Redolent of the opposition of empire and the English-speaking Commonwealth, socialist nationalism's day was done in the Labour Party, but it was to be reborn later among the Tories and UKIP. Stan Newens, former MP and left-wing stalwart, resigned from the Broad Left while staying in the Tribune Group.

Some of our proto-European Research Group 'ultras' wanted to pre-empt what Cameron's Tories did in 2014: put nation before politics when they abandoned Europe's centre-right EPP for a jumble of xenophobes, fruitcakes and closet fascists. Gorged on nationalism laced with nostalgia, Cryer, Stewart, Les Huckfield and Eddie Newman proposed to take the British delegation out of the Socialist Group. Quite where we were going was never made clear. Cryer was a zealot, driven to create the purist of sects. He was constantly suspicious of heretical thoughts and ideas, so his followers were to be put to the test until they ceded or could stomach

no more. At times he made the Socialist Party of Great Britain look pragmatic.

The continuing miners' strike drove the early agenda in the EP. My family history played a part. My first intervention was a point of order to the parliament's new president, Pierre Pflimlin, urging him to write to the Chief Constable of Merseyside to demand that proceedings be suspended against Huckfield – arrested on a miners' picket line – as the latter had parliamentary immunity while engaged in the exercise of his duties.[6] Pflimlin, who was French prime minister for a couple of weeks in 1958 before events in Algeria forced him to resign in favour of de Gaulle, was having none of it. On 10 October Huckfield was subject, not object, as he demanded a debate on the miners' strike, while Llew Smith – already with an eye to the main chance – and Alex Falconer raised at the back of the chamber the banner of the Blaenau Gwent NUM. The right, with Otto von Habsburg in the van, attempted to tear the banner down. The session was suspended.

Banner of the Blaenau Gwent National Union of Mineworkers held aloft in the European Parliament by Alex Falconer and Llew Smith.

Huckfield was back on 24 October. I asked the president for a debate on the miners' strike that afternoon.[7] Huckfield followed, protesting that the Tories and fascists were systematically blocking all avenues to a debate. In the EP the interpretation imperative meant that who controls the microphone controls the floor. We were prepared: I'd helped Huckfield smuggle in a loudhailer. When the president switched off Huckfield's mic, he swapped collective for personal and produced the megaphone from beneath his seat. The session was suspended.

The BLG provided financial support along with the political. The twelve-month levy of the thirty-two members, plus donations and appeals raised £71,920.12 for the NUM.[8] Yet solidarity with the miners didn't stop the new majority from crumbling.[9] With Christine Crawley, I wrote a response to Huckfield and Stewart's attacks on the Common Market in *Tribune*, arguing they were making a good case against entry, but that thirteen years on, the reality was that 45 per cent of British trade was with our European partners. The stable door was wide open and that horse long gone. Withdrawal itself would improve nothing. Britain's departure only made sense with the advent of a radical Labour government, forced to leave to free itself from any Brussels constraints on our industrial regeneration.

The BLG AGM of June 1985 saw Barbara Castle reneging and running. Alf Lomas was elected, but the vote had narrowed to 18–14. Meanwhile, Newens beat Norman West –the 'anointed' Broad Left candidate and Arthur Scargill's man in Brussels – 17–14 to become BLG chair, a role in which he was not a success. Most of this played out behind closed doors, but after Bob Geldof, post Live Aid, came in November and was grudgingly allowed to speak to the BLG with a TV crew in tow, the disarray was on record and the writing on the wall. Newens's problem was that he couldn't distinguish between principled differences of opinion and deliberate, sustained sabotage and wrecking.

Lomas, blithely ignoring the lessons of Broad Left, decided in the autumn that the BLG should adopt an anti-Common Market position in a long policy paper to be sent to the party back home. He was his own nemesis. It reawakened the dormant right who, energised and led by John Tomlinson and Ken Collins, proceeded to table dozens upon dozens of amendments. Determined not to be thwarted, the hard left expanded delegation meetings to fit the time available. At one Strasbourg session, the BLG spent seven and a half hours in self-stimulation while Europe's evolving politics passed us entirely by. After nigh on a year, this protracted labour bore a mouse that went off to the NEC where it was promptly ignored. The reality was that these members and fellow travellers of the Labour Common Market Safeguards Committee spoke loudly because they had nothing to say, all lungs and no wits, offering yesterday's answers to today's questions. The attempt to confirm the old anti-market position reflected the politics of incoherence, narcissism and futility.

The winds of change blew. Neil Kinnock, then party leader, had made the point in June at a *Tribune* meeting in the House of Commons that, there was no way that any party would win an election on policy of withdrawal from Common Market. By October I was telling a local Co-op members' rally that 'leaving the Common Market will not solve a single problem we face. It will not in itself create a single job or improve a single service'. Opportunity knocked for a radical socialist programme, but there was nobody there.

At the year's end, Christine Crawley, David Martin, David Morris and myself published 'Kamikaze politics or the collective madness that grips Labour in Europe', attacking the Lomas manifesto and reiterating earlier criticism:

> *This document, at best, made a reasonable case for not joining the Community in 1973, and at worst served as a collective comforter to be nursed against the threatened intrusion of the real world ... The current epithet for the British Labour members, which originated amongst the Spanish Socialists, is Los Japoneses (The Japanese) deriving from the occasional discovery in remote island jungles of Japanese soldiers who didn't know the war was over. This is a rather over generous comparison. At least [Shoichi Yokoi], who emerged from the jungle in Guam [in 1972], had the excuse that he'd been isolated for almost a quarter of a century. The same is not true of the British Labour Group or the Labour leadership.*[10]

The article continued:

> *Members of the British Labour Group have raced toy woodpeckers down sticks while the Parliament has been voting on the food aid sections of the budget. At*

> *committee meetings some have attended three quarters of the meetings, but only participated in five percent of the votes. On at least three occasions, on defence issues such as Star Wars and European Security, British Labour members have voted against the Socialist Group and Labour Group whip because, in the classic style of what Lenin called Parliamentary cretinism, they have mistaken the trees for the wood and aided the right in its enthusiasm for Reagan's Strategic Defence initiatives because of 'theological' objections to some obscure paragraph. At one stage a decision was taken to postpone agreeing that we will vote for our own Socialist Group candidate against the Tory Sir Henry Plumb in January's elections for the presidency of the Parliament ... [We need to] develop a political vision of Europe [that escapes from day-to-day activity of the BLG] governed by a form of revolutionary nihilism whose legitimation is our 'imminent departure,' whose practice is intimidatory and whose forward vision is lemming-like.*

The BLG was now, like Gaul, divided into three parts. Ours was the smallest precinct. The Campaign Group and fellow travellers – some active participants have claimed retrospectively they were just political bystanders adhering to their discipline by mere happenstance – Tribunites and the right. At the 1987 AGM, David Martin replaced Lomas, who stood down as leader. It was a three-way contest with Martin against Stan Newens and Michael Hindley: new left versus hard left versus old left. In the first round it was Martin 14, Hindley 11 and Newens 6. Christine Crawley had gone walkabout, her regular answer to hard choices. In the second round, two Newens supporters (Janey Buchan and Michael Elliott) abstained, two (Tom Megahy and Barry Seal) went for Hindley, while another two (Dai Morris and Newens himself) supported Martin, delivering Martin a fragile 16–13 victory. For deputy leader it was a repeat performance, save for Newens joining the 'don't knows,' with John Tomlinson besting Hindley 15–13. I was elected treasurer.

Phil Kelly, *Tribune*'s editor, reported Buchan's vexation, decrying that the slate had destroyed the BLG's Tribune

Group; nevertheless, he added, 'There was clearly a need for change, the behaviour of the Campaign Group members has been "abominable".'[11] The following month, David Martin and I argued 'Why we need to build a European united left ...', where we 'work with Communist Parties which are more than supporters clubs for the Soviet Union, with the Greens and their allies', offering an opening to the Partito Comunista Italiano (PCI).[12] Buchan wrote a riposte, published on the facing page, that spent its time rehashing the iniquities of the AGM rather than engaging with the politics of Europe. As an old CPGB member who'd left after Hungary in 1956, she was coming from a different era. When she referred to 'The Party', it was to that first love that had driven her away, not Labour caught on the rebound. That communism was not the one we were referencing.

Buchan's subsequent party piece when David Martin or I were present at meetings with labour movement visitors was to declare loudly that she was writing a book called 'Shits I Have Known' and that we were in it. She was also known for a trip to the African, Caribbean and Pacific Group of States (ACP)–EEC Consultative Assembly in the first parliament, when she flew to the Dominican Republic rather than Dominica. (Although I should confess that one of my staff, joining me in Beijing for a trip to North Korea, obtained the visa for the North but forgot China. She flew in and out of Beijing on the same plane.) When Janey's husband, Norman, the sterling MP for Paisley South, died in 1990, Martin and fellow Scottish MPs Ken Collins and Hugh McMahon received a letter saying that they would not be welcome at the funeral.

Open warfare was declared, with no hostages taken. In July, even Martin's right to speak as leader was forced to an 18–7 vote. The tenuous nature of the new leadership's hold was demonstrated in the October Strasbourg plenary's vote on the Galluzzi report, 'Political aspects of a European security strategy'. Despite the delegation whip to abstain, only seventeen followed with twelve against and three 'irredeemables' (Alex Falconer, Les Huckfield and Norman West) absent. Our demise was no surprise. Richard Balfe, the ultimate political flexitarian, was the weakest link. In the wake of the disastrous Greenwich by-election in February 1987, he said to Bob Cryer that the problem with Labour's candidate was that, 'Deirdre

Wood was not a proper left-winger like you and I, Bob'. Bob knew better. Balfe was to wash up a Tory member of the House of Lords. At the 1988 AGM, Balfe switched his vote for leader from Martin to Barry Seal, with Martin consequently escaping a further year of purgatory. Yet the BLG was trying to swim upstream.

There is only one looney left

In the 1987 general election I stood for Labour in Hazel Grove. For me this was not the first step on the road to Westminster, rather the start of my re-election campaign in Labour's third-most marginal European seat. I was standing neither to win, nor even enhance my CV; it was marketing and brand recognition. My Euro-constituency comprised eight Westminster seats, five held by Labour in Tameside and Oldham with respectable rather than spectacular majorities, while in Stockport all three were Tory. Stockport itself was Tory–Labour marginal, which we would finally win in 1992 with left-wing local councillor Ann Coffey, whose political trajectory deposited her in the wilderness with Chuka Umunna and Change UK. The problems were Cheadle and Hazel Grove, both Tory–Liberal marginals with Labour a bad third. The Bramhall East ward – which, counterintuitively, possessed a Labour Club – was jokingly referred to in the Euro-constituency as 'little Moscow'. In the last local elections, Labour had secured 2.8 per cent of the vote there. In Hazel Grove – and Cheadle – voters had been relentlessly pressed with the Liberal squeeze that 'Labour can't win here'. The party had even stopped handing out window posters other than to the most faithful of the congregation. All the appearance of such posters did was attract Liberal activists like bluebottles to rotting meat, looking to force home the tactical voting argument.

Our campaign worked perfectly. The electorate in Hazel Grove were told fifty thousand times via the election address and other leaflets that they had elected a Labour MEP. Despite tactical badgering, I held the Labour vote at 11.8 per cent, losing only 0.2 per cent to the Liberals, with the Tories winning by fewer than 2000. It was only later under Blair

that Labour nationally deployed people to deliberately and cynically sabotage and undermine its own vote in Tory–Liberal marginals as a way of both diverting Tory resources and creating that bigger third party as a Plan B coalition partner.

My campaign was fun. We had nothing to lose. Our eve-of-poll leaflet, borrowed from Billy Bragg's Red Wedge, pictured a demented Margaret Thatcher with the strap line 'There is only one loony left ...' and 'Get rid of her on June the 11th ... USE YOUR VOTE'. In the more serious contests it had been shunned as discourteous and disrespectful, but we didn't care. It was eye-catching and popular. On election day they appeared, stuck in house and car windows. The juice was worth the squeeze. When the European votes were counted in June 1989, we'd more than tripled our vote in Hazel Grove from 1984.

Eve-of-poll leaflet from the Hazel Grove campaign, 1987 General Election.

Seeing the Euro-phobic Conservative Party that emerged from the ashes of Brexit, it's difficult to imagine that one problem we'd faced in Brussels was Tory ultras trying to push European harmonisation beyond rational limits. Lord Arthur Cockfield was appointed by Thatcher as European Commissioner in 1984 (he didn't formally take office until 1985) and became known as 'The Father of the Single Market'. In July 1987, as I spoke accordingly in the EP debate,

> *The proposals that are being brought forward by Lord Cockfield are about VAT approximation on books, newspapers, food, children's clothes and even on funerals! The whole thing is absurd to the point of ridiculousness. Does Lord Cockfield seriously think that with the imposition of VAT on newspapers in the United Kingdom people will change from the Guardian to Libération, from the Sun to Le Figaro, or from the Salisbury Review to National Hebdo? It*

is clearly absurd. By putting VAT on funerals, does Lord Cockfield seriously think that people in the United Kingdom are going to be buried in France? By putting VAT on books, does Lord Cockfield seriously think we are going to buy our books in French, Italian, German or Portuguese rather than in English? And the same is true elsewhere. It is clearly nonsensical and this House should realise that. Just the imposition of VAT on food in the United Kingdom will take away from the pensioners more than three times the miserly rise that they received this year from the Conservative Government! We are not going to swallow it! We are not voting for this report.[13]

Reselection games

In September 1988, European Commission president Jacques Delors received a standing ovation from what had previously been seen as a Eurosceptic audience after his speech to the TUC in Bournemouth when he offered a 'social Europe' not a 'capitalists' club'. Within a fortnight, Thatcher had made her rejoinder with the Bruges speech that launched Conservative Euroscepticism. It was not self-evident that Labour activists in Greater Manchester were as politically nimble as the unions. Labour MEPs were in the early throes of the reselection process in 1988. In order to be confirmed as a candidate – in my case – each of the eight CLPs needed to vote whether or not they wished to trigger a full one member, one vote reselection contest. To be reselected I needed five out of eight. I was reasonably confident, but there was a nasty game being played by a renegade Liberal councillor, Peter Jepson, who had defected to Labour and then reinvented himself as a 'man of the left' in my own constituency of Ashton-under-Lyne.

At a poorly attended Executive Committee (EC) he orchestrated a vote, proposing the GMC pull the trigger. My supporters dealt with that when the minutes of the EC came up for approval at the next GMC as a 'correct record'. They simply rejected the minutes en bloc. I decided I needed to

tackle Jepson head on. I had off-pat a standard speech making my case, but the one for Ashton was to be tailor made. I still have my notes. I started by pointing out that in the previous year's general election, Labour had lost to the Tories for the third time running, leaving us needing to win over Labour voters who had not supported us in fifteen years – a whole generation. On the 1987 result, the Tories would have won the Euro-seat with a majority of 10,800. In Europe, we needed to campaign with the left for a thirty-five-hour week, against Tory racism, for investment in new technology and non-nuclear defence cooperation. Now it seems a quirky list, but back then it reflected contemporary concerns.

I said,

> *We can no longer sit on our luggage waiting to leave, or use Europe as a crutch to prop up backward looking politics. It would be a folly not to use it as a springboard. The reason it wasn't happening is we are fighting ourselves and not the Tories. The politics of sectarian groupings threatens the slow death of the party. For politicians most decisions are easy, only a few are hard – they are the important ones. Why are they hard? Because they are unpopular in that they go against the stream. As chair of education in Tameside I brought forward a school closure programme unwelcome with fellow Labour councillors and sections of the public alike [see Chapter 2]. There were no prizes, but it was necessary. My role inside and outside the European Parliament fighting racism and fascism has resulted in hate mail, death threats and the police watching my house. Only par for the course. Nor am I going to be intimidated by the activities of a couple of members here who trade in malicious poisonous lies, half-truths and innuendo typical of the Liberal tactics we find so offensive. If we are to win here, win in the country, win for our people, we have to move away. If you don't want to be part of it, don't vote for me.*

I won the vote handily in Ashton and in all seven of the other constituencies. The only MEP deselected was the rigid Eurosceptic Les Huckfield. His replacement Terry Wynn was as far on the right as Les had been left; hardly a Labour gain.

In November 1988 the Labour Coordinating Committee organised a well-attended and reported weekend conference in London that put together Labour's future leadership – Tony Blair, Tom Sawyer and Stuart Holland – with the likes of Oskar Lafontaine, Hedy d'Ancona from the EP Women's Committee and socialists from Italy, France and Denmark. I spoke at the concluding session alongside Karsten Voight, then SPD foreign affairs spokesperson, Larry Whitty and Frances Morrell. In *Wreckers and Builders?,* Anita Pollack claims, 'It was seen by many as a pivotal event in opening minds on the left towards the European agenda.'[14]

1989 European election campaign leaflet referencing Thatcher's plans for football fans to carry ID cards.

In the run-up to the 1989 European elections, I tried with Julian Priestley to persuade the party to see those elections as more than a second-hand referendum on the Tories with 'Euro-elections: time to go beyond "little Englandism"'. We argued that 'the choice will be made between Bruges and Bournemouth; between a narrow pinched free-for-all market Europe, fit for multinationals, as advocated by Margaret Thatcher in Bruges last September, and the other possible Europe, where social progress marches step by step with economic integration, as outlined by Jacques Delors ... to the last Congress of the TUC in Bournemouth.' We were dismissive of Thatcher's invention of the single market; it was more discovery than innovation: 'The globalisation of the industrial

economy is proceeding so rapidly that many of the measures put forward just three years ago as part of the market opening package would have had to be implemented by member states to keep themselves competitive in the world market.'[15]

During the election run-up, my campaign team had some fun with Thatcher's authoritarian solutions to domestic football-related problems, which included mandating supporters to carry ID cards to be allowed to attend matches. We produced a leaflet in Oldham Athletic's blue for the match with Swindon Town with a cartoon of Hitler telling her: 'Why not tattoo the ID numbers on their wrists?' After leafleting the fans we went into Boundary Park for the match, which ended 2–2.

Second-term charge

The 1989 European elections saw Labour beat the Tories for the first time since 1974. The previous 45–32 split of MEPs in favour of Thatcher was reversed. This time we'd done the mentoring, and anticipated the swing rather better than the national party in Walworth Road. One of my flock was Ian White, who was to win Bristol and Bath. A week before the election we spoke on the phone and Ian said, 'What am I going to do? I'm going to win and I've already got a job.' Another was Brian Simpson, running in the 'unwinnable' Cheshire East. Simpson would recount, 'There were only two of us up for selection. The other guy was from Staffordshire and nobody knew him. Even his delegates didn't show up. He was so late he nearly missed the meeting and then made an awful speech. I beat him 12–11.'

White and Simpson both won and so did I, with my majority up from 8000 to 28,000. I'd had some of my friends in the EP come over and help the campaign, including both Julian Priestley and Chris Piening.[16] I announced at the count that I was standing as leader of the BLG to open a second front against the Tories in Europe. There was another candidate looking to run, George Stevenson from Staffordshire East, but he killed his chance in the pre-meeting caucus. When pressed to commit to remaining an MEP rather than absconding to Westminster, he was deeply equivocal. In 1992 he disappeared into the anonymity and obscurity of the House of Commons.

I ran on a joint ticket, with Carole Tongue for deputy leader. On the day of the AGM we published our manifesto in the *Morning Star*, refusing to allow the Campaign Group and its fellow travellers to paint us into a corner with Labour's right. We wrote, 'The era of the small independent nation state has passed on ... The European Commission's plans for 1992 and the creation of a single internal market are a symptom, not a cause, of late capitalist re-ordering.' Industry required massive investment and increasingly this would come from an enlarged Community research and development (R&D) budget: 'only in Britain are we sufficiently self-deluding that we believe, as a Junior Minister said last year, that the best way to obtain industrial innovation is by tax relief to entrepreneurs. The Japanese are laughing all the way to the research lab.' We argued for the creation of a Community 'where we protect and enhance the quality of the environment and life. A Europe in partnership with rather than dominating over the third world. A community where everyone living in Europe has the same rights and duties, where we look outwards, rather than inwards, where we go forwards together united as all the different colours of Europe.'[17]

The 1989 intake augmented both the Tribunites and the right with the Campaign Group standing pat. There was a new element with the 'Federalist Four' – Ken Coates, Peter Crampton, Henry McCubbin and White – on the hard left, but strongly pro-European. Coates had previously been expelled from the party and had been instrumental in setting up the Institute for Workers' Control (IWC). I knew him from my minor involvement in the IWC and a more active role as a founder member in 1973 of SERA. Despite being let back into the party, there is no way he would have been allowed to stand if Labour HQ had thought there was any prospect he might win. He wasn't the only one. Walworth Road's psephological naivety made for interesting times.

The following year Ken and I were to be deported from Algeria after we joined Ahmed Ben Bella's entourage that accompanied him home from Barcelona to Algiers, ending his exile. The Algerian authorities allowed 'the president' to land, but decided the foreigners accompanying him were *persona non grata.* Having been detained for a few hours in the port, we were physically forced onto a ferry sailing for Marseille; one of the more recalcitrant was thrown bodily onto the ship's deck as it pulled away from the dock. Many of those expelled were stateless or had passports from countries requiring visas for France. Luckily, Stuart Holland was with us and he phoned French prime minister Michel Rocard's office. When the ship docked, we miscreants were taken off first, and a team of customs officials (arranged by Interior Minister Pierre Joxe) stamped passports on a production line, giving forty-eight-hour transit visas to even those with the most dubious sets of papers.

Ken Coates (left) and Ben Bella (right) arriving in Algiers by boat, 1990. Crowds visible behind with banners were estimated at 100,000 people.

This was not my first experience of Ken's political peregrinations. I had travelled with him and Ken Fleet at the end of March 1988 to the Jerusalem District Court to attend the conclusion of the trial of Mordechai Vanunu, who had blown the whistle to the *Sunday Times* on Israel's nuclear weapons programme and their hundred nuclear weapons at the Negev Nuclear Research Centre, where he worked as a technician.

A classic Mossad honey-trap saw him lured from London to Rome by a female agent, from where he was abducted by the Israeli authorities and rendered back to Israel. His trial was held *in camera*. No one, let alone us, was allowed in the court. After Vanunu received his eighteen-year sentence, we travelled down to Shikea Prison in Ashkelon in an attempt to visit. The prison gates were as far as we got.

Politics of tooth and claw

In 1989 I was elected as leader of the EPLP with the votes of the Tribunites, the right and the Federalist Four. Carole, my running mate, followed as deputy, securing for the first time an unambiguously pro-European leadership. In the aftermath, Priestley and I acknowledged that the left across Europe had performed better than expected.[18] Now, albeit with a wafer-thin left majority, we could shape the Commission's work with the social dimension marching in step with the rest of the programme. Thatcher's veto could be thwarted by the judicious use of legal bases where unanimity was not required. Stephen Hughes was the mechanic *par excellence,* taking the Working Time Directive through as a health and safety measure.[19] We also urged closer cooperation with Comecon, the Soviet Union's Council for Mutual Economic Assistance. One of my first invitations as BLG leader was to share a platform with Michael Heseltine at a *Sunday Times* business breakfast in London. I started by reiterating the opening of the *Morning Star* article: 'Labour is now the party of Europe'. Heseltine protested, the audience laughed. They weren't laughing long.

The economic and political levers no longer worked at the level of the medium-sized nation state – which included all of Europe – yet Western Europe itself was in crisis. It was old, tired and ineffective. But nevertheless, it was the only stage on which our future could be played out. There was an attraction in taking Tony Benn's Alternative Economic Strategy of 1975 – left mercantilism writ large – and transposing it from kingdom to continent, prioritising saving and creating jobs, investment in Research, Development and Demonstration

(RD&D) alongside controls on imports, exports and capital. A temporary ducking behind walls to retool, retrain and re-emerge into the world of Kenichi Ohmae's *Triad Power* (1985), where the future lay in three-way competition between the US, Japan and the EU. The balance of political forces in the EU restricted the possibility of such an economic strategy to a more cut-down approach of compromise for similar ends.

The single market was to remove the internal barriers to competition within industry, allowing creative destruction to reshape the two or three sectoral champions in each member state into a spare three or four conglomerates across the Union. In this tri-polar world there was no Mexican standoff; simultaneous cooperation and competition meant it was not a zero-sum game. It was clearly in the interest of the two running behind in any sector to partner together to catch and cap the leader.

Immanuel Wallerstein laid down the sequence. The rise and fall of great powers was a procession led by industrial union (the EU preferred to call it the single market), from which the shared industrial interests made necessary common economic and monetary policy (the EU's single currency). Industrial and economic union were the certain harbinger of Common Foreign and Security Policy (CFSP) and a step away from defence union. Each smoothly cascades down as spillover from its predecessor. Taken out of sequence, they are stillborn. Yet there was one discretionary adjunct on offer – pivotal for progressives – that the Dutch, British and American empires had lacked. Social union, forced in the space betwixt and between industry and economy, added the element that gave the project robustness and tenacity, rather than in-built seeds of decomposition, offering a more equitable share of the benefits of the economies of scale to the 'live machines' driving Europe at the competitive edge.[20]

Carole Tongue and I made the point six months later that the Campaign Group saw 'little Englandism' as the answer and the right 'Atlanticism'. Both had lost any purchase. In a globalising world, socialism in one country was even more impossible than seventy years earlier, and even as America declined as a superpower it was Germany following the opening of the Berlin Wall, not Britain, that was Washington's critical partner in Europe. François Mitterrand and the French left had learnt the lesson the hard way. We were determined Labour should not repeat their mistakes.[21]

As BLG leader I wanted us to punch our weight – which we had failed to do to date – at home and abroad. The ship needed turning. The BLG, pushed by the Federalist Four, became in June 1990 the EPLP. We stood the custom and practice of the delegation's previous decade on its head. Instead of settling our own national line on the business of parliament before engaging with the Socialist Group, now the default position was to follow the group, unless and until a specific decision was taken by the delegation to the contrary. Elected first vice-president of the Socialist Group, I was *de facto* deputy leader to France's Jean-Pierre Cot. Paul Anderson and Nyta Mann summed it all up: 'of the 45 Labour MEPs between 1989 and 1994, only thirteen voted against the Maastricht Treaty: of the rest, although most were pragmatists who did not want to miss out on anything but did not have a clear idea of where they wanted Europe to go, at least a dozen were federalists in all but name, among them Coates, Crampton, Ford, Martin, Tongue and White.'[22]

The large majority of Labour's MEPs were hard working. Unlike the House of Commons, in the EP you do almost all your work in committee, and some members stood out among their continental peers. Exceptional were Ken Collins on environment, Stephen Hughes on social affairs, David Martin both on regional affairs and trade and Carole Tongue on culture, all already mentioned, but others included Alan Donnelly on German unification, Glenys Kinnock on development (who rather overshadowed Michael McGowan, a previous chair of the Development Committee), and the warring duo Arlene McCarthy and Peter Skinner on economic and monetary affairs, with Claude Moraes coming later on justice and home affairs. Others who made special contributions in a variety of ways were Eluned Morgan, Anita Pollack and David Thomas.

Neil Kinnock welcomed our victory in the BLG. There was a photo-call with him, Carole and myself in his office in the House of Commons a couple of days after our election. I used the reconciliation to push for better and more equitable treatment for MEPs. Backed by Kinnock, the 1991 Labour Party Conference made the EPLP leader a full *ex officio*

member of the NEC, gave MEPs the same voting rights as MPs in the parliamentary section of the electoral college for future leadership elections, and representation on Labour's National Policy Forum. The invitation for the EPLP leader to attend Parliamentary Labour Party (PLP) meetings came as an unwanted bonus. The PLP met on Wednesday mornings, an impossible time for frequent attendance by any MEP. On my scant visits, interest in EPLP activities was slight, but it gave the PLP an alibi.

The party inaugurated a free-standing annual European Conference, with the first held in Brighton in 1992 with Jim Callaghan in attendance. The second was in Southampton a year later, but it was folded into the Local Government Conference in 1994 before dying a death. Absent Kinnock, Labour was to have other priorities. Only briefly distracted from Westminster's diversions and parliamentary prancing, the leadership soon reverted to Labour's default position. Brussels was no longer a second front in the fight for a better Britain, but a feint.

With Carole Tongue and Neil Kinnock in the House of Commons, June 1989.

On the NEC I sat in the 'bad boys' corner with Dennis Skinner and Tony Benn, where the duo watched perplexed at my rare intrusions pressing the case for Europe. John Prescott never forgave me for one intervention targeted at him because of his abiding Euroscepticism left over from his days on the left. His disposition towards me was not helped by the fact that

I'd previously, as BLG treasurer, tried to take back control of the former British delegation bank account containing more than £10,000, of which John was apparently the sole signatory. We never received the money. Yet my most memorable intervention was to speak and vote against Kinnock's demand to bend the rules to allow him to stand down as leader early after the 1992 election defeat. Immediately after he narrowly lost the vote, the two of us left the meeting. Outside in the stairwell he launched himself at me, waving his fists and shouting 'You little shit!' Charles Clarke had to pull him off me. But unlike Prescott, Kinnock didn't hold a grudge.

Kinnock had agreed back in 1989 that if MEPs elected departmental 'liaison members,' they could serve on the PLP's departmental teams in policy planning for the manifesto and government. The Eurosceptics were generally too lazy, too apathetic to Europe, or often both, to vie for such roles. It worked like a dream – it framed a benign form of 'dual power,' with the Liaison Committee functioning as a working executive in Brussels and Strasbourg doing the business, and the EPLP meetings reserved for Labour's situationists to play out their spectacles.

For failed aspirants to Westminster, the message was simple: 'if at first you don't succeed, become an MEP.' From the first direct elections to the EP in 1979, Europe was a dual-purpose staging post and retirement home. Used as the former, even the most hapless MEP, backed by the available resources in staff and expenses, could establish themselves in an unchallengeable position to slide smoothly into a Westminster seat behind a retiring MP in their Euro-constituency. Many did. The process crippled our effectiveness twice over. Before selection and election to Westminster, MEPs went AWOL from the EP, in many cases attending scarcely more than the minimum 50 per cent of sessions necessary to evade the parliament's financial penalties. After election they stayed on as MEPs, collecting one and a third salaries – they were only allowed a third of the second salary – yet two full sets of expenses. It wasn't a problem that correlated with politics, as left, right and centre all gobbled up the premium. Avarice had no sectarian boundaries. For some, whose political needs were ministered to by wives, husbands, girlfriends and other

family, the money – £50,000 per year – was as much prize, if not more, than the discreet charm of the House of Commons.

Those repatriating back across the Channel were not always welcome. The former Welsh NUM official and MP Kim Howells had a wicked ditty about one economic refugee, 'The Decline and Fall of the Labour Movement in South East Wales 1929–1992,' he declaimed, 'Aneurin Bevan, Michael Foot, Llew Smith.' The 'twicers' had thin skins. It was a different world back then in terms of transparency. When *Tribune* published in its diary column an attendance list of Labour MEPs, it was not seen as a reflection on the poor attendance by certain MEPs, but rather a cause for concern in an entirely different manner. Joyce Quinn, one of Labour's natural right-wingers and a twicer, demanded an internal inquiry into the 'leak' of what, amusingly, was public information.

It wasn't all a one-way street, however. Under Blair the House of Lords was brought into play with fresh vacancies for MEPs created by the offer of swapping Europe for costume drama in Westminster. Despite twenty-two sitting Labour MEPs losing their seats in 1999, there was still space for five new members to be parachuted into winning seats: Michael Cashman, Neena Gill, Mo O'Toole, Claude Moraes and Catherine Stihler (*née* Taylor). Ennoblement also served as the answer to inconvenient truths. In 1999 the Welsh Labour Party was in uproar over the preference of the diligent Lyndon Harrison over the fun-loving Joe Wilson on the Welsh list, because Harrison lived on the wrong side of the border and Wilson didn't. This was despite the fact that they'd both previously taught at the same Welsh college. The answer was Baron Harrison of Chester in the County of Cheshire.

Second MPs deselected by electorate, rather than party, could milk the sympathy vote for the next round of MEP selections. Few hankered after Brussels. Some pulled their weight, like Cryer and Huckfield who rode their hobby horses hard, but most were addicted to the Westminster pantomime. Europe was either luxury parking while awaiting the wheel of politics to turn or gardening leave easing into retirement. Kinnock agreed with my proposal to bring in new rules to ban serving MEPs from running for the House of Commons and vice versa. This held firm until well after the 1999 switch to proportional representation (PR) for the European elections.

With the new list system, using MEPs in Westminster by-elections seemed less problematic, as when elected to the House of Commons they could resign from the EP and be neatly replaced by the next candidate down the party list with no threat from the voters.

This theory proved less successful in practice. In 2003, MEP Robert Evans was allowed to contest the Brent East by-election for Labour (see Chapter 7). In what had once been Ken Livingstone's seat, Evans, an assiduous candidate, sustained a 29 per cent swing to the Liberal Democrats, who won by more than a thousand votes. In Dunfermline and West Fife in February 2006, Catherine Stihler – hustled in by the party leadership – if anything, did even worse. Here a Labour seat with a 12,000 majority became the Liberals' first ever by-election gain from Labour in Scotland on a 16 per cent swing. The NEC, led by the leadership, abandoned the practice, with later interest in standing expressed by Linda McAvan and David Martin brutally blocked. While in my view it should never have been sanctioned in the first place (the electorate does not respond well to such self-interested party games of position), the double standards screamed unfairness.

Eating with the enemy

Back then in the late 1980s/early 1990s, the British broadsheets and the BBC had a batch of correspondents in Brussels reporting on the EU's institutions. They travelled up to Strasbourg as a pack for plenaries. At the time, these started at 5 p.m. on Mondays and finished Friday lunchtime after a dog-end morning of thin parliamentary business was swiftly dispatched. By early Thursday evening, journalism was wrapped up and, by habit, those remaining congregated for dinner in an Italian restaurant, *Le Picobello.* The leaders of the gang were John Palmer and Boris Johnson, representing the political bookends of the media in the *Guardian* and *Daily Telegraph,* and sandwiched between them was Cathy Smith for the BBC and Geoff Meade for the Press Association.

I was invited to join most months along with Tony Robinson, the Socialist Group's press officer.

The dinners were an opportunity to wind down and Palmer and Johnson's verbal sparring was sport worth paying for. Boris was witty, entertaining and an enjoyable dinner companion, but his connection with reality was tenuous, and with the institutions non-existent. His Eurosceptic fables were well crafted, but built of straw. 'Brussels to ban our prawn-flavour crisps', was his precis of a Commission report suggesting the imposition of a limit to artificial sweeteners in snacks targeted at children because of well-researched fears that aspartame – used as a sugar substitute – potentiated epilepsy. He wasn't to be trusted around facts, women or countries, but you'd die laughing. To borrow Aneurin Bevan's description of Churchill, Johnson was a man suffering from petrified adolescence.

One evening a huddle of the Campaign Group had been eating upstairs and passed by us on the way out. Among them was Liverpool's Ken Stewart, well acquainted with drink. He challenged Tony Robinson, who was not entirely sober either, 'Have you put my press release out yet?' When Tony responded 'Not yet', Ken aggressively demanded, 'Why bloody not?', which led to the instant riposte 'Because it's crap!' At this point, Ken swung at Tony, hitting him hard on the cheek. Ken's comrades intervened and hustled him off. The next day it was a lead story back at home. Ken expressed surprise at the next EPLP meeting that the story had become public. Quite why he thought hitting a press officer in front of half a dozen journalists was going to be overlooked escaped all comprehension; nevertheless, he proudly passed around a copy of the *Liverpool Echo* headline, 'Our Ken hits Europrat'. Both paper and perpetrator were innocent of any embarrassment over a drunken assault by an MEP on a member of staff.

Ken had represented Speke ward on Liverpool Council. His elevation to Brussels enabled Tony Mulhearn, one of the Militant tendency's key players, to become a leading member and key strategist of Liverpool Labour Group with all that followed.[23] After the riot by Liverpool fans at the Heysel stadium in which thirty-nine, mainly Juventus, fans died and six hundred were injured, Ken resolutely defended the innocence of all those arrested from Liverpool, thus implying the

Italian injuries were clearly self-inflicted. Ken, described as 'a man of principle and forthright honesty', died in 1996 and his wife, Margaret, followed him five years later.[24] In August 2015 it was discovered that his son, also Ken, had posed as his dead mother to claim three-quarters of a million pounds from the EP as widow's pension in the intervening fourteen years.

Miner vaudeville

September 1992 saw Michael Heseltine, on behalf of John Major's government, announce another thirty pit closures, meaning thirty thousand lost jobs. In October, Arthur Scargill was invited to speak to the Socialist Group. There was an EP debate on the outcome of the Birmingham Council of Ministers meeting, where Gordon Adam, Norman West and myself attacked the proposals as political pandering that would threaten European energy self-sufficiency.[25] The Socialists put forward a procedural request for 'an early vote' on an oral question with debate to be taken by roll call at around 9 p.m. on the Tuesday, a busy day in the EP but an hour at which most were at dinner. Labour MEPs were warned of a possible Tory ambush, but you can only take a horse to water. With Scargill and TUC general secretary Norman Willis in the visitors' gallery, the vote was lost 63–62 to the great relish of the Tory presidency. Thirty EPLP members voted and fifteen didn't make their excuses. David Bowe and Collins claimed – unconvincingly – they'd been present. Bowe backed down when there was an offer to check film of the chamber. Balfe, Buchan, Lomas, Seal and Stevenson were absent without explanation or leave, while Hindley, White and Crampton claimed dinners of various degrees of insignificance. The reputation of Labour MEPs never recovered in parts of the wider labour movement. Some of the miscreants were slow learners – at least two had missed the key vote in the EP during Ronald Reagan's visit to Strasbourg in May 1985, in which the left lost by a couple of votes on a resolution condemning US policy on Nicaragua and the Strategic Defence Initiative or 'Star Wars'. That time the vote was in the afternoon, so it was shopping, not supper.

Managing the delegation's members was a job in itself. There was one member whose wandering hands meant that he couldn't be allocated female stagiaires, while Oona King, who was to work for me for several years and later was to represent Bethnal Green and Bow as its MP from 1997 to 2005 before being defeated by George Galloway, wrote in her autobiography that one EPLP member had offered her a job in exchange for sex.[26] It wasn't hard to identify the culprit. Another offered a barmaid in a Brussels pub a Parliamentary Assistant post starting the following day. Some members had inventive domestic arrangements: MEPs were given a mileage allowance for travel to Strasbourg and Brussels from home, and at least one MEP elected in southern England claimed a registered address in Scotland until threatening representations were made. There was also a daily allowance for subsistence and accommodation. It was widely believed two particular male MEPs shared a bed in a small flat near Brussels' Grand Place; the argument among their peers was whether the arrangement was motivated by sex or money.

Sinistra Italians

I had good relations with PCI MEPs from the beginning. It was the Italians who had led in giving European communism a more human face, starting with Antonio Gramsci and his demand for cultural revolution alongside the political. I'd been part of a Strasbourg Monday Dining Club in the L'Oiseau de France, set up after the 1984 elections and consisting of eight to ten Socialists, Communists and Greens. Marijke Van Hemeldonck (Belgian Socialist) and Carole Tongue were there, as was Bram van der Lek (Dutch Green) and Luciana Castellina (Italian Communist). We got interesting guests. When Jesse Jackson came to Strasbourg, he dined with us on Monday night.

Luciana had played tennis with Mussolini's daughter, been an active member of the resistance and a founder and member of the editorial board of *Il Manifesto*.[27] In 1984 she had been elected an MEP for the dissident *Partito di Unità Proletaria per il Comunismo* that was by then headed back into the PCI. It was Luciana who organised my visit to Pisa and later introduced me to Rossana Rossanda. My engagement with the PCI was heavily criticised by my Italian colleagues in the Socialist Group for propping up a party in its death throes. Yet it didn't take long to see which of the two were past their sell-by date. The March 1994 Italian elections saw the Italian Socialists virtually wiped out, while the Italian Social Democratic Party went on a common list with Silvio Berlusconi and the fascist Alleanza Nationale led by Gianfranco Fini. Consequently, I pushed for their expulsion from the PES alongside the expulsion of their only MEP, Enrico Ferri, from the Socialist Group. They were and he was.

Neil Kinnock, with Carole and myself, finally had a leadership in Europe he could work with and would work with him. He became a regular visitor to Brussels and Strasbourg and to some of the Socialist Group's further wanderings. In Rome in 1990 I arranged for him to meet with Giorgio Napolitano, a key figure among the modernisers in the PCI and later Italian president. He explained to Neil that they were trying to shift the party, with just shy of a million members, in the direction of democratic socialism. Neil, with his well-known soft spot for singing '*Bandiera Rossa*', offered his support. Literally within days, the PCI announced they would disband, which they did at their Rimini Congress in February 1991, rebranding themselves as *Partido Democratico della Sinistra* (PDS) and joining the Socialist Group and the PES in 1993. A third of the membership left to form *Partito della Rifondazione Comunista*, which itself then split between pro-European and more Eurosceptic factions over the Prodi government. In 1998, to no avail, I voted in the proportional section of the ballot for Armando Cossutta's *Comunisti Italiani.*[28] Despite my transactional support, they failed to pass the 4 per cent barrier.

In the 1994 European elections, at the request of Luigi Colajanni, the leader of the PDS delegation in the EP, I spoke at an eve-of-poll rally with Massimo D'Alema in Turin. In European elections, as with British general elections, the UK votes on a Thursday, while in most other countries, including Italy, it's Sunday. Only when the polls close in Greece on Sunday night can counting commence. We finished getting out the vote in Manchester on Thursday night and the following

morning I flew to Milan for the rally – no campaigning is allowed in the twenty-four hours before polls open. Later, we had dinner with D'Alema and his team. He'd clearly had enough of campaigning. All he wanted to talk about was yachting, and what I knew about sailing could be written on the back of a postage stamp with a six-inch paint brush. Nevertheless, he was to prove useful in 1999 in Stoke Rochford (see below). Bruno Marraza in the Socialist Group signed me up as a member of the Milan Federation of the PDS. I was there from 2003 to 2006 before we both let our membership lapse as the PDS continued to slide to the centre. Being in one party in danger of selling its soul was enough.

On the left I was also close to Luis Planas and Christos Papoutsis, the leaders of the Spanish and Greek delegations in the Socialist Group, and we worked together on a series of issues, although Luis and I had self-denying ordinance not to mention Gibraltar. Papoutsis later became Greek Commissioner and Minister. For a period, Alan Donnelly and myself dined regularly with Elmar Brok and the Belgian EPP member Raphael Chanterie.

Regal dining

In May 1992 the Queen finally came to Strasbourg to address the parliament. I'd complained two years earlier she was the only EU head of state yet to speak to the EP.[29] We didn't blame her, but Thatcher. In her speech, she said: 'Decisions need to be taken as close to the citizen as is compatible with their success but at the same time we have to strengthen the ability of Europeans to act on a European basis where the nature of a problem requires a European response. That was the necessary balance struck at Maastricht'.[30] Lunch was to follow. I was sharing a table with Jacques Delors, German Liberal Commissioner Martin Bangemann and John Major. The highest common multiple was football; Delors was Arsenal, Bangemann Manchester United and Major Chelsea. We spent a happy hour swapping banter. I had the advantage over Major, as to City and Chelsea's surprise earlier in the year we'd beaten them 4–2 at Stamford Bridge.

Security at the lunch event was laughable. Ken Stewart – again – traded his ticket to Christine Oddy, who used it to smuggle her mother in; she sat silently just down from the Queen, misidentified as a Lady in Waiting. This incompetent security was repetition not revelation. With Julian Priestley, I'd met the Queen's private secretary in Strasbourg in March. Deep into the encounter there was the politest enquiry as to how exactly members were appointed to the EP. (This was after three direct elections.) It was dangerous ignorance with disaster written all over it. Believing the EP was the continent's multilingual answer to the House of Lords, there had been no concern over controlling entry to the chamber for the Queen's speech. After all, it was the continent's B-team of the not so great and good. The Royal Household now saw a problem. There was a loose group of MEPs from 'Unrecognised Nations' and they had a staff member who represented Sinn Fein and was in possession of a plenary floor pass. Julian arranged with Enrico Vinci, the parliament's Secretary General, that all passes for non-MEPs would need 'renewing' and, to be on the safe side, a couple would go missing until the Queen was safely back in Britain.

It was to be a royal year; six months later Prince Charles paid a visit. I introduced him to a group of Lancashire miners – much to the fury of the Tories – who were in Strasbourg campaigning against blacklisting and victimisation following the 1984/85 miners' strike. Over dinner, he was remarkably sanguine, yet later that week on his return to the UK he announced his separation from Diana.

Albania intermission

In May 1991 the Socialist Group met in Corfu. Jean-Pierre Cot had to miss the dinner for Andreas Papandreou, leader of the Panhellenic Socialist Movement (PASOK) and then leader of the opposition. In consequence, I was host and needed to make introductory remarks before Papandreou spoke. With Corfu sitting immediately across from Albania, I made the joke that while we were looking forward to his address, we hoped he wouldn't be emulating his late neighbour Enver

Hoxha's seven-hour speeches. The Greeks laughed last. As the dinner was breaking up, Christos Papoutsis whispered to me that at the last party congress Papandreou had spoken for four and a half hours.

Hoxha's heirs were to get their revenge. The group chartered a boat to take those that wanted for a visit to Sarandë and Gjirokaster – Hoxha's birthplace – in Albania, which in Cot's absence again I led. When we arrived, there was a pre-planned meeting with a group of officials from the town. Thirty or forty of us and a dozen of them piled into what seemed to be a classroom with desks and chairs. I ran the meeting, which seemed to go on forever with dozens of questions and little time for answers. I'd taken off my watch to use to keep our speakers to their two minutes. Eventually, the meeting finished and I left the chair to shake hands with some of the Albanians in the body of the meeting. In those thirty seconds, someone stole the watch.

Christine Crawley (right) pictured with Albanian soldiers in Sarandë.

I returned to Albania in September. In the south of the country, around Gjirokaster, there were a quarter of a million Greek speakers in a region they termed Northern Epirus. Their political party *Omonoia* had won seats in that spring's elections, but was under threat of being banned, as religious, ethnic and regional parties had been declared illegal. Georgios Romeos, the Greek member of the Socialist Group bureau and a parliament vice-president, wanted to pressure the authorities in Tirana, and I was asked by Cot to lead a two-man delegation to do just that. We saw Ramiz Alia, Hoxha's successor, who was hanging on to the presidency by his fingernails, Prime Minister Fatos Nano and Sali Berisha, leader of the Democratic Party of Albania. They were all in their different ways refugees from Hoxha's PLA, with Berisha the former party secretary in the University of Tirana's faculty of medicine. In 1992 Berisha won the Albanian presidential election, Alia and Nano went to prison and *Omonoia* was outlawed, with six members jailed for treason after demanding Northern Epirus' union – *enosis* – with Greece.

After our visit, I raised in the EP the plight of Albania's former political prisoners – we'd met groups in Tirana – abandoned in their former camps with 'no money, no housing and no right to education. The issue is absolutely urgent and desperate and I believe the European Community has a responsibility to try and help these people, even if their political views are not the same as my own.'[31]

Baltic passage

I was only marginally more successful in the Baltic states. The EP sent an *ad hoc* delegation to Latvia, Lithuania and Estonia in the immediate aftermath of 'independence', where parliament buildings were still edged with sandbag emplacements. Our flight there was diverted to Klaipeda from its intended destination of Vilnius, because of bad weather, and my visa was 00007. All three countries needed help to 'unlock themselves from the collapsing economy of the former Soviet Union', without making the mistake of going forward to the past and trying to revive small-scale peasant farming.[32] It ultimately proved unnecessary, but we suggested the route to membership of the EU could be laid through the Nordic member states rather than behind Hungary, Poland and Czechoslovakia. But blanket amnesties for Nazi war criminals were as intolerable as the new citizenship rules in Latvia and Estonia, where Russian speakers were discriminated against and driven out. This was particularly egregious in Estonia, where around the border town of Narva the indigenous population's native language was Russian. I continued to protest in the EP and abstained on their application for membership.[33]

Ides of June

I beat the post-Castle tenure record, surviving four years as leader. Within the Socialist Group, I was being talked about as its potential leader after the 1994 European elections. That was an anathema to two factions within the EPLP, the Campaign Group and Labour's traditional right, who were both threatened in their different ways by our pro-European left agenda.

After Neil Kinnock resigned in 1992, I phoned Tony Blair's House of Commons office and urged him to run. When he declined, the field narrowed to John Smith and Bryan Gould. I threw my support behind Smith and was his campaign manager among the MEPs. At a couple of hustings in the North West I even stood in for him and debated Gould. It was a simple choice – Smith, while right-wing, didn't share Gould's antipathy towards the EU. Yet there was no warmth in our relationship. This was swiftly demonstrated after his victory. He was uncomfortable with the EPLP's political trajectory as his MEP faction. Despite the welcome distance from Gould's Europhobia, Smith was at heart a nationalist wearing a union jack rather than tartan.

At the EPLP's 1993 AGM I was challenged for leader by Pauline Green, with Smith signing off on it. She wouldn't have run without permission. The go-between was the EPLP's toxic office manager, acting as the fifth column from within. But the drive came from secret talks between Michael Hindley and John Tomlinson. According to Anita Pollack, Hindley said the Campaign Group 'wanted Ford out of the way because with the anticipated good results for Labour in 1994, he could become president of the Socialist Group and a potential later contender for the President of the European Parliament and they did not find this palatable.'[34] There was a scrabble for excuses. Wayne David argued there was unhappiness about my support for allowing some of the group's finances to fund an anti-EU pamphlet in a spirit of excessive even-handedness (see below), while the Tomlinson–Hindley axis argued, in contrast, my perceived cliquishness.

I was stabbed in the back by the right and the front by the Europhobes. Hindley, the brightest of the bunch but not as bright as he thought, explained the unholy alliance. They considered the so-called soft pro-European left as more of a threat to their vision of socialism in one country than the right, who were available to be beaten later. As 'false lefts', we threatened to seduce Labour's rank and file in a way the right could never do. For them the real enemies were on the left. As the German Communist leader Ernst Thaelman, who died in the concentration camps, said, 'After Hitler. Us!' It was this mentality – without the savage consequences – that saw in the 1928–33 Third Period the German Communist Party's *de facto* collusion in Red–Brown coalitions with the Nazis against the Socialists. Now, farce mirrored tragedy as the Eurosceptic Campaign Group and fellow travellers got their comeuppance. They were hunted to extinction by the very people they supported when New Labour replaced old with the death of John Smith.

Castles don't count

Pauline Green was elected EPLP leader with the votes of the Labour right, the Campaign Group and a couple of others who'd been sold the message that it was time for a woman, though Barbara Castle had been Labour's leader in Europe for six out of the first thirteen years. The EPLP had in the last four years enormously enhanced Labour's role and reputation in the parliament. The group had delivered to Alan Donnelly the post of rapporteur on German unification, the chair of the US delegation to Geoff Hoon, vice-president of the EP to David Martin and the chairs of three of the EP's standing committees to Labour MEPs.

I'd contributed to my demise as leader with my share of mistakes. From the beginning I was not strong enough in resisting the seduction of sectarianism. While it worked for election, it was pernicious to performance. The mantra of 'you were with us or against us' strengthens rather than weakens your opponents. Divide and conquer is a better leitmotif. A number of the Campaign Group's fellow travellers could have been won over if they'd been offered responsibilities matching their skills. That was not to be. The spoils were to be divided in the narrowest manner. After I'd first been elected

leader, I'd suggested in the Officers Group that Barry Seal, the incumbent I'd defeated 27–17, should be given the chair of the US delegation that I'd obtained for the EPLP, but Tomlinson demanded it for Hoon, who was within his faction.[35]

My mandate decided by the caucus had been to take the chair of the South Asia delegation for George Stephenson. I, as leader of the largest delegation in the Socialist Group, which was then the largest group, had the first choice of delegation. I didn't have it in me to waste that choice on India and Pakistan. I chose the US and picked up South Asia in the second round. Stephenson was furious at my betrayal of the mandate. No good turn goes unpunished. Hoon used the contacts he made in the US assiduously and they helped propel him to the post of Blair's Secretary of State for Defence and US pawn.

During my time as leader I'd offended some of the broader coalition. Ken Collins, the chair of the Environment Committee, had constantly complained that his committee was overworked. In consequence I supported proposals to split the committee. It turned out Ken was bragging rather than complaining, and was loath to surrender even an iota of responsibility. My worst offence started with Ken Livingstone's column in the *Sun* when he accused the EPLP of undertaking 'a campaign of lies and propaganda which even Dr Goebbels would have hesitated to chance his arm with', following the publication of pro-Maastricht pamphlets. I instructed the office manager to seek legal advice from Geoffrey Bindman as to whether we had a case to sue the *Sun*. The answer in the public-school comic-book world of the British legal system was NO. The EPLP was bigger than a cricket team and so could not be subject to libel. It was almost as juridically asinine as another case I was later engaged with that hinged on a judgment that a sacked vicar was not able to appeal to an industrial tribunal against 'unfair dismissal' as he was employed by God. But that's another story.

Richard Balfe, treasurer at the time, refused to release EPLP funds for the not insignificant expenses 'incurred by the Leader' in respect of Bindman's legal counsel without the sanction of the entire Labour Group.[36] Where Balfe was coming from was clear. Earlier he made a claim for parliamentary immunity to avoid giving evidence in a trial in the

UK in which Les Huckfield was being accused of misusing his parliamentary allowances.[37] The trial collapsed. Clearly, the Eurosceptics would be against, and – in retrospect – the right were already manoeuvring for position. The group agreed to cover the bill, but in winning I lost. I tied authorising the bill to the agreement of a disputed claim by one of the Campaign Group for Eurosceptic leaflets. The package passed, but it was weaponised against me at the AGM. After losing to Green 22–19, I then stood as deputy leader and bizarrely won 23–21. There were clearly enough troubled consciences to make the difference. The bonus was taking Tomlinson out.

My only reason for standing as deputy was that I'd been appointed by the Bureau of the Socialist Group as their *rapporteur* for the 1994 PES manifesto. As deputy I'd keep my place in the bureau and the responsibility for the manifesto. The group meeting in May 1993 in Aix-en-Provence, with Jacques Delors and Margaret Beckett in attendance, had prepared the ground. The manifesto, signed off by the PES Congress in Brussels in November, was a double first. It was the PES's first manifesto and the first joint statement where Labour joined the throng. John Smith figured on the front cover, looking distinctly uncomfortable. Not surprising. For the first time, there was no litter of footnotes indicating British Labour's denial of the promises contained. Herein were Labour's radical demands for the single currency, for treaty reform to give the EP the right of initiative, co-decision with the Commission and majority voting in the Council. The last we still await. It was the product of too many hands to claim much credit. Yet this prototype version of Blair's pledge card saw my priorities for Europe high up the agenda. Among the six priorities were defeating nationalism and racism, increasing R&D to put Europe at the forefront of technology, taking on the economic challenge from America and Asia, and acting as a counterweight to the activities of global financial capital and the transnationals. The manifesto also called for no British opt-outs, which was significant because the UK was known for consistently vetoing new EU legislation.

I was not alone in suffering from 'beggar thy neighbour' politics. David Martin was to face the same fate with his presidential ambitions. He ran as the Socialist Group's candidate against the Irish Liberal Pat Cox in January 2002, losing by an

unlucky thirteen. Two and a half years later in July 2004, the consensus was that this time it was the Socialists' turn. Josep Borrell Fontelles, the former leader of the Partido Socialista Obrero Español (Spanish Socialist Workers' Party – PSOE) – now High Representative for CFSP – had just been elected to the EP and was being urged to stand, but he offered to back Martin, who he'd worked with and respected, and who had served an unprecedented twelve years as one of the EP's vice-presidents, much of the time as first vice-president. The EPLP – cutting off its nose to spite its face – was persuaded by the right and righteous to nominate instead of Martin it's 'creeping Jesus' Terry Wynn who, to paraphrase Lloyd George of Neville Chamberlain, had made an adequate chair of the Budget Committee in a lean year. Borrell had no compunction in running against the undistinguished lightweight, winning the Socialist Group nomination 117–66 and then the presidency. Wynn wrote of Martin that he was 'a talented guy but as much as I genuinely liked David as a person, he hadn't really done much in the Parliament for years, except that he chaired the plenary well.'[38] Wynn never even did that. He resigned in 2006.

Institutions, like people, have five minutes of fame and then their time in the spotlight is done. For the last twenty years the EPLP, diminished by power, was a pale replica of its heyday until its final death in January 2020; no longer a battleground for fights that mattered but a slow treadmill for the production and distribution of minor honours with a litter of CBEs and OBEs to be found in the cereal boxes of departure. For a short period in the late 1980s and early 1990s, it had had far more than a walk-on part in the play reversing Labour's historical antipathy to Europe. It just did not stick.

Better lucky . . .

In May 1994 I was in Tokyo with Clare Short representing the Labour Party at the Council of the Socialist International when John Smith died. I got a call from a senior party official, former staff member Andy Rowe, alerting me to the heart attack. Within minutes Andy called back announcing his death. I had to track down Clare and tell her.

I was back in Britain for the funeral. As I'd already phoned Tony Blair back in 1992 and urged him to run, I supported him this time around for the self-evident reason that John Prescott and Margaret Beckett both had the wrong history on Europe. Although I later warmed towards Beckett the same was never true of Smith. Like with Smith, I was Blair's campaign manager in Brussels and organised his visit there to meet Labour MEPs. Without the agreement with Kinnock to add MEPs alongside MPs to the electoral college, this would never have happened (see above). Immediately before I picked up Blair with Julian Priestley, the EPLP held its AGM at which I lost out to Wayne David in my attempt to return as EPLP leader. Blair offered his condolences.

When Blair won the leadership, his first choice for his *chef de cabinet* was Julian. At the Hilton in Strasbourg, Julian agonised with me about whether to accept the offer. I was in favour, but overnight he decided against it. I later got to know Jonathan Powell, Blair's alternative to Julian, when we worked together leading a political dialogue with the head of the International Department of the Workers Party of Korea. Jonathan was Blair's best of the bunch, but Julian would have been different. Julian was to write *Putsch* (2016), a gay take on *House of Cards,* shortly before his tragic death.

Before Smith died, Pollack reports Pauline Green was in her regular leaders' meetings with Smith, preparing him to decide what posts Labour should seek after June's European elections. With Labour expected to do well, it could aim for Socialist Group leader or president of the parliament. She recommended the former and told Smith that 'both Tomlinson and Ford wanted [the post] ... Smith suggested Tomlinson was yesterday's man, that he did not entirely trust Ford,' and that other Socialist leaders recommended Green herself.[39] The obvious Labour candidate for president of the parliament was David Martin. He was, at least, to get the 'Dear John' phone call from Smith. He obviously couldn't find my number. Between Smith's death in May and Blair's election in late June, Labour had an interim leader in Margaret Beckett. The EPLP even postponed their AGM until July – not

that there would have been a majority to change anything there. Pauline Green was Smith's legacy to Europe's socialists.

The UK was to hold the EU presidency in the first half of 1998. In January 1997, with a general election looming, I stressed the urgency of ensuring Labour's preparedness for its approach to Europe:

> *Within five months Labour will have its last best hope of power in a generation. When it wins, it is determined to hit government up and running. All is ready, save for the lacuna of Europe. While Tony Blair and Gordon Brown can fall back on the promised referendum to deal with the indecision on EMU, they can't escape the crucial impact that Europe will have in other areas on a Labour government, from day one ... Some idea of the volume of work is now clear, thanks to last summer's hostilities by Britain against the EU on BSE [Bovine Spongiform Encephalopathy]. The Blanket British veto of all Council of Ministers' proposals resulted in 77 Community actions being blocked in nine separate Council meetings in a period of 23 days. At that rate, the new government, in its first 100 days, would have to make decisions on more than 350 EU proposals, many shaped by a British government no longer in office.*[40]

Blair won May's general election with a landslide and he and Labour were headed for government. Despite my warnings, the party was not prepared for Europe; the world had shifted in the generation since Labour had last been in power. I had hoped for a knight's move from Blair, making Labour the party of Europe. He had already indicated he was considering appointing a separate cabinet minister for Europe, working to ensure close coordination between PLP and EPLP and launching a broad European reform agenda. We were to get none of it. Instead, he used valuable political capital on fighting old battles not new, rerunning Gaitskell and Kinnock's skirmishes as war. He announced at the 1994 Labour Party Conference in Blackpool that Labour would be updating its constitution to make it impossible to be misunderstood or be misrepresented. It was to be a single proxy fight that, if won, would unshackle him from history; a public ordeal not as disciple but deliverer.

The taboo of Clause IV – 'To secure for the workers by hand or by brain the full fruits of their industry and the most equitable distribution thereof that may be possible upon the basis of the common ownership of the means of production, distribution and exchange, and the best obtainable system of popular administration and control of each industry or service' – was to be broken. Adopted as part of Labour's constitution in 1918, it had bedevilled the party ever after. It was a catechism that not even the one Labour government capable of responding, Attlee's in 1945, had tried to deliver. It wasn't a necessary fight, nor my choice of ground, but once battle was joined, there could be only one winner.

The EPLP had won sixty-two seats in June 1994's European elections and the anti-Europeans saw a proxy fight on a more congenial battleground. That autumn, there were discrete approaches seeking signatures for an advert opposing the abandonment of Clause IV in, some were told, *Tribune*, but others – including myself – heard the *Guardian*. I warned the party's general secretary Tom Sawyer. In early January 1995, with Blair in Brussels for a major business conference, the ad appeared in the *Guardian* at a cost of £10,000. Blair went incandescent. He met the EPLP in Brussels for the first – and last – time. He accused the Campaign Group of 'infantile incompetence' and told David Hallam, when he interrupted, to 'grow up'. MEPs were to be confined to the sixth circle of hell.

I was tasked with repairing the damage. Alistair Campbell and Tom Sawyer were both there with Blair. What was needed was a letter from a majority of the EPLP backing Blair. Getting as a foundation the thirty who hadn't signed the *Guardian* ad was comparatively easy, even if one or two whimpered – lying – that they never signed such things. Eluned Morgan's office said she was unreachable somewhere in South America. I said I'd call back in thirty minutes and I'd expect them to tell me to add her name. Half an hour later the answer was yes. The problem was turning the dissenters. Some had naively thought they could play both ends against the middle, keeping the Eurosceptic hard left off their backs in their constituencies while avoiding any clash with the leadership. The media reaction proved that wasn't to be. It dominated the

news cycle, with a media frenzy engulfing Labour MEPs. Four penitents offered themselves up: Alan Donnelly, Stephen Hughes, Hugh McMahon and then David Bowe. Brian Simpson had to be told firmly that John Prescott demanded he sign before he did. The last was Christine Oddy, whose political orientation was more weathervane than signpost. The next day, thirty-six Labour MEPs had their letter in the *Guardian*. Oddy was the serial recidivist. She had a second letter published a couple of days later, repudiating repentance.

The hardcore knew what they were doing and you could respect them for it. But many of the guileless who pandered to its organisers were to rue the day. Blair was unforgiving. After the 1997 general election, Blair pushed the PLP into adopting tough new standing orders. The EPLP at its June AGM rejected the PLP formulation, 'do nothing which brings the party into disrepute'. It was a vote too far, further infuriating the leadership in Westminster. Labour was committed to introducing PR for EP elections as a come-on to the Liberals. Better to keep them dangling, and anyway in the press of priorities it could await 2004. The EPLP's rejection of tough love saw Jack Straw brought into play, precipitating PR five years earlier than planned (see Chapter 1).

The party met at Stoke Rochford over a long weekend to interrogate sitting MEPs and candidates to draw up the regional lists for the 1999 European elections. Forty-nine of the sixty-two MEPs sought reselection. Some stood down due to age, including Stan Newens, while a number jumped before they could be pushed, including Alex Falconer, Michael Hindley and Eddy Newman. When the dust settled, the single most determining factor was whether you'd signed that *Guardian* advert. Of the twelve sitting MEPs placed in completely unwinnable positions, ten had signed. Twenty-six out of twenty-eight who hadn't signed, survived. Of the penitents, all but McMahon survived. Christine Oddy was placed seventh out of eight on the West Midland list, and after unsuccessfully taking the party to an industrial tribunal, she ran as an independent and won 4 per cent of the vote. The backbone of my speech to the selection panel was Massimo D'Alema's argument from Foreign Affairs that socialist parties must take the responsibility of power and make the necessary decisions, unpopular as they might be.

In Brussels I assembled the usual Labour suspects to draft a European framing to Will Hutton's insular *The State We're In: Why Britain is in Crisis and How to Overcome It* (1995) with a federalist flavour in *Changing States: A Labour Agenda for Europe.* Our authors' note read:

> *When Labour left office in 1979 the European Parliament was not even directly elected and the Common Market was writ small in our politics. Today it is clear that the European Union is central to our future. To try to halt the forward march of Europe is like late-eighteenth century politicians asking for a pause in the Industrial Revolution. Revisionist historians claim King Canute was merely trying to demonstrate the limits of sovereign power with his futile appeal to the tide. No one can use that defence for the Tory nationalists threatening a withdrawal from the Union.*[41]

If Blair's leadership didn't transform Labour's stance on Europe there was a second opportunity in office. Blair, to his credit, did rip up Major's opt-out on the social chapter, bought at the expense of Yugoslavia's interlocking civil wars and perpetual pilgrimages to Strasbourg, and broke Major's lock on a broad sweep of Brussels legislation. Yet there was so much more that could have been done. Opinion polls showed that the public were ready. One marker was majority support for Britain's joining the single currency. That quickly faded, but not among business, and then flowered again in the immediate aftermath of its introduction on 1 January 2002.

In April 1999 in the run-up to that year's European elections I addressed the South West TUC's Annual Conference held at UNISON's holiday camp in Croyde Bay. To no dissent, I reported visits both to Honda's Swindon plant and Nippon Seiko Kabushiki-gaisha (NSK) – the successor to my father's old employer, Hoffman – in Stonehouse, during which both urged the necessity for early membership of the single currency. There was not a mention of Brexit; nevertheless, it is all too apposite that NSK closed in May 2019 with the loss of

three hundred jobs, with Honda following in July 2021 with three thousand jobs disappearing.

I served as an MEP under four Labour leaders: Kinnock, Smith, Blair and Brown. Without doubt the most successful and most disappointing was Blair. He was lucky in opposing John Major. Major would have almost certainly lost in 1997 to any Labour leader with a pulse, but Blair had a reach into the electorate others could not match. While he will rightly never escape the stain of the Iraq War, for me the biggest anticlimax was his failure on Europe. Initially, he stepped outside and beyond 'little Englandism,' but then refused to spend political capital there. In the end, he was only visiting. Like Trotsky to Stalin, Brown would almost certainly have been worse had he been elected leader in 1994, but with Gordon there was no crisis of expectations. Smith was cool, pragmatic and transactional. For all his pro-EU reputation, built on being one of the sixty-nine Labour MPs to defy the Labour whip in 1971 and vote for the principle of EEC membership, he was driven by economic rationale alone. In his enthusiasm he was merely the other face of Hugh Gaitskell's desiccated calculating machine. The only one who had a real feeling for Europe and its political culture and way of life was Kinnock. In that, he may have been Labour's lost and last best hope. For all their fire and fury, left-alternatives within the labour movement were wedded to the nation. Migration, defence and security had no answers save at home, because they'd never ventured abroad, suffering as they did from national agoraphobia.

Addressing the TUC in Manchester.

Terminus

While I may have been surprised at my victory in the 1984 European elections, I wasn't at my defeat a quarter of a century later. After Gordon Brown backtracked and ran from his own decision to call a general election immediately following Bournemouth's 2007 party conference that came soon after his forced capture of the leadership, the writing was on the wall. The font grew bigger with the financial crisis. I protested in *Tribune* as the 2009 European elections loomed,

> *A crime has been committed and 60 million people have been collectively mugged. The current financial crisis has cost every single man, woman and child in the country something between £10,000 and £20,000. A combination of Government deregulation, greedy bankers and cowardly officials has put the future of companies, communities and families at grave risk ... Self-regulation left the lunatics in charge of the asylum with morally challenged traders and bankers devising more and more esoteric and risky ways of gambling with other people's money and pocketing the profits ... The Financial Services Authority was supposedly overseeing these people ... over several years, its officials singularly failed [to] detect any evidence that the emperor was completely stark naked ... Now Gordon Brown's Government has very little choice in terms of its broader intervention to prop up the banking system.*
>
> *Yet what remains confusing is that we seem to have a perpetrator-less crime. Who has apologised for the bankers' avarice and perfidy that has caused the present economic catastrophe? Who has been sacked, fined or sent to jail for their criminal greed, recklessness and stupidity? ... Dangerous driving is a criminal offence ... Why is there no offence of dangerous banking when its consequences can be orders of magnitude worse? Why are these dangerous bankers merely being tormented by the prospect*

> *of reduced bonuses and not the prospects of a prison cell? ... Now, with the billions of taxpayers' money the banks have received ... It is as if the Sheriff of Nottingham is riding to the banks' rescue, robbing the poor to pay the rich. ... Unless the guilty pay the price for the current fiasco, there will be a backlash. There are already signs of this beginning. People are looking for justice and retribution. It's a class issue. ... Bernard Madoff, the New York financier who defrauded his clients of £35 billion, is probably going to jail for a long time. It would be criminal if he didn't have company.*[42]

Even at this stage I knew it was going to be grim. It was clear who was under threat in the EPLP and I organised a series of lunches in Strasbourg for those facing defeat. These were, apart from myself, Richard Corbett, Eluned Morgan, Neena Gill and Robert Evans. The idea was to make a collective demand to the EPLP for targeted resources for our regions. It never went anywhere, and my pessimism was disregarded because their hope trumped expectation. Eluned and Robert stood down anyway but, unfortunately, I was all too right: all five positions were lost. The final straw with the public was the MPs' expenses scandal just a month before the election. What was revealed ranged from the unedifying via the disgraceful to the criminal. There was no excuse, but the *Daily Telegraph* didn't pay £110,000 to the anonymous 'leaker' not to weaponise the story to suit its political ends. Labour was up first and the One Nation Tories – supporters of the EU – next. The only Eurosceptic who got exposed was Bill Cash in one of the last of the *Telegraph's* daily dossiers. This all played out to the accompaniment of redundant Tory Eurosceptic Norman Tebbit's campaign urging voters to demonstrate their disgust with MPs by voting UKIP – as he would do – or Green in the coming European elections.

Campaigning in 2009 was as unpleasant as it had been in the dog days of the Labour government in the late 1970s. The result was worse. Tebbit got his way: Labour slumped to the benefit of UKIP. Labour won a sparse thirteen seats, down from eighteen, the same as UKIP, who received more votes. Half of Labour's South West list went AWOL from the count with Keir Dhillon an exception as Clare Moody and others found they were otherwise engaged as we became the first region in the UK where Labour's representation in the EP vanished.

I tried to run again in 2014. While both Richard Corbett and Neena Gill, who had lost along with me in 2009, were allowed to vie for winnable positions on their respective lists, I was blocked by Harriet Harman. In regions with one man and one woman, the next seat was an open selection. Exceptionally, in the only region with no representation, she organised to guarantee top spot for a woman. In the public vote back in 2007 for deputy leader of the Labour Party, I had placed her fifth out of six. She remembered. Again, I wasn't surprised. I ran for second place, and among my endorsers I had both Jonathon Powell and Jeremy Corbyn. The latter wrote:

> *I've known Glyn Ford ever since I was first elected to parliament in 1983 when he was an MEP and was strongly and seriously committed to fighting racism and xenophobia all across Europe. It was a pleasure accompanying him to many events focussed on marginalised and dispossessed groups on the continent. When Glyn was in the European parliament he was a serious voice for protecting our freedoms and justice and standing up for all that is best in the European Convention on Human Rights and the protection it has given to so many people who would otherwise be denied them. It's a real pleasure to support Glyn and his quest to return to the European parliament.*[43]

For a decade from 1984 to 1994, Labour's European conversion played out centre stage, first in the BLG and then the EPLP. In the end, when the baton was passed back to Labour in power it failed to bind as the siren voices from across the Atlantic drowned out the more muted, but nonetheless genuine, welcome from Brussels. To learn from our mistakes is both duty and responsibility. The EPLP's role will be a footnote, but a deserved one.

Endnotes

[1] T. H. Huxley (1888), 'On the reception of the "Origin of Species"', in F. Darwin, *Life and Letters of Charles Darwin*, vol. 2. [2] In contrast, I was later to take groups of Labour MEPs – with some other socialists – to Japan. [3] Axel Ulrich (2001), *Konrad Arndt: Ein Wiesbadener Gewekschafter und Sozialdemokrat im Kampf gegen den Faschismus (Konrad Arndt: A Wiesbaden trade unionist and social democrat in the fight against fascism)*, Wiesbaden: Zeidler, https://bit.ly/3rNLiAi (accessed 14 September 2021). [4] Anita Pollack (2009), *Wreckers or Builders? A History of Labour MEPs 1979–99*, London: John Harper, p. 88. [5] Lenin laid down in 1919 twenty-one conditions for the adhesion of socialist parties to the Communist International. [6] EP (1984), *Debates*, 27 July. [7] EP (1984), *Debates*, 24 October. [8] The British Labour Members of the European Parliament (1985), *Actions of Solidarity During the Miners Strike*, foreword by Arthur Scargill and Peter Heathfield. [9] Glyn Ford and Christine Crawley (1985), 'We can't pretend that Europe doesn't exist', *Tribune*, 1 March. [10] Glyn Ford et al. (1986), 'Kamikaze politics or the collective madness that grips Labour in Europe', *Tribune*, 12 December. Date and spelling corrected from original. [11] Phil Kelly (1987), 'New leadership for British Labour Group at Strasbourg', *Tribune*, 19 June. [12] David Martin and Glyn Ford (1987), 'Why we need to build a European united Left ...', *Tribune*, 8 July. [13] EP (1987), *Debates*, 9 July. [14] Pollack (2009). [15] Glyn Ford and Julian Priestley (1989), 'Euro-elections: time to go beyond "little-Englandism"', *Tribune*, 12 May. [16] Chris Piening was to die tragically young. In his 1997 book *Global Europe; European Union in World Affairs* (Boulder: Lynne Rienner), he made the point that North Korea was one of only two countries with whom the EU had no relations. I clearly took on the challenge. [17] Glyn Ford and Carole Tongue (1989), 'Labour in Europe', *Morning Star*, 20 June. [18] Glyn Ford and Julian Priestley (1989), 'We can open a second front in Europe', *Tribune*, 23 June. [19] Labour MEPs were lobbied hard to vote against when it came up with Blair in office. [20] Hazel J. Jones (1980), *Live Machines: Hired Foreigners and Meiji Japan*, Vancouver: University of British Columbia Press. [21] Glyn Ford and Carole Tongue (1990), 'Uniting to forge a progressive European home', *Tribune*, 16 February. [22] Paul Anderson and Nyta Mann (1997), *Safety First; The Making of New Labour*, London: Granta, p. 139. [23] Peter Taaffe and Tony Mulhearn (1988), *Liverpool: A City that Dared to Fight*,

Minneapolis: Fortress Press. [24] Wayne David (1996), 'Obituary: Kenneth Stewart,' *Independent*, 6 September. [25] This draws heavily on Pollack (2009), pp. 197–199. [26] Oona King (2007), *House Music: The Oona King Diaries*, London: Bloomsbury. [27] Luciana Castellina (2014), *Discovery of the World; A Political Awakening in the Shadow of Mussolini*, London: Verso. She gives a slightly jaundiced and not entirely accurate description of the life of an MEP in Luciana Castellina (2009), 'European?,' *New Left Review* 55, January/February. [28] Through my wife I was able to become a dual-nationality Italian citizen in 1997, and was therefore eligible to vote. [29] EP (1990), *Debates*, 15 May. [30] EP (1992), *Debates*, 12 May. [31] EP (1991), *Debates*, 10 October. [32] Glyn Ford and Gary Titley (1991), 'Europe's Baltic dilemma,' *Tribune*, 29 November. [33] European Parliament (1993), *Debates*, 12 February and 25 April. [34] Pollack (2009), p. 200. [35] Minutes of the BLG's AGM on 20 June 1989. Accessed from the Labour History Archives and Study Centre (LHASC) in the People's History Museum, Manchester. [36] Letter from Richard Balfe to Dianne Hayter, 7 October 1992. Accessed from LHASC. [37] EP (1992), *Debates*, 6 July. [38] Anita Pollack (2016), *New Labour in Europe: Leadership and Lost Opportunities*, London: John Harper, p. 156. [39] Pollack (2009), p. 205. [40] Glyn Ford (1997), 'Labour must get ready for Europe,' *New Statesman*, 10 January. [41] Ford, Kinnock and McCarthy (1996), p. xiv. [42] Glyn Ford (2009), 'Bankers deserve trial and retribution,' *Tribune*, 13 February. [43] Email from the office of Jeremy Corbyn MP, 1 May 2013.

5 Ranging Asia

> Glory is fleeting, but obscurity is forever
>
> Napoleon (alleged)

Japan was on globalisation's roller coaster. It wasn't the robots building robots in the dark at FANUC's plant that was most instructive, but the pattern of visits I made over a decade and more to Nissan's Zama plant – which had been on Deng Xiaoping's Japanese itinerary in 1978 – as automation drove efficiency to extinction. In 1983, on my first tour, the plant in Shinagawa employed five thousand workers who swarmed around the one-and-a-half-mile production line like extras in *Modern Times*. The next visit saw the workers culled, now sandwiched between robots that were humanised with taped pin-ups. The third saw naked robots all the way, policed by rare custodians overseeing their mechanical charges. There were no further visits. In 1995, four months after Nissan concluded a technical transfer and licensing agreement with China's Nanjing Auto Works, the Zama plant closed.

Seoul survivor

Japan opened the door to North East Asia. Chris Drake, a friend married to an emigre Korean musician, pressed me to visit Seoul in 1984 to meet with opposition leader Kim Dae-jung, who had flown back from exile in the US in early February that year and was now being held under house arrest. Back in August 1983 when Benigno 'Ninoy' Aquino, an opponent of Filipino president Ferdinand Marcos, flew into Manila to serve the jail sentence Marcos had imposed, he was shot and killed on the tarmac. There was a fear that South Korean president Chun Doo-hwan had similar plans for Kim. The latter had long been the centre of a growing opposition to Seoul's military-cut dictatorships, and there had been at least two previous assassination attempts, with a dramatic 1973 abduction in Tokyo, a death sentence and imprisonment. Kim was supposedly complicit in the Gwangju uprising in 1980 and was convicted of 'inciting rebellion'. Chris argued that the more attention and visitors Kim received, the more difficult it was going to be for any 'accident' to happen.

With Kim Dae-jung, Strasbourg 2001.

Off I went, rather nervously, to Seoul and Donggyo-dong. The rather modest bungalow on the corner of two narrow streets was ringed by riot police modelling the latest in black body armour. Yet my passport parted the sea and I was allowed to the door. Kim was charismatic, exuding a quiet authority. The only person I've met who bettered that was Nelson Mandela. Kim had with him a group of prospective candidates from his new Millennium Democratic Party, readying themselves for the legislative elections in January 1985. The meeting ended with them leaping in and out of threesomes with the two of us for photos. Kim and I continued to work together for a quarter of a century until his death in 2009.

In December 1986 I returned to Korea, this time as an MEP. By this point the British embassy had an enthusiasm to assist, in contrast with their absence the first time around. I was picked up outside the Lotte Hotel by the ambassador, with a chauffeur-driven car and fluttering Union Jack all set to whisk me to lunch with the party leader and subsequent president and Nobel Peace Prize winner in the National Assembly. I was told in not so many words that I was lucky to be granted an audience with such an esteemed figure – clearly, the embassy's historical memory had failed. When we arrived, waiting at the top of the wide red carpeted internal stairs was Kim, who embraced me warmly – taking the ambassador aback.

I had a see-saw relationship with South Korea. Close to the progressive opposition, I caused resentment among the conservatives with my interference. It was my own fault. Apart from my friendship with Kim I'd been an irritant to the South's 'elected' dictator Chun Doo-hwan. President from 1980 to 1988, Chun visited the UK in April 1986 and I wrote in *Tribune*, 'When this man sent in the troops to smash a strike, 2,000 people died. What is he doing at Number Ten?', giving the tortured background and urging a boycott.[1] More importantly, I tabled a resolution in the EP condemning his role in the Gwangju massacre, which passed with little opposition, all coordinated with Kim and his office. In 1988, when Chun finally fell, I was unforgiving.[2] Chun was sentenced to death in August 1996 for his role in the massacre. In a fitting symmetry, his sentence was subsequently commuted at the instigation of Kim, whom Chun had sentenced to death back in 1980 in the wake of Gwangju.

In the mid-1990s, with a trip to Japan in the offing, I decided to take the opportunity to visit Seoul to meet with opposition and the trade unions. I'd told the South Korean embassy in Brussels I was going. While I was in Tokyo, they called my Brussels office and spoke to a Japanese member of staff I had at the time. They told her they wanted to help make sure everything went smoothly and asked if she could let them have a copy of my itinerary and programme. She did. The result was everyone on my list of meetings was visited by the security services and advised to be unavailable. Those that ignored the injunction spent several days in detention.

There was no overnight democratisation in South Korea, rather it was taken inch by inch. Chun gave way to his hand-picked successor, former general Roh Tae-woo, whose quasi-democracy in turn produced the semi-democracy of Kim Young-sam, who had merged his 'opposition' party with Roh's conservative authoritarians. I had met Kim Young-sam in opposition. He wasn't the same calibre of man as Kim Dae-jung, who won in 1998 more despite the system than because of it. The Security State even then put limits on Kim's freedom to act.

Kim was awarded the Nobel Peace Prize in 2000 for his rapprochement with Pyongyang and Kim Jong Il. Yet the National Security Law and the Security State remain sacrosanct and resilient. In 2012 the same forces intervened to subvert Moon Jae-in's election chances in favour of Park Guen-hye, the daughter of the former dictator Park Chung-hee (in power 1963–79). I had dinner with her in 2006 at the EU ambassador's residence when I thought she was in a strong position to become the Conservative candidate for the 2007 presidential election. I was agreeably surprised to discover how open she was to engagement with Pyongyang despite that North Korean special forces had in 1968 killed her mother in the crossfire of a failed assassination attempt on her father. I thought she could play Nixon to the North's Mao. I was wrong about both. She was forced to wait in line for 2012, then proved as obdurate towards the North as her immediate predecessor, Lee Myung-bak. It all ended in tears when she was impeached for the corrupt practices of herself and her Rasputin-like aide, Choi Soon-sil. Her chief crime was stupidity.

South Korea's presidents are familiar with prison. Chun Doo-hwan, Roh Tae-woo, Lee Myung-Bak, Park Guen-hye and Kim Dae-jung were all jailed. The difference was that Kim did his time before he was president, the others after. Park was pardoned by President Moon Jae-in in December 2021.

Island storm

In 2009 I saw the other face of South Korea. After asking about the Seoul–Tokyo dispute over the Dokdo/Takeshima Islands,

I was immediately offered a visit, but I replied that I didn't have the time. That problem was short-circuited, with Seoul providing a helicopter. We flew from Seoul to Ulleungdo, had lunch at a beach restaurant and a practical demonstration that Dokdo was visible on the horizon, and then on to the islands. We met the police detachment and saw their field artillery – which seemed rather over the top – the post box and then my phone rang to demonstrate mobile phone coverage. It was an Estonian colleague thinking I was in Brussels. The fisherman's house was in view, but there were no signs either of fish or the islets' husband and wife population. In international law inhabitable islands generate more rights than dots of rock. This explains why two Royal Marines and a naturalist were landed on Rockall by helicopter in September 1955. The speck was incorporated into the County of Inverness by the Island of Rockall Act 1972.

This Seoul–Tokyo clash is as much about history as resources. While the waters adjacent to the Dokdo/Takeshima Islands are rich in fish, particularly squid, it's the fact that the islands were the first part of Korea annexed by Japan at the beginning of the twentieth century that makes the dispute so emblematic for the South. North and South agree on little, but on the ownership of Dokdo they are as one. In the receptions to both the Foreign Ministry and the Blue House in Seoul, there is a live feed from Dokdo on the screens. It's eminently missable, unless you are inordinately fond of seagulls.

Burmese daze

At the beginning of December 1994 Kim Dae-jung set up, with Cory Aquino, Sonia Gandhi and Oscar Arias Sanchez, the Forum of Democratic Leaders in the Asia-Pacific. I was the only European politician invited to the founding conference in Seoul. Immediately following, it was planned that a small delegation would travel to Yangon with a message of support for Aung San Suu Kyi. Kim couldn't go at the last minute and I ended up going alone. I didn't get to see Suu Kyi, but the British ambassador, mindful of potential incidents, took me in hand and offered accommodation in the residence. Hanging above the headboard in my airy bedroom there was a small, framed notice: 'Aung San [Aung San Suu Kyi's father] slept in this room in 1945.' I sold my Johnnie Walker Red Label and my 555 State Express, as recommended by *Lonely Planet*, and I got to meet U Nu, the former prime minister and opposition leader. My letter from EP president Klaus Haensch to Aung San Suu Kyi remained undelivered.

It was not until the late 1990s that, on a semi-clandestine visit with Glenys Kinnock – we came in with a camerawoman, pretending to be three teachers on holiday – I finally met Aung San Suu Kyi. The Quai d'Orsay (French Foreign Ministry) was arguing against EU sanctions on Myanmar, claiming they would hurt ordinary people. Some thought the less ordinary people they were most concerned about were closer to home: Total's shareholders and their oil concessions. After meeting some Burmese opposition figures in the ladies' toilets of one of Yangon's new luxury hotels, we crept off to 54 University Avenue Road where, in front of camera, 'The Lady' made her support for EU sanctions very clear. We flew back to Bangkok and showed the footage at the International Press Centre, and again the following week in the EP in Strasbourg. Myanmar got sanctions and we each got a sixteen-year visa ban. A *Times* front page in 2010 produced a list of those who'd had their ban lifted. I was in excellent company, with the likes of Desmond Tutu and Glenys Kinnock.

Heroes can, however, be zeroes. Aung San Suu Kyi became the country's de facto prime minister in 2016 and remained in office until her arrest in February 2021. During the lead years of Burma's generals, from 1988 to 2010, the country's Muslim minority, the Rohingya, were oppressed, discriminated against and murdered in their hundreds. It was the coming of 'democracy', the easing of state oppression on the population as a whole that released the mobs, led by Buddhist monks from the 969 Movement, to rape and murder tens of thousands and drive out almost a million Rohingya from Myanmar. The army was complicit, but not the cause. At best, Aung San Suu Kyi did nothing; at worst, she colluded with Buddhist 'fundamentalism's' base instincts in her open Islamophobia. Where were the pro-Burmese demonstrators protesting genocide when you needed them?

KEDO misdemeanours

In the mid-1990s the EU became the key to unlocking Tokyo's coffers for the Korean Peninsula Energy Development Organization (KEDO). In 1994 Bill Clinton did a deal with the North, the Agreed Framework, whereby Pyongyang would abandon its nuclear weapons ambitions, close and ultimately disable its Yongbyon nuclear reactor and come into compliance with the International Atomic Energy Agency's non-proliferation treaty; in exchange, the US would offer security guarantees and organisation of the construction of two proliferation-resistant light-water reactors in the North by 2002 with, in the interim, delivery of half a million tonnes per annum of heavy fuel oil (HFO). This was all packaged by the US within the rubric of KEDO. The problem was the question of who would foot the bill. Seoul had little option but to take the lion's share and was ordered to pay two-thirds, but Clinton was neither willing, nor able, to pay for more than the HFO. In fact, as it later turned out, once the Republicans took control of Congress after the midterm elections he couldn't even reliably pay for that.

In June 1994 the LDP, learning from Britain in 1931, formed a coalition between its 223 MPs and the JSP's 70; the JSP leader Murayama Tomiichi took the Ramsay McDonald role as prime minister (serving from June 1994 to January 1996) – in place, but not in power. The LDP were back and the JSP's death was foretold. Murayama was to destroy his party even more comprehensively than Nick Clegg managed to do the Liberal Democrats with his Cameron coalition. Yet some good came of it when in August 1995 Murayama went further than any other leader before or since in expressing his regret for Japan's actions during the Second World War, conveying his 'deep remorse' and stating his 'heartfelt apology.'[3]

Washington demanded Japan bridge KEDO's financial gap, but Murayama said it was impossible without other serious contributors. The US needed a fall guy and Brussels was dressed for the part. With the EU promising to chip in €250 million, Tokyo offered a billion dollars. The deal was to be killed by Bush in 2002, but not before Clinton's cash was cut off by Congress. I was the rapporteur for the Energy, Research and Technology Committee (ERT). With the EP coming to discuss the renewal of the annual European contribution, I had a call from Blair asking me to increase the budget line to deliver more EU money to KEDO. The funds were needed to pay the HFO bills Clinton couldn't meet in Washington. I agreed to Blair's request, even though it wasn't strictly legal, as the Commission and I both knew, with the budget line falling within the auspices of Euratom and being strictly ring-fenced for nuclear programmes. Brussels was more prepared to go the extra mile to save the US Agreed Framework than Bush.[4]

No secrets

Hwang Jang Yop, former Ideology Secretary and the pen behind Kim Il Sung's *Juche*, defected to South Korea via Beijing in February 1997 as Kim Jong Il was about to finally take up the presidential reins three years on from his father's death. I was travelling to Seoul prior to the EP's summer recess with the EP's delegation to the Association of Southeast Asian Nations (ASEAN) and the Republic of Korea and, as rapporteur for the KEDO project, I pressed the South for a meeting. When I arrived, Seoul set one up on the promise that I would tell no one before or after. The delegation secretariat was told one morning I wasn't well, and I was subsequently whisked off in an anonymous black car that then deposited me on a street corner, from where the ritual was repeated. The third leg saw me delivered to a large, nondescript residence where I had my encounter. Hwang, then the highest-ranking North Korean anyone could talk to, was still a 'Catholic,' but Pyongyang had anointed the wrong Pope. He contended three million had died during the 'Arduous March' in the North. He may have been right, but he had his own agenda. The meeting concluded, I joined the delegation at the National Assembly at lunchtime, after a miraculous recovery. As promised, I told no one where I had been.

In October I was in Pyongyang and was invited, as usual, to the Swedish ambassador's residence (the British didn't appoint an ambassador to North Korea until 2002). After I arrived, he beckoned me out into the garden where he

reported that the Foreign Ministry had told him of my meeting with Hwang Jang Yop in Seoul. The next morning in the car with the North Koreans I very deliberately mentioned my interview with Hwang. It taught me a lesson: North and South were so interpenetrated that the only way to walk the line was to have no secrets. This was only reinforced a few years later when one of my regular contacts in the Workers' Party of Korea's European Department, Ri Ung Gil, said he'd decided I was OK after he had listened to one of my press conferences in Seoul.

My twenty-year-long political engagement with the North has been detailed both in *North Korea on the Brink: Struggle for Survival* (2008) and *Talking to North Korea: Ending the Nuclear Standoff* (2018).[5] Pyongyang has its characters, ranging across a clutch of four American 'defectors' who deserted from the US military and crossed the line to the North, to the Japanese Red Army Faction who more than half a century ago hijacked a domestic flight from Fukuoka with the intention of diverting it so as to join Cuba's revolution, but ended up appropriated by Kim Il Sung when the size of the fuel tanks dictated a short course (see below).

Irina Kalashnikova and James Dresnok (wearing his Kim Il Sung badge) in Pyongyang, 2008.

I interviewed James Dresnok, one of the American four, in Pyongyang in August 2008. He and the US Army had a troubled relationship from the off. As punishment for some minor infraction, 'I was forced to clean an armoured truck with a toothbrush and a bucket of water. It was 42 below zero. That's when I first thought of crossing to a communist country. But if you went to the DDR [East Germany] they interrogated you and sent you back.' While his thoughts of defection appeared more driven by unhappiness than ideology, he noted, 'I'm not a communist, but I'd like to be one.' He waited his chance. Up in the demilitarised zone (DMZ) in 1962 with a court-martial for forging his officer's signature looming, he went North, where he became a TV and film star. He was typecast as an 'evil American', playing a POW camp commander named Arthur Cockstud in the iconic *Unknown Heroes* (1978–81), which told the story of a spy in Seoul during the Korean War. He expressed that he'd have liked to see the US again, but knew it wasn't going to happen. 'I love my country. I love my town,' he said, but he knew he'd be arrested as soon as he set foot in the country. Even if he could make it home, he wouldn't have expected a warm welcome: 'even my brother has disowned me.' He was not a fan of Robert Jenkins, a fellow US deserter who played Dr Kelton, the mastermind behind the Korean War, in *Unknown Heroes*. Jenkins had bad-mouthed Dresnok after leaving for Japan in 2004 with his wife, Soga Hitomi, a former abductee.[6] Dresnok described him to me as a 'cunning son of a bitch ... he's as fake as a three-dollar bill.'

I also met two of the North's long-term unconverted prisoners, U Yong Gok, who spent more than forty-one years in the South's prisons, and Hong Myong Gil (thirty-eight years). U was captured in 1958 while returning to the North after liaising in the mountains with the last of the partisans. He was not held as a POW, but as a 'special prisoner.' Hong was arrested in 1960 as a leader of the 'Revolutionary Party for Re-unification' and, like U, held incognito. Their families thought they were dead until 1975 and their wives had, in the meantime, remarried. In the late 1960s there were over eight hundred 'special prisoners.' U and Hong, with about forty other recalcitrant survivors, were released by President Kim Dae-jung in 1999. U went straight to Pyongyang, while Hong initially stayed in

U Yong Gok and Hong Myong Gil.

the South before, isolated, ostracised and alone, he opted to travel North.

I also met Kim Yong-suk – a victim of Tokyo rather than Seoul – who as a thirteen-year-old orphan was bought from her mistress to serve as a 'comfort woman' in Shenyang. Here she was forced to service up to forty Japanese soldiers daily for five years. Twenty of the twenty-five women in her brothel died. She still has the scars from the cigarettes stubbed out on her body.

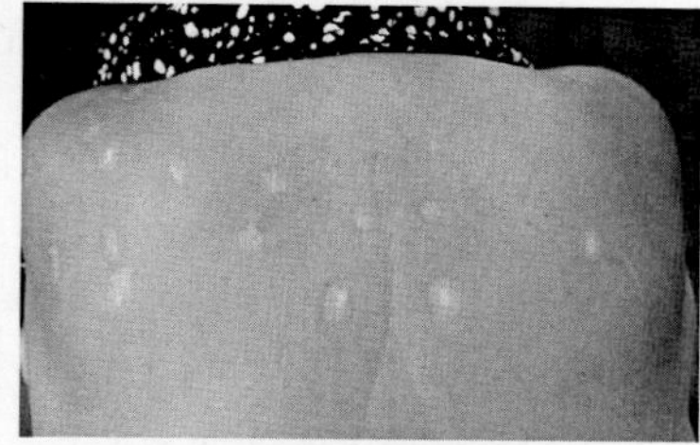

Kim Yong-suk's cigarette-burn scars from her time as a comfort woman.

Saving grace

It's always natural to question whether one ever made a difference. It's just possible I may have done in 2017, but stopping calamitous events always works better as a spectator sport. Kurt Vonnegut has my sense of the absurd. First, in *Mother Night's* (1962) the central character has been a double agent deep inside the German Nazi Party. With no one left alive to vouch for him he's imprisoned by the Israelis in the same cell block as Adolf Eichmann and is tortured by the guilt that in a perverse way they are right to lock him up: he may have done more to help Hitler than undermine him. He ultimately takes his own life. My other favourite is *The Sirens of Titan* (1959), in which aliens from the planet Tralfamadore are marooned with their spaceship on Saturn's largest moon, Titan. They need a replacement part for their craft, but their only resource is weak telepathy. However, over centuries they manipulate human history to drive mankind into space until, finally, an exploratory mission lands on Titan. Before departing, one of the crew after drinking a can of coke tosses the ring pull. The aliens now have the part and can finally head home. The seemingly inconsequential can be pivotal.

This Vonnegut digression relates to a visit to Pyongyang from 21 to 23 November 2017, where we met with our usual interlocuter, Ri Su Yong – vice-chair of the executive of the politburo and head of the International Department of the party. The situation was already tense – there had been a steady stream of missile tests throughout the year, including the Hwasong-14 in July demonstrating the range to hit Chicago and a hydrogen bomb test in early September. Ri warned us that what they were about to do would send Trump crazy. He argued that the US was gearing up for a pre-emptive strike and the North – unlike Iraq – would not sit and wait for Washington, ponderously readying itself for war, to deploy. They had their own tripwires and timetable. For them the evacuation of US non-combatants was a sign of intent and they would themselves pre-empt. We went on to Seoul, Tokyo and Washington. On 28 November, while we were in Japan, Ri's promise was fulfilled with a Hwasong-15 launch that demonstrated the range to hit anywhere in the US save Florida. If the US had not already been making kinetic plans in November, they were now. On 4 December there was a meeting in the White House. During the conversation, in a throwaway remark, we pressed Ri's admission into service to demonstrate the danger of unforced errors on both sides.

It was only months later in September 2018, reading Bob Woodward's *Fear* (2018), that I learnt what we'd done. On 4 December 2017, H. R. McMaster, Trump's national security advisor, 'had received a warning at the White House. Ri Su-yong, the vice chairman of the politburo, had told intermediaries "that the North would take the evacuation of US civilians as a sign of imminent attack." Withdrawing dependents was one of the last cards to play.' The possible tweets by Trump about this exact matter then 'scared the daylights out of the Pentagon leadership' because a 'tweet about ordering all military dependents out of South Korea could provoke Kim. The leader of a country like North Korea that had only recently acquired nuclear weapons and had many fewer nukes that a potential adversary, could be trigger-happy. A use-it-or-lose-it mind-set could take hold. The tweet did not go out.'[7]

Learning in the North

Earlier I'd been responsible for my son Alessandro's gap year. His previous work experience had included a spell with Koryo Tours in Beijing and teaching in a school in Djourbel, Senegal. He decided on a break between school and university and asked my opinion. I said as long as at least half of it was doing something serious I was in favour. He asked for suggestions and I proposed North Korea and offered to explore options. Shortly after, I was in Pyongyang meeting with Kang Suk Ju, then head of the International Department of the party, and I asked if it would be possible for Alessandro to do a semester at the Kim Il Sung University. Kang said he'd get someone to look into it. They came back to me with an easy yes, but it turned out not to be that simple. The university was not keen: they just saw trouble, but Kang told them they didn't have the choice.

In the late summer of 2014 I travelled with Alessandro to Pyongyang. We were to spend a couple of weeks touring around before I left him to the mercies of dormitory cooking and a 24/7 Korean roommate. It was a bargain – $2250 covered six months' tuition, accommodation and food. The only extra was a fee for taekwondo lessons with one of the North's leading blackbelts. All I can say is that Alessandro survived the experience; he told the story for himself in a TedTalk.[8] With his experience with Koryo and North Korea, he was frequently called on by them as a locum tour guide.

Having spent five months sharing a room with Ri and a dormitory with a collection of around thirty students – including young army officers on secondment, and a small cohort from China for whom economic necessity meant learning Korean in Seoul was not affordable – Alessandro has a unique insight into North Korea's youth. My favourite story from his time in Pyongyang was his conversation with his roommate over bowing before the statue of Kim Il Sung every morning on entering the university. He enquired as to what would happen if you failed to bow. Nothing! So why bow? It's the Great fucking Leader isn't it! At night he dreamt of skiing down mountains, Kim alongside.

Eating Japanese

I spent twenty-five years on the EP delegation with the Japanese Diet. As mentioned in Chapter 4, when I was in Tokyo in 1983 my friend Satofuka Fumihiko had me talk to a semi-Trotskyist faction within the JSP called Rentai (Solidarity). When the EP delegation was meeting with Rengo (Japanese Trade Union Confederation) several years later, I kept hearing *'rentai'* being interpreted as cooperation. Here my colleagues, after an earlier encounter, were convinced that I spoke Japanese. When I intervened to say 'solidarity' was a better translation, my fate was sealed, only compounded when in response to my question I heard 'consumption tax' and knew the answer, saying 'fine' before the consecutive interpretation even kicked in. I established the practice of the Japanese and European political families breakfasting together before delegation meetings on the same basis as in the EP. As expected, on most issues we had more in common with fellow progressives than fellow Europeans.

I equally argued in *Tribune* that if we removed the blinkers of history and language, we shared more with Japan than the US:

> *While I was in Tokyo, it struck me forcibly that Europe has more in common with Japan than the United States ... The US today is a country beset by the onset of religious fundamentalism ... In some states 4 out of 10 people describe themselves as born-again Christians ... And justice is not only blind, it is deaf and dumb as well. Judicial apartheid means the black and the poor – they are often one and the same – fill death row, while millionaires can purchase their innocence with gaggles of fat-cat lawyers ... Japan, on the other hand, is a secular country where religious tokenism is the norm ... More importantly, it is a rational society where real thought rather than mumbo-jumbo conspiracy theories rule. Where Elvis is dead, the communists are not trying to poison the water supply, and the 'Zionist occupation government' is a far-fetched plot for a cheap novel, rather than the foundation of political strategy.*[9]

The result of my quarter-century consistent presence as a member of the EU's delegation with the Japanese Diet was the establishment of a rapport with a group of Japan's politicians across the political spectrum via the Diet's parallel European Friendship Group. One of the first and most impressive was the late Hata Tsutomu, who was later responsible for finding a Japanese publisher for my *North Korea on the Brink*. He was, in a sign of high favour, to give me an invitation impossible to refuse: to join him in a Japanese bath. A sceptical LDP (*Jiminto*) representative from Nagano, he was to lead a breakaway group of forty-four LDP MPs in 1991 to form the Renewal Party. By August 1993 he was deputy prime minister in Japan's first progressive government since shortly after Japan's surrender in the Pacific War, as a thin slice in the eight-party coalition led by Hosokawa Morihiro (August 1993 – April 1994), all assembled and masterminded by Ozawa Ichiro, the éminence grise of Japanese politics. Hata followed Hosokawa as a sixty-four-day prime minister (April–June 1994) in a desperate attempt to stop the unstable coalition from collapsing. He died in 2017.

As soon as the log-jam was broken with Hosokawa, I quickly arranged to travel to Tokyo with Luigi Colajanni on behalf of the Socialist Group. We saw nine cabinet ministers in three days.[10] It was a unique conjuncture that ended up being fumbled. With Clinton in the White House and Delors serving the end of his ten-year neo-mercantilist sentence (1985–95) in the Berlaymont, there was means, motive and opportunity for a global united left. I was the Socialist Group's representative on the Socialist International's Asia-Pacific Committee and we pushed. I was there in Tokyo with Clare Short three months later in May 1994 representing the Labour Party at the Council of the Socialist International.

No one saw the opportunity and seized the time. Washington and Brussels both lacked the imagination and Tokyo suffered from the London bus problem. No progressive prime minister in generations, then three coming along in twelve months. The Asia-Pacific Committee did persuade the Council to authorise a delegation to North Korea. I was to go to Pyongyang with JSP leader Doi Takako, but she postponed it at the last minute as she wasn't prepared to share a commercial flight from Beijing to the North with relatives of hijackers (see below). There were assurances that it was to be quickly rescheduled. We're still waiting.

Hata Tsutomu doll.

Hata was symbolic of a wider ferment as Japan transitioned to a post-war generation that had lost the lived history of the war as adults and the contrition that it carried. They found a self-confidence and outward vision that had been long missing. Hata, while serving as the LDP's finance minister in 1990–91, led the charge to abandon the country's sclerotic electoral system that was making Japan ungovernable. The post-war system had initially fostered rebuilding, rehabilitation and economic take-off under the tutelage of corporatist capitalism in the form of the *Zaibatsu* industrial conglomerates, but what had once facilitated now inhibited. America's tether was too short. The monolithic LDP and the 1955 System were crumbling as the absurdities bred stagnation, abuse and corruption.

The consequence of multi-member constituencies with single, non-transferable votes was to create finance-driven factionalism and indecisive leadership within the LDP and the impossibility of change outside. It was an elected aristocracy with seats inherited, being passed down the generations. The opposition JSP's last and only period in power had ended in 1948 with the fall of Katayama Tetsu's government. The breakthrough with the 'everyone apart from the LDP' government forced change. A new electoral law saw the end of multi-member constituencies with non-transferable voting and instead a mixed system with three hundred single member constituencies and two hundred seats allocated by proportional representation from eleven regional blocs. The two sides exchanged books in 1994. The LDP's rising star and future prime minister Hashimoto Ryutaro led with *Vision of Japan* and Ozawa countered with *Blueprint for a New Japan*. The faction system is far from dead, but its iron grip has been broken.

Manga mania

Political factionism and corruption weren't limited to Nagatacho – the Diet district. They were also the stuff of comics. In the five years from 1990, Fumimura Sho (writer) and Ikegami Ryoichi (illustrator) published the twelve volumes of *Sanctuary* (later published in English in nine volumes), in which two childhood friends who escape the killing fields of Cambodia determine to deliver a new Japan.[11] One, Hojo Akira, takes the dark path via the Yakuza while the other, Asami Chiaki, follows the political road. By Volume 2, Hojo is a Yakuza boss, but it is Volume 9 before Asami is prime minister and then – like in all the best manga – he promptly dies. Later, I was impressed to see a full set of *Sanctuary* on display in the Diet office of Gotoda Masazumi, an LDP liberal from Shikoku, whose constituency I was later to visit.

In 2002 I had two encounters with Moriyama Mayumi, former Chief Cabinet Secretary and the first woman to serve as Minister of Justice (2001–3), who revealed much of Japan's misogyny with her *What I Saw in the Cabinet* (1991). We were to discuss the matter of the Japanese plane hijackers. Nine members of the Japanese Communist League – Red Army Faction hijacked Japan Airlines flight 351 flying from Haneda Airport to Fukuoka in the Yodo-go incident in March 1970. They commandeered the plane on behalf of *Ashita no Joe* (Tomorrow's Joe), a working-class manga hero of Japan's New Left. It was the cultural equivalent of a hijacking in Britain on behalf of *Citizen Smith*'s Wolfie. They'd been on their way to Cuba to join the revolution. Unfortunately for them, the plane was not capable of flying the Pacific. They ended up in Pyongyang where their wish to join Castro's revolution met the response 'the revolution's here.' They did not even get to meet Fidel when he visited in 1986.

The Red Army Faction group included Takahiro Konishi, who I met half a dozen times in Pyongyang, and Wakabayashi Moriaki, bass player in the cult avant-garde rock band Les Rallizes Dénudés.[12] The band had come out of Kyoto's Doshishi University and consisted of four communist revolutionaries. Their MO was 'total cultural assault' with their twenty-minute 'Smokin' Cigarette Blues' easily capable of emptying a concert hall. The group's frontman, Takashi Mizutani, was apparently meant to be one of the hijackers, but overslept. Never has languor brought greater reward. Wakabayashi's second problem was he was a hardcore Liverpool FC fan, devoted to Steven Gerrard. On one visit I brought him a Liverpool shirt with Gerrard's name and number. On a second occasion he turned up in a Pyongyang pizzeria wearing the shirt of the Japanese national team, which was not something that went down well in the North. Early in their stay there was training in unarmed combat, including karate training that lasted until you were rendered unconscious. They swiftly moved on to other things. By 2000 the four remaining hijackers wanted to return home to face years in prison – one of the other hijackers caught years before, served five years. They just wanted assurances they would not face accusations of involvement in the abduction of Japanese citizens to the North.

Moriyama first met me in the ministry where her officials, unwilling to engage, quickly closed down the discussion about the return of the hijackers to Japan. She then offered a private meeting in her Diet office. At the second time of asking it was a polite, rational rejection, even if I did not accept

the premise. The Koizumi government was determined to maintain maximum pressure on Pyongyang. Washington had the North on its 'Terror State' list because they were harbouring the 'hijackers'. Logically, if Tokyo facilitated their return, the North would no longer be harbouring terrorists and the US listing would lapse. Two decades on, the four hijackers are still in Pyongyang, having long abandoned any hopes of any happy returns.

Around the same time, in the run-up to the 2002 World Cup, hosted jointly by Japan and South Korea, Tokyo announced that to combat English hooligans they would be automatically refusing entry to anyone who had a record of having been deported. I explained to Moriyama my 1990 Algerian adventure when I had been expelled after returning to Algiers with ex-president Ahmed Ben Bella. She gave me her private mobile phone number, but I never needed it. Immigration proved less of a problem than Brazil posed Germany as I watched Europe lose 2-0 to South America in the final.

Changing places

I also built up a personal, less political, rapport with Nakayama Taro, an LDP MP from Osaka. He had served as foreign minister during the Iraq War (1990–91) and was responsible for gifting Bush Senior $11 billion as Japan's mite. It was an expensive ticket for a guaranteed ringside seat for presidential inaugurations. When I met him, he was chair of both the EU delegation in the Diet and, more importantly, the Lower House's Constitutional Affairs Committee. There he was pushing through legislation to enable referenda as the first step to amending the US-imposed constitution of 1947. It was Japan's generosity in Washington's war that had set the process in motion. Tokyo's contribution was unacknowledged and unremarked. Ozawa's *Blueprint*, as a result, argued hard for Japan to become a 'normal' country, a sentiment echoed at a lower pitch by Hashimoto. Government and the main opposition were as one. The problem was Washington.

The US-imposed constitution of 1947 included, under Article 9:

> *(1) Aspiring sincerely to an international peace based on justice and order, the Japanese people forever renounce war as a sovereign right of the nation and the threat or use of force as means of settling international disputes.*
>
> *(2) In order to accomplish the aim of the preceding paragraph, land, sea, and air forces, as well as other war potential, will never be maintained. The right of belligerency of the state will not be recognized.*

Washington regretted that presumption all too fast. The US would ideally have liked Tokyo to have provided much more than mere 'rest and recreation' and provisions for the Korean War. There was some semi-clandestine assistance with shipping, but that was as far as it went. The problem was the triple lock that Washington had placed to constrain any reversion by Tokyo: a two-thirds majority in both houses of the Diet and consequent ratification by an affirmative referendum.

If you can't move the mountain you can skirt around it. Article 9 has been ground down over the decades to a point of virtual irrelevance. The Japan Self-Defense Forces appeared early; a notional 1 per cent limit on defence spending came, was innumerately interpreted and then went; while in 2007 the Defense Agency stepped up to become a fully fledged Ministry of Defense. Meanwhile, when the EU enquired, Japan's Supreme Court, the guardian of the constitution, made it clear that it would bend over backwards to avoid ruling creeping militarisation 'unconstitutional'. As a consequence, Japan's defence spending places it number six in the world. What worries Tokyo's politicians is not power, but projection. 'Out of area' operations are still unacceptable to civil society. Japan did send troops to Iraq in 2004–6, but in non-combatant roles, 'guarded' by British troops.

Until Nakayama set to work there was no legal basis on which to break the third lock and hold a referendum. It took years, but he delivered in the end. I sympathised with the objective. There was more than a touch of racism about Article 9; it effectively said that Japan was a bloodthirsty nation, while the Germans and Austrians had just been misdirected

by Hitler and his acolytes. The same provisions were never contemplated in Europe. Yet 'normal', as in Ozawa's conception, has its limit. It doesn't stretch to pre-emptive, let alone preventive war.

What attracted me to Nakayama was that his vision extended far beyond enabling Japan as Washington's helpful ally. He'd read Ohmae Kenichi's *Triad Power* (1985). A 'normal' Japan could seek to look increasingly to its own global interests, which would mean the ability to lean away from Washington and towards Brussels. Younger LDP members agreed. We exchanged staff: I put Elodie Sellar in Nakayama's office in Tokyo and Keiko Nakajima came to the EP. Elodie was there when Koizumi Junichiro came door-knocking for Nakayama's vote for prime minister.

Captive communication

Government and opposition in Japan both used my knowledge of North Korea. Nakayama had me address the LDP's research group. I later briefed former prime minister Murayama when he was preparing to lead an all-party delegation to Pyongyang in 2000, which proved to be the precursor to the Kim–Koizumi Summit in September 2002 and the Pyongyang Declaration. After the LDP group, I later did the same for the Democratic Party of Japan (DPJ) and their international secretary, Fujita Yukihisa (see below). Later I met with Cabinet Office Senior Vice-Minister Nishimura Yasutoshi – a friend and constituency neighbour of Gotoda – and Ishikawa Shoichiro, vice-minister for the abductee issues.

It all went wrong for Japan when they were invited by Beijing to join the Six-Party Talks. The three key issues for Tokyo and Pyongyang were the North's nuclear weapons and medium-range missiles, the abductees and the legacy of the past – Japan's occupation of Korea from 1910 to 1945. The talks, which started in August 2003 and limped on until 2009, were for Pyongyang sabotaged by Tokyo. The problem was Abe Shinzo. Chef de cabinet to Koizumi Junichiro, he was in the room in 2002 when Kim Jong Il had magicked five abductees from nowhere. It was a gesture of goodwill by Kim with disastrous unintended consequences. Instead of being read as demonstrating Pyongyang's pity, rather it proved their perfidy.

Tokyo had claimed the North had abducted seventeen Japanese, while Pyongyang now confessed to thirteen with five alive and eight dead. The remains of some of the dead were returned, but this only made matters worse. Tokyo produced its own 'dodgy dossier' using outdated techniques and inexperienced junior staff to conclude that the remains were fake. *Nature*, probably the world's most prestigious scientific journal, in response published an editorial in 2005 arguing that Japan's 'interpretation of the DNA tests has crossed the boundary of science's freedom from political interference', and that 'dealing with North Korea is no fun, but it doesn't justify breaking rules of separation between science and politics.'[13] From 2002 on, this all prompted virtual mass hysteria in Japan. Fanned by Abe as prime minister, it swept out of control. Anyone who'd ever gone missing had now been abducted by the North. The numbers sought climbed close to an impossible nine hundred.

With Jonathan Powell, Kang Suk Ju and Par Nuder.

Japan's Communist Party (JCP) had been first to press the issue in the Diet as early as 1988. They had fallen out with the Workers' Party of Korea (WPK) twenty years earlier over Kim's personality cult and military adventurism as his 'Southern advance' strategy threatened a second Korean War with his guerrilla units deployed to the South. The JCP proved more pragmatic than Abe's LDP. For them the prime focus had to be protecting Japan from the threat of nuclear weapons hoisted on the North's missiles. For Abe, in contrast, the abductees

came first. They were all alive and they all had to be returned, although apart from Yokota Megumi, the youngest and most famous of the victims, all the initial twelve 'unaccounted for' were years beyond the North's late-sixties life expectancy, with one in his mid to late nineties. With the Six-Party Talks poisoned by Tokyo, the North walked.

Even after killing the talks, Tokyo continued to kick the corpse. As part of the political dialogue organised with the WPK's International Department in 2014, we brought the North's former Six-Party Talks chief negotiator Kang Suk Ju – then the International Secretary of the party – to Europe to visit Berlin, Brussels and Bern. In Berlin it just so happened that then Japanese foreign minister Kishida Fumio was sharing the same hotel. The morning after their arrival, the Korean delegation looked sleepless in Berlin. Separately, Tokyo and Pyongyang both denied each other. Yet a few weeks later the North offered a further investigation into the fate of the remaining abductees. Nearly twelve months on, back in Pyongyang we asked Kang how things stood. He replied, 'it's over'. The investigation was finished and would not reopen, having failed to find any of the 'missing' abductees. A week later in Tokyo the vice-minister for the abductee issues refused to accept Kang's message. To date it has proved all too true, but with Kishida being from a different current in the party and therefore not carrying the same baggage regarding the issue, there may be some hope.

Abe made his political career on the back of his intransigent line on the abductions. But in the end, he had no room for manoeuvre. The same was true of his chosen successor, Suga Yoshihide. But barely a year after Suga's succession, his burgeoning public unpopularity forced him out. With that, the short Abe dynasty died. Suga was replaced by Kishida, the last senior Japanese politician to deal directly with a counterpart in the North. Kang, on his Brussels leg, chose beauty over beast, preferring Bruges to Waterloo. I spent several hours alone with him in the back of his car driving to Europe's northern Venice where, among other things, he confessed that his favourite novel was *Gone with the Wind*. It can only have been Kang who told one US envoy, 'Frankly, Scarlett, I don't give a damn.'[14]

Socialist Seppuku

If the 1993–94 progressive government had been farce, the second was tragedy. The DPJ, led by Hatoyama Yukio, won 308 seats to the LDP's 119 in August 2009's general election – with Nakayama losing his seat. For the first time since its formation in 1955, the LDP was not the largest party in the Diet. It was the worst defeat for a governing party in modern history. The result had been well foretold. In the 2007 Upper House election, the DPJ had surged past the LDP. They had a mandate for change and now the majority to deliver.

I knew the DPJ and Hatoyama. Several years earlier I'd travelled at his invitation to his constituency in Hokkaido to speak at a conference on space policy. The irony passed me by at the time. My later scepticism regarding Hatoyama as prime minister showed in *Tribune*: 'Hatoyama's wife believes that she was once abducted by aliens. We can only hope that progressives from Europe and the US can work with the new Japanese government to build a global progressive forum that addresses issues of security and climate change, economic recovery and development in a way that allows us to be grateful they didn't take her husband as well.'[15] Japan had an interesting take on why so many Americans believed they had been victims. It was like fishing – when an American was hooked, they were hurriedly thrown back. The rest you keep.

Hatoyama turned dithering into an art form. Almost the only inescapable policy commitment he and the DPJ had was to relocate the Futenma US marine base, with close to twenty-five thousand military personnel, not further north on Okinawa in Heneko, as planned by the previous government, but outside the prefecture. Procrastinating, he hawked the base around the country. To his evident surprise, nobody wanted it. He tried Tokunoshima in the Amami Islands, part of Kagoshima Prefecture. There were immediate mass protests and instant opposition from Kagoshima's governor Yuichiro Ito.[16]

I'd long been a friend of Okinawan musician Kina Shoukichi, an exponent of Okinawan folk-rock who played an electric sanshin. As a peace activist he was a seasoned campaigner against the US bases littering Japan's poorest and smallest prefecture, using the slogan 'Turn weapons into musical instruments'. More controversially, he favoured

independence for the Ryukyu Islands (Okinawa is the largest of them). He ran his own club in Naha where he played a nightly set with his band Champlose, including his million-selling hit 'Hana'. In 2004 he was elected to the House of Councillors for the DPJ on his anti-base platform. In May 2010, under pressure from Washington, Hatoyama broke the campaign pledge regarding independence for Ryukyu and resigned as prime minister the following month. After the May statement, Kina promised to destroy Hatoyama. But instead, Hatoyama destroyed him. In his Upper House re-election bid in July – after the new DPJ prime minister Kan Naoto confirmed Hatoyama's betrayal – Kina was swept aside, losing 60 per cent of his former two hundred thousand votes. One can only conclude that the aliens that took Hatayama's wife leaned heavily to the right. Hatoyama did more to destroy the future of the left in Japan than anyone since General MacArthur in the late 1940s, and the latter had the excuse that he was doing it deliberately. That said, Hatoyama's successors were to make their own marks.

With Yukio Hatoyama – holding 'Changing States'.

It was musical chairs. Hatoyama was replaced by Kan Naoto, who then gave way to Noda Yoshihiko. With the party crumbling as blocs of MPs flaked away, Noda called an early election at the end of 2012. The LDP only held the honour of the worst defeat for a governing party for a brief three years. The DPJ lost 251 seats and were reduced to a rump of 57 MPs. Worse, they immunised Japan's voters against any further temptation to experiment. Apart from Hatoyama himself, one survivor in the Upper House was his close advisor, the former senior vice-minister for finance Fujita Yukihisa. Fujita became the party's international secretary, and we continued to work together on North Korea (see above). In early 2009 he had forced Prime Minister Aso to acknowledge that his family mining company had used allied POWs to dig coal during the war. Fujita did get himself in trouble when he seemed to question the events of 9/11. At his request, I provided support in a press statement that defended his political work.

I travelled further to the Yaeyama Islands. Among them was Ishigaki, where the mayor was Ohama Nagateru, elected with support of the JSP. I visited three or four times as part of the tour itinerary with small groups of Labour MEPs. The tour template was Tokyo, Hiroshima for the Peace Memorial Park and Museum, Naha for Kina and Governor Ota's Okinawa Prefectural Peace Memorial Museum – situated where the end of the battle for Okinawa saw hundreds of women and children jump (or pushed) off the cliffs to their deaths – and then Ishigaki before flying back to Tokyo. One long evening on Ishigaki, Dr Ohama took us to meet his fishermen's support groups. We sat on benches under a garage canopy and ate the freshest sashimi straight from the boats, washed down with Orion beer and adder liquor chasers. It was priceless. I then made it to Yonaguni, the last island in the chain and only sixty kilometres off Taiwan, whose mountains loom large on the horizon. There I shared a hangover with the deputy mayor, who was pre-eminent in Japan's carp competitions. In 1945 Ishigaki and Yonaguni saw bombing and strafing from British elements of the naval fleet; another world, another time.

North East Asia Economic Forum

It was through Nakayama Taro that I was introduced to the North East Asia Economic Forum (NEAEF). Nakayama proposed I go with him to their annual conference in Alaska. I travelled to Anchorage as a rider to a Japanese Foreign Ministry delegation where I met the late Lee-Jay Cho, NEAEF's conductor in chief. The forum's footprint was huge. China, Japan and the Koreas were the core, with a periphery of Mongolia, Primorsky Krai, Hawai'i and Alaska. The origins

were back with the Tumen River Project – which was subsequently taken over by the UN – that had looked to economic integration to buttress peace. Largely unconsciously, it was employing the dawn logic of European integration to North East Asia. The financial vehicle was to be a new North East Asia Development Bank. Lee-Jay, a Korean-American, spoke (apart from English and Korean, of course) fluent Chinese and Japanese and had a network of connections without parallel. He was at one time the director of the East-West Center in Hawai'i and had been a key player in facilitating the opening of Chinese–South Korean diplomatic relations in 1992 with Jiang Zemin.

NEAEF's annual conference toured the Eastern hemisphere. I was there in Shenyang, Beijing, Tianjin and Haikou, Busan and Seoul, Honolulu, Anchorage, Osaka, Sendai, Vladivostok and Ulaanbaatar. The regular attendees included Steve Cowper (former governor of Alaska), George Ariyoshi (former governor of Hawai'i), Nakayama, and B. Ganbold (former Mongolian ambassador to South Korea). In 2014 I organised a side trip from Shenyang to the Rason Special Economic Zone in North Korea on the triple point with China and Russia. An economic and social enclave, Rason was 'lite' on ideology and heavy on chancers and Chinese. NEAEF still continues under the charge of Denise Konan, Dean of Social Sciences at the University of Hawai'i.

With Julian Priestley, Lee-Jay Cho and the NEAEF.

China atrocities

Through Mark Seddon, then editor of *Tribune*, I was invited to a conference organised by the International Department of the Chinese Communist Party on EU relations in December 1998. Slightly to my surprise, I ended up leading the European side. There were two better candidates in Ana Gomes, a former diplomat and MEP, and Maria Joao Rodrigues, a former minister in the Antonio Guterres government and key player in formulating the Lisbon Strategy. Both Portuguese, neither would give way to the other, and with the organisers under department head Zhang Zhijun demanding to know who was in charge, I was 'elected' by default.

At the end of the conference the department took me on a two-city 'atrocity' tour, the first unfamiliar to most and the second all too well known. I was flown up north to Harbin where, in the ice and snow, I went to Pingfang and the former headquarters of Japan's Unit 731, a covert biological and chemical warfare R&D centre, where up to ten thousand prisoners were killed including American POWs – or 'logs', as the Japanese termed them – during experiments.[17] After the war the perpetrators were captured, some by the Soviets and others by the US. Moscow's prisoners made the cast of the Khabarovsk War Crimes Trial (1949) where the key players received twenty-five years. Meanwhile, Washington's criminals, including the unit's head Ishii Shiro, received pardons from General MacArthur in exchange for exclusive access to their research findings. From Harbin it was down to Jiangsu province. Here the horrors on display were in the Memorial Hall of the Victims in Nanjing Massacre by Japanese Invaders, built in 1985. The hall commemorated the two months from December 1937 when the victorious Japanese army raped, tortured and killed close to three hundred thousand men, women and children.

The dog's bollocks

Years before, I'd visited Xichang and one of China's space launch facilities with the late Stan Newens MEP, where we

looked up at the ill-fated Long March 2E rocket that was to demonstrate that Beijing's aerospace industry's capacity for hubris matched Britain's. During our trip we were entertained with the farther shores of Chinese cuisine. When I – tongue in cheek – complained to Stan that he'd eaten my turtle paw, he looked horrified. The Koreans – North and South – went further. I have a *Best Recipes of Pyongyang* book that includes tangogi soup, the primary ingredient of which is dog meat. I also knew of a restaurant adjacent to the Koryo Hotel that offers the whole animal sliced and diced in every way imaginable, including the inimitable testicles. In the South it was Busan's speciality of live squid freshly chopped and writhing, which works well for those whose chopstick technique wants improvement – the food does half the task, grabbing the chopstick for itself. You do, however, have to prise it off the roof of your mouth and are advised to chew hard, otherwise there's a danger it sticks in your throat and you choke to death. To be fair, the live squid was preferable to Busan's Irish pub's offering of a toasted ham and cheese sandwich battered and deep fried then sugared. What part of Ireland that hailed from is beyond me, but it compares unfavourably with Aberdeen's deep fried Mars bars.

Japan's contribution to this litany of provender is *fugu*. This is one of a variety of pufferfish whose liver contains deadly toxins. To the surprise of no good promoter, the tastiest part of the fish is next to the liver, and a trained chef can give you a tingle of the tetrodotoxin poison. Miyagawa, a Japanese psephologist who I worked with on electronic voting, always insisted on taking me to a *fugu* restaurant for dinner when in Tokyo. I'd eaten it previously, but the first time I went with him I dutifully went through the *gaijin* ritual and said I'd heard it was dangerous. His response was to say his uncle had died eating it the previous year. It turned out a group of friends had caught a fish and tried slicing it themselves, absent anyone with the minimum three years' training required by professional chefs, with fatal consequences. The poison, for which there is no antidote, paralyses the muscles, with its victim fully conscious as they slowly asphyxiate. Miyagawa favoured *torafugu*, the most poisonous.

I was a member of the EP's Animal Welfare Intergroup. I once complained that Air Lingus had force-fed me pâté de foie gras on a flight from Dublin to Brussels. But my more extended venture was with the Tiger Campaign, who were complaining that the demand for tiger skins and tiger products in China was driving illegal poaching in India and Nepal with the lucrative export market. The campaign was aware of my China connections and I was asked to press the Chinese authorities to do more. I dutifully arranged to meet with the Ministry of Natural Resources' State Forestry Administration the next time I was in Beijing. Well briefed, I made the plea. Tigers were in danger of extinction and the use of their skins in religious vestments and the bones and organs in Chinese medicine were only exacerbating the problem. China, I insisted, had to do much more. The response left me nonplussed: 'We arrested forty-three smugglers last year and executed them.' It's unusual to be literally lost for words. I made my excuses and left, muttering under my breath my opposition to the death penalty.

Tibetan travails

In 2005 the International Department said I could visit anywhere I wanted in China. Never one not to abuse an opportunity, I proposed Aksai Chin. This for Pakistan is Chinese territory, while for India it is Chinese-occupied Kashmir, and both the cause and platform for the latter's 1962 China War and the skirmishes that broke out again in 2020. Not to my surprise, the offer was honed: anywhere I wanted in China apart from Aksai Chin. I was directed towards Tibet, which at the time was largely closed to visitors. It was the first of three visits.

The third visit was the most fascinating. Organised again through the International Department, in July 2008 I brought a delegation of Elmar Brok (German, EPP) – the seemingly perennial chair of the EP's Foreign Affairs Committee – and Philippe Morillon (French, ALDE), who had commanded UN forces in Bosnia. I'd previously been with Morillon on a Committee on Foreign Affairs (AFET) delegation to Afghanistan (see Chapter 7). The delegation was to meet in Beijing with senior People's Liberation Army figures before travelling to

Lhasa and Shigatse in the aftermath of the 14 March riots in the province. The disturbances, which involved thousands of young Tibetans, saw a score of Muslim Hui and Han settlers killed and their stores, schools – we visited the partly burnt-out Lhasa No. 2 Middle School – and one of the two mosques destroyed or damaged before the protests were brutally put down by the authorities. It was the mosque favoured by Chinese Muslims that bore the brunt, while the one patronised by the descendants of Kashmiri refugees was left alone. The same was true of the stores, with Han Chinese shops selectively torched. There were dozens of deaths among both victims and rioters.

As usual we announced our visit to the EU's ambassador and the relevant member states when we landed in Beijing. The unanimous response from the European diplomats was dismissive; there was no way the Chinese authorities were going to permit the visit. Tibet was closed and journalists expelled. But with no cancellation twenty-four hours before departure, there was a dawning realisation that we just might be going. There was a rush of requests to join the visit. The party response was 'if only you'd asked earlier'.

Beijing had poured money into the province's infrastructure with the Qinghai–Lhasa railway, opened in 2006, only one part of the largesse. The economy was booming and the Tibetans had done well with hundreds of thousands dragged out of poverty. The problem was the Han Chinese settlers had done better. Traditional social structures were broken and a growing group of fashion-conscious, alienated youth were prey to dreams of secession as a solution to their angst. I wrote a piece called 'Money can't buy you love'.[18] Full pockets don't fill hearts and minds, and the road to terrorism was open. Yet I wondered how this radical next generation could meld with the conservative traditionalists in exile on the other side of the mountains in Dharamshala. I'd met the Dalai Lama in Manchester some years earlier and, subsequent to this visit, was asked to meet Lobsang Sangay – who was later to become the Tibetan prime minister in exile – in Brussels after he read the article. There is an ever-yawning gap between the two geographies and generations. What Beijing fails to understand is the Dalai Lama is the last ageing barrier to a turn to terror by young militants in Tibet.

In Lhasa, with the help of Zhang Lijia,[19] we set up a meeting with Tashi Tsering in Barkhor one evening.[20] Outside our hotel on the outskirts, the first three taxis we flagged down, with Han Chinese drivers, refused the fare. Tensions were still high. But get there we did – eventually. Tsering merits a book and a film. As a peasant boy he was cynically recruited by 'talent spotters' visiting his village as a dancing boy for the Potala Palace, but he then fled Tibet in 1959 with the Dalai Lama and the help of the US Central Intelligence Agency (CIA) to exile in Dharamshala. Later he moved to university in the States before returning to China to join the Cultural Revolution's Red Guards. Subsequently arrested, he spent years in prison as an 'American spy'. On his release he completed the circle and returned to Lhasa to open a carpet shop, where we met him. His profits went to setting up schools in remote villages and preparing the first comprehensive Tibetan–English dictionary.

Socialist splits

My travels benefited from rivalry at the top of the Socialist (now Socialist and Democrat – S&D) Group. In 2004 the former Danish prime minister Poul Nyrup Rasmussen was elected an MEP by the people of Denmark and as president of the PES by member parties. In the EP Martin Schulz was starting his seven and a half years as leader of the S&D. This created a spicy rivalry. Which was Mary and which the lamb was never clear, nevertheless 'everywhere that Mary went, the lamb was sure to go'. Schulz took an S&D delegation to China to meet senior officials and the Three Gorges Dam. Rasmussen upped the ante with a PES trip that may have disappointed in place (Shanghai) but made up in person (President Hu Jintao). As the group's self-made China hand, I was the only overlap in the delegations' membership. In 2018 I was to meet Xi Jinping in Shanghai. Yet for all this, looking with old eyes as we were, the sheer scale and pace of change escaped us all.

Greater India

I'd spent time in India during the latter part of my spell at Manchester University when we were looking at sites for the deployment of ocean thermal energy conversion plants. India was interested and its Andaman and Nicobar Islands appeared an ideal location. But visits back in the early 1980s were extremely restricted as the islands were designated an 'Inner Line Zone' to protect the indigenous Jarawas, Onge and other tribes. It was Denis Healey's intervention with the Indian authorities that delivered the permits we needed. Nothing came of our visit except for an appreciation of the plight of these local tribes, who were threatened by encroaching 'civilisation'. Mass tourism is turning them into the inhabitants of a human zoo, parading naked for gawking visitors. This is one population for which less is very definitely more.[21]

I returned to the subcontinent via Pakistan. In east Manchester there was a large Kashmiri community; in Oldham in particular almost all had their roots in the city of Mirpur in Azad Kashmir. By chance, the call for migrant labour for Oldham's mills was published there. Tens of thousands came from the district in the late 1950s and early 1960s. By the 1980s, they and their children were active in the Labour Party. A normal Labour Party ward meeting would attract ten members or less, but put Kashmir on the agenda and you'd have a hundred. I was invited to visit Pakistan by one of the Kashmiri groups along with Bryan Davis, the MP for Oldham Central and Royton. After Islamabad it was Muzaffarabad and Mirpur. We were allowed to meet everyone, although it was very clear that the secular Jammu-Kashmir Liberation Front (JKLF) in Muzaffarabad, who supported an independent Kashmir, existed only on sufferance. Pakistan wanted more Kashmir, not less.

Mirpur stuck in my memory for reasons of taste not revolution. We arrived hot and bothered after a long car journey. We weren't stopping overnight, just doing a series of events. We were early, so were put in a shared hotel room to rest. We didn't get much, and the atmosphere was hot, damp and noisy. The wait seemed interminable. Eventually, it was into the centre where we sweatily debouched into the lobby of some multi-story block and were whisked up to a banqueting suite seating men in their hundreds. It turned out we were two hours late! No explanation was ever provided. An endless chain of speeches followed as we waited to break a long fast. Finally, the speeches ended and food began. It was competitive eating. Course followed course with ever-shrinking gaps between arrival and departure as part eaten plates were whisked away by racing waiters. An hour's perorations were topped by visiting a feast rather than eating one. Suddenly the top man stood up. It was over. Shaking our way through a procession of hands, the delegation was ushered into a lift to depart. To our surprise, we went up rather than down. Three floors higher we were ushered onto an identical set with a different cast, where the whole performance was reprised with slow speeches, fast food and sharp conclusion.

That trip rather awoke the Kashmiri community in Britain and Europe to the opportunities afforded by the EU. I was part of a group of British Labour MEPs that organised a conference in the EP for the Kashmiri diaspora in October 1993 that included among its guests the JKLF founder and chairman Ammanullah Khan, who had previously been expelled from Britain in 1986. As Khan was being driven to his hotel with George Stevenson MEP, the Belgian police stopped the parliament car with guns drawn and arrested Khan – despite his Belgian visa – on an Interpol warrant issued at the request of New Delhi for his connection to the assassination of Kashmir University Vice Chancellor Mushir-ul-Haq in Srinagar in 1990. He was eventually released and allowed to return to Pakistan. I missed the 'fun' – I was in a Socialist Group bureau meeting discussing the 1994 European election manifesto.

Kashmir had arrived and didn't leave – it became a standing issue. Subsequently, I went on an AFET delegation back to Muzaffarabad where we were helicoptered up to the Line of Control on the Pakistani side to face Indian troops a few hundred metres away. India, not to be outdone a few months later, mirrored the exercise from their side right down to the helicopters. The difference was the two provincial capitals, Muzaffarabad and Srinagar. Both were poor and rundown, and while the former looked neglected the latter felt and smelt like occupied territory with its walls and fences, soldiers and security.

EurAsia

The last forty years has seen empire recede in the rear-view mirror while an oncoming Asia looms ever larger ahead. Japan was unknown to most politicians, let alone ordinary citizens, back in the 1980s. It was around then that I was told, 'you know they even have karaoke in Japan'. My response was to explain that when Japanese travel abroad and get homesick they go to McDonalds for home cooking. Since then, manga and anime have swept the West. The Republic of Korea, once seen as a low-income country that was the destination of choice for Japanese sex-tourists, is now an economic and cultural giant with the products of its *chaebol* filling the aisles and K-pop the airwaves. Meanwhile, China just overshadows everything.

Early in my time in the EP I was often quizzically asked about my involvement with the region, 'Why do you bother with the Far East?' I'd reply, 'With the world's largest country; biggest democracy; second-richest country; largest Muslim state; most dangerous stand-off along the Korean peninsula's DMZ, why not?' It's not all necessarily for the good, as Washington inveigles Brussels and London into a joint enterprise offensive against Beijing, but today the question should be, 'Why on earth aren't you interested in East Asia?'

Endnotes

[1] Glyn Ford (1986), 'When this man sent in the troops to smash a strike, 2,000 people died. What is he doing at Number Ten?', *Tribune*, 18 April. [2] Glyn Ford (1988), 'Ex-dictator's fate is crucial for stability in South Korea', *Tribune*, 16 December. [3] Statement by Prime Minister Tomiichi Murayama, 'On the occasion of the 50th anniversary of the war's end', 15 August 1995. [4] All elaborated in my *Talking to North Korea* (2018). [5] *North Korea on the Brink* was translated into Japanese and Korean (published in Tokyo and Seoul), while *Talking to North Korea* was translated into Korean. [6] Robert Jenkins with Jim Frederick (2008), *The Reluctant Communist: My Desertion, Court Martial, and Forty-Year Imprisonment in North Korea*, Berkeley: University of California Press. [7] Bob Woodward (2018), *Fear: Trump in the White House*, New York: Simon & Schuster, pp. 301–302. [8] Alessandro Ford (2016), 'A North Korean Tale of Friendship | Alessandro Ford | TEDxUHasselt', YouTube (uploaded 13 April), www.youtube.com/watch?v=ltoeQXf_gnI (accessed 11 March 2022). [9] Glyn Ford (1996), 'God's own version of the Weimar Republic', *Tribune*, 12 July. [10] Glyn Ford (1994), 'Taking the Orient Express', *House Magazine*, 7 February. [11] Fumimura Sho and Ikegami Ryoichi (1990-1995), *Sanctuary*, Big Comic Superior, Tokyo: Shogakukan Inc. [12] See Julian Cope (2007), *Japrocksampler; How the Post-War Japanese Blew their Minds on Rock 'N' Roll*, London: Bloomsbury. [13] For more detail see my *Talking to North Korea*, pp. 222–227. [14] Sophie Pinkham (2020), 'Something resembling normal life', a review of *Friend: A Novel from North Korea* by Paek Nam-nyong, *New York Review of Books*, 3 December. [15] Glyn Ford (2009), 'Earthquake shakes Japan', *Tribune*, 11 September. [16] I discussed this in 'Make or break for Japan's left', *Red Pepper*, 22 June 2010, www.redpepper.org.uk/make-or-break-for-the-japan-s-left/. [17] Glyn Ford (1989), 'Review: *Unit 731* – Peter Williams and David Wallace', *Tribune*, 17 March. [18] Glyn Ford (2010), 'Money can't buy you love', *EU Reporter*, March/April. [19] Lijia Zhang (2008), *Socialism is Great!: A Worker's Memoir of the New China*, London: Atlas. [20] William R. Siebenschuh and Tashi Tsering (2003), *The Struggle for Education in Modern Tibet*, Lampeter: Edwin Mellen Press. [21] Jonathan Lawley (2020), *A Road to Extinction: Can Paleolithic Africans Survive in the Andaman Islands?*, London: EnvelopeBooks; and my Christine Marple (pseud) (1983), 'Letter from Port Blair', *Far Eastern Economic Review*, 25 August.

6 Science Politics

> Split the Lark – and you'll find the music.
>
> Emily Dickinson

Why did Britain build the Brabazon and Concorde rather than Boeings or Airbuses? London and England were a family with the wrong people in charge, as Orwell put it so aptly in *The Lion and the Unicorn.* They extrapolated straight lines from positions history was already abandoning. It was class travel not mass travel, quality over quantity and speed over payload.[1] The Americans never had the same suffocating problems of social status. While Europe's establishments had compromised themselves as fellow travellers with Hitler and been pushed aside in the post-war world, Britain's establishment had been providentially deprived of the prospect of treachery. Had Britain fallen to the German Reich, there is little reason to doubt that there would have been orderly queues of aspiring collaborators forming outside Gestapo headquarters.[2] The level of collusion with the Nazis in the only part of Britain to be occupied by Hitler – the Channel Islands – was so disconcerting that Churchill swept it under the carpet. In contrast to Europe's new beginning after the war, deep politics in Britain was on pause until normal programming was resumed in 1951 as the Tories crept back into power with more seats but fewer votes than Labour.

Our relative decline was sufficiently slow and steady that we scarcely noticed as year on year we slipped out of manufacture into service and tumbled down the tables of comparative wealth. After the Suez fiasco in 1956 the 'special relationship' with Washington became one of master and servant, even if we were on first name terms. The future was to be driven by technology; about this in 1964 Harold Wilson was right, but those charged with delivery got it wrong. Their mistakes were, first, favouring theory over practice and, second, scale and nation over market. Schooled in grandeur, the decision-makers inevitably ensured the money gravitated towards 'big technology' projects – military and civilian – that proved duds.

The problem on the left was deeply embedded attitudes to science and technology that stretched from Marx to Methodism. This was a threat from when the genie of progress was released into the world, even if it was not to exhibit for a long century and more.[3] The twin fictions were that science was neutral and technology progressive; summed up in demands for science that had no limits and more expertise. The Haldane principle that decisions about research spending should be made by scientists rather than politicians was unmatched in other spheres of government. The military did not get to choose their wars, while science had full command of workplace, process and product, with civil society left to watch from the sidelines. This technological determinism left only a partial politics as the Fabian mantra 'the inevitability of gradualness' ran its course. True there was accelerator and brake – although why anyone, apart from a reactionary, would want to slow progress was impossible to comprehend – but no steering. Science and socialism were in a symbiotic relationship of mutual dependence, although it was clear who was horse and who rider.

Labour walked the walk without deviation or interruption, but much repetition. There was a moment, though, in the early 1980s. The party's Home Policy Committee set up a Science and Technology Subcommittee in November 1981, 'to develop policies in the field of science and technology – subjects which have been neglected in the Party's policy-making for a number of years.'[4] The membership was drawn from the scientific and educational trade unions, Labour's house-trained businessmen in the 1972 Industry Group and friendly academics. I served as one of the last and was later, with Steven Rose, part of the drafting team that prepared a speech for Neil

Kinnock on science and technology policy. The subcommittee's interim report to the 1982 Party Conference in Blackpool, to no one's shock, complained of a 'lack of appropriate investment in science and technology' that 'simply underlines the need for socialist planning to overcome the barriers to faster progress thrown up by private enterprise'. Yet there was a hint of heresy: 'a key objective is the establishment of a democratic framework for science and technology in which government, management, trade unions, and the scientific community itself jointly influence the general direction of research and development'.

There were two alternate readings. The first saw a 'capitalist utopia of common national interest' while the second implied a pluralism of interests served separately on a mediated menu. This harked back to 1976, Mike Cooley and the social shaping of innovation with his alternative corporate plan to avoid redundancies at the defence manufacturer Lucas by switching production to 'socially useful products'. The 1983 Labour Party Manifesto reduced this down to: 'ensure that research and development are directed towards society's needs, with a reduction in the present high proportion of defence research'. This weak shoot of hope was long dead after three more leaders and general election defeats.

The trickle-down theory of scientific innovation proved as fallible at delivering products to the market as trickle-down economics was at delivering equality. The dress code favoured white coats over oily dungarees. C. P. Snow's *The Two Cultures* with its complaint that, unlike Germany, post-Victorian education in Britain focused on the humanities to the neglect of science, missed the mark. The failure wasn't so much philosophy rather than physics, or classics and chemistry; it was to neglect the applied sciences. German technical education focused on application over discovery with the applied science universities (*Fachhochschulen*) in the vanguard. Neither did it hurt that Germany's R&D budget in terms of GDP was 60 per cent greater than that of the UK.

An academic team from my department at Manchester University had published *Wealth from Knowledge*, a study of eighty-four technical innovations that had won the Queen's Awards for Industry in 1966 and 1967.[5] They found no cases where pure science had pushed innovation. Applied science was the mother, and 'product champions' the father of innovation. A prize was offered for providing an example to the contrary. It remains unclaimed. Pure science intellectually tidies up after the event, providing retrospective understanding and hinterland, but the evidence is no catalyst for competition. Science owes more to production than production to science. At its most brutal, RD&D and its close confidant applied science are central to industrial policy, while pure science should look to support in the cultural chapter of the budget. Bread or roses, pure science is poetry, applied prose.

Science for the people

Science is beyond good or evil as another element of culture and society that must endlessly struggle to escape the embrace and capture of social norms and values. In that I favour Aleksandr Bogdanov over Lenin, the target of his *Materialism and Empirio-Criticism: Critical Comments on a Reactionary Philosophy*.[6] Lenin makes 'matter' ahistorical, while for Bogdanov scientific knowledge shapes and is shaped by society. Science was abused by the likes of Cyril Burt in the race IQ/nature versus nurture debates, in which Burt designed his results to fit the thesis that intelligence was inherited, and the 1944 Education Act expedited the rest. The point is less that Burt 'massaged' his data, but that his credulous work was adopted without question and tasked to justify the basis for Britain's elitist school system.[7] The same sleight of hand was the eugenics movement where American 'science' underpinned racism at best and genocide at worst. In the Deep South in the US, it provided the intellectual foundations for the Jim Crow laws, while in the Third Reich it became the tool of the anti-Semitic judicial establishment, even if Berlin attenuated the harshness of the US Confederate States.[8]

Science and technology are a good thing, and the more the better was long the prevailing opinion, save among knots of irredeemable reactionaries and nostalgics. The twentieth century's punctuations of the Great War and, more especially, its successor conflict that gave the world Holocaust and Hiroshima, saw this substituted by the use/abuse model. Bad

people misemployed the products of the laboratory, good people didn't. The Nazis and the Soviets were ahead of the game, wearing their ideological glasses of race and class, seeing in the first case 'Jewish science' to be rejected and in the second Lysenkoist horticulture wherein, in a throwback to Lamarck, plants across generations could be educated not to feel the cold. Post-1945, the West's version of racist science was passive, not active. National Socialism drove Jewish professors and their ideas from the universities of Germany, while the West, as Joseph Needham demonstrated encyclopaedically in his *Science and Civilization in China*, just pretended it wasn't there.

The late 1960s and 1970s saw this new neutrality of science put to the question. The production of science was the result of political decisions and thus was inherently tainted by the process. Science was as much part of the political struggle as education, law and foreign policy. It was neither autonomous nor disinterested, but deeply complicit. This could be seen in the work of Hilary and Stephen Rose, whose book *The Radicalisation of Science: Ideology of/in the Natural Sciences* (1976), building on Boris Hessen's seminal paper 'The socio-economic roots of Newton's "Principia"' that was presented at the Second International Congress on the History of Science in London (1931), illustrated the point. Some went further. I even had a soft spot for Paul Feyerabend's anarchist *Against Method* (1975) that argued that science was in the end irrational. Feyerabend was a joy to read. How could anyone not love a philosopher who entitled a book chapter 'More Marxist fairy tales from Australia'? Nevertheless, the ideas were definitely a bridge too far.

Thomas Kuhn's *The Structure of Scientific Revolutions* (1962) demonstrates incommensurability rather than irrationality in the evolution of science. Short periods of revolutionary science alternate with long spells of normal science where slow incremental accretion was the standard.[9] Science was a hidden kernel buried under layers of contusion, confusion and collusion. Practitioners had to unwrap the parcel before redressing it to suit the future. My own faltering attempts to explain the concept to non-scientists in two diverging directions was 'Science in society: even the truth is relative' in *Socialist Review* (July 1978) and 'A framework for a new view of Islamic science' in *Adiyat Halab* (Volume 4–5, 1978–79). Nevertheless, it was a start. Newtonian physics was an everyday approximation of Einstein's paradigm shift, while the unrolling of quantum physics was to see the world anew as relations and events rather than substance. Heisenberg's sojourn on the bleak wastes of Helgoland produced that vision.

The argument for new democratic structures where people choose alternative pathways seemed distant from reality. How would it work? I rather favoured the Dutch science shops that provided demand-driven bottom-up community-based research at university level. Yet there was a problem of scale – it was all too small. I thought we could adapt the 1971 Rothschild Report on the purpose of government funded research. Previously, the Haldane principle saw command and control of research funds in the hands of the practitioners; Rothschild transferred 25 per cent of funding back to government departments for them to serve as surrogate customers. I'd make it close to 100 per cent and distribute it between sectoral business associations, trade unions and civil society to allocate to the universities and research laboratories. One can imagine that the NUM might have commissioned research on the dangers of pneumoconiosis rather earlier than the mine owners or the men from the ministry.

So my theory and practice in science policy was shaped by this intellectual niche and its activist wing in the British Society for Social Responsibility in Science and the Radical Science Collective with *Science for People* and *Radical Science Journal*. This was all rather too 'new' Left for the CPGB, who countered with their *Science Bulletin; Communist Science and Technology Journal*. They all faded away by the 1980s, although the US *Science for the People* revived in 2019 in word and deed after a long thirty-year intermission. Socialist science wasn't the only fruit – I further explored Islamic science in a series of articles.[10]

The reins of science are tight, and the blinkers are on. Nevertheless, the restraints don't limit the future to any single destination. William Morris was more lyrical than the Stone Roses, but a touch unremitting: 'Science – we have loved her well and followed her diligently, what will she do? I fear she is in the pay of the counting house and the drill sergeant, that she is too busy and will for the present do nothing.'[11]

First committees

Considering this scientific background, there were for me a series of questions European science was required to answer: who (1) chooses, (2) monitors, (3) evaluates, (4) promotes post-innovative performance, and (5) lifts the dead hand of competition policy? I searched for answers in Brussels. In 1984 I served on the ERT and the External Economic Relations (REX) committees, the latter the precursor of what was to be the International Trade Committee. I shared the former with the assiduous Gordon Adam from the 1979 cohort of MEPs and Norman West from the NUM (an accomplice of Arthur Scargill) who smuggled foreign funds into the UK for the union. The head of the Committee Secretariat was Julian Priestley.

I attempted to impose my theory on European science, including the Framework Programme (FP1, 1984–87, €3.8B; FP2, 1987–91, €5.4B) the Joint Research Centres (Ispra in particular – see below), Star Wars and the Human Frontier Science Programme and Scientific and Technological Option Assessment (STOA, report October 1985, launched March 1987). I set out my stall early on, writing with Ken Green in *Tribune*.[12] We complained of both the quantity and quality of Europe's R&D. We were barely spending 2.5 per cent of the budget on research and spending that badly. The limited funds were being concentrated on the narrow dictates of high-technology fashion and elite science. This was nuclear power rather than alternative energy, with an almost religious obsession with nuclear fusion that was so long on promise and papers and so short of practical results. Aside, it was charity, 'out relief', for Europe's multinationals as we underwrote their research programmes.

The fusion fable continues today with ITER in France. In what was to prove my final parliamentary term, there was a battle between Paris and Tokyo for the siting of the next generation fusion facility. The winner was to be awarded a disproportionate slice of the bill. In the case of Paris, the EU was to share that prize. During one of the EP delegation meetings with the Japanese Diet in Tokyo, I announced that I was backing Japan's bid – after all, it was a waste of good money and it would be better that it was Japanese yen rather than euros.

We welcomed the early commitment by Viscount Étienne Davignon, the soon to depart Commissioner for Industrial Affairs and Energy, to up spending to 4 per cent of the budget, to promote the European Strategic Programme on Research in Information Technology (ESPRIT) and scientific exchanges, but what was really required was the democratisation of the process of deciding what is to be done. Alongside the scientists, trade unions, the workforce and consumers needed a say. As I'd said earlier in criticising the UK's overemphasis on military R&D, 'science is too important to be left to the scientists.' New technology needed to be encouraged in the workplace alongside protection and retraining of the workforce – something that was to appear later as the European Commission's Objective 4. Human-centred choices would have given priority to rural transport over Concorde and heart disease over heart transplants.

There were other problems. First the EU's competition rules hamstrung effective R&D. Japan had picked up the model of the UK's sectoral stale and starved research associations and ran them hard in a different direction. Major Japanese corporations first co-operated then competed at successive phases of the innovation process. They ran together for the first three laps of the course and only when the bell rang did they break and sprint to the finish. All of this was on show in Japan's science city, Tsukuba. The first phase of mutual aid was outlawed in the EU in the self-harming of a competition policy that benefited the competition at the expense of domestic industry. Only now, two generations on, does the European Commission, with its drive for strategic autonomy, finally recognise it needs to break those rules.

The second issue was post-innovative performance. Europe made groundbreaking innovations but allowed others to capitalise on those initial breakthroughs with the stream of technical enhancements and modifications that rang the global cash registers. In Kuhnian terms, Europe was good at 'revolutionary' science but was unable to deliver on 'normal' science because of our failure to embed our scientific researchers among technologists and engineers on the shop floor. Japan didn't make that mistake.

The third was monitoring and evaluation. Scientific research is, by its very definition, haphazard and uncertain. Some ideas work, a few fail completely, while others make chance discoveries off to the side of the initial direction that merit further exploration. Yet the bureaucracy and rigidity of the Commission's decision-making processes meant that getting grants was extremely difficult, but once given they were rarely taken away. I wanted that reversed: they should be easier to get and harder to keep. There should be ongoing monitoring and evaluation that could spur what was working, reorientate what would benefit from redirection and terminate – without rancour – the rest. Instead, the emphasis was on ticking boxes on cross-border research with projects involving institutions from multiple member states prioritising, in effect, social programmes over science. There were virtual PO box institutions in some smaller member states that received a slice of the Commission's largesse for lending name and nation to application.

Worst of all were the joint research centres, like Ispra in Italy. Left over from the Union's initial enthusiasm for all things nuclear – including the chimera of fusion – they had scrambled to diversify. But nuclear scientists don't always retrain easily into other scientific disciplines. An attempt was made to revitalise Ispra with a generous early retirement programme. It was too generous. The 'young guns' grabbed the offer of leaving a tired institution with a healthy financial package to seek scientific pastures new, while those with few prospects stuck fast. It was the only early retirement scheme I'm aware of that left the average age of the staff older at its end than at its beginning. More recently, Ispra found a niche in the promotion of 'non-animal' testing.

Curious counterparts

The ERT committee had a fascinating assortment of members. One was Manolis Glezos, elected in 1984 on the PASOK list. He had been one of the two anti-fascists who had climbed the Acropolis in 1941 and torn down the Swastika flying there. Sentenced to death, he was never caught. After the war his support for the Communists got him a second death sentence from the new Greek government, which was subsequently commuted to life imprisonment. In the post-war period he spent eleven and a half years in prison and four and a half in exile, a poor exchange for the Lenin prize and being featured on a Soviet stamp. On the committee we had a shared interest in geology and, before he stepped down to promote direct democracy back home, he fed my smoking habit – back then MEPs could smoke in committee – with an unhealthy supply of Greece's distinct Karelia cigarettes. He was to return to the EP in 2014 at the age of ninety-one, this time representing Syriza.

Another was Michel Poniatowski, the committee's chair. A Polish prince, he had been a controversial Minister of the Interior (1974–77) under Valery Giscard d'Estaing, accused both of the sins of commission and omission. He sent in the gendarmes to suppress a small nationalist 'rebellion' in Corsica and in the ensuing firefight two gendarmes were killed. In 1977 the Gaullist deputy Jean de Broglie was assassinated and Poniatowski was accused of being all too well aware of the death threats and failing to act to protect de Broglie. He stepped down as minister a couple of months later. It was Poniatowski who facilitated the emergence of Jean-Marie Le Pen's Front National (FN). He agreed to merge his RPR-UDF list with the FN for the second round of the Dreux municipal by-election of September 1983, saying, 'The fascist danger in France does not come from the right, but from the left.'[13] The FN had 16.7 per cent of the vote, and the media storm that followed carried Le Pen's party to 11 per cent in June's European elections, giving them ten MEPs. Despite the ideological chasm, Poniatowski would invite Benedikt Härlin (see below) and myself for dinner from time to time, especially when the committee was travelling. His Polish connection delivered us an audience with Pope John Paul II. Nevertheless, there was a shadow over him. Dinner generally had two armed gendarmes at the restaurant's entrance.

Benedikt Härlin, together with Michael Klöckner, had come from prison to parliament. The two had both been central to the publication of German left-wing magazine *Radikal,* Härlin as editor and Klöckner as journalist/accountant. They were arrested in 1983 because one of the

magazine's articles – published anonymously – was judged to have been aiding and abetting a terrorist organisation, namely Germany's Baader–Meinhof Group, and were sentenced by the Berlin Higher Regional Court to two and a half years without parole. The verdict was not overturned until 1990. For many on the left, these prison terms were draconian and posed a threat to press freedom. Consequently, the Greens put both on their list for the 1984 European elections. Victory triggered parliamentary immunity and they were released to serve five years in the EP instead. Härlin went native and Klöckner AWOL.

Energy Research and Technology Committee meeting at the Joint Research Centre in Ispra. Left to right Phili Viehoff (The Netherlands, S&D), myself, Anne-Marie Lizin (Belgium, S&D) and Rolf Linkhor (S&D, Germany).

Härlin became an active ERT member and a friend. He came and campaigned for me in the run-up to the 1989 European elections – much to the fury of East Manchester's Greens – on the grounds that with first past the post the Greens couldn't win and it was far better to have me than a Tory. I had dinner one evening in Strasbourg with the two of them. Klöckner spent the evening smoking serial joints. Within six months he became a rare bird in the parliament before disappearing entirely.

Härlin wrote a piece – as did Poniatowski – for the issue of *Science and Public Policy* I guest edited in 1988 and we travelled together on an EP delegation to China. His

'Biotechnology in Europe' stands the test of time, talking as it does of the dangers of allowing the patenting of life, the myth of the 'gene–technology gap' in Europe and the fact that EU agriculture needs bovine growth hormones to enhance milk yields like it needs a hole in the head as we threaten to drown in milk lakes. 'Designer plants, super-cows and ultra-pigs, insecticide viruses and new vaccines, bacteria as little helpers to clean up dangerous wastes in the environment ... will genetic engineering lead us to a new Eldorado and provide us with a biotechnology paradise out of a bottle?' The problem was public control with the absence of independent experts not tied to industry, while 'the less politicians really know about a technology, the more easily they are convinced our future will depend on it.'[14]

Star Wars

The EP's committees were permitted to meet once a year outside the parliament's normal meeting places of Brussels, Strasbourg and Luxembourg. In September 1985 the ERT was in an Athens hotel when it was agreed the committee would prepare an 'own-initiative' report on Ronald Reagan's Strategic Defence Initiative (SDI), more commonly known as 'Star Wars.' I was keen to become the rapporteur, but looking around as the vote loomed, the Socialists appeared short of bodies to win the coveted post. I hurriedly called around the rooms and got Norman West out of bed to vote. His interest in the committee was strictly limited to coal and little else. It worked. I won with a single vote to spare. Apart from destabilising the US–Soviet stand-off, whose essence was encapsulated in mutually assured destruction, SDI threatened to subvert the trajectory of European science and technology in the interests of Washington's military-industrial complex while denying Europe access to the full fruit of any technological spin-offs.

Star Wars lit up civil society. The Socialist Group agreed to sponsor a fact-finding trip by myself and Reinhold Hack, the group's staff member servicing the committee, to Washington DC and California in late January 1986 to meet with scientists

and officials, Congress and industry. On my birthday the two of us were around a table in NASA's Washington HQ, just starting our meeting when the door burst open and someone rushed in holding a transistor radio broadcasting a disconsolate commentary. The space shuttle *Challenger* had blown up a minute after launch. As we listened in silence, people congregated, while hope bled to resignation. We stayed for our allotted hour then made our excuses and left, leaving them bemused over what might have gone wrong. It was months before Richard Feynman, the physicist on the Rogers Commission investigating the disaster, proved the guilt of inflexible O-rings, frigid with the cold. Yet neither then, nor subsequently, did the *Challenger* disaster dent the matchless confidence that Star Wars' technologies would, like shooting fish in a barrel, take out a rain of incoming intercontinental ballistic missiles.

Washington was keen to keep Europe on board with SDI. We were to double as outpost and cash cow. SDI might be the 'high frontier' in the States, but in Europe it would be on the ground. The British and the German governments had signed memorandums of understanding (MOUs) to participate in developing the technology. These were one-way streets, a form of technological osmosis. European knowledge and expertise would feed into the US programmes with no reflux, rather an intellectual black hole sucking in everything with nothing escaping. One active promoter of SDI was the Hungarian physicist Edward Teller, 'the father of the hydrogen bomb' and Director Emeritus of the Lawrence Livermore National Laboratory. In the run-up to the vote on SDI in the EP he was dispatched to Strasbourg to lobby MEPs. I countered with Mary Kaldor, one of the founders of END. The three of us spent almost two days arguing, teasing out our positions between Teller's intermissions as he plied the more tractable EPP and Liberals. It was like meeting Dr Strangelove in the flesh. He was the nuclear warriors' nuclear warrior; a man who had never met a nuclear weapons programme he couldn't endorse. Mary said, at the end, she now understood why her father Nicholas Kaldor described Teller as an impossible man. The two had been at school together in Budapest during and immediately after the First World War. In the end, Teller's cavalry came from the left field.

The programme caused concern in the EU both technologically and politically. First, it was feared that the tens to hundreds of millions of dollars that would flow into the American high-tech R&D sectors would just widen the knowledge gap between Europe and the US. In political terms, it was feared that SDI would escalate the arms race and provoke critical destabilisation. These issues were rooted in the reality of the Star Wars programme: despite its avowed defensive intentions, the reality was that it strengthened America's offensive threat. The proposed budget for European involvement in SDI was $300–1000 million for the first five years, providing an obvious red flag for the economic benefits of joining.[15]

A Christmas card I produced of a 1987 general election poster by Gould-Mattinson that the party disavowed after a single appearance – several were returned by irate Tory businessmen.

On top of this, American industry made it clear there was no sharing. To avoid European and Japanese companies gaining a competitive edge from the spin-offs of SDI work, foreign involvement would be limited to research sectors where state-of-the-art technologies were unavailable in the US. Thus, foreign industries had little prospect of serious returns from MOUs, with lots to lose and little to gain. Absent an MOU, direct contracts were also available between individual companies and the US government, with the allied government acting as postbox and police, channelling classified material

to the companies and vetting their employees. Here Europe's defence industry had to go head-to-head in bidding against its US competitors with the hidden hand of Washington pressing heavily on the US side of the scale.

Star Wars posed a real threat to the Soviets, as the developing technology had the potential to protect US missile silos and hardened targets, giving the Pentagon an effective first-strike capacity for the first time since the 1950s. While research was permitted under the 1972 Anti-Ballistic Missile Treaty, testing and deployment would breach the agreement. It was a signal to the Kremlin that the White House was not serious about arms reductions talks. Because of the necessity for American launch sites to be placed within close range of the USSR, any superpower war would start in Europe.

The former French foreign minister and European Commissioner Claude Cheysson saw a hidden agenda: 'In the name of the threat which they pretend hangs over the United States and Europe, it will be possible to inject considerable sums into scientific and technological research. The Americans wish in this way to recover their leadership in certain areas of the high technology of tomorrow.'[16] The EU was to voluntarily enter into the same form of dependent sadomasochist relationship London had with Washington, but on a Europe-wide scale. The EU was to submit to a form of intellectual and technological bondage to the US, where Washington carried off the results with Europe unable to share or utilise the technology produced absent US authority. Equally, the very scale of funding exclusively available to the American scientific and technological community far outweighed anything in Europe. This could only result in a significant competitive boost for high-tech industries in the US. Perversely, some European governments argued the necessity for their companies and research institutes to participate in SDI to maintain a stake in the development of these new technologies, despite grave reservations about the military and political aims. Involvement would still come at a high price, with the diversion of European scientists and technicians away from European projects, and their self-inflicted seclusion in caches of American R&D within European companies.

In late March 1986 I travelled with the Japanese delegation to Tokyo. There Chris Drake, a friend working in a Japanese university, proposed that I write a guest editorial for Japan's biggest selling daily, the *Asahi Shimbun*. On 8 April they published 'An appeal to the people of Japan – don't play Star Wars.'[17] I argued Reagan's initial claim that the creation of an impenetrable umbrella would render nuclear weapons redundant was nonsense. Star Wars would accelerate, not slow, the superpower arms race. Washington was desperate for Tokyo to sign an MOU, but I was adamant they shouldn't do it. Japanese industry knew all too well that they were only being offered the crumbs from the table, and the US had no interest in allowing Japan – or Europe – to gain a competitive edge. It was for this reason that Japan's industry had proposed as an alternative the Human Frontier Science Program (HFSP). The only people backing Star Wars in Japan were the hand-picked members of Prime Minister Nakasone's think-tank, the Niju-Isseiki Vijon No-kai (Twenty-first Century Vision Study Association).

The SDI report was adopted in the ERT on 23 April 1986. The plenary debate was on 14 May, with the vote the following day. On behalf of the Socialist Group, I'd tabled the key paragraph 'No European participation in Star Wars' as an amendment, but this was defeated on the chairman's vote. Again, a party line vote, rejected 176–174. EPLP internal faction-fighting saw abstentions from the most unforgiving of Labour's Europhobes: Alex Falconer and Bob Cryer.[18] Teller got his way: sectarian talking points had it over the struggle for peace. In my plenary speech on the Wednesday, I conceded that SDI would work, just not as advertised. The realists in the Pentagon knew it was no impenetrable shield, but rather a new element in air tactical defence. After a first strike, even a leaky defence against the enemy's remnant second-strike weapons would mean the war would be 'won' by whoever hit the button first.

The plus side was that Star Wars alerted some in Europe to the yawning technology gap with the US, and the need for Europe to develop a coherent and well-resourced RD&D strategy. Europe was falling behind and, increasingly – outside the odd industrial sector – could not compete technologically with Japan and the US. In 1984 the French government had proposed EUREKA as a sort of civil parallel to Star Wars. I had long argued that case. While EUREKA initially

looked promising as such a vehicle with the European Community boosting R&D funding, in the end it disappointed with no overarching technological vision. Its resources were spread too thinly, project selection lacked coherence and lack of oversight saw projects surviving into their intellectual dotage.

I explained some of this in *El País*.[19] The US and Japan were advancing two distinct technological trajectories, with Tokyo spurred to respond to Washington's commitment to Star Wars as both military project and a surreptitious subsidising of its electro-mechanical high-tech industry. Japan's civil HFSP, in contrast, was to be built on international research collaboration in biology. Both were looking for EU participation. Admittedly, Tokyo's funding was six times smaller than Washington's, but that was not the crux. First, Star Wars would have EU companies not as partners but as mercenaries, with the results of research flowing to the US and no technological return back home. Second, it was hope not expectation that saw massive innovative spin-offs into civilian industry. The common view among the science policy establishment was that the space race had given the world the non-stick frying pan and little else.

論壇

日本のSDI参加に反対

核の恐怖知る大国の責任果たせ

グリン・フォード

An Appeal to the People of Japan – Don't Play Star Wars, op-ed Asahi Shimbun, 8 April 1986.

Japan's offer was a better fit for Europe, but even to take that up required the EU to get serious and stop squabbling over pocket change for FP2 and make real resources available. My 1988 EUREKA report demonstrated the necessity both for more funding and less top-down equivocation. This ruled it out as the motor to drive the EU's technological future. Instead, Brussels needed to create a European Technological Community with projects at its core that were environmentally sound and job-creating; that brought the industrial competitiveness of the EU's smaller nations up to level with the best, while pushing Europe to match and surpass American and Japanese technology at least in the majority of industrial sectors.

In committee I continued to push for Brussels to sign up to Japan's HFSP. In the end, supported by thirteen countries plus the EU, the programme established its secretariat in Strasbourg.[20] The Japanese White Paper on Science and Technology Policy (December 1986) laid down its key objectives as solving human problems and enhancing the quality of life for all. Its different approach was summarised by the importance it laid on the shift towards technologies that stimulate 'greater involvement in intellectual pursuit and creative family life.'

HFSP aimed at investigating the processes of nature and seeing how these could be replicated in the laboratory, then applying them to develop new technologies. This represented both Japan's coming out as an international scientific player and confirmed its willingness to promote alternative approaches where the focus – reflecting Japan's domestic practice (see above) – via the Ministry of International Trade and Industry, was pre-competitive R&D, pushed to within the shadow of marketisation. It worked, but it wasn't the answer. In its first ten years, Japan provided 82 per cent of the funding, setting an impressive precedent for R&D funding designed to marry the search for jobs with innovation.[21] It side-stepped the chronic duplication of effort prevalent in Europe, although that lesson remained unlearnt. Much of this was promoted by my regular column in *Research Fortnight*, assisted by one of the committee's staff members, Gordon Lake, who I'd known and worked with at Manchester University in the late 1970s and early 1980s. He was to die in tragic circumstances in 2002.

The Echelon affair

One hot issue in the radical science movement back in the late 1960s/1970s was the nature and extent of state surveillance.[22] One of the key texts was *The Technology of Political Control* (1977).[23] The EP – at the initiative of Rolf Linkhor, the Socialist coordinator on the ERT in the mid-1980s – decided

to follow the lead of the US Congress and establish an interface between science, technology and politicians. In 1972 Congress had established, encouraged by Edward Kennedy, the Office of Technology Assessment (OTA) to provide members and committees with authoritative analysis of complex issues where science and technology overlapped with politics. The whole idea was predicated on the use/abuse model of science and technology. Science was 'neutral', and as the National Rifle Association claims, 'guns don't kill people, people kill people'. My own more muscular position was outlined at the head of this chapter.

OTA closed in 1995, technically defunded – such an expressive euphemism! – after the 1994 midterm elections that saw the Republicans storm to victory under Newt Gingrich's 'Contract with America' banner. While one swallow does not make a summer, it did in retrospect signal the opening of a partisan divide that was two decades later to give birth to Trump. The claim was that OTA was wasteful and hostile to Republican plans. I offer no solace to the party of Lincoln, but they were half right: OTA exposed waste rather than created it. OTA had put the brakes on many a rash Republican programme founded on 'scientific' sand. 'Alternative facts' are so vulnerable in the face of reason. Unforgotten and unforgiven in the Republican's elephantine memory was OTA's comprehensive evisceration, over 325 pages, of the pretensions of Reagan's SDI programme.

In 1987 the EP launched its pale shadow: the Office for STOA. After the 1994 European elections I served on the STOA panel representing the Civil Liberties Committee. Nicky Hagar's *Secret Power: New Zealand's Role in the International Spy Network* had appeared in 1996, exposing 'Five Eyes' global espionage. In 1997, harking back two decades, I proposed an updating of the OTA's 1977 study. The updated study, 'An Appraisal of the Technology of Political Control', was nodded through by the panel. As normal, the work was contracted out, going to the Omega Foundation and Steve Wright, who had been in my department at Manchester University. The report, when it appeared, proved explosive. I had – mistakenly – presumed confirmation that Washington was long into equal-opportunity espionage would be nothing new to MEPs.

The report highlighted the Echelon electronic spy network, through which the 'Five Eyes' (US, UK, Canada, Australia and New Zealand) spied on the world for Washington, stating: 'The Echelon system forms part of the UKUSA system but unlike many of the electronic spy systems developed during the Cold War, Echelon is designed for primarily non-military targets: governments, organisations and businesses in virtually every country. The Echelon system works by indiscriminately intercepting very large quantities of communications and then siphoning out what is valuable using artificial intelligence aids like Memex.' In theory – at least – the five didn't know each other's targets. They each had their own 'dictionaries' run by the satellite interceptors and the product was downloaded to the recipients unread.

STOA immediately approved a comprehensive follow-up with a further five-part study of which Section 2, the Echelon section, was awarded to Duncan Campbell, an investigative journalist specialising in intelligence and security matters. It was subsequently published as 'Development of Surveillance Technology and Risk of Abuse of Economic Information.' It was a gift that kept on giving. Even Nicole Fontaine (EPP, France), the parliament president, waxed indignant. The EP, rather reluctantly, established a thirty-six-member Temporary Committee on the Echelon Interception System, with Carlos Coelho (EPP, Portugal) as chair and Gerhard Schmid (PES, Germany) as rapporteur. Having initiated the whole process, I was impertinently nominated by the then EPLP leader to the committee as a substitute. I refused. It wasn't just in the EP where the issue resonated. The farrago triggered parliamentary inquiries in France, Belgium and Italy. I produced a chapter for an edited volume titled *Human Rights and the Internet*, widening the remit to look at racism, pornography and paedophilia alongside covert spying and control by governments.[24]

In May 2001 a delegation from the committee was dispatched to Washington to meet officials from the CIA, National Security Agency and Department of Commerce. All were cancelled at the last minute by the US government, although the delegation did get to meet Nancy Pelosi, then in her role as Vice-Chair of the House Intelligence Committee, and Clinton's former CIA director James Woolsey. The US was

not the only member of the awkward squad. Both the British and Dutch governments refused to respond seriously to the committee's questions, although a committee delegation did at least get to meet Home Secretary Jack Straw in London.

The committee adopted its report in July 2001 and it went to the plenary that September. It proved a hot potato that no one from the major political groups and parties wanted to touch. Coelho later grumbled that 'everyone has chosen to forget this report and its conclusions'. The report had noted that the Echelon system had the capacity to carry out quasi-total surveillance with the ability to intercept any telephone, fax, internet or email message around the world and this global capacity was because of 'Five Eyes' collaboration. In case anyone had the slightest doubts, in March 2000 Woolsey told a press conference in Washington that of course the US used intelligence gleaned from satellite interceptions to aid US companies around the world – it was the only way to counter Europe's traditions of bribery and corruption.

Here's a conundrum. Edward Snowden's courage, commitment and sacrifice is to be applauded, but his *Permanent Record* (2019) was little more than a footnote to the EP's Echelon report, and even *The Technology of Political Control* more than forty years earlier. There is a serial amnesia that affects the political class who determine to forget what they prefer not to know. Russian and Chinese interference in democratic processes across the globe are amateur hour in comparison with Washington's activities since 1945. Here institutional memory seemed particularly short. Back in 2001, Philip Agee, the CIA whistleblower from the mid-1970s, came to Brussels and made the same point.[25]

Designing Descendants

During my first term as an MEP I was invited to present a BBC science programme on 'Gene Therapy'. Recent advances had made it possible to slice and splice the genetic code to correct faults causing a variety of illnesses. These cutting-edge experimental procedures were being used to treat various cancer patients in the National Institutions of Health (NIH) in

Washington DC. It was in itself a breakthrough, but it opened up major ethical issues as to the limits imposed on the use of the technique. Non-heritable somatic gene cells could be repaired in individuals with a faulty genetic code, but equally such cells delivering traits with the normal range could be enhanced. This posed a series of ethical questions. Where did the limit lie between repair and enhancement? Was it acceptable in making a necessary repair to enhance? You could choose to make your baby grow tall and therefore grow rich. In the US there is a positive correlation between height and wealth as Jeremy Rifkin, one of our interviewees, complained.

This was bad enough, but worse followed. Operating on germ cells, rather than somatic cells, meant repair and enhancement were inherited. While few would baulk at the repair of somatic cells, by the time individuals were paying millions to design their own descendants, for the overwhelming majority those red lines would have been well and truly crossed. A subsidiary issue was how insurance companies and others would handle gene mapping of clients. Would life insurance companies use evidence of adverse traits to impose premium charges on these individuals? Would chemical companies find it cheaper to select staff with a high resistance to chemical poisoning rather than to clean up the production environment? We filmed in the laboratories, the NIH and interviewed doctors, patients and consumer advocates. The programme asked the questions. We are still waiting for the answers.

Later in the EP I was to clash with the German SPD MEP Evelyne Gebhardt, who was running a campaign to ban the sex-testing of foetuses. I was entirely with her in stopping amniocentesis's use for selective abortions by those parents pushed by cultural coercion and – at the time – China's one-child policy to kill for a boy. However, in a limited number of cases there were sound medical reasons for sex determination and there was an example in my extended family with a variant of juvenile Tay-Sachs syndrome. Here boys – not girls – would because of a genetic disorder, have a fifty percent probability of suffering from the destruction of the nerve cells in the spinal cord exhibiting as seizures, and the gradual loss of hearing, speech and movement. Onset was between five and ten and from the first symptoms death would take three

to four years. Any family having watched its passage in one male child, should not be forced to spend a decade watching and wondering whether nature would impose the burden a second time.

Politics as sausages

It wasn't Otto von Bismarck who said, 'Laws are like sausages, it is better not to see them being made,' but rather the American lawyer-poet John Godfrey Saxe back in the 1860s. Yet it anticipated the EU institutions. In 1990 the ERT appointed me rapporteur for the revision of the Commission's Stimulation Plan for Economic Science (SPES), in which it looked to increase funding and widen the remit. At one level I was sympathetic, yet the promised evaluation of outcomes to date had not been presented to parliament, and the plan's wider footprint failed to stretch sufficiently to take on board the EP's demands for a better political balance among the projects selected and the incorporation within SPES of the economics of technical change and innovation. SPES was by no means the worst of the Commission's programmes; in fact, it was better than most. Nevertheless, a bird in the hand. We asked for SPES to be withdrawn. This would be a first: the Commission had never previously withdrawn a research proposal on parliament's request.

In committee my report was adopted unanimously, urging the Commission to withdraw its proposal as premature. It supported – subject to a positive evaluation – incorporating a fuller proposal within FP3. I met with Filippo Pandolfi, the Commissioner for Research and Development, who was accompanied by a clutch of Commission officials during the January plenary, to make my apparently futile plea. I was told that some staff were called back from leave for the meeting. Before we started the formal business it was clear Pandolfi was preoccupied. He admitted he just learnt that he had been caught, in a written answer to a parliamentary question tabled by the Labour MEP Llew Smith the previous September, misleading the parliament as regards a report evaluating wave energy.

He asked for my advice on how to extradite himself. I suggested a fulsome apology in plenary, admitting his unfortunate error, following which I would immediately intervene and state on behalf of the Socialist Group that we fully accepted the apology and as far as we were concerned the matter was closed. This amicably settled, we moved onto SPES. I said I wanted it withdrawn. Immediately, without a word from his officials, he responded 'yes.' The following morning in plenary we played our roles in the first act, with Pandolfi sweetening the pill by offering wave energy an additional ECU 1.2 million and a series of seminars.[26] The final act followed in February when the second shoe dropped. Pandolfi, in replying to the debate, announced he would propose to the College of Commissioners that the SPES proposal be withdrawn.

How did we do?

Quantitatively, the R&D element of the Union's budget has soared. Étienne Davignon's FP1 (1984–87) had a budget of €3.3 billion. The latest seven-year Horizon programme has €95.5 billion on the line. Institutionally, R&D is now built deep into the system. As early as 1986, the Single European Act incorporated a research chapter into the treaties, while 2000 saw the designation of a European Research Area and seven years later a European Research Council (ERC) to promote 'frontier research.' The two step-changes were 1984's ESPRIT programme that started a whole new line of work for which we have Davignon to thank, and 2006 when there was well over a doubling in research funding.

Qualitatively, there is less to celebrate. Fundamental research was a small fraction of FP1, but almost forty years on is now close to a fifth of the budget. Some of the ERC work is to be applauded, but the term 'frontier science' can so easily be weasel words for going back to basics. Direction is still in the hands of the same people. The ERC's argument that their programme restores some agency to the scientists themselves is a poor substitute for widening agency directing or financing R&D choices. Nevertheless, here the EU is doing no worse, if no better, than its member states, save the Dutch

with their science shops. At least – apart from the legacy of ITER – Brussels has avoided feeding and suborning its R&D funds to a parade of technological 'white elephants.'

Endnotes

[1] This was less true in the military sector. See my review of David Edgerton's *England and the Aeroplane* (1994) as 'Good in technology', *European Labour Forum*, Summer 1994. [2] See my review of Tim Tate's *Hitler's British Traitors* (2019) as 'Avarice and ideology', *Chartist* 301, November/December 2019. [3] See J. B. Bury (1920), *The Idea of Progress: An Inquiry into Its Origin and Growth*, London: Macmillan. [4] Glyn Ford (1992–93), 'Images of science and progress', *ENDPapers* 23, Winter. [5] J. Langrish et al. (1972), *Wealth from Knowledge: A Study of Innovation in Industry*, Stuttgart: Macmillan. [6] See Chapter 5 in Carlo Rovelli (2020), *Helgoland*, London: Allen Lane. [7] Glyn Ford (1978), 'Science in society: even the truth is relative', *Socialist Review* 4, July/August. [8] See my review of Stefan Kühl's, *The Nazi Connection* (1994) as 'An abuse of science', *European Labour Forum*, Winter 1994/5. [9] Thomas Kuhn (1962), *The Structure of Scientific Revolutions*, Chicago: University of Chicago Press. [10] Glyn Ford (1985), 'Peeling the ideological layers of science', *Afkar Inquiry* 2:8, August; (1984), 'Rebirth of Islamic science', in Ziauddin Sardar (ed.), *The Touch of Midas: Science, Values and Environment in Islam and the West*, Manchester: Manchester University Press; and (1978), *Review of Islamic Science: An Illustrated Study* (World of Islam Festival, 1976) by Seyyed Hossein Nasr, in *Gazelle Review* 4. [11] William Morris (1977), 'The Lesser Arts', Speech to the Trades' Guild of Learning, 4 December. [12] Glyn Ford and Ken Green (1984), 'A socialist science policy for Europe', *Tribune*, 7 December.

[13] Claude Julien (1984), 'Nouvelles chasses vieilles sorcières', *Le Monde Diplomatique*, January, www.monde-diplomatique.fr/1984/01/JULIEN/37795 (accessed 17 November 2021). The RPR-UDF was a union of two right-wing French political parties: Rally for the Republic (RPR) and Union for French Democracy (UDF). [14] Benedikt Härlin (1988), 'Biotechnology in Europe', *Science and Public Policy*, December. [15] Glyn Ford (1986), 'Star Wars secret could cost us dear', *Guardian*, 17 February. [16] E. P. Thompson (ed.) (1987), *Star Wars*, London: Penguin. [17] Glyn Ford (1986), 'An appeal to the people of Japan – don't play Star Wars' (in Japanese), *Asahi Shimbun*, 8 April. [18] Pollack (2009) gets this wrong, naming Alex Smith as one of those involved. Smith did not become an MEP until 1989. [19] Glyn Ford (1987), 'SDI, Eureka y Fronteras Humanas', *El País*, 28 September. [20] The EEC's fi-

nancial participation in HFSP coincided with the Fourth Framework Programme for Research and Technological Development (1994–98). *Telecomworldwire* (2000), 'Euro 1.5 million grant for EU participation in Human Frontier Science Program', *Telecomworldwire,* 20 September. [21] Richard Nathan (1999), 'Japan celebrates ten years of the HFSP', *Nature Medicine* 5:1, January. [22] See the section 'Science in society' in Chapter 3. [23] Carol Ackroyd *et al.* (1977), *The Technology of Political Control,* London: Penguin. [24] Glyn Ford (2000), 'The European Parliament and human rights on the internet', Chapter 3 in Steven Hick, Edward Halpin and Eric Hoskins (eds), *Human Rights and the Internet,* Stuttgart: MacMillan. [25] Philip Agee (1987), *On the Run,* New York: Lyle Stuart. [26] EP (1991), *Debates,* 24 January.

7 Hard Power, Soft Power and Trade

Si vis pacem, para bellum (If you want peace, prepare for war)

Renatus, De Re Militari

The toolbox of international relations has a series of instruments at its disposal. These are coercion, co-option and mutual economic interest. The EU spends the money, but fails to deliver on the first, punches above its weight on the second and on the third had – until very recently – a proactive, offensive and successful policy of trade promotion. If Europe is to voice its power, the three legs of the stool on which it stands must be equally strong and bound together in common purpose.

Tough choices

I supported both the first Gulf War's Operation Desert Shield (August 1990 – February 1991) and the October 2001 US invasion of Afghanistan, Operation Enduring Freedom. Both were, in my view, just wars in conception, if not in execution. Iraq's seizure of Kuwait was unacceptable and needed to be resisted, even if two decades earlier a similar Iraqi venture into Iran saw a welcome from Washington. During Desert Shield I was leader of the EPLP. There was precious little support among Labour MEPs for Kinnock's endorsement of Bush's military zeal, even under the imprimatur of the UN. It was a

fait accompli. The irrevocable build-up of troops and equipment was fully underway long before the UN Security Council voted for 'all necessary means' to force Iraq out of Kuwait. The war was preordained. In our last vote before military action, support for Labour's position in Westminster couldn't muster more than an unlucky thirteen votes in the EPLP.[1] Ambushed outside by waiting journalists, I argued that I appreciated why some Labour MEPs were sceptical, yet one of my best friends, a councillor back in Tameside, had a son on the frontline. The logic was unsound, but they seemed to buy it.

Afghanistan in the beginning was easier, not that we didn't jump the gun again. I got a call from a contact in the Armed Forces Parliamentary Scheme from inside Afghanistan weeks before we 'invaded'. Yet there was an evidential chain of cause and effect. Osama bin Laden and Al Qaeda were responsible and proud of the carnage unleashed on America on 9/11, and they were deeply entrenched in Afghanistan with the ruling Taliban refusing to expel them. There was just cause. Questionable was the war's subsequent metamorphosis with expeditionary force turning into an army of occupation, while retribution stepped up to remaking and remodelling the country. Overreach and overstay made the cure worse than the disease as Afghanistan became the unacknowledged martial side dish to Iraq. In an afterthought, Afghan women were weaponised by the West to justify conquest while turning a convenient blind eye to their oppression in Bin Laden's homeland. That was all to come.

I was part of an AFET visit to Kabul, Mazar-i-Sharif and Kandahar in 2003 that was led by Philippe Morillon, the former French general who had commanded the UN forces in Bosnia (1992–93). We flew out from Kabul to Kandahar and Mazar-i-Sharif, and met the latter's colourful warlord Abdul Rashid Dostum and the country's monochrome president Hamid Karzai. Retrospection is a perfect science, but from Bagram air base, the armed convoys and soldiers riding shotgun that we needed to travel around town and the guards necessary to shop in Fish Street, all suggested President Karzai's fetch didn't extend much further than Kabul. The general situation didn't get better. The allies misled millions, building a house of cards that promptly collapsed immediately once external support was removed, sacrificing their fools to the mercies of a misogynist cult.

My opposition to the second Gulf War and Operation Enduring Freedom in March 2003 was more straightforward. Some years earlier, I'd been in a delegation to Syria and Iraq under the auspices of the Arab League. We had a long meeting with Tariq Aziz, Iraqi foreign minister and a Chaldean Catholic. There was no question Saddam Hussein's Ba'athist regime was barbaric. Towards the end of the Iran–Iraq War in 1988, they doused the Iranian occupied Kurdish town of Halabja with mustard gas, killing men, women and children in their thousands, which was immediately, roundly and rightly condemned by the EP; even if Tony Blair failed to sign the corresponding early day motion in the House of Commons. Saddam's treatment of dissidents was savage. Yet for all that, the Ba'athists were no Islamic fundamentalists – some, like Aziz, were not even Muslims. It was a semi-secular ideology with a light touch of Islam and I knew from my work on the arms trade (see below) that the West had encouraged, resourced and subsidised Saddam's Iran–Iraq War (1980–88) as a proxy fight against Islamic fundamentalism. What had changed in the meantime was Washington's interests and inclinations rather than Saddam's.

The notion that Saddam was acting in consort with Al Qaeda was for me as credible as the Papacy conspiring in joint enterprise with the Reverend Ian Paisley. I had been in Strasbourg in October 1988 when the said Reverend was forcibly removed from the chamber, screeching and screaming 'the Antichrist' as Pope John Paul II began his solemn address. In May I went on record, sceptical of the 'transparently thin case for Iraq – Al Qaeda links made in the *New Yorker* 25 March.'[2] Certainly, some in Washington were hunting a reason for war after Saddam threatened to denominate his oil sales in euros, which would have threatened, in the long term, the dollar's lock on global trade.

The goalposts were moved with claims that Saddam had weapons of mass destruction (WMD). It was both indisputable and unlikely. In 1983 during the war with Iran, Donald Rumsfeld went, with Reagan's blessing, to help prop up Saddam's regime, which was losing the war to Tehran and its Revolutionary Guard. Subsequently, billions of dollars poured into

Baghdad along with cluster bombs and anthrax. Yet there was justified scepticism that these WMDs survived through the first Gulf War and its aftermath. Hans Blix, as head of the UN Monitoring, Verification and Inspection Mission, scoured Iraq in 2002 looking for WMDs, to no avail. Absence of evidence is sometimes evidence of absence.

This time I was the EPLP foreign affairs spokesperson and thus a member of Labour's foreign affairs team that met weekly in the Foreign and Commonwealth Office (FCO). Headed by Jack Straw as foreign minister, its other members included the ministers of state Denis MacShane and Baroness Symons of Vernham Dean, their parliamentary private secretaries and the party's foreign affairs staff. In the long march to war, cued by Bush's State of the Union address describing Iraq, Iran and North Korea as the 'Axis of Evil', the constant call was for hard evidence of WMDs to quell the growing scepticism among backbench Labour MPs. The 'dodgy dossier' (or, more formally, *Iraq – Its Infrastructure of Concealment, Deception and Intimidation*), praised before its release both by Tony Blair and Colin Powell as quality research, was designed to still those credulous voices. Published in February 2003, it was the cobbling together of a mess of material that had as its bottom a thirteen-year-old US student thesis. Powell's own performance two days later at the UN seemed more convincing with 'facts and conclusions based on solid evidence'. Both dossiers were bespoke military fairy tales crafted and drafted to retro-fit evidence to justify decisions long made.

Looking from the inside out made things appear worse, not better. With the 20 March invasion I'd had enough. Many were prepared to defend the indefensible, but I refused to be one of that number. It wasn't so much the illegality of the war – few wars meet that yardstick – but the moral bankruptcy and the full spectrum of imbecility on military, political, economic and cultural grounds. In contrast, Gary Titley, then EPLP leader, delighted in the foreplay: 'We must prepare to go to war. I am particularly proud of the courage, nerve and clear-sighted vision that have been shown by my party leader and I wish a few more party leaders would do the same.'[3] I therefore resigned as Labour's foreign affairs spokesman. Richard Howitt was only too eager to leap into my still-warm seat.

The hawks and patsies had their revenge and reward after the 2004 European elections. Titley addressed the survivors of a disappointing election and argued that Labour's nineteen MEPs needed to work to maximise their influence in the Socialist Group (S&D). He would do whatever was necessary to help. I gullibly took him at his word, telling him I'd been approached by several Socialist MEPs asking me to stand as coordinator and foreign affairs spokesperson for the group. Subsequently, Gary told me he had, unfortunately, only been able to secure a single full-member's place on AFET, which had to, of necessity, go to Richard Howitt. It didn't add up. There was alternative arithmetic on the right. Britain's Conservatives, with twenty-seven MEPs, secured four seats. On that maths, with nineteen MEPs Labour had a reasonable claim for three, at the very least two places. Reduced to a substitute on the committee, I was ineligible to stand as coordinator. It went to Veronique De Keyser, one of the S&D MEPs who'd offered me her support.

A single market in arms: production, exports and conversion

To step back, in my second term in the parliament I'd been a member of the Security and Disarmament Subcommittee of AFET. The change of name from the Political Affairs Committee came in 1992. There I was responsible for a trio of reports on the arms trade, the first for the committee itself (1989) and the second and third for the subcommittee in 1992 and 1994. Until 1989 there was no consensus on security and defence. It was an impasse, with neither the federalist right's demands for an independent, integrated EU defence policy and capacity nor the left nationalist arguments for less defence spending and more arms conversion commanding a majority. I thought it possible to square the circle by assembling a package that gave something to both camps. The starting point was the Cecchini Report of 1988, 'The Cost of Non-Europe in the Single Market.' A single market for arms could deliver for both: Europe could spend less and get more. There could be a viable European military deterrent that freed up both labour and capital for the high-tech civil economy.

I have an aversion to war, but I'm not a pacifist. I'd share Aneurin Bevan's position: 'I am not and have never been a conscientious objector. I will fight, but I'll choose my own enemy, and my own battlefield, and I won't have you do it for me.'[4] In Washington, might overshadows right, as martial strength towers over debilitated diplomacy. Thus, for a country whose prime tool is military, the answer to every question is armed force. It's Maslow's hammer – if the only tool you have is a hammer, every problem is a nail. Therefore, the EU needs its own independent security and defence policy reflecting interests that will not always align with Washington and the capability to protect and project those interests. Am I in favour of a European army? Absolutely. Do I want to use it? Only rarely, with war the last resort.

The defence budgets of the then twelve member states combined made the EU the world's second-biggest military spender. Few would have credited it. EU member states spent the money singularly and badly. There was only the most basic interoperability between the military forces, and worse, in planning to fight the last war rather than the next, the larger states, in particular, procured the wrong weapons and equipment. As Yugoslavia shattered into history's ethnic fragments, the EU lacked the heavy lift capacity to intervene in its near abroad, leaving us spectators to Serbian and other atrocities and the journey's end for the hundreds of thousands fleeing the slaughter. We were dependents of Washington. Clinton hesitated before reluctantly intervening and, after the event, George W. Bush said he wouldn't have intervened at all. If that wasn't a wake-up call, no one had yet invented the alarm.

Incompetence is a fault, but waste a sin. There were free-standing independent arms industries in every large member state – and some of the smaller – with captive national markets. Yet demand in many sub-sectors was so limited, manufacturers were reduced to batch rather than mass production, absent economies of scale. In the struggle to boost demand for the required production runs, reckless arms sales were extended to the good, the bad and the ugly. The biggest threat to the Falklands Task Force in 1982 was French military technology rather than Galtieri's conscripts, with the British fleet facing Argentina's Super Étendard fighter jets from Dassault-Breguet armed with Exocet anti-ship missiles from Aèrospatiale. Resolving this paradox was simple. The creation of a single market in arms would – over time – deliver intra-European operability, economies of scale and an end to the imperative to export. The bonus was that the creative destruction of this wider market would liberate tens of thousands of the most highly qualified scientists and engineers available to be siphoned off into tomorrow's industries; shifted out of Europe's military-industrial complex and into the high-tech civilian economy, they would enhance EU competitiveness with the US and Japan, as common arms production and procurement saw less delivering more.

There were two stumbling blocks to arresting our persistent self-harming. First was Article 223 of the Treaty of Rome, or rather more precisely its Section 1(b), allowing member states to disavow the merits of the single market to advantage domestic arms manufacturers on the grounds of 'the protection of the essential interests of its security'.[5] Second was 'neutrality'. Back then it was just Ireland after Sean MacBride turned down Ireland's invitation to NATO's founding conference in 1949, but spread with enlargement like a rash to Austria, Finland, Malta and Sweden. Neutrality between Washington and Moscow made some sense before the arms race blew up the Soviet Empire, but neutral as regards your own security has a senseless imprudence. European problems require European solutions. Following Russia's invasion of Ukraine in February 2022 the earth finally moved. Both Finland and Sweden applied to join NATO in May, while in June Denmark voted, with more than a two-thirds majority, in a referendum to end its opt-out on European Defence and Security Co-operation.

Round One

My first report for the Political Affairs Committee on European Arms Exports noted a slackening in the growth of global arms sales since the late 1970s. The fall in commodity prices had left Global South governments strapped for cash. Others had completed their military inventory back then and were now only updating and renovating. At the same time

there was increased competition with the club of European arms manufacturers gaining new members from Greece, Spain and Austria. Developing economies, like Brazil, South Korea and India, were looking to import substitution and indigenous industry, manufacturing and buying at home rather than abroad. Even assessing the extent of the trade lay between difficult and impossible. Governments were even at times reluctant to supply data specifying what constituted a 'military export,' while the complexities of countertrade (see below) and offsets made anything more than an educated guess of trade volume impossible.[6]

The report attempted to assess and summarise the arms industries and export policies of seven member states, incorporating a case study of EU arms exports in relation to the Iran–Iraq war. Europe leant towards Saddam Hussein and away from the Ayatollah Khomeini. Iraq was the West's proxy partner in fighting Shia fundamentalism and securing future fuel supplies through Saddam's attempt to annex Iran's oil-rich Khuzestan province. Iraq's sixteen million people were scarcely a third of Iran's forty-eight million, but in terms of delivery of military equipment in quantity and quality it was Baghdad that dominated a buyers' market.

When Iraq invaded in 1980, Tehran was in the chaotic aftermath of its 1979 revolution, with depleted military stocks and morale. Its equipment was last-generation US hardware from the Shah's time, with spare parts consequently at a premium.[7] The American hostage crisis in 1983 made the bad worse. Meanwhile, in 1986 Iraq sourced 55 per cent of its arms from the USSR, 20–25 per cent from France. Indeed, 'During the course of the war France sold more than $5.6 billion worth of arms to Iraq,' for which Iraq paid with a mix of countertrade and cash.[8] Iran, in contrast, struggled to source arms and spare parts even on the illegal arms market. They turned to Beijing and Pyongyang, where what was lacking in quality and sophistication was compensated in availability. Starting in 1986, these two supplied 70 per cent of Iran's arms. It was North Korea's inconstant Hwasong-5s that were Tehran's answer to the more up-market questions posed by Baghdad in the 'War of the Cities.'

The West's preference in favouring Iraq over Iran did not prevent certain member states from, either wilfully or unknowingly, supplying both sides. Arms merchants with consciences are rarer than Persia's manticores. Dollars know no politics. Even when they were acquainted, first-exporters have little ultimate control over end user or end target. The report concluded – rather weakly – that the necessity for export sales as a way to reduce unit costs through longer production runs could be alleviated by European political cooperation in security and defence, laying down a common arms export policy 'necessary for maintaining European security', which would simultaneously strengthen the effectiveness of arms embargoes.[9]

Round Two

When the first report was drafted, Gorbachev was still in the Kremlin and the Soviet Union in existence. By 1992 it was a world transformed. This second report, focused on the interaction among arms production, arms exports and arms conversion, largely spoke for itself. Initially seen as an addendum to my first report, it was hijacked by what proved an armistice in the long Cold War, and conflict in the Gulf, while in Brussels the completion of the single market was back high on the agenda.

> *With regard to the single market, high-technology industry is reorganising itself into a smaller number of larger corporations. Article 223 of the Treaty of Rome is endangering this process and undermining European competitiveness in areas where there are dual-use technologies. The very Europeanisation of industry with longer production runs in the defence industry also removes the imperative to export by sharply lowering production costs. And of course, we also have the experience of the Gulf War, where we faced our own weapons across the desert.*[10]

It called for the deletion, or at least a restricted interpretation, of Article 223. The prospect of half a million workers in the wider defence sector losing their jobs in the next two or three

years argued for intervention on moral, technological and economic grounds.

> *The pool of skills available for use by the European Community must not be allowed to evaporate. In Europe we require these groups to be moved into new high-technology industries, the industries where we are going to compete in the future. If it was right for the Community to intervene in the sunset industries in the past, the steel industry, the coal industry, the textile industry and the shipbuilding industry, with a whole series of programmes, it must be just as important, if not more important, and equally right, that we intervene to allow the sunrise industries of the future to be created ... What we really want are proposals from the Commission to deal with the problems of conversion in the arms industry in consultation with the workforce.*

If the Commission seized the time, threat could become hope. Decisions on arms exports needed a political and humanitarian overlay when selling to third-country governments:

> *We need to look at their human and civil rights record and make sure that they will not be used to oppress populations that are unhappy with governments that are tyrannical. We need to look at the security situation in the region in question and not add fuel to regional conflicts. We need to make sure that we limit arms exports so that countries have a defensive capability, but not the capability for offence. [For Central and Eastern Europe and the former Soviet Union] we need to give aid and assistance to them in helping with the arms conversion programme, so that instead of producing tanks, they can produce televisions. We need to give advice to them as to how industries which have been cost-plus in the past, and with priority access to raw materials, can become competitive.*

> *We also have to deal with what is now a flea market in second-class, second-hand weapons, some of which, I am sure, are ending up in former Yugoslavia. These are being sold for little more than scrap value in exchange for hard currency from the countries of Central and Eastern Europe and the former Soviet Union ... We require an intervention scheme to buy up and scrap those weapons that are becoming available on the market. It will be cheaper to do that than fighting wars directly or by proxy in the future.*[11]

The report concluded, 'one of the most important things we can do is to start to create the institutional architecture whereby we can speak with one voice rather than twelve'.

Round Three

Two years later in 1994 the world had clicked on again, although the messaging reverberated from before: the world had seen the collapse of the Soviet Union and the end of the superpower stand-off, a Gulf War fought by the Allies against Iraq, and the outbreak of the interlocking set of civil wars in former Yugoslavia and the ex-Soviet Union.[12] Now there was no excuse for inaction with an economic moment of opportunity; keeping together the teams of highly skilled scientists and engineers would mean 'they can start the new high-technology industries of the future to compete with Japan and with the United States'. Retraining and arms conversion were needed both in EU countries – such as the UK – and those of Central and Eastern Europe. In the latter, I suggested buy-back should be used to take conventional weapons out of the market. More dangerously, I noted, 'we have now virtually third world countries with nuclear capacity and we must use carrots and, if necessary, sticks to ensure the destruction of these weapons as a step towards removing the threat from around the world'.

All three reports were carried with good majorities in committee and plenary. Hans-Gert Pöttering (EPP, German), the

subcommittee's chair and later EP president, was only too delighted for the log-jam to be finally broken. Today the Union remains the world's second-largest military spender. The budget is still spent in twenty-seven different ways, hostage to national preference.[13] Nevertheless, there is progress. Article 223 lives on, renumbered in the new Treaty on the Functioning of the European Union as Article 346, yet member states are now goaded forward by Josep Borrell, the High Representative for CFSP, after the dead hand of London was lifted.

I proselytised the messages from Genoa to Glasgow, Brussels to Brighton. UNITE the Union had me speak to their Defence Industry Group, who were all too familiar with Mike Cooley and his Lucas alternative corporate plan (mentioned in Chapter 6), which proposed to replace weapons manufacture with the production of socially useful products. I also did a series of events with the NGO Saferworld and one of its senior staff Struan Stevenson, including at the Labour Party Conference in Blackpool. I was slightly taken aback when in 1999 Struan appeared in Strasbourg as a Tory MEP. Further afield, I travelled to Miami and Istanbul with the EP's delegation to the NATO Parliamentary Assembly. At the first of these, there was an American proposal to make the use of 'dirty bombs' crimes against humanity. I suggested, to much laughter, that maybe the crime was worse if a nuclear weapon actually worked to specification. Washington's representatives let the matter drop.

Europe's forward march was on show when in 2008 a subcommittee delegation visited Thessaloniki and Nicosia to inspect some of the first battlegroups established under the EU's Common Security and Defence Policy. Welcomed by UN Secretary-General Kofi Annan in 2004 as a help to the UN in tackling trouble spots, they comprise eighteen battalion-size units that went operational in 2007, whose component parts are drawn from variable geometry coalitions of member states. Two are on standby for instant deployment. While the troops are ready, it's the politicians that are tardy. It was certainly wise to avoid the quagmire of Libya, but their utility in the Democratic Republic of the Congo seemed self-evident to everyone apart from Europe's foreign ministers. Instead, the EU has been all at sea. Off the Horn of Africa, Operation Atalanta – formally EU Naval Force

Somalia – is Brussels' counter-piracy deployment, launched in December 2008 and still on station today. Nineteen member states – plus the UK while in the EU – have been part of the force cooperating both with the US and NATO.

Thwarting Trident

European defence and security should reflect today's and tomorrow's collective interests and be a substitute for national pretensions rather than merely feed the beast from the past. One of Blair's last acts as prime minister was to call for a vigorous debate on the Trident missile programme. David Martin and myself were happy to engage. We wrote in the *Morning Star*:

> *We are not arguing military spending should fall, rather the opposite. If anything, British defence spending should rise, but it must be used to give us the capacity to fight tomorrow's battles rather than yesterday's wars that never were, and it must help us create a European Union Common Foreign and Security Policy (CFSP) that allows us in the absence of the US to intervene in our own 'near abroad.' Renewing Trident is arming Britain to fight the wrong war ... Tomorrow's wars will be fighting the Taliban and Al Qaeda whose weapons of choice are the assassin's bullet, the terrorist bomb, rather than the ICBM. You cannot take them out with heavy footprint nuclear weapons, rather requiring the delicate stiletto of Special Forces and precision guided weapons ... Britain should be taking the lead in promoting continent at the expense of country as it is this that will ultimately make our country more secure in contrast to the narrow nation state approaches left over from the Cold War.*[14]

In retrospect, Gordon Brown had counted the votes long before the conclusion of the debate. In the interests of pandering to male machismo, he was determined Britain would waste

its money on weapons to fight yesterday's wars controlled by proxies in Washington rather than reshore the purchase point back across the Atlantic to Europe and the technology for insurrectionary conflict and not country-on-country wars.

Ford Major

Training with Clare Ward MP as part of the Armed Forces Parliamentary Scheme on the Macal River, Belize.

It took me decades to realise that the problem with military conflicts are the politicians, not the soldiers. Many politicians are so unknowing, they neither appreciate military capacity nor its limitations. It was not entirely their fault. Conscription in Britain ended in 1960, with the last national servicemen discharged in 1963. The result was that with the passage of time, fewer and fewer MPs – particularly on the Labour benches – had any military background or experience. In 1989 the former Conservative MP Sir Neil Thorne set up the Armed Forces Parliamentary Scheme, designed to expose serving politicians to first-hand experience. Initially restricted to MPs and members of the House of Lords, it was extended to British MEPs when Geoff Hoon, a former MEP himself, became Secretary of State for Defence in 1999. I was its first recruit, 'joining' the Royal Marines as a major. My mentor was Major Andy Mason who shepherded our cohort through its paces.

To graduate the programme, you needed twenty-two days in the field. There was cold-weather training in Romania, where – I think – I learnt how to build and shelter in an igloo. Tropical training took place in Belize, where I was allowed to take off and fly a fully loaded helicopter – for some reason there was a reluctance to let me land it. I swam a crocodile-infested river in full kit, with my rifle perched on top of my floating kit bag, with soldiers on both banks ready to shoot any of the river's reptilian inhabitants who got overly inquisitive.

They weren't needed, but that didn't mean I wasn't pleased to see them. The upside was a visit to the Mayan ruins of Xunantunich by helicopter. It did not land, rather winched us down and came back a couple of hours later to literally pick us up.

We invaded Portugal from HMS *Ocean*, flying in low on helicopters to bundle out as they hovered in the dark, and later exfiltrated by wading out to the ship's landing craft that were bobbing offshore – I presume someone had told Lisbon we were visiting. Too realistic was a visit to Kosovo, where in Pristina the Royal Marines were part of the NATO-led Kosovo Force keeping the warring communities apart. I was sent out on patrol with a group of marines whose weapons were loaded with live rounds. This was not a drill.

I guarded Britain's nuclear weapons in Faslane. There you were in full kit on one minute's notice. There were five layers of security and after breaching layer three, things became serious with shoot-to-kill orders. Protestors could make their point and jump a couple of fences, but there was a limit. The threat scenario they prepared for was a breach by a team of six to eight who would pick up a 150-kilogram bomb, with four carrying it away on a litter as the others steered them out. Just as I arrived, Green MEP Caroline Lucas phoned me. I'm sure we had company on our call. Later I was invited to the UK Defence Academy near Swindon to debate Europe with UKIP's Godfrey Bloom – a man whose views were so far onto the further shores of politics that even UKIP was eventually forced to withdraw the whip. Ex-Territorial Army, he had the audience on his side until he suggested those failing to share his views were 'traitors.' Not a word to use lightly in a military setting, sympathy died and his tide of support went out.

Indonesian exploits

Edward Bulwer-Lytton was not entirely accurate when he said in 1839, 'The pen is mightier than the sword.' Nevertheless, he had a point. The year 2004 saw the first peaceful transition of power in Indonesian history with direct presidential elections. Two hundred and seventy million people make the archipelago the world's fourth-largest country and largest

Muslim state, with just shy of a hundred and fifty million electors, spread across six and a half thousand inhabited islands arching across three time zones from India to Australia. I was there as the EU's chief election observer. Brussels has long seen election observation missions as a value-for-money means of promoting stability and democracy. In elections, the root problem lies not with winners revelling in victory, rather with the opposition wallowing in defeat. They – and their supporters – need to acknowledge they have lost and lost fairly. This was not understood by many in the West prior to Trump's demonstrable tantrums after his November 2020 defeat by Biden.

Brussels only sends a European Union Election Observation Mission (EUEOM) when invited. That does not mean some invitations are not dragged from grasping hands. The invitation from Jakarta was squeezed out of Megawati Sukarnoputri's government like old toothpaste from a tube. EU Commissioner for External Affairs Chris Patten made it clear that any absence of Brussels oversight would have political and economic consequences. Indonesia's foreign minister Nur Hassan Wirajuda reluctantly proffered the invite. The EUEOM was gatecrashing the party and the host was less than thrilled. Bringing Wirajuda around took time and tobacco. During one of our first meetings, we discovered we'd both spent time in Pyongyang. He complained how cold and miserable he'd been one winter, isolated in North Korea's state guesthouse on the periphery of Pyongyang. I knew exactly how he felt: it had been my place of custody on my first visit. Wirajuda confessed he resorted to smoking. When we met again for the next phase of the elections I presented him with a carton of two hundred *Glory*, Pyongyang's finest. I'm pretty certain he never smoked them, but relations skipped to a different level.

EP observation missions saw between four and eight MEPs spending a short week centred around election day. EU missions, in multi-round elections, could stretch to six months and more. It had been during the Cambodian elections in 2003 – when I had been the EP's chief election observer (see below) – that I had recognised the value of EUEOMs and the controlling hand of the chief observers. It was around then when the EU decided that in future all chief observers were to be MEPs with an independent mandate. When the Indonesian elections came in sight, I phoned Patten and lobbied for the post. He put my name forward to the Council of Ministers and it was nodded through. It was to be – at the time – the EU's largest ever EOM, where over the immediate election period with expat and local staff we had over thirteen hundred staff on the ground. I spent eighty-four days in country. Even at that scale, the cost of the entire mission was three and a half hours' spending in Iraq.[15]

I'd first been to Indonesia in 1999 as a UN expert advising the newly 'liberated' parliament on redrafting its rules of procedure. I had recommended 'radical rules' that would allow MPs to speak without permission from their party leaders, and I cast the gravest doubts on the democratic merits of maintaining a bloc of appointed army officers among the parliament's members. I was grateful that the composition and nature of the UK's House of Lords had passed the Dewan Perwakilan Rakyat (People's Representative Council – DPR) by.[16] This army/police bloc disappeared with the 2004 election.

The EU was far from having an exclusive franchise on election observation with other – sometimes complementary, sometimes competing – missions from the Organization for Security and Co-operation in Europe (OSCE), the Republican National Committee, the Carter Center and a bureaucracy of governments all joining in. Initially, the yardstick to be met was 'free and fair' elections. Experience quickly demonstrated this was too narrow a window. A number of countries, including Indonesia and its neighbour Singapore, easily met and matched those criteria with election carnivals lasting a fortnight or so, where the world was turned upside down and repressed parties and politicians were allowed to stand, fleetingly campaign and even on occasion get elected.

The real constraints on 'free and fair' were past and future. The years running up to an election would see unremitting press, publicity and propaganda in favour of the ruling party. But for those foolish enough to confuse fiesta with normal business there was a comeuppance. Results were closely monitored, and constituencies, villages and even polling stations where the opposition did well – let alone had the temerity to win – faced reprisals. Retribution by omission saw no new roads, medical centres or schools, with all government

investment frozen. Thus, from 2000, Brussels adopted a wider and deeper remit for EOMs. This subtler sieve was the ability to vote, stand and campaign, access to the media, the impartiality of the electoral commission and the state, and polling, counting and resolution of disputes.

Jakarta's system had its flaws and imperfections. The most significant clustered around the ability to stand. The long Indonesian nation was burning its democratic candle at both ends. Aceh was in the throes of a thirty-year-long insurrection with the Guerakan Acèh Meurdèka (Free Aceh Movement – GAM) seeking independence, while Irian Jiya (West Papua) faced a disorganised low intensity conflict with similar aims. As a result, in order to stifle their political manifestations, Jakarta drafted rules for party formation to prevent the emergence of regional parties.

The ability of individuals to stand was compromised with health and education tests. The first disbarred a previous president, Gus Dur (Abdurrahman Wahid), for his partial blindness. David Blunkett was no help. The second were towering social barriers for people without formal education and women. This was institutionalised in Aceh in the form of a Quran reading test organised by clerics that saw not a single female candidate pass. True, this could be side-stepped by self-declaring as a non-Muslim candidate, but this cure was worse than the disease. In a province where 98 per cent of the population are Muslim, it was not a vote-winning strategy.

Worse was the ban on former members of the Partai Komunis Indonesia (PKI) and their descendants from standing. In many provinces, it was even unclear as to whether they were allowed to vote. It was history. Back in 1965 under President Sukarno, the PKI was one of the three legs – along with the army and the forty-million-strong Muslim organisation Nahdlatul Ulama (NU) – of an uneasy coalition propping up a left-leaning regime that was a thorn in the side of London and Washington with its threats to US oil interests and the territorial integrity of Malaysia with Sukarno's *Konfrontasi* (Confrontation) policy. An incoherent and cack-handed failed *coup d'état* on 30 September by elements of the PKI was a pretext for mass murder, egged on by black propaganda from Britain's security services that would have been farcical if it hadn't been fatal. The result was a savage genocide with between five hundred thousand and one million of the PKI's two million members and sympathisers sadistically murdered. Started by the army, with the knowledge, complicity and support of not only Britain but also America and Australia, the death squads' work was then subcontracted out to NU – who had turned on their erstwhile allies – various Christian groups and village gangs. The butchery bested Stalin, Hitler and Mao at their most savage. A 'luckier' million ended up in concentration camps where tens of thousands died of starvation, disease and brutality. The survivors and their descendants remain second-class citizens.

Early on in Jakarta, I insisted on calling on the most prominent victim just to make the point to the authorities. Pramoedya Ananta Toer had fought the Dutch in Indonesia's war of liberation and spent two years in prison as a result. Following independence, he had become the country's most famous novelist and a political irritant to Sukarno. Arrested as a communist after the failed coup, he served another stint in prison, this time well over a decade, and was only released in 1979 into house arrest where he remained until 1992. For the decade 1969–79, he was held in a remote island penal colony, denied even pencil and paper. His answer was to write his books in his head, reciting them like a *hakawati* to fellow inmates. The result was four novels – the *Buru Quartet*, named after the island where he and thousands of others were incarcerated, brutalised and died – and *A Mute's Soliloquy*, his prison notebook. In 2004 the ban on his books in Indonesia was just beginning to lift. He was deaf, and so for him were the politicians, thus he expected nothing from the election. He may just have been mildly surprised.

The election was to have three phases. In April there were to be simultaneous elections for the national parliament – both the lower house DPR and the upper house regional representative council, Dewan Perwakilan Daerah (DPD) – alongside the provincial and district assemblies. Then to follow in early July and late September was a two-round presidential election, for which only parties that had obtained 5 per cent of the national vote could nominate presidential candidates. The April elections were the largest and most complex ever held on a single day worldwide. The Komisi Pemilihan Umum (General Elections Commission – KPU)

managed the enormously challenging task of delivering more than 600 million ballot papers in 2286 variations to over half a million polling stations, where 148 million voters were entitled to vote for the two houses of parliament (DPR, DPD) as well as provincial and regency councils with a total of 350,000 candidates running for office.

My responsibility was to make political decisions relating to the mission, and draft the interim and final reports with my core team judging the election's bona fides. During the campaign, parties boosted audiences at their rallies with the provision of 'petrol money' to even those arriving on foot. I was pressured to condemn the practice. Instead, I went on national TV urging voters to take the money and then cast their vote elsewhere.

The electoral system chosen for April was dysfunctional. The root of the problem was the decision to have open rather than closed lists of candidates – allowing individual voters in theory to override the preferences of party managers. This increased the complexity of the count by several orders of magnitude, as with more candidates than Luxembourg has voters, it generated four hundred million results, the overwhelming majority of which read zero; as a consequence, the count was not finalised for a month. Worse, it served no purpose. The threshold required to climb the rungs of the open list was set so high that the mission was not aware of a single case where any candidate of any party beat the system and got elected.[17] Other problems followed. Nazaruddin Sjamsuddin, the chair of the KPU who I met frequently during my time in Jakarta, had other things on his mind. In May and December 2005, he faced two trials for financial corruption associated with the printing of those ballot papers. The result was seven years imprisonment and a fine of twenty billion rupiah (close to €1 million).

In the run-up to July's first round of the presidential elections, I met the two leading candidates: the challenger Susilio Bambang Yudhoyono (known as SBY) from the new Partai Demokrat (Democratic Party – PD), and the incumbent Megawati Sukarnoputri from the Partai Demokrasi Indonesia – Perjuangan (Indonesian Democratic Party – Struggle – PDI-P). Wiranto, the candidate of the political wing of the military, refused to meet me. His Partai Golongan Karya

(Party of the Functional Groups – Golkar) had finished a bad first in the parliamentary elections because the PDI-P had managed even worse as voters switched in numbers to the smaller parties. SBY's PD had beaten the barrier with 7.5 per cent. The result was Golkar and Wiranto were bitter when they finished third in the presidential contest with only 22.2 per cent of the votes after the first round, behind SBY on 33.5 per cent and Megawati on 26.6 per cent. Wiranto blamed the KPU and the EUEOM, claiming 5.4 million votes had been stolen. The Constitutional Court didn't agree and upheld the initial result. The second round in September saw SBY – and his deputy, Jusuf Kalla – win with 60.6 per cent to Megawati's 39.4 per cent.

We faced difficulties in getting all our observers where we wanted them, thrice thwarted by civil society, corporations and government. There had been resistance from the authorities over the nationality of our initial deployments to both Aceh and Irian Jaya. The problem in Aceh was Swedish. Stockholm had granted political asylum to the GAM leaders of the insurrection. In Irian Jaya it was the Dutch, with the province their colony until 1969, when in a highly contentious plebiscite, tribal leaders were coerced into opting into Indonesia. After my rapprochement with Wirajuda, I provided him with the CVs of our long-term observers in the two provinces. They were neither Swedish, nor Dutch, and the barriers to deployment were raised.

The other problems were with individual polling stations and districts. This was particularly acute within the large *madrassas* (Islamic schools). The schools were closed off to outsiders – especially women. At two of them, 100 per cent of all possible votes went to the same Islamic candidates – unnerving and impressive. At others, our observers arrived thirty minutes after the polls opened to find everyone had voted. We could never pull off the same feat in the UK with voters forgetful or indifferent, having a mind of their own or simply misreading the ballot paper. Polling stations on land owned and controlled by mining multinationals were equally inaccessible. The Grasberg mine, near Timika, is the world's largest gold mine and the second-largest copper mine. Majority owned by Freeport-McMoRan, with reserves of a hundred billion euros, its management kept tight control. Observers

could fly into Timika but no one would take them from the airport into town absent the company's authorisation. The response was the final report's Recommendation 26: 'Polling stations should only be established in places accessible to the general public and where the KPU can exercise its authority'.

Immediately prior to the second round of the presidential elections, a suicide bomber blew himself up outside the Australian embassy, reputedly the number-three target after the US and UK embassies. At the time, I was in a meeting with Wirajuda. We entered the Foreign Ministry from the organised chaos of Jakarta and emerged unprepared for total pandemonium. I'd been in the Australian embassy only a few days before. Nine people died and over 150 were injured. Two days later, the mission was due to have 140 and more short-term observers fly in for a two-day briefing before dispersal across the country. I had to decide whether to postpone or cancel their arrival. We went ahead, but it was now to be in and out. They stayed one night in Jakarta and then into the field. They were all being accommodated in a hotel overlooking the British embassy – an oversight not repeated by our *new* security officer for the subsequent Aceh mission.

Indonesian poster for the 2004 elections illustrating the voting process where rather than using a written X, a hole is punched for the party/candidate of choice.

The EU mission had company. There were at least half a dozen others from Australia, Japan and the United States all doing the same. We set up a coordinating committee, which I chaired – our operation was four or five times larger than the rest combined. At best for some it was political tourism, at worst for others it was straight tourism with no politics. Shortly before the first round of the presidential elections, we asked group coordinators to share their deployment plans to ensure that, overall, there was as close to total coverage as possible. We discovered that one of the recently created provinces had no one, so I redeployed one of our teams there. Jakarta was over-represented by a factor of four. This was logical, as most of the teams had eminent individuals arriving late and leaving early, and in Indonesia internal travel was not to be taken lightly. Despite all their differences, there was all but total unity among the other missions as to where electoral malfeasance was to be focused. Bali had sixteen times more observers than the average.

One of the US teams was from the Carter Center, and Jimmy Carter himself and his wife, Rosalynn, flew in. I spent time with them as we were both asking for the same meetings with people like SBY, so it proved convenient for the Indonesians to lump quantity and quality together. Carter was knowledgeable and engaged with Indonesian high politics, yet the Carter Center had no more than ten people on the ground. This team certified the election as 'free and fair' with SBY the winner, almost as the last votes were being cast. We had put several hundred times their effort into our work and were still receiving reports from our teams monitoring the counts at polling-station level as Carter was boarding his plane home after his press conference.

Our biggest problem in the first round was more cock-up than conspiracy. In Indonesia you vote with a nail not a pencil, punching through the ballot paper in the box next to your choice. In the first round of the presidential elections, the ballots were handed to voters folded with SBY's box on early display, before voters fully unfolded the A3 paper. Millions punched his name without completely unfolding their papers, spoiling their ballots in the process as they inadvertently punched a second hole, thus voting twice. It threatened to be Indonesia's version of Florida's hanging chads and undermine the integrity of the result. We quickly urged the KPU to rule that such ballots were acceptable where the voter's intention was clear. They did, and after local officials revisited and recounted the ballots, we got a result.

I covered the country from Banda Aceh to Jayapura (Papua) via Ambon, Bandung, Denpasar, Makassar, Medan and Surabaya. Makassar's oil, the Victorian hair conditioner, was easy to resist, although it evoked memories of form long outliving function with the antimacassar defence that decorated my parents' three-piece suite as a child. The most surreal episode was in Wamena, central Papua, where we travelled to a village of one of the highland tribes. The women wore grass skirts and nothing else and the men were limited to *kotekas* (penis sheaths made from gourds). In Aceh there had been pubic covers for young girls, but they'd fallen out of fashion. I was paraded around the village on the shoulders of the women as the leader of my tribe and the men with bows and arrows hunted and shot a small pig, which provided lunch. Interest in the elections was not high. At the end of the mission, my core team presented my deputy and myself with our own *kotekas* emblazoned with the EU flag.

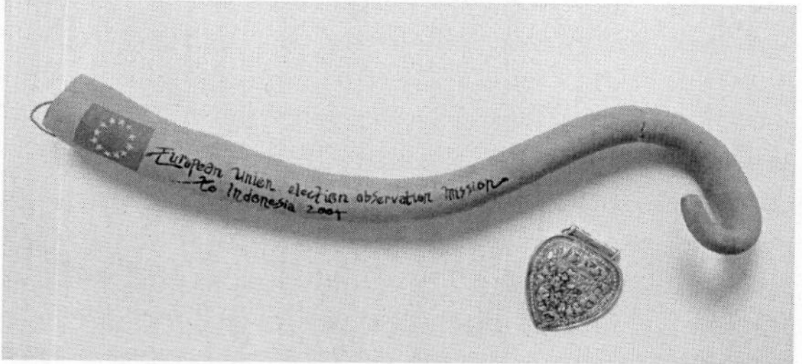

A Dani koteka I was presented with by my core team when the EUEOM concluded and a pubic cover from Aceh.

Despite the siren voices of pedants and perfectionists, it was clear to me that there was a rigour in the process and a numerical robustness to the result that merited an unequivocal endorsement of the outcome. The report said, 'some procedural shortcomings and isolated cases of fraud did not affect the integrity of the result.'[18] Nevertheless, we were fortunate that it was so clear cut. There was unquestionably some limited fraud, but not enough to affect the result in any way. The incumbent winning by a wafer-thin margin might have been another matter. Here a comparative outsider with no real party machine crushed both the political wing of Indonesia's military and the Sukarno dynasty's incumbent. Politically, it was a win for Indonesia and the EU. We had watched over the shoulder Indonesia's first ever peaceful transition of power and seen democracy consolidated.

Aceh's electoral tsunami

Success delivered a sequel. SBY's deputy was Jusuf Kalla, who served as the bridgehead between the Islamic parties and Golkar. SBY had no majority in the parliament, but Kalla in this ingrained transactional state pulled together a grand coalition around SBY's victory that included almost all save the PDI-P. As a concomitant, he re-engaged in the Aceh peace process. Talks were already underway, before 2004's Boxing Day tsunami devastated the province and Sumatra. Even so, the disaster stepped up the pace to peace. The war had lasted thirty years (1976–2005) with an estimated fifteen thousand lives lost, the bloodiest period being 1989–91 when ten thousand were killed. Put in the context of the UK, the death rate was 50 per cent higher than in Northern Ireland during the Troubles. A deal was on the table between Jakarta and the rebel GAM early in 2005. There was light, yet no tunnel: the desired outcome was clear, but in the absence of trust the problem was process. The deal was to be in two phases. First, the surrender of arms by GAM, while the government removed its 'non-organic troops' and resettled combatants. Second, fresh elections for governor and the provincial council where for the first time 'independent' candidates would be allowed to stand. The elections in April 2004 had all too graphically demonstrated the political divide. Amien Rais's National Mandate Party, the political wing of the hardline Islamicist NGO Muhammadiyah, overall finished fifth with less than 7 per cent, but received over 56 per cent in Aceh.

If the Aceh peace process was to work this time around, a third-party mediator was required that was acceptable to both Jakarta and GAM. The only two that fit the bill were the EU and ASEAN. Brussels' case was helped by the EUE-OM's performance in 2004. The result was the EU, along with ASEAN, deployed the Aceh Monitoring Mission (AMM) as part of its Common Security and Defence Policy to provide

oversight for the first phase of the peace process. It had its bizarre aspects. Off of mainland Aceh was the large, sparsely developed island of Simeulue. Here GAM's writ had never run, but they smuggled arms there early in the peace process in order to make a point in subsequently shipping them back for surrender. The island was twice lucky. Having effectively ducked the civil war, it also escaped the tsunami. A tidal wave – *semong* in the local language – had devastated the island in 1907. Burnt into folk memory was that when the sea suddenly retreats, head for the hills. That legend saved all but six lives.

At the conclusion of that first phase, the AMM were to step back into the shadows and – exceptionally – an EUEOM was to take over. Brussels normally does not monitor local and regional elections, but in the context of the AMM an exception was made. As the chief observer in 2004, I got the call. Getting into Aceh for the legislative elections had been difficult, but this improved for the presidential elections and I'd visited the province during the first round despite access being still checked and controlled. Now we were back in 2006, not only with permission but positively encouraged to roam the whole province. In charge of the AMM was the EU's Pieter Feith.[19] We passed the baton over a period of twenty-four hours, during which my team and I were briefed. Pieter enquired if I'd like to keep the snipers on the roof – I declined the offer. But I did seek guidance as to access to alcohol. Sales in Aceh were not entirely outlawed on account of the small Chinese and Christian communities, and some of the local restaurants with sturdy doors served wine and beer that vanished at the sound of heavy knocking.

This led to an interesting conversation with the shariah police, where emphasising how much Yusuf Kalla was committed to the success of our mission, I pre-emptively reassured them that were there any issues with individual members of the mission I guaranteed they would be out of the country within twenty-four hours. We wanted no prospect of our observers being threatened with caning for adultery, gay sex or drinking. Whether this had a result I'll never know, but in the end there were neither arrests nor signs that our observers behaved other than in their normal discrete manner.

Brussel's judgement was that Indonesia's domestic airlines had safety records that left so much to be desired that it was inadvisable to use them. The alternative was neither attractive nor safer. A forty-minute hop or eight hours of driving on bad roads with worse drivers made the choice. No one was forced to fly, yet none to my knowledge refused. On election day, the mission hired a helicopter to make it possible to cover as much ground as possible. Our first stop was Takengon, a town next to Laut Tawar Lake. I'd visited it earlier in the campaign after a case of arson against a polling station had been reported. It was here that the ceasefire a decade earlier had broken down. When I saw the lake appear below, I thought 'we're here'. The helicopter circled three, four times. The deafening noise made it impossible to hear anything, so the pilot passed me a note: 'I can't find the airport. Can I land?' The question answered itself, and we descended into a local football stadium, with a casual match in progress. The pilot was promptly arrested – a far cry from the reception by civic dignitaries we were expecting. As one of my staff endeavoured to get him un-arrested, the rest of us passengers found a couple of polling stations to observe in the immediate neighbourhood. Explanations accepted and pilot released, we took off for our next stop on our itinerary with no sight nor sound of Takengon's welcoming party.

In the late morning I received a phone call from Irwandi Yusuf, the former GAM leader whose faction had won the battle for him to be the 'unofficial' GAM candidate for governor, urging me to call off the election because of massive ongoing fraud. Somewhat bemused, I explained that we had no power to intervene in the process. At that point there had been no reports of anything other than the most minor problems. Half an hour later, he called me back telling me to disregard the call. Clearly, he had initially been paying too much attention to the capital, Banda Aceh, the centre of Indonesian colonisation from GAM's perspective. It proved the only district he lost in the entire province with overwhelming support everywhere else. The provincial elections, held at the same time, proved more complicated. These were again two-round elections, and mainly because of GAM-on-GAM contests in a number of districts, no first round winner emerged. We came back in 2007 with a reduced team to oversee the handful of districts with run-offs.

There were some spots on the sun, even if it was a bright shiny day. In the MOU between GAM and Jakarta it was agreed the army would be kept as far away from the election as possible. Military personnel were not allowed within three hundred metres of polling stations. Nevertheless, one of our observers on election day had a photo of an NCO, name tag visible, carrying a ballot box from a polling station. At a press conference in Banda Aceh, I provided the press with the picture and publicly asked the head of the military for an explanation. The assembled media gave me a round of applause and no coverage. Instead, the public heard one side of a conversation. I was publicly attacked, with no explanation, by a spokesman for the armed forces in the same media for questioning the military's integrity and neutrality.

Disparate observations

On behalf of the EP, and others, I did a number of missions both before and after Indonesia, including South Africa, Kenya, Cambodia (twice), Ukraine and Haiti. South Africa was with the Association of European Parliamentarians with Africa, and Ukraine with the OSCE. They all had their moments. South Africa was my first and, in retrospect, totally unique. April 1994 was more a procession than a poll, more a coronation than combat. True there was a car bomb close to our hotel in Johannesburg a couple of days before the polls opened. But the explosion was drowned in the festivities. I was sent with Neil and Glenys Kinnock to Bela-Bela, then known as Warmbaths, and its rural fastness in the Limpopo District, the poorest, most Black, least white district in South Africa. Here, out in the middle of nowhere, we found long strings of men and women sitting patiently waiting hour upon hour, sometimes days, for delinquent election material to finally appear.

The votes were meticulously counted, aggregated and dispatched to a central black hole. Days later, a perfectly calibrated result was proclaimed. It was an African National Congress (ANC) landside that fell just short of the two-thirds required for them to be in a position to unilaterally amend the Interim Constitution. F. W. de Klerk's National Party finished second with just over 20 per cent of the vote, allowing him to be elected deputy to Nelson Mandela, while Chief Buthelezi's Inkatha Freedom Party won forty-one out of eighty-one seats in his KwaZulu-Natal Province. It was psephological fiction and political triumph. The ANC made sacrifices for the greater good. Two or four per cent either way could have seen black-on-black or white-on-black civil war. Up in Limpopo with the proportional representation election system, the ANC won thirty-eight out the forty seats. I smoked a lot – because Neil had 'given up' – so every time Glenys hovered into view I was passed, like a baton in a relay race, a part-smoked cigarette. In the interregnum between the vote and the result there was a long evening's drinking with Thabo Mbecki – the coming man – who revealed none of his US-style science denial that was to warp and taint his presidency.

In Kenya on Boxing Day 2002, a group stood around Mwai Kibacki's hospital bed on the eve of the presidential election he was to win with a landslide, pushing aside for the first time Jomo Kenyatta's Kenya African National Union that had ruled for the four decades since independence. Kibacki had been injured at the beginning of December in a motorbike accident and returned to his home district of Nyeri on the lower flanks of Mount Kenya. A comparatively wealthy urban area in Kikuyu territory, here the votes were weighed, not counted. He was to survive a rough political ride, much of it his own making until 2013. Back in 2002 I had a soft spot for Simeon Nyachae, whose party came a poor third with less than 6 per cent of the vote. He was running for FORD – People Party, the Forum for the Restoration of Democracy.

In Cambodia in summer 2003, the EU's chief observer Robert Evans was to lose Labour, and himself, its Brent East seat. Evans was Labour's candidate for the by-election and prevailed on the party to push the date of the election back a fortnight from early until mid-September to enable him to travel to Phnom Penh. The extra fortnight allowed the Liberal Democrats to build enough momentum to edge past Labour with a stunning 30 per cent swing. As it was, Evans departed sharply after Cambodia's polling day; as the EP's chief observer, I was left holding the baby, with a furious Sam Rainsy stalking the EUEOM offices claiming massive

systematic fraud and demanding the EU endorse his allegations. It was here I had my electoral epiphany (see above).

At Mwai Kibacki's bedside on the eve of December 2002's election. Left to right, myself, Emma Nicholson MEP, Jim Nicholson MEP and Michael Wood from EP.

Hun Sen's Cambodian People's Party (CPP) certainly used their deep roots in the Cambodian countryside to the fullest. While the Sam Rainsy Party had overtaken Norodom Ranariddh's Royalist National United Front for an Independent, Neutral, Peaceful, and Cooperative Cambodia (known by its French acronym FUNCINPEC), mopping up the alienated internal migrants crowding Phnom Penh's sweatshop factories and winning the capital, Rainsy's vicious anti-Vietnamese racism had – thankfully – not cut through to the CPP's rural voters. Rainsy and Hun Sen were two peas from the same pod. The only difference would have been that the fate of Myanmar's Rohingya could have been visited on Cambodia's Vietnamese had Rainsy prevailed.

During the mission I sent myself up to Anlong Veng in the country's north-west corner abutting Thailand. In the previous elections in 1998, 'Brother Number Four', Ta Mok, was commanding the last remnants of the Khmer Rouge in the nearby Dangrek Mountains. We drove up to this last redoubt, also the site of Pol Pot's last resting place. On the map, the narrow road continued back in an arc short of the border. Yet in our path there was a Thai border post blocking the way. A hundred kilometres away, the Thais and Cambodians had been fighting and dying over the Preah Vihear Hindu temple. Here in Anlong Veng, sleeping dogs were left to lie.

On election day, my first polling station was the one closest to Pol Pot's former camp. Back in 1998, voting in this district was understandably patchy, with the Khmer Rouge killing seven voters in a series of attacks. When I returned to Brussels, the EP cash office indicated that the receipt for two nights in Anlong Veng's 'best' hotel – situated next to Ta Mok's old house – didn't conform with parliamentary rules. I pointed out the total was four US dollars. They paid.

Boxing Day 2004 saw me as part of the OSCE observation mission headed up by US Congressman Alcee Hastings – who I was to meet again as part of the Congressional Black Caucus – in the Ukraine, watching the rerun of the presidential poll between Viktor Yanukovych and Viktor Yuschenko, both backed by their own oligarchs. Yanukovych had won the first time around, but the Supreme Court ordered a rerun following the 'Orange Revolution' protests. At the second time of asking, Yuschenko won 52–44. Ukraine's future civil war and Russia's intrusion was written in the results. We learnt East was East and West was West, with votes that were mirror images of one other. The west went for orange and the east for Moscow. My deployment on the day was eighty kilometres north of Kyiv, on the edge of Chernobyl's thirty-kilometre exclusion zone. It all came back to me twice, first when I watched the HBO mini-series over Christmas fifteen years later and again with the Russian invasion and their occupation of the disaster site.

Haiti saw concurrent presidential, senate and house elections in February 2006 with second rounds as necessary two months later. Rene Preval was trying a comeback after his 1996–2000 presidency. He had been succeeded by Jean-Bertrand Aristide in a chaotic and disputed election boycotted by the opposition. Four years later, Aristide was overthrown. The result was an interim president and long-promised and long-delayed elections. In the first round, which saw a 60 per cent turnout, Preval finished massively ahead of a string of thirty-four challengers. Early returns gave him just over half the vote, but late results eroded his lead to a point where he ended up with a fraction under the 50 per cent required to avoid the run-off. Second was Leslie Manigat with 12 per cent. The reaction was rioting on the streets of Port-au-Prince, with us EP observers gingerly exiting via Toussaint Louverture

Airport over broken glass and promises, despite the presence of the Chinese-manned United Nations Stabilisation Mission in Haiti. A week later the Provisional Electoral Committee, numerate and percipient, excluded blank ballots from the count. Late returns, when Preval was already known to be on the edge of victory, had seen a positive flood of blank papers. The decision pushed Preval up and over the threshold. Again, a political rather than juridical decision that worked.

A Cap-Haïtien school featuring the 2006 general election by Rody Xavier (2006).

During the first round I'd been in Jacmel, an old French settlement, in the south on the coast and up the long Jacmel valley and Bainet. Here the turnout had been close to 75 per cent. At a party meeting in Bath a couple of weeks later, I was asked what could be done to improve the usual woeful turnout for the coming local elections. Using Jacmel's hinterland as my mirror, I suggested ten-mile hikes and five-hour waits was the answer. If Jacmel itself was Haiti's Brighton, my location for the second round of the House elections was dourer: after starting in Saint-Marc I was then off to the barren, hilly, drought-riven island of Gonâve. The island wasn't so much left behind and forgotten, as never found. It made the Cité Soleil ghetto in the capital look good. No wonder that under the French, no colonists chose to live there. Gonâve's inhabitants' interest in the election matched the capital's interest in the islanders. Less than 10 per cent voted.

Trading places

I served two separate terms on the EP's trade committee with a long hiatus between. It was the ERT committee in my first parliament (1984–89) and then the International Trade (INTA) Committee in what was to prove my last term. In the first incarnation I drove the report – described earlier in this chapter – on EU–North Korean trade, and I was the committee's rapporteur on countertrade. This was the practice of bartering goods and services without hard currency changing hands, favoured by developing countries with neither foreign exchange nor credit. Countertrade comes at a price. Back at Manchester University I'd had involvement in a contract the department was given to justify a 'technology premium' on a swap of oranges for aircraft. The very idea of such a premium is ludicrous, but the side with the whip hand could exploit its strength. It was this that piqued my interest. Nowadays, up to eighty countries are engaged, and estimates suggest countertrade accounts for between 5 and 15 per cent of global trade. It's generally frowned upon by the West as a practice utilised, more often than not, by countries of concern for products of concern. Like in the Manchester University example, one side of the deal is all too often military goods and equipment. Yet for too many the expensive option is the only option.

If my first venture was offensive, with the second I played defence. The object of my ire was the Moorhouse Report on EU–Japan trade. James Moorhouse was an old-school pro-European Tory who in 1998 was to defect to the Liberal Democrats. His report was a mishmash of ignorance, misunderstanding and misapprehension embedded in an after-image of Japan from a quarter of a century before as a low-wage sweatshop. I'd been living in Tokyo not much more than a year before and I knew salaries and costs. It was a different world from the one Moorhouse recalled. I exploited my position as a 'former Japanese civil servant' – my spell at Todai had me as an employee of Monbusho, the Ministry of Education. My fickle co-conspirator was Carlo Galluzzi, a prominent Italian Communist, chair of the EP's Japanese delegation – much to Tokyo's bemusement – and another member of ERT. He tabled a hundred amendments to the report while I prepared more than twice that number, with the help

of a Japanese stagiaire, Kyoko Sakuma, I borrowed from Stephen Hughes. When the situation in the committee turned brutal, Galluzzi withdrew his amendments. But I wasn't to be intimidated by Moorhouse and his group. I refused to withdraw my two hundred and upped the ante by taking over all of Galluzzi's. Moorhouse withdrew his report. He came back twelve months later with a new script which now had some connection with reality. This time, instead of rerunning the procedural filibuster, we opposed the report that narrowly carried in plenary. A decade later – in September 1997 – we were both on the same page with a second report that passed virtually unanimously.

At the second birth I continued to work on Japan and the Korean Peninsula (although this time South rather than North), also ASEAN as well as the economic partnership agreements. I was appointed rapporteur for the EU–ASEAN free trade agreement (FTA), which almost from the off proved a deal too far. ASEAN's ten member states ranged from economies with GDPs matching those of EU nations to some of the poorer, 'less-developed' countries, while political systems covered the full spectrum from democracies to dictatorships, via authoritarianism and post-Cold War communism. One particular obstacle was Myanmar, under military rule and EU sanctions. Vietnam was lead negotiator, but tightly tethered by the rest of ASEAN. Nothing was agreed until everything was agreed. It was the unwilling, the unable and the undesirable in pursuit of the unobtainable. Over time, I visited – or met – every one of the ten trade ministries, and it was clear not even the most skeletal framework agreement was possible. The grandiose bloc-to-bloc ambitions had to be dismantled to match the possible. It worked, and at the time of writing the EU has FTAs in place with Singapore (2018) and Vietnam (2019) and stalled negotiations with the undesirable (Philippines and Thailand), the unwilling (Malaysia) and the unable (Indonesia). All that is missing are the three troublesome less-developed countries, Myanmar, Cambodia and Laos, and easily missed Brunei. There is fresh talk of an EU–ASEAN FTA. That's a prospect if the EU's deep dive in 2022 into the quagmire of the Indo-Pacific persuades Brussels to be less fastidious.

An FTA with the Republic of Korea was negotiated in parallel, where I represented the S&D Group. It proved a massive success after provisional application in 2011. For the EU, a €10.5 billion deficit in trade in goods in 2010 was balanced by 2018, with a €5.6 billion surplus in services in 2017 and a more than doubling of inward foreign direct investment, making the EU Korea's biggest investor. For Seoul, the EU came to be its third-largest export market; more importantly, the very process of negotiation rescued the moribund United States–Korea FTA that had been cast away in the US Senate as American industry feared the worst.

In 2008 Baroness Cathy Ashton was parachuted into the role of European Commissioner for Trade as a stop-gap appointment after previous incumbent Peter Mandelson ransomed himself to Gordon Brown as the Prime Minister desperately cast about for anyone or anything that might save the floundering government that he was responsible for scuttling. My relations with Peter had always been quixotic. Back in 1989, shortly after I was elected leader of the EPLP, Peter had stopped me sitting on the platform at that year's Labour Party Conference on the first day because I was wearing a leather jacket. I think it was *The Times* that reported that I had no problem the next day with an Armani suit in tow. Equally, when he was Trade Commissioner he much resented opposition to some of his proposals from David Martin and myself. Yet for all that, he was clear headed and rational, seeing the logic when I argued that Korean fridges had 'side-by-side' doors for sensible ergonomic rather than competitive reasons with the small residential footprint of most families in East Asia, and he dropped the tariffs imposed on Korean models alongside those from the US. When I asked him for a first meeting with Chinese Vice-Minister Zhang Zhijun, who was responsible for the International Department of the Chinese Communist Party, he had me join.

In order to become Commissioner, Ashton had to go through a confirmation process in INTA before being signed off by the EP. The S&D coordinator Erika Mann asked me to manage the process. Gordon Brown's options to replace Mandelson with a credible figure were constrained by his dread of triggering a by-election he could well lose, which would further erode his government's already rocky standing.

He turned to the Lords and Ashton, whose CV was void of international experience. The Tories were out to get her, seeing Brown as the wounded politician at bay that he was. Here they should have had the Christian Democrats in the EPP on board as they were still hoping that Cameron might see sense and renege on the promise to the Tory ultras, needed to buy their votes for the Tory leadership in 2005, to take them out of the EPP after the 2009 European elections.

Ashton faced a two-hour grilling in INTA with more than twenty MEPs putting her to the question. I marshalled the S&D, sympathisers and fellow travellers, and we designed chronology and content to match her briefings and comprehension. She got a punishment beating from Britain's Tories, but easily survived. Their mistake was to go domestic with allegations of financial mismanagement during her period as treasurer of CND in the 1980s. There was no cut through with continental MEPs. The Tories were firing on the wrong position: she was far more vulnerable to forensic interrogation on detailed trade policy. However, she did herself no harm in her pre-emptive surrender to INTA of the powers parliament was to gain over trade policy with the ratification of the 2007 Lisbon Treaty.[20]

In the end, as the final questioner of twenty-three, there was little, if anything, to mop-up. I therefore reverted to my own interests and asked her about opening negotiations on an EU–Japan economic partnership agreement (EPA). Her response was anodyne and noncommittal. Privately, she subsequently explained a breathing space was necessary after any Korea FTA. While both Seoul and Tokyo offered substantial economic gains, the European industrial sectors which would suffer with a Korean deal were the self-same ones that would be hit by a Japanese EPA. It was a pause, and not postponement. Japan's EPA entered into force in 2019.

My final foray and swansong as an MEP was as rapporteur for the interim economic partnership agreement (iEPA) with the Pacific and as S&D spokesperson on the iEPA with Eastern and Southern Africa. The need for these negotiations were a result of the World Trade Organization (WTO) ruling a decade earlier that the EU's favouring through the Lome Convention of the ACP block of former colonies was discriminating against other less-developed countries outside of the ACP. The new deals with regional groups of countries had to be WTO compliant, with ACP members disgruntled at the loss of their privileged position. There was no alternative. The EP played the card Ashton had offered in her hearing to anticipate Lisbon's grant of veto powers to the parliament, and agreed to withdraw any deal the EP rejected. There was no need. The offer in itself gave us the leverage to gain the concessions needed to mitigate the worst. Speaking in the debate in March, I noted that when I'd attended the ACP Parliamentary Assembly in Port Moresby six months earlier, only Papua New Guinea and Fiji were on board, and the latter reluctantly at that.[21] In addressing the Eastern and Southern Africa iEPA, I thanked Daniel Caspary (EPP, Germany), the rapporteur, for accepting my amendment to incorporate the Chagos Islands in the deal. The population, driven into exile by a British Labour government in the late sixties, to suit the US military's forward deployment on Diego Garcia, adding a further speck to America's pointillist empire. They are still campaigning for a right of return.[22] The campaign's leader Oliver Bancoult, with four others, was finally able to visit under the auspices of the Mauritian government fifty years on from his exile in February 2022. Yet a permanent return is still a long way off.

In the Pacific it all turned out better than forecast. Four eventually signed up – Papua New Guinea (2011), Fiji (2014), Samoa (2018) and Solomon Islands (2020) – with Tonga and Timor-Leste signalling in 2021 their intention to join. Eastern and Southern Africa saw an early rush with the Seychelles, Mauritius, Madagascar and Zimbabwe signing up immediately in 2009, to be joined belatedly by Comoros in 2017. As for the Chagos Islands, despite an International Court of Justice ruling in 2019 that the UK's occupation was unlawful – reinforced by a UN General Assembly resolution urging that the archipelago be handed back to Mauritius, and the 2021 the International Tribunal for the Law of the Sea ruling that the UK has 'no sovereignty over the Chagos Islands' – the islanders and their descendants remain in the Seychelles, Mauritius and poverty.

Endnotes

[1] The vote inside the EPLP on the EP's Common Resolution on the Gulf was thirteen in favour (Adam, Balfe, Collins, David, Donnelly, Ford, Harrison, Hoon, Titley, Tomlinson, Tongue, Wilson and Wynne), sixteen against (Barton, Buchan, Coates, Crampton, Elliott, Hindley, Hughes, McCubbin, McGowan, Morris, Newens, Newman, Oddy, A. Smith, L. Smith and White) and eight abstentions (Bowe, Green, Martin, McMahon, Pollack, Read, Simpson and Stevenson). The other eight were absent or ran away. [2] Glyn Ford (2002), 'Democrats' thriller in Manila', *Tribune*, 31 May. [3] Pollock (2016), p. 126. Despite the sycophantic fawning and a well-resourced campaign, Titley failed to be nominated to the House of Lords after he stood down in 2009. Gordon Brown was clearly not a fan, but Titley's reputation as an employer won't have helped, particularly when one of the employees was Stephen Kinnock. [4] Michael Foot (1975), *Aneurin Bevan*, vol. 1, London: Faber, p. 50. [5] Any Member State may take such measures as it considers necessary for the protection of the essential interests of its security which are connected with the production of or trade in arms, munitions and war material; such measures shall not, however, adversely affect the conditions of competition in the common market regarding products which are not intended for specifically military purposes.' EC Treaty (Treaty of Rome), Art 223(1b). [6] Glyn Ford (1989), 'Report on behalf of the Political Affairs Committee on European arms exports' (Doc A2-0398/88). [7] Apart from the covert arms transfers revealed by 'Irangate' with five shipments of US arms worth $30–87 million between August 1985 and November 1986. [8] See my report: Glyn Ford (1986), 'Report on behalf of the Committee on External Economic Relations, on counter-trade' (Doc A2-117/86). [9] Glyn Ford (1989), 'Report on behalf of the Political Affairs Committee on European arms exports' (Doc A2-0398/88). [10] Glyn Ford (1992), 'Report on behalf of the Committee on Foreign Affairs and Security on the Community's role in the supervision of arms exports and the armaments industry' (Doc A3-0260/92). [11] The EU was later to put money aside to buy up nuclear material from the former Soviet Empire and provide opportunities to its nuclear scientists and engineers. [12] Glyn Ford (1994), 'Report on behalf of the Committee on Foreign Affairs and Security, on disarmament, arms export controls and non-proliferation of weapons of mass destruction' (Doc A3-0111/94). [13] World Bank (2020), 'Arms exports (SIPRI trend

indicator values)', https://data.worldbank.org/indicator/MS.MIL.XPRT.KD (accessed 2 November 2020). [14] Glyn Ford and David Martin (2007), 'The case for Trident makes no sense', *Morning Star*, 10 April. [15] The EU spent €5 million on the Indonesian EOM. See European Commission (2004), 'European Union Election Observation Mission to Indonesia for upcoming election', 27 February. [16] Indonesia weighted its parliament with the security services, while the UK went for family – the Lords – and education in the Commons with its university seats that were only abolished in 1950. [17] Stephen Sherlock (2004), 'The 2004 Indonesian elections: how the system works and what the parties stand for', a report on political parties, Canberra: Centre for Democratic Institutions. [18] European Union (2004), 'Final Report for the European Union Election Observation Mission to Indonesia.' [19] Aceh's EOM cost €2.4 million. See European Council and Commission (2007), 'EU Annual Report on Human Rights', Brussels: European Communities. [20] The lessons and opportunities Lisbon offers for reshuffling the EU's institutional architecture have been touched on in Chapter 1 and will be again in Chapter 10. [21] EP (2009), *Debates*, 30 March. [22] See David Vine (2009), *Island of Shame: The Secret History of the U.S. Military Base on Diego Garcia*, New Jersey: Princeton University Press; and Glyn Ford and Richard Gifford (2009), 'Islands of shame', *Tribune*, 16 October. I travelled with the Chagossian leader Olivier Bancoult in 2010 to the US Congress to lobby members of the Congressional Black Caucus on behalf of the islanders.

8 Racism and Fascism

I am, somehow, less interested in the weight and convolutions of Einstein's brain than the near certainty that people of equal talent have lived and died in cotton fields and sweatshops

Stephen J. Gould, The Panda's Thumb (1980)

I was not the only surprise victor in the June 1984 European elections. In France there was a breakthrough by Jean-Marie Le Pen's FN that saw them elect ten MEPs. They joined with others on the far right, present in the previous parliament, from the Movimento Sociale Italiano (MSI) and a solitary Greek from the pro-Colonels' party Ethniki Politiki Enosis, to form the Group of the European Right.[1] Previously isolated on the fringes, the far right now had a platform and a voice.

These parties had their own 'stars'. Le Pen, the FN leader, had been elected as the second-youngest deputy on the petite bourgeoise populist and anti-Semitic list of Pierre Poujade for the 1956 National Assembly elections, before subsequently taking a furlough from the assembly to go to Algeria. As a lieutenant responsible for military intelligence there, as a holiday to hell, he tortured suspected members of the pro-independence Front de Liberation Nationale.

There were other equally unsavoury MEPs in the group. They had a collaborator who had fought with the Waffen SS, Gustave Pordea, whose place on the Le Pen list had been bought by the Unification Church and who turned out to be a Romanian spy; Jean-Marie Le Chevallier, meanwhile, ended up as the FN mayor of Toulon. Several of their MEPs – Yvan Blot, Jean-Yves Le Gallou and Bruno Megret, among others – were associated with the Research and Study Group for European Civilization (GRECE) and the Club de l'Horloge. These two French far-right think-tanks were opposed to multiculturalism, liberalism and capitalism, while promoting national preference and 're-information'. The only difference was that GRECE favoured paganism over the Club de l'Horloge's ultramontane Catholicism.

My bête noire was Bruno Gollnisch, who arrived in the EP in 1989 and stayed for thirty years. When Jean-Marie Le Pen stood down in 2011, Gollnisch ran from the even-further right against Marine Le Pen for leadership of the FN at the Tours Congress. Backed unanimously by France's trio of far-right papers – *Minute, Rivarol* and *Présent* – he received 32 per cent of the vote. Gollnisch was a Holocaust sceptic/denier. Following an address by Israeli prime minister Yitzhak Rabin in a debate on racism and xenophobia, one speaker mentioned *The Diary of Anne Frank*, at which Gollnisch interjected, bawling 'half of it is a forgery!'[2] Yet he was a serious intellectual, a professor of Japanese language and civilisation in the notorious humanities division of Jean Moulin Lyon 3 University, with a Japanese wife. We were born on the same day and he would stalk me on the Japanese delegation, telling our bemused hosts that we were the Janus's faces of the EU. When he discovered my daughter was in Lyon for her language year abroad from Cambridge, he pressed his mobile phone number on me, in case she ever needed help. She didn't.

The Italians were no better. The leader of the MSI was Giorgio Almirante, who had been the chef de cabinet for the Minister of Propaganda in the Salo Republic, the one period of Mussolini's rule where anti-Semitism was to the fore. His nemesis on the right, Pino Rauti, was there in tandem. Rauti was earlier associated with Stefano Delle Chiaie and the 'strategy of tension'. The latter had been tried for involvement in the Piazza Fontana bombing, although he was acquitted for lack of evidence. When Almirante stood down in 1987, Rauti ran for the leadership but lost 727–608 to Gianfranco Fini, Almirante's designated successor and another fascist

MEP who arrived in the EP in 1989. Fini was to serve as deputy prime minister under Silvio Berlusconi from 2001 to 2006.

Almirante died in May 1988. I was in Rome with the ERT committee and played truant to observe the funeral cortege as the leadership of the MSI marched through a phalanx of tens of thousands lining the streets giving their 'roman salutes'. They were accompanied by MEPs from the FN and Ulster Unionist MEP John Taylor, who the previous year had joined the Group of the European Right. Fascist salutes didn't seem to bother him, but then he had previously been a member of the anti-immigration Monday Club. About twelve months after Fini became an MEP, a journalist from the French left-wing paper *Libération*, Francesco Cerri, invited the two of us to debate. Fini got his retaliation in first with a firm 'No!' Yet for me 'no platform' was a tactic, not a strategy. I demonstrated against Nick Griffith's invitation to the Oxford Union, while supporting Harlem Désir debating Le Pen (see below). The first was trying to break through into the public arena, the second was already deeply rooted there.

Funeral procession for Giorgio Almirante MEP, leader of the neo-fascist Movimento Sociale Italiano, Piazza Navona, Rome 1988. 'Roman salutes' can be seen at the right while in the van are French MEPs from Jean-Marie Le Pen's Front National, including Martine Lehideux MEP and Jean-Marie Le Chevallier MEP.

Evrigenis report

The Group of the European Right's birth in 1984 demanded a reaction. We forced the parliament's hand through an unsung provision in the rules of procedure – only deployed once before – allowing a Committee of Inquiry to be established at the request of a quarter of the members. The British delegation passed the proposal to the Socialist Group who endorsed it. We rapidly signed up the left, and despite protestations from the mainstream right and threats of lawsuits and worse from Le Pen, who claimed they would use 'all means possible' to stop the committee's work, the EP was faced with the reality of a Committee of Inquiry into the Rise of Fascism and Racism in Europe (1984–86) in need of both a chair and rapporteur.[3]

What goes up must come down. The EP president Pierre Pflimlin told the Socialists that, as the instigators, they had ownership. The parcel was passed by Rudi Arndt, the Socialist Group leader, back to the British delegation, who duly passed it to me as the initial culprit. Labour's ultras urged me to play it short and hard: orchestrate a spectacular bust up, denounce the right for colluding with fascism and move on. After all, actually achieving anything would threaten to distort their image of the EP as mere talking shop. I chose to play long. At one of our first meetings, I had Harlem Désir from SOS Racisme speak to the committee. Its *Touche pas à mon pote* badge was as recognisable in France as the Anti-Nazi League's (ANL) roundel. It was the start of a friendship that survives today.

There was an early distraction. December 1984 saw me weigh in, decrying the Benelux tradition where on St Nicholas's Eve (5/6 December) the saint has tagging along behind him 'Zwarte Piet', variously depicted as servant, freed slave or Italian/Spanish chimney sweep who puts on blackface and red lipstick and threatens to abduct the bad and ply the good children with sweets. With the brutal colonial histories of Belgium and Holland, Zwarte Piet, was racism in the flesh. Yet that was not what my Low Country colleagues, or their voters, saw. I was categorically denounced by their domestic press and media, for what now would be 'political correctness', in

my slandering of a parochial folk figure. Time talks. In 2020 in the wake of Black Lives Matter, the majority of civil society in the Low Countries finally discarded their blinkers and saw Zwarte Piet for what he always was: a cultural pariah.

The committee had its rare birds. My favourite character was Otto von Habsburg, an MEP representing Bavaria's Christian Social Union (CSU) and the man who – save for Germany's defeat in the First World War – would be king, or rather Kaiser. A committed European, and sympathetic to refugees, he was a ferocious opponent of both Nazis and Communists. After the Anschluss he was sentenced to death by Hitler's courts and fled into exile in the United States. When he died in 2011, aged ninety-eight, his body was entombed in the Imperial Crypt in Vienna while his heart was buried in Pannonhalma Archabbey in Hungary. In the committee he was always making the most extravagant demands, and on one occasion I accused him of being a closet Trotskyist. From then on, he greeted me with a clenched fist salute. He was as conservative as they come and I was seen to be well on the left of the Socialist Group; we ended up as a mutually supportive double act. Much of the EP's procedure rests on harvesting specified numbers of signatures from MEPs. If Otto and I had signed a request, our political span left 80 per cent and more of the parliament at our mercy. There would be barely a member of the EPP who would baulk at adding their name to a proposal championed by Otto, while centre and left would be directed to look across the page to me. On this basis, together we got half the MEPs to sign a written declaration demanding action to combat growing anti-Semitism in Europe.[4] Unlike with Westminster's early day motions, this was now EP policy and it was followed up with Commission and Council.

Frank-Ludwig von Stauffenberg, who also represented the CSU, was less amenable. Frank-Ludwig was the son of Claus von Stauffenberg, who led the July 1944 attempt on Hitler's life and was executed following its failure, having joined the conspirators in 1942. Claus was no democrat, yet it was his very heroism and courage that perversely served in the immediate post-war period to distract from German nobility's wider collaboration with Hitler. An opinionated, deep-dyed conservative, Frank-Ludwig was, if for self-evident reasons, a committed anti-fascist. He frequently tossed his 'get out of jail free' card into committee debates: 'My father died because he tried to rid the world of Adolf Hitler'. Eventually, it all got too much for one of the Socialists on the committee, who retorted, 'It's a pity he spent the previous four years invading Europe for him'. True but unhelpful. Instant uproar ensued, as the committee collapsed into cross recriminations, demands for apologies and threats of walkouts. I spent ninety minutes successfully stopping the last, but got nowhere near any apology. In the end we were saved by the interpreters and their trade union spirit. At 1 p.m., as was their right, they promptly turned off their microphones and went for lunch. There was no way I was going to ask for any indulgence and linguistic imperatives closed that particular committee meeting. By the time we met again a fortnight later the issue was gone, but not forgotten.

Experts

The Committee of Inquiry decided to invite a series of experts. With no prospect of finding any agreement across the political groups and members on who these experts should be, we retreated to the EP's default mechanism and carved up the invitations among the groups using the D'Hondt system. It was an eclectic bench that ranged from right to left through Jean-François Revel and Andrè Glucksmann to Professor Stephen Rose and Ernest Mandel via Oscar Luigi Scalfaro, then Italian Minister of the Interior and later president, plus Simon Wiesenthal.[5] Opposition to the committee's work was not limited to the far right. Ambalavaner Sivanandan, the director of the Institute of Race Relations, advised Rose to have nothing to do with us. Luckily, my earlier work with the professor on radical science prior to becoming an MEP saw him override the injunction.

Revel, himself an apostate socialist, argued Nazism and fascism were rooted in socialism, with their natural opposition therefore traditional conservatism. He asserted that racism is natural and it is anti-racism which is not, while it was extreme left terrorism of Belgium's Cellules

Communistes Combattantes and Portugal's People's Forces of 25 April with their subversion and destabilisation that were the most serious and most important threat to Europe. Glucksmann wanted balance, arguing that Hitlerism came from left and right, as the racist concentration camps of Germany were mirrored by the left-wing camps of Russia and Cambodia. In 1933 the Red Army starved to death seven million Ukrainians. Anti-Semitism, as Bebel said, was 'the socialism of idiots. The real Fascist danger comes from the current inarticulate and incoherent political class failing to address the problems facing us all and not the presence of a few fascists.'[6]

From the first CoI on racism - James Spence, myself, Derek Prague MEP, Robert Chambeiron MEP, Dimitrios Evrigenis MEP.

Rose, in sharp contrast, attacked scientific racism. In his view, there was neither science nor race in the concept; it was a scavenger ideology feeding on the crumbs. Race, he contended, was a social construct, as 'more than 94% of genetic variation takes place within socially defined races than between them.'[7] Rose echoed Glucksmann in disparaging the inadequacies of orthodox parties, but for him it was the synergy of nationalism and racism, monetarism and science that needed to be broken as they danced a quadrille together, alternating to take the lead in tacit conspiracy. Meanwhile, Mandel's road to fascism had numerous steps. The first was in incoherent parliamentary democracy, the second a connected or coincidental economic crisis. These were, for him, already present. The third was desperado organisations passing a threshold of credibility where 'big business' became willing to pay an 'insurance premium' to ward off left-wing alternatives as the fascists drew on the imperial roots of ultra-nationalism and racism to justify the reimportation of brutal colonial discipline to master the real and imaginary enemies within.

Scalfaro's invitation was triggered by his equivocal position on a number of terrorist bombings and massacres in Italy. What colour and shape was terrorism? Red or black, circle or line? Scalfaro wasn't sure. There was European terrorist cooperation on the left threatening NATO, and sometimes left and right terrorists worked together. The problem was institutional. While the security forces in Europe worked together, the politicians lacked the political resolve to act, hidebound by rules and paralysed by doubt. Wiesenthal argued that Nazism, an order of magnitude more dangerous than fascism, had never died; rather, its reckoning with history was adjourned with the start of the Cold War. He asserted that Hitler did not invent racism or anti-Semitism, the difference was the technology the Fuehrer had at his command. National Socialism, according to Wiesenthal, did not begin with gas chambers, it began with leaflets against immigrants; but because the German populace were complicit, it ended in the Holocaust.

It didn't take me long to realise that the pen was mightier than the gavel. The directing mind was the rapporteur. Dimitrios Evrigenis was a Greek Christian Democrat who had been jailed by the Colonels Regime (1967–74) during the Greek dictatorship. Despite his conservatism, he had first-hand experience of the realities of neo-fascism via the junta. A former Deputy Minister of Education, judge at the European Court of Human Rights and a member of the UN Committee on the Elimination of Racial Discrimination, his selection by the EPP was fortuitous for his experience and the cover it provided on the right for our work. He was a polyglot and when asked about his linguistic shortcomings he replied, 'I don't speak Dutch.' I worked easily with him, although we were never close.

I drew on my own background to manage the politics of the committee. Before council committee meetings in Tameside, Labour Group members met to debate and agree the line. I called pre-meetings of the Socialist, Communist

and Green MEPs plus Jeff Ulburghs (the observer from the Non-Inscrits). The key players were Robert Chambeiron (French Communist, a resistance fighter with Jean Moulin, who had earlier helped with clandestine arms deliveries to the Spanish Republic), Bram van der Lek (Dutch Pacifist Socialist Party in the Green Group), Marijke Van Hemeldonck (Flemish Socialist), Willi Rothley (German Socialist), Heidi d'Ancona (Dutch Socialist), Giorgio Rossetti (Italian Communist, who with the rest of the PCI was to join the Socialist Group in 1993). Unlike Tameside, we had a language problem, but there was political support among the interpreters and a small group volunteered their services unpaid.

Outcome

The Evrigenis report went to the plenary in December 1985, swiftly followed by a further debate in January 1986 in the immediate wake of Spain and Portugal joining the Union. It was adopted all but unanimously.[8] There were forty-one recommendations; institutional and information (data collection), education and social integration, mainstreaming and monitoring. The report explored the situation and causes of racism and xenophobia in EU member states, plus Austria, Norway, Sweden, Switzerland, Turkey and Eastern Europe. As for the UK, the proximate cause of its racism and xenophobia was history, empire and the ensuing immigration. The high bar of the first past the post electoral system closed off electoral politics, radicalising street violence. Britain's far-right groups were catalogued and racial attacks recorded, the promotion of football hooliganism noted and institutional discrimination explored.

As I told the plenary, anti-racist groups 'of all political and religious persuasions are already using the report as a basis for joint European activities'.[9] The report's powerful content was betrayed by its weak close. Nevertheless, it was an enormous advance. In the first directly elected parliament (1979–84), the entirety of its attention to combating racism was a single written question by the Belgium Socialist Raymond Dury.

From the beginning it was clear we could expect no help from the other institutions. The Council was opposed and the Commission dismissive. The key question the report had to address was Community competence. For Evrigenis and the committee, the Community's basic primacy of law and fundamental rights argued a competence it had failed to exercise. That was the crack in the door – it was just a long time opening. The report prompted 'A Solemn Declaration against Racism and Xenophobia' (June 1986) from the three institutions, but progress then paused.[10] Evrigenis tragically died on 25 January 1986 and Pflimlin in his tribute during the parliament's next session noted, 'you will all retain an abiding memory of the remarkably objective, conscientious and scrupulously fair manner in which he acquitted himself of his duties as rapporteur for the Committee of Inquiry'. The president was right. The report went as far as Evrigenis was prepared to go and, more significantly, as far as that parliament could at the time be taken. That crack and that precedent were to prove critical.

The Socialist Group produced its own pamphlet in 1986 – *Against Racism and Fascism in Europe* by Andrew Bell – that took a rather harder line than Evrigenis.[11] It quoted the FN's Bernard Antony: 'the modern world is once again facing the Jewish problem. Jews are at the centre of contemporary debate. Marx and Rothschild can be said to represent two sides of the same coin ... Another aspect of the Jewish problem is the propensity of Jews to occupy all the key posts in western societies'.

Ford report

In 1988 the Commission submitted a watered-down proposal to the Council for a resolution on racism and xenophobia to encourage member states to adopt anti-discrimination legislation. The Council diluted it further, and an elephantine gestation period ultimately brought forth a mouse. It was clear where some of the member states were coming from. Athens' position was easily summarised: 'We don't have a

dog. It hasn't bitten anyone. If it did, it was their fault.' Greece was not alone.

After the 1989 European elections – in which I was elected leader of the British delegation and first vice-chair of the Socialist Group – it was clearly time to advance to the next staging post. This would require more confrontation than consensus. Playing nice wouldn't work twice. As I said in public debates, 'Trade unions didn't get the right to organise from parliaments who decided it was a good idea. Women didn't get the right to vote because someone thought it was time. They got it through campaigning and struggle. Europe's thirteenth state will only get their rights from the same process.' I put in a demand for a second Committee of Inquiry on Racism and Xenophobia (1989–90) with 147 MEPs signing. This time I was the rapporteur.

Our continued pre-meetings agreed we should look to a maximum of ten to twelve recommendations. This was to prove a forlorn hope. In practice, each group – and in some cases each MEP – wanted ten to twelve different recommendations. We ended up with seventy-seven.[12] As was subsequently said, 'The volume and breadth of the Committee's recommendations made it difficult to generate and sustain momentum for any single recommendation or set of recommendations.'[13] That stricture was all too true.

I arranged for the committee – deliberately and provocatively – to travel to Marseilles to take evidence. Le Pen's FN were less than impressed. The French fascist paper *Présent* announced me as a 'personal enemy of Le Pen in Marseilles.' The local FN organised a demonstration to try to disrupt our final press conference, but it went ahead thanks to steel barricades and the French riot police. The EP was sufficiently nervous that they organised with the French authorities for me to be accompanied by two police bodyguards for the duration of the visit. One evening I had dinner with a friend living in the area, and I found it disconcerting having the two of them dining 'lite' at the next table.

This time there was to be no consensus. The only question was where the line would be drawn. The Socialists, the members of both Communist groups (Euro-communist and 'Stalinist') and Greens voted in favour, while the centre-right shattered. Dimitrios Nianias, a Greek in the European

Democratic Alliance from Dimokratiki Ananeosi (Democratic Renewal, a split from New Democracy), voted in favour; Jean-Thomas Nordmann (Liberal), the committee's chair, voted against; Nicole Fontaine (EPP) – a future president of the parliament – abstained; while Patrick Cooney from Fine Gael, also representing the EPP, declined to take part in the vote. The others absented themselves. There was to be a very belated minority report by Nordmann.

The committee's report was both popular and hated. On the Monday of October 1990's Strasbourg plenary, the session's chair, in answer to a complaint that copies of the report were unavailable to MEPs, responded, 'we have produced three editions of the Ford report with a total of 11,000 copies which is more than corresponds to the number of Members of the House. We have not been able to produce it at a speed proportionate to its success but work is now in progress to produce more copies.'[14]

Total debate

The very nature of the EP normally attenuates the cut and thrust of debate. The act of interpretation creates a temporal hiatus as long as that between lightning and thunder. The linguistic comprehension gap, dilution of language and narrowing of lexicon as the safety net for the surrogate messengers, seated in the interpretation booths circling the chamber, kills all spectacle and presence. Outside of voting time, attendance is transactional. Yet here, over three days of manoeuvring, debating and voting, the parliament's politics and language were red in tooth and claw, vitriolic and vengeful.

The battle lines had the left on one side, the far right and Liberals on the other with the centre-right largely spectating. The fascists and fellow travellers now nested both as the cuckoos in the renamed Technical Group of the European Right and as the defenestrated among the Non-Inscrits. In the previous parliament the French and Italians had shared the Group of the European Right, but in 1989 the German Republikaner had jumped Germany's electoral threshold and entered the EP. They were revanchists, claiming Italy's

German-speaking periphery for a 'Greater Germany', making it impossible for Italy's MSI to share the same space. Le Pen betrayed his Italians and chose the heirs of Hitler over Mussolini, leaving the latter stranded in the limbo of the EP's Non-Inscrits.

There were two interconnected clashes with the Liberals. These were personified around the committee and group chairs. In the committee, the Liberal chair Nordmann had taken umbrage late, voting against the final report with no prior warning. Subsequently, he went on record at a press conference we did in Paris, stating that he could have supported the recommendations absent the reference to the granting of voting rights to immigrants.[15] He was under pressure within his group. The French had at the last European elections parachuted in the former president Valery Giscard d'Estaing, who had promptly been anointed group leader. Giscard and I had history from the off. When he arrived in the EP, the parliament's protocol services decided this particular new member needed special treatment, decreeing that he needed not one but two lifts cordoned off to assure his speedy access to the chamber. This was abandoned under my vigorous protests.[16]

Back in France, Giscard had found it expedient to rail against 'invasion' not 'immigration' and had called for the two-hundred-year-old 'law of the soil' (*jus solis*), by which those born in France gain French citizenship, to be replaced by the 'law of blood' (*jus sanguinis*), requiring French parentage. Privately, he excused his xenophobia as a way of staunching voters' flight to the right. The FN MEPs goaded him mercilessly as a belated convert to their cause.

Giscard was thought to be job-seeking, and in January 1992 there would be a vacancy for a right-wing president of the EP. The Socialists and the right had been alternating the post since direct elections and the incumbent was the Spanish socialist Enrique Baron. The presumptive heir was the German Christian Democrat Egon Klepsch, a man for whom 'pedestrian' was far too sprightly a term. Giscard eyed the post and recognised that votes from the far right might help to deliver. In the end Giscard didn't run, retiring from the parliament shortly after it was blessed by Klepsch. Giscard was to get his reward a decade later, appointed by the European

Council to the post of President of the Convention on the Future of Europe, whose endgame was the Lisbon Treaty.

Marijke Van Hemeldonck, a Jewish Socialist from Antwerp and a committee stalwart, persuaded me before the session started to co-sign a Socialist Group press release that she'd prepared in the run-up to the debate, complaining about Giscard's failure to condemn Le Pen, describing him as Napoleon had Talleyrand: 'shit in a silk stocking'. Constantly egged on by Gollnisch, the EP's right in general and the Liberals in particular – abetted by the odd British Tory – went apoplectic and the left went missing. For three days, each session of the parliament opened with demands to the president that we be forced to apologise. Finally, when the debate and vote on my report was concluded and the whole imbroglio died down, I walked across the chamber to Giscard and offered my apologies, 'if my remarks ... have caused him personal hurt', and said the same to the parliament.[17] The Greek Christian Democrat president of the session said: 'The subject was discussed in the enlarged Bureau, and Mr Giscard d'Estaing expressed the wish that explanations should not be made public. I presume that you did not know that he so wished, but that is all the more reason why I consider your statement does you honour'. Marijke Van Hemeldonck was unabashed. In the debate she had concluded, 'Mr de Donnea, Mr Gollnisch, Mr Wijsenbeck, I did not mention any names, but if the silk stockings fit, wear them! *(Protests)*'.

The Belgian Liberals were, if anything, worse. They'd been found with their hand deep in the extreme right's cookie jar of xenophobic tropes. Nordmann in an initial intervention complained of my 'outrageous language', which 'unfortunately bears witness to his injured pride and disappointment at his failure to get the report adopted unanimously'. He hadn't lost the plot; he had clearly never found it. A second intervention saw him play catch-up, arguing, 'it is Mr Ford who bears the heavy responsibility of not having attempted to find a position that could have been unanimous and having turned the struggle against racism into an instrument of partisan confrontation ... If we give voting rights to foreigners here while allowing them to keep those rights at home, Mr Ford, that is to give them greater rights than those enjoyed by Community citizens and, in doing so, to exacerbate the feelings of

frustration and xenophobia which will mitigate against the efforts to fight racism and xenophobia.'

Yves Galland, a French Liberal who was to succeed Giscard as president of the group, argued that to even consider voting rights was to offer Le Pen 'an electoral highway that he is certain to exploit': 'Those who wanted this report and who will be voting for the motion for a resolution tabled by the four political groups will bear a heavy responsibility: responsibility for having divided Parliament ... and for the publication of documents that will stir up racist and xenophobic feelings.' Consequently, the Liberal Group voted against, with the exception of Simone Veil, the elected parliament's first president, who refused to vote: 'Today what an appalling, wretched spectacle we have seen from the House!' Veil reacted, concluding, 'I want nothing to do with a report which is a charade and at the same time merely skims the surface of this grave evil which dishonours our societies.'

I emphasised to the plenary the political nature of the issue: 'Racism is scientifically nonsensical, morally wrong but, most importantly, politically dangerous.' The report tried to institutionalise anti-racism and anti-discrimination, particularly in relation to immigrant communities. Perhaps it was no surprise that it lent towards UK approaches to tackling racism and discrimination. The report contained justified criticism of the European institution's failure to take up any of the earlier Evrigenis report's forty recommendations. We exposed and explored media representation of and for ethnic minorities, infested as they were by racist images and stereotypes, while the availability of advice and services in migrants' mother tongues was far less common than English and French material in West Germany for occupying troops.

The EP's Legal Affairs Committee was to have responsibilities added to its terms of reference (Recommendation 1), while in the Commission it would be the president (14). There was to be a directive prohibiting the dissemination of anti-Semitic and racist material (32), a European Year of Racial Harmony (20), a Residents Charter and Card (33), with a Community-funded European Network to Combat Racism and Xenophobia (34) and European Migrants Forum (39). Member states were urged to make the acquisition of citizenship easy and cheap after five years' residence (62), alongside the contentious consideration of voting rights, at least in local elections, first to all Community citizens and then to all 'legal immigrants' also after five years' residence (64). Finally, to nail the pretext of lack of competence, the next Intergovernmental Conference was to explicitly introduce competence into the treaties in respect of third-country nationals in the Community, and the EP was to investigate taking the Council to the European Court of Justice (10) for its failure to respect the June 1986 Solemn Declaration with the outcome of the Resolution on Racism and Xenophobia (see above).

Yet the institutions and their unions also had in-house work to do. Recommendation 7 was 'That consideration be given, in negotiations with the trade union organisations concerned, to amendment of the Staff Regulations for officials of the European Communities to open the way for those from third countries with permanent resident status in one of the Community countries to permit employment as established Community officials.' The institutions were all too slow but began to look more like the communities they were supposed to represent, and Black MEPs appeared from places other than Overseas France.

Again, there was a country-by-country survey, but also an attempt to tease out the transnational linkages. One focus was the international skinhead movement, which was born in the UK in the late 1960s when 'Paki bashing' was paired with a visual subculture of shaved heads, bomber jackets and steel-toecapped Dr Martens. Racist music, centred around Skrewdriver and its lead singer, Ian Stuart, was a British export to West Germany, Belgium, Holland and Scandinavia. The racist skinhead cult expanded across Europe, as unemployment fed tensions that resulted in violence against migrants in France and Hungary. To celebrate the 1993 arson attack on a migrant family in Solingen that killed five women and girls, the English band No Remorse recorded an album in 1996 titled *Barbeque in Rostock*. The UK anti-fascist magazine *Searchlight* closely monitored the growth of these fascist gangs, and I later wrote the introduction to their *White Noise: Inside the International Nazi Skinhead Scene*.[18]

I accepted that the report had its imperfections – 'every hedgehog is a gazelle to its mother! Clearly in a 300 page report, there are some minor points which require amendment

and clarification' – and asked members to submit their concerns in writing. On the left there was broad support. No socialist offered any criticism, while some of the Greens and Communists argued it didn't go far enough. There were racists and xenophobes hiding in plain sight. Within the regionalist Arc en Ciel group was to be found the Lega Lombarda – Alleanza Nord, who would subsequently unambiguously descend into xenophobic populism, but at the time were trying to hang on to the tatters of their progressive credentials.

Among the centre-right, the EPP were supportive. Nicole Fontaine commented, 'Mr Ford has picked up the torch. It was not in easy circumstances that he did so ... Mr Ford has performed an important task. We must acknowledge the fact that he tried to achieve a consensus. However, our group cannot go along with him all the way.' The Portuguese MEP Lucas Pires, speaking for the EPP, echoed Fontaine: 'we should like, before anything else, to congratulate our colleague, Mr Ford, the Chairman [*sic*] of the Committee of Inquiry, and the other members of the committee on their good work, which we find overall positive notwithstanding some nuances and odd points that could have been approached slightly differently or from another point of view. In truth, racism and xenophobia are two mortal enemies in any free and democratic society. Its reappearance on the European scene is therefore a reason for worry and alarm.'

The others on the traditional right were more enigmatic. I said, 'there was some talk about hard hitting determination. It seems to me that some groups' hard hitting determination is about as threatening to most members of the Front National as being savaged by a dead sheep.' The Reverend Ian Paisley opposed because the report failed to recognise that 'the left-wing Sinn Fein/IRA are carrying out a campaign of racist genocide against the British people of Ulster.'

The extreme and neo-fascist right was venomous. Gollnisch argued process in seven separate interventions; but the parliament lacked the competence for such an investigation. As far as Fini was concerned, I was 'lying, blinded by ideological hate,' and should 'go to the Kremlin to get paid.' According to Antonio Mazzone (MSI): 'What you are outlining and proposing to future generations of Europeans is a life as a people without a fatherland, a life in which the memory of their forefathers and the values of diversity would be watered down in a horrible humanity swarming in great cities that are increasingly polluted and inhabitable.' Cristiana Muscardini (MSI) claimed: 'Mr Ford is not just a racist; he is an inveterate liar.' Jean-Marie Le Chevallier (FN) thought that I was a 'racist, troublemaker and falsifier,' and a 'mediocre spokesman of a decadent left.' Yvan Blot (FN) demanded the EP 'set up a committee of inquiry into the actions of professional totalitarian anti-racists like Mr Ford.'

Bernard Antony's (FN) 'thoughts turn to those thousands of my compatriots, men and women, small children and old ladies fallen victim to theft, rape and other crimes, attacked by the dregs of society who would have been dealt with far more harshly in their countries of origin than they are here ... In my library I keep readily to hand the books of the finest of French storywriters, Alexandre Dumas, who felt no urge, though as West Indian as Harlem Désir, to found SOS Racisme.' For Karel Dillen (Vlaams Blok) the report was 'a *document humain* of left-wing manipulation and disinformation, half truths and whole lies ... In more tragic circumstances he [Ford] would have rivalled the grand inquisitors, the sinister Vichynski of the purges of Moscow, the equally sinister Freisler of the German *Volkgerichtshoft*, who incidentally also came from the extreme left wing.' In an earlier intervention, she claimed that 'the blind have been exposed as political pygmies too often and for too long, and listening now to Mr Ford I could not help thinking back to Nietzsche's *Thus Spake Zarathustra* and to his *Geschichte vom bleichen Verbrecher*. But for him also wisdom comes too late.' Thus, I was an example of the latent careless evil in humankind, willing without compunction to deceive and defraud.

I responded that I was 'proud that the MSI who gave us the Bologna bombing through some of their factions, the FN whose members and supporters murdered a French Socialist Party worker at the last elections, who attempted to bomb SOS Racisme headquarters in Toulon and whose leader attempted to smuggle guns out of the United States, do not like the work I am doing.' The joint resolution between the Socialist Group, the Green Group, the European United Left and the Left Unity Group was adopted.

Further steps

The issue of free movement was covered in the report. It was my view that ignoring the rights of migrant workers – European residents, but not European citizens – was ignoring the rights of what I termed, at the time, Europe's Thirteenth State. Arbitrarily diced and sliced as legal in a single member state, but inevitably attracted to work in economic hotspots across no longer functioning borders, they were ripe for exploitation by unscrupulous employers. This underpinned the vital importance of a European Social Charter, and the reason for my dislike of the Schengen and Trevi groups. In plenary in June 1990, I'd made my stance clear on this structural oppression: 'The people most affected by the problems of racial harassment and racial discrimination are those people who are not nationals of one of the twelve Member States of the Community.' Without treatment equal to that received by everyone else, they faced exploitation and the creation of an 'under-class that will drive down the social wage throughout the Community.'[19]

The Schengen group operated behind closed doors, producing no reports or minutes for the parliament to review. I had protested its democratic deficit in November 1989: 'We are frankly fed-up with these semi-clandestine groups like the Schengen group and the Trevi group who meet and make decisions on behalf of the people of Europe without being accountable in any way.'[20] By 1991, to anticipate, we were warning against the creation of a 'fortress Europe.'[21] We had a long march to come.

Round Two

Twelve months after the initial debate on my report there was a second round with the publication of the final text. The far right stayed the course with new contributions from Germany. Harald Neubauer (Die Republikaner) spoke, saying, 'I wish to repudiate most emphatically the monstrous accusations that have been made against me,' although he failed to respond to my request seeking him to confirm or deny membership of the NSDAP/AO – a US and European coordinating network distributing neo-Nazi propaganda.[22] Neither did Le Pen disavow the report in *Globe* magazine that had stated: 'He believes the Americans built the gas chambers in Buchenwald after the War.' I did correct an error, for which I received no thanks. I had initially identified MSI leader Giorgio Almirante as a cabinet minister in the Salo Republic and now correctly labelled him as 'chef de cabinet for the Minister of Propaganda.'

In my speech I argued that the EU institutions needed to go further and faster. The creation of the European Migrants' Forum was necessary, but not sufficient. The Council were dragging their feet; John Major was the culprit, blocking all social chapter legislation, but others were hiding behind him. The difference between Council and Commission was evident from their two Socialist spokesmen. For the Council, Piet Dankert – a former president of the EP – was detached, in denial and passed the parcel. While racism and xenophobia must be tackled at local, regional and national level, there was no real European dimension to the fight. Jacques Delors, Commission president, regretfully confirmed as much.[23] Responding to criticisms of the Commission's inertia from the French Green Djida Tazdaït, Delors said: 'I repeat that I share your feelings here – we have to remember that we live under the rule of law. We are not 100 per cent competent in these areas. Far from it. But we have stressed that at length. We supported the Joint Declaration against xenophobia and racism. I think that you have to be fair in your criticism, despite the feelings which, fundamentally, I share.' I concluded my initial contribution with: 'Victims of racial hatred offer Europe far more than they could ever possibly take: enterprise, art, culture, science and many other things. Look around Europe, look at what we have gained from those who have come here in the past and imagine what we could gain in the future.'

The extreme right hadn't shifted their bilious stance from the previous year. Le Chevallier (FN) lamented the situation had gone 'from bad to worse' with 'illegal immigrants, asylum-seekers and all who are attracted by the magnet of social advantage' provided by Europe: 'It is the Islamic invasion which is to be feared and resisted. As far as the increase in racism and xenophobia is concerned, this is an artificial

debate based on half-truths which seek to obscure the real issues.' He demanded the truth about the desecration of Jewish graves and bodies in the Carpentras cemetery, pointing the finger not at the far right but at 'Israeli fundamentalists'. In 1996 five members of the French and European Nationalist Party (PNFE) were arrested for the desecration. The PNFE contained many former members of FN and had links with both the British National Party (BNP) and Vlaams Blok.[24]

Franz Schönhuber (Die Republikaner) argued that, 'as far as the description of the situation in Germany is concerned, the Ford report is not a report, it is a pamphlet, and a bad one at that!' A former member of the Hitler Youth and the Nazi Party, he defended Die Republikaner as 'a constitutional party and nothing Mr Ford says or does can change that'. Schönhuber continued: 'To sum up, as always the rule is *vae victis* – it is tough to be a loser! The victors regard patriotism as a virtue, the vanquished see it as chauvinistic, racist and the like. Just imagine the howls of protest – anywhere, but particularly in this Chamber – if I had, by analogy to the statements of the French politician Giscard d'Estaing, spoken about German blood rights. Rosenberg's "Myth of the Twentieth Century" would immediately have been made my bible. For the rest, the faded Nazi "blood and soil" apostles in Valhalla will, with a blood-curdling laugh, have admitted the French ex-President to membership of their Wotan association.'[25]

Cristiana Muscardini (MSI) had read 'the latest work of political science fiction by Mr Ford'. She protested my representation of the MSI as 'a tiny extremist and racist group', and said that 'like a good colonialist, he [Mr Ford] has probably forgotten to mention in his report, that there are other movements in Italy which could possibly be considered racist ... Actually, the Albanian refugees were put in the stadiums by the Christian Democrats and the Socialists'. She dedicated the final seconds left 'to the victims of racists, like Mr Ford'.

The French Liberals, however, had found a different hymnbook twelve months on. In the context of requesting the inclusion of Nordmann's minority opinion in the report, Yves Galland said, 'you are the rapporteur of one of the most important reports approved by this house'. Meanwhile, Simone Veil was 'now speaking in a personal capacity and on behalf of some members of my group who, like me, will vote in favour of the report'. Even Nordmann said, 'I should also like to thank the President of the Commission for being present at this debate which is an extremely important one and all the more so in that while Mr Ford's report may not have received unanimous approval on some points, the Commission has not raised any objections to the recommendations made to itself and the Council. Hence our eagerness to be informed of the action taken in relation to the most useful measures suggested in the report'. No explanation for the shift was given, but many were cognisant that in January/February in Paris and Lyon three National Assembly by-elections saw FN surge into second place with 25–28 per cent of the vote. The Belgians failed to follow where their French neighbours led. As early as November I mordantly offered to help Giscard in hunting down the 'perpetrators of this vile calumny' and fraud that purported to be election material from the Belgium Liberal Party, which contained the most awful racist and xenophobic statements.[26]

As one commentator was to say: 'The Evrigenis and Ford reports were critical first steps in the recognition of issues related to immigration, racism and discrimination at the EU level. Although they did not lead to immediate legislation on the part of the Commission, they were the building blocks that would lead other actors to step in and take action on these issues'.[27]

Kahn Committee

With increasing racist and xenophobic riots and violence in Germany, France and other member states, including the arson attack in Solingen, Helmut Kohl and François Mitterrand, under pressure, pushed the Council at their 1994 Corfu Summit to establish a Council of Ministers' Consultative Committee on Racism and Xenophobia.[28] Each member state – and applicant country – was to have a representative along with the EP. I was the EP's full member with Dutch EPP member Arie Oostlander as substitute. Its chair was to be Jean Kahn, the French president of the European Jewish Congress.

Initially, I was sceptical. In *Searchlight*, following the committee's first meeting, I complained about the narrow terms of reference, which were 'to make recommendations, geared as far as possible to national and local circumstances, on cooperation between governments and the various social bodies in favour of encouraging tolerance, understanding and harmony with foreigners.' The danger was of the committee degenerating into nothing more than a public relations exercise for Kohl and Mitterrand in the run-up to their respective elections. It was clear that the problems of racism and xenophobia could neither be adequately addressed through intergovernmental cooperation, nor by merely fostering a tolerance of 'foreigners.'

The Kahn Committee met monthly in the Council's Justus Lipsius Building, across from the Commission's Berlaymont, and produced its final report in May 1995. The fight was institutional and political. Race relations fell within the 'Third Pillar' of the Maastricht Treaty, but the demand was that in the treaty revision at the 1996 Intergovernmental Conference, these would be brought within the First Pillar, thus placing discrimination on grounds of race on a par with sexual discrimination. This would bring it indisputably within the remit of the EP and the European Court of Justice, and rescue it from the murky behind-closed-doors compromises of intergovernmentalism with indisputable EU competence.

This final report delivered all of the above, plus a Race Relations Directive protecting all European residents, and a directive banning Holocaust denial and the distribution of race hate material. These were all topics from the committee's May 1995 hearings with representatives from six anti-racist organisations, including *Searchlight*; the German churches; the European Centre for Research and Action on Anti-Semitism; European Migrants' Forum (set up as a result of the recommendations of the Committee of Inquiry); and UNITED, the European anti-racist network based in the Netherlands. All emphasised urgency in the face of a rapidly deteriorating situation.[29] The medicine proved too strong for the patient's taste, and the Kahn Report was left to moulder on the table at the Cannes Summit in June 1995.

One issue for the committee was the establishment of a European Monitoring Centre on Racism and Xenophobia

(EUMC). The climate had shifted sufficiently to make outright opposition impossible. Instead, it was to be killed by kindness. Some member states' representatives argued its work was so important that its footprint should become that of the Council of Europe – covering the likes of Albania, Azerbaijan and Ukraine – and its responsibilities should be widened to incorporate all forms of discrimination, both with no increase in the budget. This widening was convenient for coy member states, as the worst of the near and not so near abroad would misdirect away from failings back home. The proposal of making the EUMC a 'joint venture' between the EU and Council of Europe was successfully resisted in favour of 'cooperation' and it was all signed off at the 1996 Florence Summit.[30] The Consultative Committee was given the mandate to continue its work until the EUMC – to be, by mischance, based in Vienna – was up and running in June 1998.[31]

Under its first director, Beate Winkler, the EUMC proved a valuable resource for monitoring racism and discrimination across the Union, providing – much to the chagrin of certain member states – the hard data and consequent exposure that had been missing for the Committees of Inquiry. The EUMC set up RAXEN, a network of national focal points in member states that fed information into the centre. It was the centre that in 2003 drew up but never adopted the working definition of anti-Semitism that in the hands of the International Holocaust Remembrance Alliance was used to eviscerate Jeremy Corbyn's leadership of the Labour Party.

In 2007 the pallid opponents got their way and EUMC's remit was extended, transforming it into the European Union Agency for Fundamental Rights (FRA). We had won the battle against widening the remit beyond the EU, but not the war on diluting the issue beyond racism. Nevertheless, the FRA, a worthy institution, does such good work without annoying its paymasters, and is now part of the pattern of the EU's institutional wallpaper.

The Intergovernmental Conference in Messina started the process that led to the Amsterdam Treaty, ratified in May 1999. Article 13 finally provided the EU with that unambiguous legal base to combat discrimination on grounds of racial or ethnic origin, religion or belief, disability, age or sexual orientation. Delors's question of competence had finally

been answered. The mountain went to Mohammed and the Commission moved.

In 1994, in response, the EP established the Civil Liberties and Internal Affairs Committee (LIBE), which I served on until 2002; it had within its remit responsibility for addressing all forms of discrimination. I gave up my full place on ERT and dropped to substitute, and left AFET for LIBE. The Delors III Commission in January 1993 saw Ireland's Padraig Flynn named as Social Affairs Commissioner; he stayed in the post for the 1995 Santer Commission. Early on, serendipitously, he made a sequence of ill-judged comments on race and gender equality that left him sharply at odds with the EP. This worked to our advantage as, in turn, he was forced to overcompensate; in the end, he proved incredibly helpful. In late 1995 Flynn informed the EP of the Commission's proposal to designate 1997 as 'European Year Against Racism.'[32] It had taken a decade to get there – it had been an Evrigenis demand in 1986 – but for all that was nonetheless welcome. It put racism on the EU's visible agenda, even as accompanying legislation was sidelined. The year had two strands, one supporting existing programmes at national level and a second involving political, cultural and sports events, alongside seminars and conferences.[33]

This meshed nicely with the new Commission nominated after the June 1999 European elections. Labour, in a fit of pique, had abruptly abandoned first past the post for a flawed and uneven regional list system, and I'd subsequently been relocated from Manchester back to the South West (see Chapter 1). It was more chance than necessity; nevertheless, for the party it proved fortuitous. The number of Labour MEPs elected slumped to twenty-nine, but under the old system we would have had not much more than half that number.

Craven in Vienna, catastrophe in Budapest

The new Commission President was Romano Prodi. Early on, Europe's mettle was tested and was – at the last – found wanting, although not before it gave the EU's populists and national revolutionaries a scare. This all followed from

October's Austrian elections. The Social Democrats (Sozialdemokratische Partei Österreichs, SPO) had lost ground, but the shock was the surge of Haider's extreme-right Freiheitliche Partei Österreichs (FPO) that had pushed them 400 votes - out of 1.25 million - past the conservative Österreichische Volkspartei (OVP) into second place.

Austrians were entranced by Haider's charismatic populism and turned off by the relentless clientelism of the long-serving grand coalitions in equal measure. Haider had previously been forced to resign as governor of Carinthia back in 1991, after saying Hitler's employment policy was better than that of the SPO government. Months of negotiations ended in January with the formation of a coalition between OVP and FPO. The former's Wolfgang Schlüssel became chancellor and Haider stepped aside as FPO leader. Few were fooled. It would be the first time since 1945 that a 'fascist' party would serve in government. I tabled a resolution in the Socialist Group urging the EU to invoke Article 7, suspending Austria from membership on the grounds of the threat to democracy posed by this new government. The resolution passed, despite qualms from SPO MEPs, and went to the subsequent EP plenary. It was incorporated into a joint resolution backed by four other political groups condemning Haider's racism and xenophobia, and demanding Article 7 be triggered.

The *Guardian* quoted me arguing: 'Some say that it is not right for us to interfere in Austrian politics. They are wrong. Some say we have to accept the outcome of democratic elections - but elections do not always make democrats.'[34] Pressure from the EP, and elsewhere, forced the Council's hand and sanctions against Vienna were imposed on 4 February, while a Wise Men's Committee, consisting of former Finnish president Martti Ahtisaari, former Spanish foreign minister Marcelino Oreja and the German international lawyer Dr Jurgen Frowein, was established to report on the situation in Austria.[35]

Inevitably, the new government's actions proved my suspicious mind correct. The EUMC, now newly opened in Vienna, saw the de facto sacking of the Austrian representative, Professor Anton Pelinka, from the management committee in June 2000. Pelinka had been a rather pedantic force for

moderation on the Consultative Committee. Haider sued Pelinka for defamation (see below) after the latter had said in a TV interview that Haider had downplayed the actions of the Nazis.[36] Pelinka won his case. While the management committee adopted a resolution expressing regret at Pelinka's forced departure, the European Council hid behind the fact that sanctions were technically between member states and Vienna, doing nothing slowly.

Sanctions were lifted in September after the release of the Wise Men's report. It argued that – despite the FPO's open xenophobia and coordinated use of the libel laws to intimidate their ex-parliamentary opposition – Austria's commitment to European values remained and FPO ministers were working to deliver the government programme. It concluded that the sanctions should be ended because continuation would be counterproductive, in promoting growing nationalism. The report's recommendations were sweetened by the call for 'the introduction of preventative and monitoring procedures' into Article 7, 'to avoid a similar situation from developing in the future.' The report was adopted and the sanctions went.

It was a lost opportunity for Europe to lay down and define rule-of-law norms and minimum democratic standards. It set the precedent for Victor Orbán who, since resuming the Hungarian premiership in 2010, has eaten away at these norms and values from the inside, leaving only a dry husk on open display. Hungary's government pretends to be a democracy, and Europe's politicians pretend to believe them. Lenin once remarked that business would happily sell the rope that would be used to hang it. Europe's leaders feed Fidesz (Hungarian Civic Alliance) the funds that, along with a little coercion, allow Orbán's state capture. As such, Fidesz and their fellow travellers in Poland and Slovenia threaten the Union's very integrity.

The EP had its Anti-Racism Intergroup across multiple parliaments. I was its president, co-president when Harlem Désir became an MEP, and then faded into the shadows as more and more member states saw people of colour join their cohort of MEPs. My last significant parliamentary role was as part of the EP Delegation to the UN World Conference against Racism in Durban in late August 2001. The EP urged the EU representatives to take a positive line, emphasising 'condemnation of attacks on immigrants and members of minority communities', and, more significantly, the 'recognition of the long-term suffering and continuing impact caused by Europe's historical and contemporary experiences'.[37]

I was a double delegate, simultaneously representing the ANL at the parallel NGO forum. It was a jamboree with almost ten thousand there from around the globe. Contentious points of discussion were reparations for slavery and equating Zionism with racism. Washington was against both, but the second was an easier public call. They walked out over it and Israel followed in their wake. The reference was voted out of the UN World Conference's declaration, and while it was agreed to declare slavery morally abhorrent, there was no call for retroactive reparations from colonial powers. The even more discordant NGO forum's declaration declared Israel a 'racist, apartheid state', with demands for reparations limited to the transatlantic slave trade, turning a blind eye to the heavy traffic from Africa to the Dar al-Islam. Both declarations disappeared in the smoke of 9/11 three days later. Nevertheless, it was symbolic of how far the world had travelled in a generation.

Street fighting racism

My anti-racist work was made possible with the help of my staff: Salma Ahmed, who had worked alongside me at the university, Graham Atkinson, Steve Tilzey and Sarah Chilton, among others. Graham had been a long-time deep entrist inside Europe's far right and Nazi groups. After he came out, a meeting he helped organise at UMIST in the 1970s was attacked by National Front members and sympathisers. He ended up needing more than a hundred stitches in his face after he was bottled. Steve, to the contrary, had stayed onside. He had been part of the International Socialists *squadristi*, who were later expelled for their physical force approach to tackling the fascist threat. After one particularly brutal encounter he had been arrested, charged and jailed.[38]

I – and my constituency office – were regularly threatened. We reported all incidents to the local police and received

advice on security. As early as 1987, the *Oldham Chronicle* was reporting that Werneth Park Study Centre was daubed with obscene graffiti after I'd spoken there at an Oldham Campaign Against Racism and Fascism, with swastikas punctuating 'Ford dies' and 'We are watching you'.[39] During one particularly tense period, after Combat 18's *Redwatch* had published my name and home address and invited people to 'visit', the local police told me they would be watching the house. A couple of weeks later my doorbell rang early one morning. It was my neighbour from across the road telling me that someone had stolen the wheels off my car and left it on bricks. Clearly the local constabulary's eyesight needed testing. I was due to speak later at a public meeting at another community centre in Oldham when the fascists found their paint brushes for a second time. On the eve, the outside walls were daubed with 'Ford is a Jew', 'Kill the Jews' and, to complete the syllogism, 'Kill Ford'.

Police protection for Euro-MP

GRAFFITI-scarred walls and windows at Werneth Park study centre — part of the anti-Ford campaign.

LOCAL Euro-MP, Mr. Glyn Ford, victim of a race-hate campaign, has been given police protection.

National Front sympathisers daubed Werneth Park study centre with obscene graffiti, after Mr. Ford sponsored a recent meeting there of the Oldham Campaign Against Racism and Fascism.

Checks

Some of the paint-sprayed messages between swastikas say "Ford dies" and "We are watching you!"

Police are now keeping regular checks on Mr. Ford's Ashton home, where he lives with his wife, Hazel, and five-year-old daughter, Elise.

TARGET OF 'RACE HATE' CAMPAIGN

Mr. Ford, who represents Greater Manchester East (including Oldham) was on Common Market business in Strasbourg when the right-wing vandals struck.

He has already been the target of obscene callers and hate-mail from extremists.

Following the latest assault, Mr. Ford believes that he is now singled out for special attention by NF followers.

And he is concerned for the safety of his family.

"I am sure that there is great personal animosity against me. There are precautions which one can take — and I am taking them," he says.

"There is the safety of others to consider, as well as my own. It is unusual for anything to happen ... but it could. It would be foolish to take any risks."

Mr. Ford is often in the public eye with his strong anti-racist views.

"I have spoken at a number of OCARF meetings and am on a committee of MPs reporting to the EEC on the growth of racism and fascism in Europe," he says.

"I was also one of the signatories to a newspaper advertisement trying to get the planned NF march in Oldham last July banned by the Chief Constable."

Hooliganism

Mr. Ford believes that he is the latest focus of the local NF, "continuing to act out its hooliganism".

On a lighter note, he adds: "They have taken a dislike to me ... which obviously means that I must be doing something good.

"But I have a conveniently short name for graffiti artists — perhaps it would be different were I called Winterbottom."

Oldham Chronicle, 24 June 1987.

Yet the only time I was physically attacked was in Ashton-under-Lyne prior to becoming an MEP. The local Labour Party had organised an anti-racist meeting in the town hall. A group of National Front supporters – including Anthony David Jones, a local member of their 'Honour Guard' – turned up and were refused entry. They returned thirty minutes later – minus Jones – armed with metal bars and clubs. We were lucky. There was a disco upstairs in the town hall and on the way in they'd attacked one of its bouncers thinking he was with us. His colleagues waded in on our side along with Dave Hallsworth and others from the local Revolutionary Communist Party who were in the audience, and the National Front contingent were put to flight. We'd called the police during the attack and forty minutes later a solitary female officer turned up. But the attack served a purpose. Ashton's MP, Robert Sheldon, who had been a reluctant speaker at the meeting, became markedly less sceptical about the threat from the far right.

The House of Commons MPs were unhelpful in promoting the anti-racist agenda. This was not entirely true of the four Black and minority ethnic MPs – all Labour – elected at the 1987 general election: Diane Abbott, Paul Boateng, Bernie Grant and Keith Vaz. Two engaged with our work, two didn't. Paul and Bernie were both there when it mattered and fully committed. Paul preferred to limit himself to the parliamentary side, while Bernie was happy wandering the streets of Paris late at night with militants from SOS Racisme. I only got nervous when Dacia Valent, a Somali-born former police officer who had served as part of the VIP protection service and represented the PCI in the EP, told tales of her and Bernie meeting Colonel Gaddafi. She had a soft spot for David Martin. Meanwhile, Keith Vaz's engagement with the EU was even half-hearted during his undistinguished spell in his only government post as Minister for Europe. The other exceptions were Alf Dubs and Virendra Sharma, in Alf's case both before and after his time in the Commons.

I travelled the UK on speaking engagements. I spoke for the ANL in Edinburgh with Steven Rose against the work of Christopher Brand, a self-confessed 'scientific racist' in the university's psychology department. I also made appearances for the TUC in Manchester and London. It seemed I was popular at the Labour Party Conference; for instance, in 1992 I was listed as speaking at more fringe meetings than anyone else. That year I ranged across racism, Europe and the arms trade. I was later asked to give the International Brigades Memorial Lecture in Stoke Town Hall.

One organisation who engaged me early on was the Student and Academic Campaign for Soviet Jewry. I went with them on two trips to Moscow to argue with Soviet authorities over their treatment of Jews. The travellers were a very mixed bag. I remember Charles Moore, who was to become the editor of *The Times* and biographer of Margaret Thatcher, Sir Anthony Kershaw (the Stroud MP who I'd spent much of my youth working against), Paul Boateng (later to become Britain's first Black cabinet minister) and Barbara

1996.

Castle. I remember the horror on Moore's face when there was a suggestion he share a room with Boateng, but he voiced no objection. My other two memories of the visits are first flagging down 'taxis' by waving packets of western cigarettes as we made our way through the snow to meet with Yelena Bonner – a human rights activist on her own account and the wife of Andrei Sakharov – in her cramped, dingy apartment. Second was a meeting with Soviet officials where we made our demands for the right of Jews to emigrate to the UK. Pretentions were exposed when we were asked how many we wanted – ten, twenty, thirty thousand or more? Kershaw hurriedly backtracked, explaining the UK was not open to mass migration. The campaign's concerns were limited to a select list of notables.

I travelled Europe extensively. In France I spent time with Harlem Désir, and later Fode Sylla, from SOS Racisme, whose slogan was *'Touche pas à mon pote'* ('Hands off my mate').[40] At the 1985 'Concert SOS Racisme' on the Place de la Concorde, I addressed a quarter of a million people, and at the Sorbonne I spoke alongside Jacques Delors. I was there for their congresses when hundreds discussed and debated late into the night. On one occasion I remember speaking at 3 a.m. before heading back to Manchester on the morning plane. Harlem asked my advice as to whether he should run for the Parti Socialiste in the 1999 European elections. I recommended he did. He stood and was duly elected, and by 2011 he was the leader of the party as first secretary. Fode Sylla, Harlem's successor as leader of SOS Racisme, was elected in the same elections on the list of the Parti Communiste Francais. These were the disciplined party wing of the anti-racists.

In terms of the anarchic autonomist wing of French politics, I was for several years invited to the week-long summer festival organised in the Longo Mai commune in Forcalquier,

Provence, by the Comite Europeen de Defense des Refugees and Immigres (CEDRI). Longo Mai had been set up in the early 1970s by Roland Perrot, a friend of Jean Giono (author of *The Man Who Planted Trees*, 1953). The 'head' during my spell of working with them was Philipp Bouchardeau, son of Hugette Bouchardeau, the Parti Socialiste Unifie Minister of Environment in the first Mitterrand government. CEDRI had their own radio station, Zinzine, which broadcast the proceedings live to the region; one suspected the audience for six hours of speeches a day, particularly mine in English, might have been slight. But they could deliver high-profile speakers. Twice I was there with Bruno Kriesky, the former Austrian Chancellor, and once with Jean Ziegler from the Swiss National Council. CEDRI had other bases in Basle and Carinthia. I went at their invitation to Klagenfurt to campaign against Jorg Haider, the FPO leader. His political base was Carinthia and it was from there that he ran his vicious, discriminatory campaign against Austria's Slovene-speaking minority, which was only a few tens of thousands strong. Haider was removing dual-language road signs and attempting to close schools where Slovene was the language of instruction. I described him as 'a fascist in a lounge suit', which took off as my trademark. Haider was notoriously litigious, but by quoting me, any action would need to name me, and it was believed he wouldn't try to sue an MEP with all the ambiguities over parliamentary immunity. He didn't. This experience stood me in good stead when the FPO edged into government with Austria's traditional conservatives (see above).

With Harlem initially, and later Fode, we had extensive European tours, to Italy, Spain, Germany, Sweden and Denmark. I still have a poster from a visit to Pisa organised by Luciana Castellina and the PCI announcing the presence of 'Glen Ford' and Harlem's French MP friend Julien Dray. In

Stockholm, at the invitation of *Dagens Nyheter*, I apparently spent time with Steig Larsson, the creator of the formidable Lisbeth Salander in the *Girl with the Dragon Tattoo* series. I'm mortified that I have no memory of him or the encounter.

The PSOE delegation in the Socialist Group organised a small group to go to Spain's African outliers, Ceuta and Melilla, where hundreds of refugees arrived every month from Algeria and sub-Saharan Africa. Despite the vicious violence of Algiers' Islamists at the time, the first were thrown back to their fate under protest. In contrast, the sub-Saharan Africans were held in squalid camps for months on end, before being drawn off in batches to the mainland with one-year work visas; they would then promptly disappear north in search of their colonial patrimony. This was the perfect exemplar that proved the necessity for EU policy rather than 'beggar thy neighbour' pragmatism.[41]

Fode organised a delegation to Andalusia from the Anti-Racist Intergroup in September 2000, to follow up the race riots in El Ejido. After a Moroccan immigrant had been accused of stabbing a Spanish woman in February, the town saw some of Spain's worst race riots, lasting three days, as gangs of white youths looted and burnt the shops, homes and mosques belonging to the town's fifteen thousand (mainly undocumented) migrant workers from Algeria and Morocco. Many had been taken on for horticultural work on minimum wages after indigenous labour spurned the jobs, growing salad vegetables in plastic tunnels in tropical jungle heat and humidity for export; it would have been a soul-destroying existence. The national and provincial authorities did try to step in after the riots, but the local authority was obdurate, and they had voters on their side. In elections that March, the right-wing Partido Popular saw its vote climb from 46 to 64 per cent. Only a week-long strike by the workers saw local employers and authorities make restitution for the damage done. During our visit we found that the uneasy accommodation between the two sides was holding – just. The reality was both the local population and migrant workers were the victims, exploited to the benefit of a limited number of local and provincial employers who had stood aside, as the two groups clashed, counting their cash.

In the UK there was growing interest in the European dimension to fighting racism and the extreme right. Yet the arrogance of 'English exceptionalism' persisted, with the UK in the role of detached spectator looking in shock and awe at events in mainland Europe, with little concern or comprehension that the same would be visited on England in the following decades. The spectre of the UKIP, the election of two BNP MEPs and the Brexit Party failed to haunt. I'd worked with the ANL from its foundation in 1977, and they approached me to take on the role of National Treasurer after the death of Ernie Roberts in 1994. A decade later the ANL was folded into Unite Against Fascism. Again, I toured the country, most notably at Trafalgar Square four or five times and in Victoria Park, London, in April 2008. We also, along with *Searchlight*, brought up the tail of the Remembrance Day Parade.

Interestingly, English sectarianism was a match for the Germans. One very active Green MEP, Claudia Roth, a prominent anti-racist who was to go on to spend almost ten years as one of the party's two co-chairs, came to Manchester and I took her along to a Labour Party meeting.[42] There were loud protests about 'outsiders for other parties', although quite what vital political intelligence she might have been expected to pick up at an Ashton CLP GMC escaped me. She was eventually allowed to stay. When I did my return visit to Berlin the shoe was on the other foot and I was the one allowed to remain on sufferance.

Marching with to left to right myself, Joke Kniesmeijer (Anne Frank Foundation), Leon Greenman (Auschwitz Survivor) and Gerry Gable (Searchlight) at the Remembrance Day Parade in 1987.

Labour colluding in institutional racism

In March 2001, the BNP staged an 'Equal Rights for Oldham Whites' rally outside the local police station, where the police 'helpfully' confirmed that of the 572 racist incidents in the previous year, 60 per cent of the victims had been white. The following month the mugging of Walter Chamberlain, a white pensioner, by four Asian youths was the spark. On the Saturday, Oldham Athletic's last match of the season saw their 'Fine Young Casuals' hooligan group – with their links to the National Front, BNP and Combat 18 – join their Stoke City counterparts the 'Naughty Forty' and run amok, attacking Asian market stalls and rampaging through the Muslim neighbourhoods. The scenes were repeated three weeks later – with the help of itinerant thugs from Combat 18; on this occasion, just as it seemed it was being brought under control, the police mysteriously withdrew, and it all kicked off afresh. By then, forewarned and forearmed by precedent, Asian youth responded in kind with petrol bombs and the rest. Later the BNP distributed confidential police videos of the riots provided by sympathetic serving officers.

At this point Labour sided with perpetrators over victims. Government chose to collude with, rather than confront the institutional racism of Britain's police. Two interventions I made in the EP at the end of 2002 and beginning of 2003 speak for themselves. In December I said,

> *Mr President, as you may be aware, there were a series of disgraceful riots in Oldham in the summer of 2001, provoked by members of extreme right-wing groups such as the British National Party, the National Front and Combat 18. Film footage that appears to be that compiled by the local police has got into the hands of the local British National Party who are distributing it. Apart from the understandable security concerns of those involved, the apparent collusion between members of the local police and the British National Party can only cause concern to those who hope that the perpetrators on both sides will be dealt with by a system of justice that is*

> *blind to politics. I hope you will raise the matter with the British authorities.*[43]

I was forced to come back a month later:

> *Mr President, as you may recall, last month I raised the issue of the extreme right-wing British National Party claiming that sympathetic serving police officers in Oldham have provided confidential police videos of the riots in that town, obviously calling into question evidence given by such biased officers in the ongoing trials. It turns out that, instead of investigating the claims that the BNP had received such material, the police have obtained an injunction imposing a ban on the showing of the videos, which I understand, but also on the reporting of the fact that BNP is making such claims and even on the fact that an injunction has been obtained. Will you write to the appropriate authorities expressing Parliament's concern that this attempt to bury a problem, rather than to investigate it, is not the way to deal with these issues?*[44]

But the then Home Secretary David Blunkett had done exactly that, burying the problem in the depths of the British judicial system.

I'd been one of the leading figures in the left-leaning Greater Manchester Labour Coordinating Committee in the early days after its foundation in 1978 along with Graham Stringer, who was to become the leader of Manchester City Council and later MP for Manchester Blackley and Broughton from 1997 and LEXIT supporter (but that's another story). We had both David Blunkett and Charles Clarke, who was to succeed David in the Home Office, to speak in the downmarket The Britons Protection. If you'd asked me who I thought would bend to expediency first, I'd have had to put my money on Charles. I was wrong and I owe him an apology. When he was Home Secretary, we kept in touch over my work with the ANL. David was swallowed by his boxes and his libido – he was forced to resign in 2004 after his office was found to have intervened in the visa application of his lover's nanny.

The Oldham riots in 2001 were used by the far right to create an agenda around a series of myths that they proved incapable of carrying forward. Others like Nigel Farage and Boris Johnson picked up these racist batons and ran with them. The fables of parallel lives, failures to integrate and 'no go' zones were told, re-told and embellished. Yes, groups of white lads wandering the terraced streets of Werneth were not welcome, but they had only mischief in mind. The Asian taxi drivers called out to non-existent fares on the then all-white Fitton Hill estate and having their cars bricked didn't feature. On the other side, the 'left behind' white working class were provided with a road to empowerment through the appropriation of an exclusivist national identity.[45]

Rock Against Racism Northern Carnival 15 July 1978. March to Alexandra Park with the Ashton-Under-Lyne CLP banner.

Labour's establishment was marginally better than the Tories, but they were more accomplished at hiding it. Back in 1987 there was the *Spycatcher* affair with Peter Wright, whose book Thatcher banned in the UK, although it was published in Australia and the US.[46] Even quoting from the text was prohibited. I had a dozen copies shipped in from Australia which I distributed to fellow Labour MEPs. Together we tried to insert sections into the EP's version of Hansard during the debate and vote on the Starita Report on high-speed trains. The British press was still free to quote EP proceedings. The then president of the EP Henry Plumb, a Tory grandee who'd been made a baron by Thatcher less than six months earlier, ordered these references to be stricken from the record. I intervened to protest the following day, again quoting Wright on Harold Wilson: 'The plan was simple. In the run-up to the election which, given the level of instability in Parliament, must be due within a matter of months, MI5 would arrange for selected details of the intelligence about leading

Labour Party figures but especially Wilson, to be leaked to sympathetic pressmen, using their contacts in the press and amongst union officials word of the material contained in MI5 files and the fact that Wilson was considered a security risk will be passed around.'[47] This Plumb didn't censor by expunging from the EP records and it was gratefully picked up by John Palmer, the *Guardian's* European editor.

One memorable occasion was the thirtieth anniversary rerun of the Rock Against Racism festival. The first time around I'd been one of eighty thousand marchers. Second time I was a speaker. This was during Gordon Brown's 'dead men walking' phase of the last Labour government as they clung to office like drunks to a lamp post. The audience were in no mood for compromise. Some speakers had faced bottles lobbed in their direction from the hardcore clustered around the stage who were annoyed at interruptions to the music or them. When I'd spoken at Glastonbury at the Left Field, Jon McClure, lead singer of Reverend and the Makers, advised me to speak off the back of the band – when the band is dismantling its gear rather than keep the audience waiting when the next band is on stage. It was good advice. That tactic, along with an introduction from Unite Against Fascism's Weyman Bennett, who urged people to pay attention as I wasn't the normal Labour MP, saw my ten minutes of fame pass without incident. One of the other speakers was Tony Benn. I asked if he'd speak for me in Bristol – his former constituency – during the coming European election campaign. Neither my views nor position matched his requirements. I lost without his help.

Speaking onstage at Rock Against Racism, Victoria Park, London, 27 April 2008.

When SOS Racisme was at its peak there was an attempt to transplant it over to the UK, but it never took. The only relic was a very memorable version of their *Touche pas à mon pote* badge designed by Neville Brody who was the graphic designer for *The Face*. I never got to question him, but I see echoes in his work of my favourite Italian Futurist, Fortunato Depero (1892–1960). Through Graham Atkinson and Steve Tilzey I ended up in a few meetings with the 'physical force', Anti-Fascist Action. They were certainly people you wanted on your side, but they had an unhelpful green tinge with the sectarianism of Irish politics.[48]

I also remember a trip to York one March to commemorate one of the worst anti-Semitic massacres of the Middle Ages when in 1190 during the Crusades, the city's entire Jewish community was trapped by a mob inside Clifford's Tower of York Castle. Up to 150 men, women and children were killed or committed suicide to avoid forced baptism. It was reported that the extreme right was organising a counter demonstration and attack on the commemoration event. I arrived by train across from Manchester to be met by one of the students who had invited me to the event, and they rather nervously walked me to the tower, where the daffodils were just emerging. There was a thin crowd fronted by a row of skinheads. Introduced to the organiser I immediately whispered, 'Who the hell are these?' Apparently, to my relief, it was 'Skinheads against the Nazis', but it was only when my return train pulled out of York that I relaxed.

Palmers and Panthers

In the US I collaborated with Buzz and Alice Palmer and the Congressional Black Caucus, in particular Alcee Hastings and Barbara Lee, attending and speaking at conferences in Chicago, the University of Illinois in Urbana and Springfield, at Howard University, Washington DC, and New York. Alice had been a State Senator in South Chicago's Thirteenth District and Buzz the founder in 1968 of Chicago's Afro-American Patrolmen's League (AAPL) in the wash of Martin Luther King Jr.'s assassination when Mayor Daley, in the response to the ensuing riots, ordered a shoot-to-kill policy for suspected arsonists. The AAPL aimed to build relations between the police and the Black community and protect the Black leadership, including Jesse Jackson, when visiting Chicago.

Buzz worked with Dick Durham, the 'Marxist' editor of Elijah Muhammad's *Muhammad Speaks*, filling its centre pages with leftists and progressives. Durham had earlier pioneered Black radio's *Destination Freedom*, while Buzz was later close to Leonard Muhammad, Louis Farrakhan's chief of staff. When Palmer met Black Panther Fred Hampton, he was told by Hampton that he was the more likely of the two to be assassinated as he was the more dangerous. The AAPL ended up the following year protecting the evidence as Palmer was the first Black officer on the scene after the raid on Chicago's Black Panther headquarters that killed Fred Hampton and Mark Clark. This evidence was to prove the murder conspiracy between the FBI and Chicago Police Department. Through them I met Congressman Bobby Rush (Chicago First), a survivor from the Chicago Black Panther leadership, and Danny Davies (Chicago Seventh).

Rush was the House Representative who Barack Obama took on in the primaries as one path to high office. Rush crushed him in his solidly Black district. Danny Davies informed me when I attempted to talk trade that, on principle, he voted against all trade bills. I did not get anywhere near Obama. I actually got closer to meeting Farrakhan: Buzz had arranged a meeting and we got as far as Farrakhan's front door in South Chicago, only to be told he was unwell. We were due to talk about race and North Korea; the Black Panthers had previously had their Beijing and Pyongyang moments with Eldridge Cleaver.[49]

It was a long and complicated story, explained in detail in David Remnick's Obama biography *The Bridge*, but basically Obama had used a gang of lawyers to block Alice returning to stand for her State Senate seat after she had lost in 1994 to Jesse Jackson Jr. in the primary for the Chicago Second House seat.[50] It was, therefore, no surprise to find that in the 2006 primary campaign, Buzz and Alice were the leading Black campaigners for Hillary Clinton, nor that I received a letter from Hillary thanking me for a copy of *North Korea on*

the Brink they had given her. Her policies, however, made it manifest she hadn't read it.

Inter-Parliamentary Council Against Antisemitism

In late December 1995, I travelled to Jordan with a delegation from the Inter-Parliamentary Council Against Antisemitism (IPCAA) along with its (later discredited) president Greville Janner. I was there as the chairman of the EP Group of the IPCAA; also present were Arne Melchior MP (Denmark), Andreas Khol MP (Austria), Deborah E. Bodlander (US House of Representatives) and Douglas Krikler (director of the Maimonides Foundation). The delegation had been invited by Crown Prince Hassan bin Talal, the first Arab and first Muslim leader to join the Council. The trip was sold as an opportunity to initiate discussions with a group of Muslim parliamentarians from various countries to set up a parallel council to deal with Islamophobia, with IPCAA operating on a consultative basis. When we arrived, however, we were instead to meet only Jordanian parliamentarians.

The Jordanians made clear their concerns about rising Islamophobia in Europe, and their hopes to educate non-Muslims on the tolerance and pluralism of Islam. They presented us with a working paper on the establishment of an inter-parliamentary council against Islamophobia which, on behalf of the IPCAA, we offered to study. During our meeting with the Royal Institute of Inter-Faith Studies, the conversation focused on the distribution and sale of the *Protocols of the Learned Elders of Zion* in the Arab and Muslim world. One representative said that anti-Semitism was a Christian invention, not Muslim, and that the book was authored by Christians. I responded that while that may have been the case, virtually the only places where the book remained openly on sale were in the Arab and Muslim world, and at Islamic student society meetings in Europe. It had been banned elsewhere as an anti-Semitic forgery and only sold underground by neo-Nazi groups. The idea for an inter-parliamentary council against Islamophobia was stillborn, but the need remains.

CLASS of 2014

The newly established left/trade union think-tank the Centre for Labour and Social Studies (CLASS) asked me ahead of the 2014 European elections to draft a pamphlet addressing the question of how the European left could deal with the threat posed by xenophobia. Little was new. I felt the key was to re-engage with traditional core supporters who we were neglecting, leading to them being politically marooned. With Labour convinced they had nowhere to go, it pandered to triangulation's seductive hunt for the soft centre. The growth of fascist right and fascist lite parties in number and size was palpable across Europe as they recruited the discards of the 'third way.' As I noted in a piece for CLASS: 'While these parties are of varying degrees of toxicity, they all pose a serious threat to the continued political effectiveness of the traditional left for two main reasons. This is firstly due to the fact that they privilege family, order, race and nation, and secondly as they make inroads into the left's old working-class base.'[51]

The myth of the magical ceiling to right-wing populist support was baseless. They were shape-shifters, transforming themselves with ease and capable of showing concurrent images. There was a shiftless complacency among parts of the left, believing their growth came from the right. They were corralling the votes of those we thought 'had nowhere to go' and in doing so remotivating many who had long lost their way to the ballot box and some who'd never known it in the first place. They were the first falling bricks from Labour's red wall. It all played out in South West England where I was standing. UKIP were making inroads and I persuaded the Devon Labour parties to produce a specific anti-UKIP leaflet, which we would need permission from the party to publish and distribute. The regional director demonstrated the party's political illiteracy and innumeracy. In refusing permission, he argued the leaflet was so effective it would drive UKIP voters back to the Tories at our expense, seemingly forgetting it was a proportional representation election.

In the CLASS think piece, I wrote: 'The main threat lies in the four main themes of the policies of these far-right parties: Euroscepticism; anti-immigration; a cocktail of reactionary social policies; and a cynical exploitation of fear of crime

and other insecurities.' In Britain at least, the tabloid media fanned the flames. The way forward, I felt, was that, 'First we must expose xenophobic parties for what they are, second we must address the concerns of their voters and thirdly we must mobilise those threatened by their policies and very existence in politics.' Europe's divide was not sex, race or nation, but wealth. Hope lay with the young. I continued:

> *We should also recognise that there is a mirror image of xenophobes out there – young and internationally minded, liberal thinking and socially open individuals. They don't see the relevance of traditional politics and politicians, but it is their lifestyle that bigots threaten as much as that of the working class. They have been mobilised around opposition to the BNP and National Front – it was the Anti-Nazi League that ran with the 'NF No Fun' logo. If you want Government – local or national – back in your bedrooms, schools and theatres ignore the populist right. If you want to stop a new 'Section 28' go out and vote even if for the moment you want to hold your nose.*
>
> *If we want to defeat the threat we have to organise. The Front National took off in France as it filled the vacuum on the streets left by the political class. We have a job to do. Don't moan, organise! The European elections are assumed to be a triumph for UKIP as it roots itself deep into English politics. Even now it's not too late to blunt Farage's victory and start the fight back against 'yesterday's' values against UKIP and others dressed in Eurosceptic clothes. We have to set out a progressive vision for Britain's role within Europe, one that encourages tolerance, collectivism and solidarity to repair the damage done to social cohesion by divisive austerity policies. We have to reclaim the EU as our own issue, something worth fighting for, rather than letting those on the right use it to support their small-minded values for electoral gain. Ultimately, we, on the left, have to introduce an alternative narrative, 'Our Europe, Not Theirs.'*

What is to be done?

Compared to where we started, progress on recognising and combating the evils of racism has been enormous, but there's still a protracted path to follow. Racism was thrice denied by the great and the good. It was, and still is by some, believed to be a problem among the less enlightened 'over there', but not 'over here'. This is not just the explicit take of the *Daily Express* and *Daily Mail*, but even implicit in the likes of the *Guardian*. A few weeks after my Committee of Inquiry report was published, the latter paper reproduced a two-page spread from a Danish newspaper on racism there. Close reading revealed it was the Danish take on the committee's report, a fact which had entirely passed the *Guardian* by.

They were not alone. The UK was imperious and unaccepting in disavowing reality, putting a curious credence into English exceptionalism eradicating the threat of far-right populism and xenophobia in Britain. 'We only saw it coming afterwards', was the stunned reaction to both 2001's northern mill town riots and the subsequent political fallout. The BNP came to councils and the EP, alongside UKIP, who promptly captured the former's voters with a resonance of village greens and cloth caps appealing to subterranean English nationalism, before Boris bested them in 'getting Brexit done' and in doing so stealing away the opportunity for Britain to be third in the trinity of the EU's enemies within alongside Hungary and Poland.

From Raymond Dury's solitary question in the 1979–84 EP, the racism/anti-racism antithesis is now inescapable. It's unrelentingly in our feeds, on our screens and in our newspapers, day after day after day. There is little escape from notice of endemic discrimination and institutional racism, but precious few signs of engaging with the structural and institutional transformation necessary to address the issues facing communities and congregations rather than convenient celebrities of colour. Institutional racism in the police is well recognised now, but with courage twenty years ago could have been a generation ahead of today's game. The deployment of front-page 'celebrity' solutions to historic and systemic wrongs begs the question of how to tackle deep-seated institutional racism. The danger then is that

we allow racism to wriggle free from its state function as a self-serving wedge to divide class, and thus see solutions in the mirage of an enlightened establishment, rather than as part of an organised and united struggle against the same.

Endnotes

[1] The Regime of the Colonels or Greek junta was a fascist dictatorship that ruled Greece from 1967 to 1974. [2] EP (1993), *Debates*, 1 December. [3] Le Pen referred the matter – unsuccessfully – to the European Court of Justice on the fittingly appropriate date of 1 April 1985. [4] Official Journal of the European Union, No. C 1871117, 18 July 1988. [5] André Glucksmann's son Raphaël was elected in 2019 as an MEP on a joint list with the French Socialist Party, and at the time of writing is the scourge of Beijing as the chair of the EP Special Committee on Foreign Interference in all Democratic Processes in the European Union, including Disinformation. [6] Proceedings of the public hearings held by the Committee of Inquiry into the Rise of Fascism and Racism in Europe, 1984–85. [7] Proceedings, 1984–85. [8] The results were 286 for, 1 against, 1 abstention; see EP (1986), *Minutes*, 16 January. A good record of the state of play at the time is to be found in Geoffrey Harris (1990), *The Dark Side of Europe: The Extreme Right Today*, Edinburgh: Edinburgh University Press. Harris was the Socialist Group staff member servicing the committee and used its work as the basis of his book. [9] EP (1986), *Debates*, 15 January. [10] EP (1986), 'Annex 1: Joint Declaration by the European Parliament, the Council and the Commission against racism and xenophobia,' European Union Anti-Discrimination Policy: From Equal Opportunities between Women and Men to Combating Racism, 11 June, www.europarl.europa.eu/workingpapers/libe/102/text5_en.htm (accessed 4 September 2020). [11] Andrew Bell (1986), *Against Racism and Fascism in Europe*, Strasbourg: Socialist Group in the European Parliament. It also infuriated some of our Spanish members as it named a prominent PSOE member as a former Franco collaborator. [12] Glyn Ford (1992), *Fascist Europe: The Rise of Racism and Xenophobia*, London: Pluto Press. [13] Terri E. Givens and Rhonda Evans Case (2014), *Legislating Equality: The Politics of Antidiscrimination in Europe*, Oxford: Oxford University Press, p. 70. [14] EP (1990), *Debates*, 8 October. [15] Recommendation 64: That Member States consider granting the right to vote and stand, at least in local elections, first to all Community citizens and then to all legal immigrants with five years continuous residence in the country. [16] Stephen Clark and Julian Priestley (2012), *Europe's Parliament: People, Places, Politics*, London: John Harper, p. 130. [17] All quotes in this section are drawn from EP (1990), Debates, 8–10 October, unless otherwise indicated. [18] Nick Lowles and Steve Silver (eds) (1998),

White Noise: Inside the International Nazi Skinhead Scene, London: Searchlight. [19] EP (1990), *Debates,* 13 June. [20] EP (1989), *Debates,* 23 November. [21] EP (1991), *Debates,* 9 October. [22] All quotes in this section are from EP (1991). *Debates,* 7, 9 and 10 October, unless otherwise stated. [23] Earlier, I'd shared an *SOS Racisme* platform with Delors in Paris at the Sorbonne. The tenor of his intervention there had been less equivocal. [24] Anon. (1991). 'Les attentats contre les foyers Sonacotra devant la cour d'assises des Alpes-Maritimes – Les commanditaires occultes de Gilbert Hervochon,' *Le Monde,* 30 October. [25] Alfred Rosenberg, one of the principal ideologues of the Nazi Party and editor of their paper *Volkischer Beobachter,* published *The Myth of the Twentieth Century* in 1930. [26] EP (1991), *Debates,* 18 November. [27] Terri E. Givens and Rhonda Evans Case (2012), 'Race and Politics in the European Parliament,' in Terri E. Givens and Rahsaan Maxwell (eds), *Immigrant Politics: Race and Representation in Western Europe,* Boulder: Lynn Rienner, p. 111. [28] Johan Leman (1996), 'Europe's consultative commission on racism and xenophobia and the slow progress towards a European antiracism observatory,' *Loyola of Los Angeles International and Comparative Law Review* 18:3, p. 603. [29] Glyn Ford (1995), 'Hearings hear call for European legislation on racism,' *Searchlight,* July. [30] Glyn Ford (1996), 'Internet reveals Nazis' international links,' *Searchlight,* August. [31] Council Regulation (EC) No. 1035/97 of 2 June 1997 establishing a European Monitoring Centre on Racism and Xenophobia. [32] EP (1995), *Debates,* 25 October. [33] European Commission (1996), 'Press release: 1997 European Year Against Racism,' 5 December. [34] Ian Black (2000), 'Europe rallies against Haider coalition,' *Guardian,* 4 February. [35] W. Hummer (2000), 'The End of EU sanctions against Austria – a precedent for new sanctions procedures?,' *European Legal Forum* 2, November/December. [36] Council of Europe (2005), Case of Wirtschafts-Trend Zeitschriften-Verlags GMBH v. Austria, ECHR, 27 October. [37] EP (2001), '6. World Conference Against Racism,' *Official Journal of the European Communities,* 16 May. [38] Dave Hann and Steve Tilzey (2003), *No Retreat: The Secret War Between Britain's Anti-Fascists and the Far Right,* Lancashire: Milo Books. [39] 'Police protection for Euro-MP; target of "race hate" campaign,' *Oldham Chronicle,* 24 June 1987. [40] Harlem Désir (1985), *Touche Pas à Mon Pote,* Paris: Bernard Grasset. [41] Glyn Ford (1998), 'A Spanish dilemma,' *Frontline,* 28 August. [42] Claudia Roth continues her anti-racist work and in 2021 was the target of a false flag planned assassination by a former army officer pretending to be a refugee. [43] EP (2002), *Debates*, 16 December. [44] EP (2003), *Debates*, 13 January. [45] Makin-Waite (2021). [46] Peter Wright with Paul Greengrass (1987), *Spycatcher: The Candid Autobiography of a Senior Intelligence Officer*, Sydney: Heinemann. [47] EP (1987), *Debates*, 17 September. [48] See my review of *Beating the Fascists: The Untold Story of Anti-Fascist Action* by Sean Birchall, 'Physical Force: Putting the Boot into the Far Right in Britain', *Tribune*, 20 May 2011. [49] See Yuk-sa Li (ed.) (1972), *The Speeches and Writings of Kim Il Sung, with a Foreword by Eldridge Cleaver*, New York: Grossman; and my review of Robeson Taj Frazier (2015), *The East is Black: Cold War China in the Black Radical Imagination*, in *Asian Review of Books*, 5 March 2015. [50] David Remnick (2010), *The Bridge: The Life and Rise of Barack Obama*, London: Picador. [51] Glyn Ford (2014), 'Think piece: How can the European left deal with the threat posed by xenophobia?', Centre for Labour and Social Studies, April.

9 Vignettes and Curiosities

> I'll play it first and tell you what it is later.
>
> Miles Davis

Football

For a long time I was able to use a line at public meetings in my constituency, 'I hate football [long pause] – I'm a Manchester City season-ticket holder'. It always got a laugh. They're not laughing now! My passage through life has long been punctuated by the referee's whistle. It started when Swindon Town were promoted to the second division for the 1963/64 season while I was at Marling. A group of us started to travel up on the train from Stonehouse and Stroud for Saturday 3 p.m. matches. I was at Wembley in March 1969 when then third division Swindon beat Arsenal 3–1 in extra-time in the League Cup final. There was a flirtation with Oxford United – their city had better bookshops – but it was the Robins that were to choose my Manchester team for me.

When I moved to Stockport in 1973 you could still just turn up and pay at the turnstiles to get into any match. I was seduced by the 'Swindon reject' Mike Summerbee at City and ended up standing on the Kippax. My first match was a Wednesday night 1–0 win over Coventry with Summerbee, Bell, Lee and Marsh on show, but no Law. Marsh scored the only goal from the penalty spot. Both Church founded, City was the Protestant team – founded in 1880 as St. Mark's (West

Gorton) – and United the Catholic. That worked, as after all I was a Protestant sceptic. My father was a football fan, and when he came to visit it was *de rigueur* to see a match. The pecking order was City then United, depending on who was at home. One weekend we were reduced to Bolton Wanderers. We were at United v Sunderland when they spent a year in the second division in the mid-1970s. On that day, 2–0 down at half-time, United came back to win 3–2.

I followed City through thin and thinner. The nadir for me was a League Cup away match against Barnet during a torrential downpour in autumn 1994 when we lost 1–0, conceding a goal after twenty-eight seconds. It was worse than even York and Wycombe in Division Three, yet not as bad as losing 2–1 to Mansfield Town in December 1998 in the Auto Windscreens Shield. The only redeeming feature was that while I was present at the first three, I was thankfully in China for Mansfield. I was away again for City 3 QPR 2 in 2012 when we became champions for the first time since 1968. Thankfully Mansfield had not been on TV, but I found QPR in an Irish Bar in Sanlitun.

I met some of the City hierarchy. Chairman Peter Swales invited me into the boardroom – at the time wives and girlfriends were hived off to alternative accommodation – where his only query was, 'You don't really stand in over there?', pointing towards the Kippax, the huge terrace of choice along the far side of the pitch where the City hardcore congregated. During the Francis Lee era I became friendly with Colin Barlow, and when City were short of a goalkeeper I recommended they enquire after Brazil's Claudio Taffarel who I'd read in *La Gazzetta dello Sport* had been reduced to playing in an outfield position for Italy's Reggiana. Apart from a flurry of calls, nothing came from it, and instead of Taffarel – who'd got a World Cup winner's medal the previous summer following his heroics in the final penalty shoot-out – we ended up with John Burridge, at forty-three the oldest player ever to play in the Premier League. Thaksin Shinawatra, I met twice – once in Brussels when he was the Thai prime minister, when he came to lobby me as the EP's rapporteur on the EU–ASEAN FTA, and on a second occasion when I took the head of the World Taekwondo Federation to meet him after a City–Newcastle match at Maine Road. A former Korean assistant of mine was working for the federation.

Just over a year after the Brussels meeting, I was in Tokyo when the 1999 Intercontinental Cup Final was being played between Manchester United and Palmeiras, a Brazilian club founded by Italian immigrants. I bought a ticket and the green scarf of the South American side. United won 1–0 and the fifty thousand neutrals were regaled by the United fans chanting 'Hello, hello, we are the Busby boys. Hello, hello, we are the Busby boys. And if you are a City fan, surrender or you'll die. We all follow United'. As almost certainly the only City fan in the stadium, I took it personally!

Apart from City, I always check the Plymouth Argyle result – my father's team – and have a soft spot for Milanese giants Internazionale. I also follow from afar Europe's two most renowned anti-fascist teams, Hamburg's St Pauli and Tuscany's Livorno where the PCI was founded in 1921. I have the t-shirts: St Pauli's features their broken swastika motif and Livorno's Che Guevara. The fans at the latter's Armando Picchi Stadium have even been known to flourish large North Korean flags on occasion. There seems to be an unfortunate correlation between progressive politics and regressive football. While St Pauli are generally mediocre performers in the German Bundesliga second division, Livorno put them totally in the shade, going bankrupt in 2021 and being reborn in the semi-professional fifth tier of Italian football. The first step on the long march back to Serie A started in 2022 as they finished top of the Eccellenza Toscana Girone B division. Yet St Pauli have their moments; after leading the German second division for most of the 2021/22 season they snatched failure from success, collapsing on the run-in to finish fifth.

North Korea also has a football connection. During the 1966 World Cup in England, the only match I saw live was a dire 0–0 draw at Villa Park between Argentina and West Germany. But up in Middlesbrough, North Korea beat the Italians 1–0 after an earlier 1–1 draw with Chile. In the quarter finals in Liverpool against Portugal they roared into a three-goal lead before Eusebio put them to the sword with four goals, Portugal eventually winning 5–3. I watched in grainy black and white. I was later to carelessly present a video of the match to Kim Yong Nam, North Korea's Head of State. Whether he was amused was far from clear.

In 2007 North and South Korea were drawn in the same qualifying group for the 2010 World Cup. I suggested to two friends that it would be rather fun to go to the North to watch the home match. Keir Dhillon and Stuart Emmerson were up for it, so off we went the following March via Beijing, only to discover when we arrived that after Pyongyang had refused to allow either the playing of South's anthem or the *Taegeukgi* flag to be flown, FIFA had moved the match to Shanghai. We had no way to get there, so decided we'd watch it on TV. It wasn't being shown. Even the 0–0 result wasn't available in Pyongyang until two days later. I guess if they'd been thrashed, we might still be waiting.

The UK's FCO were in an engagement phase in late 2008 and were keen to connect not just with their Ministry of Foreign Affairs (MFA) but also with the people who made the decisions, namely the International Department of the WPK. The problem was that they wouldn't accept an invitation from the FCO. They needed a political invitation, so I was approached and asked to invite them, which I duly did. A group of five came over, led by Pak Kyong Son, a vice director in the International Department. They had a briefing on the proposed Severn Barrage – the west coast of the Peninsula has an enormous potential for tidal power – refused to visit Oldbury nuclear power station (which shares a design with the DPRK's Yongbyon plant) after I had painstakingly obtained ministerial clearance from Bill Rammell, visited a community centre in Cheltenham that overlooked GCHQ and were dragged up to Stoke to watch City.

At that match in the Potteries, we were deep among the City fans and the raucous behaviour was a shock for both delegation and FCO minders. The match was bad enough. Despite Stoke having a player sent off after half an hour, they went ahead on the stroke of half-time. At the break, Pak went off to the gents. When he hadn't returned after ten minutes, I went looking and found him transfixed there as the City fans, packed in the toilets for an illicit fag, pogoed to the chant of 'Stoke, you're a fucking joke'. I rescued him, but he might have been better off staying where he was. The fans were wrong: Stoke held on to win 1–0. Worse, after the match we were held back by a police cordon as we came out of the Britannia Stadium to give Stoke's fans time to disperse. Marialaura De Angelis, who spent a decade with me working on North Korea and Japan, was having a sneaky roll-up when she was accused of smoking dope. At this point, our FCO minders made themselves scarce, leaving us to argue our way out of the situation and wonder if we might have a rather interesting diplomatic incident to contend with. Although retrospectively it might have served them right. The police finally satisfied it was nothing other than dodgy tobacco, we were allowed to leave, at which point our minders miraculously reappeared.

In October 2012 I had a small group from the North Korean Embassy visit the Forest of Dean and I took them up to Birmingham to see City play at West Bromwich Albion. Again we were among the City fans, this time behind the goal down towards the corner flag. It wasn't going well. In the middle of the first half, James Milner was sent off, while in the middle of the second, Shane Long scored for West Brom. Ten minutes from time, Edin Dzeko was brought on for Gareth Barry and promptly scored in front of us. A leather-jacketed skinhead grabbed Hyon Hak Bong, the ambassador to EU and UK, in a tight, enthusiastic embrace, with an equally intimate repeat when Dzeko scored a second in injury time.

Hyon began to get into the swing. He was present when City won 3–1 at West Ham a year later and insisted on driving us back – bus lanes all the way – into Central London. The following April, immediately after Steve Gerrard's slip gifted Chelsea a 2–0 victory over Liverpool that put the Premier League title back in City's hands, City won by the same score at Crystal Palace with goals from that man Dzeko again and Yaya Touré, with the ambassador a full-blooded participant in the hand gestures and 'Yaya Touré, Kolo Touré' incantation. I was by this point getting my visas issued in the back of the embassy car.

At the beginning of January 2016, I invited the ambassador to a Watford match at Vicarage Road. He couldn't make it, but suggested his number two come instead. I knew Thae Yong Ho from a couple of earlier matches. The weather was dreadful, pouring with rain, and everyone including Thae got soaked. Rather like the West Brom match four years earlier, City came from behind, winning 2–1 at the death. When I saw the ambassador in late April for dinner he was in a state, explaining that Thae had disappeared some weeks previously and all the FCO would say – after serial enquiries – was that he was 'safe'. Prior to his disappearance, Thae had been informed he was to be recalled to Pyongyang over financial irregularities. The ambassador wanted my advice. It was obvious Thae had defected, and I told the ambassador to take control of the story by breaking it himself. Of course, he never followed through as Pyongyang buried its head in the sand and the story finally broke that August. Thae and family had been whisked out to Germany by MI6 for a lengthy debriefing and then on to Seoul.

Thae's wife was related to O Paek Ryong, part of the family-and-friends circle around Kim Il Sung, explaining why Thae got the extended 'soft' foreign postings so coveted by MFA staff. While he was stuck at number two, his wife and their two sons were in London. There were reports that in the aftermath Ambassador Hyon had been recalled to Pyongyang and executed – on par for most journalism dealing with the North. Hyon was scheduled to return anyway at the end of his normal tour of duty. I had dinner with him that December in Pyongyang with Ri Su Yong, the party's Vice-Chair for International Affairs. What was true was that Hyon's promised promotion to Vice-Foreign Minister for Europe never happened and he was shuffled sideways into the MFA's research wing and onto retirement.

In 2018 Thae wrote *Cryptography from the Third Floor Secretariat* (in Korean), a rather balanced account of the North compared to that of most defectors. It is finally scheduled to appear in English. In the 2020 National Assembly elections he was elected in Psy's conservative Gangnam constituency for the right-wing United Future Party. Back in 2015 Kim Jong Chol, Kim Jong Un's elder brother, had come to London for an Eric Clapton concert and Thae had been his minder. Putting up with Clapton once might be bearable, but Kim insisted on coming back a second night for more. It was then the paparazzi caught them. A better briefing might have saved them. At a gig back in 1976, Clapton had spewed racism into the laps of his audience, calling Britain a white country and for the foreigners and 'wogs' to leave, while lauding Enoch Powell.[1] Clapton's diatribe saw 'Rock Against Racism' set up as a counter. Thae came with his heavy security detail to an event I was speaking at in Seoul in 2019 and I asked him whether it was Watford's rain or Eric Clapton's singing that had proved the final straw. No reply was the answer.

At the Stoke vs Manchester City match, 31 January 2009, with the Workers' Party of Korea Delegation along with Keir Dhillon and Marialaura De Angelis. On my left is Ri Ung Gil and on Marialaura's right is Pak Kyong Son. City lost 1-0.

Fine French football

During my last parliament (2004–9) I was for a while chair of the Sports Intergroup – with Tory Eurosceptic MEP, and Boris Johnson's future chief whip, Chris Heaton-Harris as secretary. Earlier I had campaigned against both all-seater stadiums and mandatory IDs for English football fans. Finally for the 2022/23 season 'safe' standing for home fans at Premier and Championship grounds in England is being reintroduced. Away fans since the post-Hillsborough Taylor Report had long played fast and loose with the definition of all-seater. The threat that fans refusing to sit during matches would lead to subsequent stadium closure led visiting supporters, while persistently standing, to barrack the home fans with chants of 'sit down or they'll shut your ground.' I also campaigned against the financial sleight of hand where top English clubs bundled together match tickets with expensive travel packages organised by cronies, dressed up as an excuse to manage the threat of hooliganism.[2]

A group of MEPs took the French Football Federation to court – and retrospectively won – over discrimination in ticket sales for the 1998 World Cup that prioritised French nationals and Visa card holders. The following July, I demanded a Commission Statement after the Commission announced they were fining the French €1000 for making €200–300 million profit by ignoring Community Law. Three days later, Neil Kinnock spoke for the Commission. I said in response,

> *Madam President, I thank the Commission and Commissioner Kinnock for being available to make this statement following my request earlier in the week. While I welcome the fact they are here to make the statement, I am disappointed in its content.*
>
> *I am told I do not like football: I am a Manchester City season-ticket holder. I am told that the Commissioner has similar problems with a rumoured enthusiasm for Cardiff City which may explain some of the difficulties we both face. Nevertheless, I agree that the French Football Federation put on a wonderful feast of football. The French 'rainbow team' did much to confound the xenophobics and racists who, like Mr Le Pen and our unlamented former colleague Mr Mègret, believe that to be French is to be white. Yet importantly, there clearly was a breach of competition rules on a massive scale. Commissioner Kinnock talked about 180,000 tickets being made available to football fans across Europe. That was after 600,000 tickets were sold on a discriminatory basis. The organising committee deliberately and provocatively ignored early on the requirement that all citizens of the European Union be treated equally, and clearly breached Article 82 of the Treaty. In doing so, they massively increased their profits, selling tickets in corporate blocks as small as one. You could not buy a ticket by telephoning and paying FF500, but for FF5000 you could get the same ticket and the equivalent of a school dinner – I have had corporate hospitality before. If Commissioner Kinnock is asking me if I believe that the European Commission could actually help grassroots football better than*

the multinational corporations who actually rely on the profits, I would actually vote for the European Commission. It may not be a very popular move but I have seen very little evidence of the people who are making multi-millions of pounds out of football putting it back into football. They are putting it into franchising and other things.

This also endangered the security of thousands of football fans. It turned tens of thousands of French men and women into amateur ticket touts. If they bought their allocation of four tickets each for a major match and sold them on the black market, they had enough money for two of them to take a two-week holiday in Australia. It was very difficult to imagine that French men and women would not pick up tickets and sell them in that way and clearly that was happening. In these circumstances, therefore, does the Commissioner not agree that football fans will think it is absolutely ludicrous, the €1000 fine – which was about the black-market price for a ticket for England–Argentina – that ticket touts will think that this is good news and that genuine football fans will be disappointed? Can he not confirm that we could have fined the French football authorities something between FF100m and FF200m, which was something like 10% of the extra profits they made? Does he not believe that the excuse that the organising federation no longer exists is actually a facile one when clearly it is the responsibility of the French Football Federation?

Does he not agree that the message to the organisers of Europe 2000, to the organisers of Europe 2004 and the possible organisers of the Mondiale 2006, whether in Germany or the United Kingdom, is that they can ignore the rules, maximise profits and in the end, all it costs them is the small change? Should the Commission be treating football differently from any other multi-billion-pound industrial operation? It seems to me that if this had been in the telecommunications sector or elsewhere, the notion that we would have come back with a symbolic fine in circumstances where people had increased their profits by £200m or £300m would have been as ludicrous as the symbolic fine appears to football fans.[3]

The scant compensation was that they actually paid up!

The EP supported the Bosman ruling, which ended serfdom in soccer (albeit of a rather up-market variety). Prior to the ruling, I long argued that the Treaty of Rome's free movement provisions meant EU nationals could not be counted as foreign by UEFA or the Premier League.[4] I told City management this repeatedly, but despite the evidence of parliamentary questions they initially refused to act. Finally, City contacted me and asked if I could get a letter from Padraig Flynn, the commissioner responsible, addressed to them saying that the UEFA regulation on three foreign players (the '3+2' rule) was a breach of the European treaty. This I did and delivered. The letter was cashed in, as I remember, at a home match. Losing 1–0, we brought on yet another foreign player and deservedly continued to lose. But the Premier League had been outplayed by the Commission. With the Bosman ruling, the '3+2' rule was officially no more.[5]

I was interviewed by Dave Wallace from the fanzine *King of the Kippax* in 1998 when City were at their worst.[6] He asked me if I thought we'd ever get into Europe again. The answer was 'absolutely'. Before you knew it, I was proved right. At the end of the 2002/3 season, City were awarded a place in the UEFA Cup as England's fair play champions. The following season's European campaign started at home with a match against Welsh side Llansantffraid FC, rebadged as Total Network Solutions, with City ultimately winning 7–0 on aggregate. I finally attended my first City match on the European mainland with a trip to East Flanders where Sporting Lokeren were beaten 1–0 to complete a 4–2 aggregate victory. I luckily only made the home leg of the next tie against Groclin, where a 1–1 home draw married to 0–0 away saw City eliminated in Poland on UEFA's now abandoned away goals rule.

My one regret was using EU competition law to help Wimbledon FC's owners emulate American football's franchises and up sticks from South London to the glories of Milton Keynes. I always thought John Betjeman would have retargeted his 'Come friendly bombs and fall on Slough! / It isn't fit for humans now' if the new town had been built in the 1930s rather than the 1960s. Associated enquiries on dual ownership of Sparta Prague and AEK Athens led to me watching the immigrant-formed Athletic Union of Constantinople (AEK) in their Nea Filadelfeia stadium when I was in Greece with the Socialist Group.

Olympic bidding

Manchester bid for the Olympics both in 1990 and 1993. The first time around I wasn't involved. They were up against five other cities that September in Tokyo. Atlanta beat Athens in the fifth round to be awarded the 1996 games. Manchester went out in round two having come ahead of just Belgrade, although in the first ballot they'd only narrowly trailed Melbourne and Toronto. They decided to go again. The second time around, part way into the process, I was pulled in. The voters were the just shy of a hundred members of the International Olympic Committee (IOC) who whittled down the candidate cities to a conclusion by serial secret ballots. Things have changed, but back then it was a sinecure for life. I was initially approached as a possible conduit to Franco Carraro, one of the two Italian IOC members, who had been Mayor of Rome and Minister of Tourism for the Partito Socialista Italiano. I never got very far with him, but it turned out my other contacts were better. Apart from Carraro, my prime targets were Mohamed Mzali, a former Tunisian prime minister in exile, the two Japanese, Igaya Chiharu and Okano Sun-ichiro, and the North Korean Kim Yu Sun.

On the eve of another September vote in Monte Carlo I was able to organise, through North Korea's embassy to UNESCO in Paris, dinner with Kim. I went along with Graham Stringer, the leader of Manchester City Council, who I'd known for years. We'd both been active in the late 1970s in the

Labour Coordinating Committee in Greater Manchester in its left anti-Trotskyist phase, organising meetings with the likes of Charles Clarke and David Blunkett. The other dinner guest was Bobby Charlton, a star of England's World Cup victory in 1966. When I'd travelled to Turkey for the first time in the late 1960s I'd taken a ferry from Istanbul on a three-day voyage along the Black Sea coast, disembarking at Hopa, only eighteen kilometres from the border with the Soviet Union. We'd called at half a dozen other ports on the way, one of which was Rize. Here we went ashore and sat in a cafe sipping Turkish coffee and 'chatting' to the locals. Their English was grim, our Turkish far worse. When they discovered we were from the UK they started intoning 'Bob Charly, Bob Charly!' We were totally bemused, until one mimicked dribbling a football. Twenty years later Bob Charly and I were having dinner.

Kim was accompanied by Chang Un, the head of North Korea's national Olympic committee who was to succeed Kim on the IOC when he resigned after the 1993 vote. Kim, a former squad member of the North's football team, had retired before the glory of 1966. We talked football, which back then wasn't even an Olympic sport. It was the only topic we had in common, with Bobby a Manchester United stalwart and Graham a hardcore fan. It was years in the future before I discovered it had worked – to a degree. I saw Chang in Pyongyang a decade later and asked him about the outcome of our dinner. Beijing was first choice – hardly a surprise – but if China went out it had been agreed Pyongyang's vote would switch to Manchester. I suspect that, apart from the Chinese, we were the only bid team to court Pyongyang.

I also had lunch with Okano. This was when I was in an abstemious phase and not drinking. I still managed to resist when he ordered a £300 bottle of wine on a bill we were picking up. Okano said he was going to vote for Manchester, but IOC members make politicians look principled – giving lying a bad name. I'd have put my money on Pyongyang over Tokyo.

Mzali was a different kettle of fish. He had been a controversial prime minister under President Habib Bourguiba from 1980 to 1986. When he was dismissed, he fled to Paris in exile; his wife, Fethia Mokhtar – who herself had served as Minister for Women – and their six children were stranded in Tunisia, forbidden to leave. In June 1993, Tunisia's then president Zine El Abidine Ben Ali – who was to survive until the Arab Spring swept him away in 2011 – was in Strasbourg to give a solemn address to the EP. I tabled a resolution, due to be debated the same day as his address, condemning his government for holding the Mzali family hostage. On the Monday his entourage descended on my office keen to mitigate the damage. We came to an accommodation. The following morning, I intervened in the plenary, 'Madam President, there was an urgency tabled by the Socialist Group with respect to the family of the former prime minister of Tunisia, Mr Mazali [*sic*], complaining that his family had not been allowed to leave Tunisia. It now appears to be clear that if it ever was the case, the Tunisian Government has put no barriers in the way of his family now leaving. Therefore we wish to withdraw the resolution.'[7] In the run-up to the Olympic vote, when the Arab IOC members met to agree a common candidate, Mzali said that he was under an obligation to support Manchester.

Manchester's 2000 Olympics bid Exhibition in the European Parliament, Strasbourg December 1992 (left to right) Lyndon Harrison MEP, myself, Sir Bob Scott, Sir Christopher Prout MEP, John Major, and the Lord Mayor of Manchester Councillor Bill Egerton.

This time, Manchester was a poor third out of five, well behind Sydney, who beat Beijing by two votes. Beach volleyball was added to the catalogue of Olympic sports to give the games an Aussie flavour. Manchester peaked at thirteen votes in round two. I was responsible for one, maybe two of those votes. Allowing for our bankers, Princess Anne and Dame Mary Alison Glen-Haig (Britain's own IOC members), if the rest of the bid team had done as well, the Olympics would have been coming home. It was not a dazzling performance, but Barcelona had five attempts before it finally delivered the games. Manchester chose not to go a third time, but passed the baton to London, stepping down to bid instead for the Commonwealth Games.

It was at the 1994 Victoria Games in Canada where Manchester made its case, political and sporting, and I was reunited with 'Bob Charly', getting a singular picture with him and my daughter in a City shirt. Manchester's pitch to marry sport and development, to use money from Britain and Europe to provide training facilities, basic equipment and coaching offered to make its Commonwealth Games more than just Olympics for losers.[8] It proved to be third time lucky. The Commonwealth Games Federation awarded Manchester the games in November 1995 at its meeting in Bermuda. In summer 2002 almost four thousand athletes christened what was to become Manchester City's new stadium.

Masonic bodge

Transparency had been a concern of mine since I was first elected to Tameside Council. I learnt from experience. When I was chair of education, an attempt was made to stitch up a senior appointment with a massaged short list consisting of an 'adequate' internal candidate propped up by four others who would have been lucky to make any long list. Shortly before the interviews, I was tipped off he was an active Freemason, as were the more senior staff in that part of the education department. We went ahead, but I refused to appoint, arguing we could do better. Tameside re-advertised with the, then, maximum allowable strapline that as the authority was short of women and minority officers, we would particularly welcome applications from both. At the second time of asking, we appointed a Black woman candidate from London who was head and shoulders above our first best option. The bonus was that she was also unlikely to be a lodge member.

As a result of this recruitment farrago, I persuaded the Labour Group to change the council's standing orders, forcing councillors to declare whether they were members of the Freemasons or any similar organisation. There was no consequence for declaring membership, but those that refused to declare – and a couple of Tory councillors did – were excluded not from the council itself, which would have been illegal, but from all council committees. The local 'alternative newspaper', *Tameside Eye,* mocked our efforts, but subsequently published a list of suspected and known local Freemasons.[9]

The EP and staff had a Masonic group that dined every plenary Monday at Le Pont des Vosges in Strasbourg. Along with Les Huckfield MEP, I proposed a similar injunction on MEPs to that in Tameside, but my thoughtless transposition proved an embarrassment. I had not appreciated the schism between the Anglo-American and Continental Masons. The former was the result of a US-led split that occurred shortly after the American Civil War as the Continental Masons first banned discrimination on grounds of 'colour, race or religion' – but not sex – and then followed by admitting atheists. In the southern US the Masons were white supremacy for gentlemen. In the EP we rightly got nowhere. Jewish Socialist colleagues argued that Freemasons had taken the lead in hiding and helping the Jews under German occupation, while in Spain during the Spanish Civil War and the long tail of terror that followed, Franco hunted down the anti-clerical Masons.

Lobby lists

Back in 1984 there was neither any register of members' interests in the EP, nor any register of those lobbying the EU institutions. The lobbying process – I say as a gamekeeper turned poacher – is in itself not the problem. Rather it was the absence of openness and transparency that kept the activities of both the lobbyists, and the small minority of MEPs acting as their creatures, hidden in the shadows. What was important was not the big picture – in favour of Star Wars or against – rather the small. The hot money is spent not on 'yes or no', but in the verbal jungle, where displacing decimal points, suppressing Oxford commas and massaging explanatory footnotes can be worth millions. As the EP gained more power and the Commission accepted up to 80 per cent of parliament's amendments in whole or part, the dangers attendant on a failure to regulate were all too clear. What was needed was the disinfectant of the bright sunlight of public disclosure. No one whose taste buds weren't completely shot came into the EP for Belgian coffee at its most unpalatable or sandwiches barely fit to eat – all enter with an agenda. A series of MEPs on the left, in particular Marc Galle and Alman Metten (both S&D), argued from as early as 1990 that the EP needed to put its house in order.

Cartoon from French magazine Les Inrockuptibles, 1996.

The committee responsible was Rules of Procedure, where Galle was the chair from 1989 to 1992 and he started the process. Progress was glacial: after four years of work MEPs suspended consideration of his report because it was 'too close to the elections'. Post-1994 I took up the mantle as rapporteur

– following Galle's retirement – with a committee 'own-initiative' report on the control and registration of lobbyists.[10] Resistance continued in public and private; there was opposition, obstacles and obstruction. One creative diversion came in the form of objections on the grounds that the report did not go far enough. It was a tack Ken Livingstone had tried when I challenged his Euroscepticism at a Labour conference fringe meeting – the EU was not international enough.

Early on there was a push to exclude the great, the good and the unprofitable from any regulation. Greenpeace and the Environmental Intelligence Agency were closer to my perspective than British Nuclear Fuels and the Heritage Foundation, but there was absolutely no reason to catalogue them differently. All were engaged on the same mission: to shape legislation in their favour. My initial report – referred to as Ford 1 – was sent back to committee by plenary as going too far for the centre-right.[11] The resultant public backlash meant a sharp rebound. Six months later, in July 1996, a marginally tweaked report – Ford 2 – sailed through plenary with a solitary vote against. There was an addendum. What had passed in July had been a framework document to be filled out with a series of further reports. The following May I was back in plenary with my report on a code of conduct for lobbyists to cement in the gaps and set up an annual pass for those registering.[12]

In the January 1997 debate in plenary, I'd made the point that the declaration of members' interests needed to be 'published in an accessible manner and not kept behind closed doors in Luxembourg, Brussels and Strasbourg, forbidden to the photocopier, fax and telephone. We want to see this information available to the people of Europe through the new communications technologies of today'. We may have won in the public battle, but the stay-behind resistance deep in the EP continued its rearguard action to neuter its efficacy. The EP quaestors were using the ludicrous justification of data protection legislation to restrict the register's availability to the EP's working places. The register could be viewed, but not photocopied, although note taking was allowed. The newest technologies at the disposal of Europe's public were to be the pen, pencil and notebook.

I became part of the story. In January 2001 the British comedian Mark Thomas sent in a researcher to copy out the juicy details for the benefit of the British public via his own website.[13] I had the Labour Party Regional Office on the phone demanding to know why I was writing for *Communist Research Fortnight*. I thought it was a joke, but they were not amused. Thomas had misread 'Columnist, *Research Fortnight*'. I would have written it off as the shoddy work it was, but the party was insistent that I demand a retraction. Our comic didn't help himself, arguing it was my fault with my bad handwriting. I more forcefully pointed out the original was typed, and it was settled to the benefit of a few hundred pounds to a trio of South West charities.

It wasn't long after that the pen and pencil gave way to electronics. Since then, the whole system has seen a series of further extensions and elaborations to the demands on both MEPs and lobbyists. The one area that remains inadequately policed is the role of the special interest groups and the intergroups. While Rule 35(4) specifies an annual declaration, this is more honoured in breach than delivery. Here is a scandal waiting to happen. Similarly, under Annex 1, Article 3, when MEPs have an unregistered benefit from one of these groups, they are supposed to orally declare an interest. It doesn't happen. Silence may not be golden, but its sound hides many a transgression.

Revenge served cold

For some years, I was both on the editorial board and a columnist for *Tribune*. In my column on 1 November 1996, 'Today your love, tomorrow the world,' I took issue with the claim by Ian Buruma in the *New York Review of Books* that future prospects for European deepening and democracy were increasingly bleak. Looking at London, he described Tory nationalism as intolerant, xenophobic and vainglorious – nothing wrong there – but then argued the situation would be no better under Labour, citing as evidence the fact that, 'The July issue of the Labour Party newspaper *The Tribune*

[*sic*] had as its main feature an admiring interview with ... Sir James Goldsmith.'[14]

While Buruma, who I entertained when he'd earlier visited Brussels, is one of my favourite writers, here he was wrong. I argued the interview (published in *Tribune* on 21 June 1996) was not to praise Goldsmith, but bury him. Nevertheless, I chose to highlight a warning to potential fellow travellers of the left about the kind of man they were cuddling up to. Goldsmith had been elected to the EP in 1994 representing the authoritarian and deeply conservative Majorité pour L'Autre Europe who, with Danish xenophobes and Dutch misogynists, promptly formed the Europe of Nations Group, which he led. His Referendum Party was the toast of the BNP and infiltrated by former members of the National Front. Worse was his hypocrisy. His book *The Trap* in English 'reads like a tract from Bill Cash and the Eurosceptics', while its French version, *Le Piege*, 'insists that "European authorities need strong powers", that the Tories suffer from "colonial nostalgia" and that France offers the best hope for a European future.'[15]

The consequence of my article was a letter from the neocons' libel lawyers of choice, Carter-Ruck, threatening to sue me, but not *Tribune*. Carter-Ruck and *Tribune* had done a deal for an apology, destruction of any remaining copies of the offending edition and a sycophantic interview with Sir James for a future edition. I went to Geoffrey Bindman, the socialist counter. His advice was simple. I had a good, but far from watertight, prospect of winning the case. The concern was, if I lost, I'd be effectively bankrupt; if Goldsmith lost, he wouldn't even notice, any reparations subsumed in the rounding errors of his bank balance. The advice – which I took – was to issue an apology that, while it didn't go as far as Goldsmith demanded, Bindman believed would be sufficient for his legal advisors to tell him pursuing me further would be counterproductive as prospects of victory shifted in my favour. I duly issued the carefully crafted apology, which did not extend to his minions named in the piece – such as Marc Gordon, his campaign director, an apologist for apartheid South Africa – on the grounds that without the shelter of Goldsmith's chequebook they would back down, which they duly did.

Goldsmith's money delivered the Referendum Party well short of a million votes in 1997's May Day general election. It cost him £20 a vote. The psephologists claim he cost the Tories something between four and sixteen seats, but in the Labour landslide it was scarcely noticed. Goldsmith fared as badly as the rest of his flock with 3.5 per cent of the vote in Putney, where David Mellor lost to Labour. However, Goldsmith was ill and immediately after the election retreated to his Spanish farm. He tried to resign his position as an MEP, but the problem was he was unwilling or unable – or both – to go through the proper procedures and sign a letter of resignation in front of the parliament's Secretary General, Julian Priestley. The matter was referred to the EP's Committee on Rules of Procedure, where I was Socialist Coordinator, for a decision. At our pre-meeting it was all cut and dried. Goldsmith resigning would save the EP money. When the committee itself opened and we got to the item, there was an intervention from his group spokesman, saying that it was Goldsmith's wish not to die an MEP. That did it. In July he died still representing France in Brussels.

Jack Straw – foster father of Brexit

Great men are rare, but fools there are aplenty. The chance juxtaposition of events has history tell a different story. On that basis one could blame Jack Straw for Brexit. His involvement may have amounted to little more than a one-night stand, but it nonetheless had his DNA. After the 1997 election, Jack was summoned to Number Ten believing he was about to become Minister of Transport. On his way he was doing last minute revision on planes, trains and automobiles. To his surprise he emerged back on the street as Home Secretary.

The European elections were two years away, and it was clear that at some point Britain needed to address the electoral aberration that was our first past the post system. We alone were responsible for the wild swings – from sixty Tories to sixty-two Labour – that unbalanced and distorted the EP's political centre of gravity. The growing demands for increased powers for the parliament were hampered by the resulting misrepresentation. In Westminster the view was that after eighteen years of the Tories and Thatcher, this was neither a priority for parliamentary time nor business. There was no urgency to introduce proportional representation for the 1999 European elections. While there was a strong possibility Labour's MEPs would take an unnecessary beating for the party in these midterm elections that could be mitigated by PR, their fate was of little consequence to Labour's leadership. The feeling was the matter could be best left for the 2004 elections, with concessions pulled like teeth from duly obligated Liberals desperate for PR.

Blair had had an early run-in with Labour's MEPs during the Clause IV debate (see Chapter 4). He was far from enamoured by the EPLP and collectively we were condemned to the sixth circle of hell. More importantly, in Westminster he wanted to tighten discipline over Labour's MPs. The PLP duly obliged with a change to its standing orders. When the same proposal was put to the EPLP, it was rejected – albeit narrowly. That was that. Within days it was announced that the government was to introduce legislation to introduce a PR system for 1999. In terms of the EP and the accrual of power, it was a gift. But no good deed goes unpunished – domestically it was a disaster.

The policy was reactionary, nothing more than a snap response to party management problems. Preparation was at best slipshod and likely non-existent. If Jack had smoked, one could have looked for his notes on the back of a fag packet. He decided on a regional list system – which did have logic and precedence from the EP perspective. However, it destroyed rationale and purpose in refusing to challenge England's regional power brokers, instead producing a wildly inequitable jumble. Avoiding the obvious approach of creating a series of constituencies with between three and five seats, and instead pandering to the regions, it resulted in a proposal so distorted that it was in effect a series of different systems whose psephological impact depended on where you were registered to vote. Worse – in certain regions – it was an electoral door to UKIP xenophobes and the BNP neo-fascists. I know all this because as a member of the EP's Committee on Civil Liberties, Justice and Home Affairs, I was the 'link' between the

EPLP and the Home Office. Straw was repetitively warned and didn't listen.

The North East was to have three seats and the South East eleven. Thus, to guarantee election in the North East required 25 per cent of the vote while in the South East it would take just 8 per cent. A third party would struggle in the former and a fifth or sixth party would have hopes in the latter. The voters came and delivered UKIP its preordained breakthrough in a contextual election, with Nigel Farage winning a seat in the South East and UKIP picking up a second seat in the South West. Plaid Cymru and the Greens joined UKIP in gaining their first MEPs. Labour slumped from sixty-two to twenty-nine seats, but without proportional representation it would have been worse, falling into the mid-teens. I would have narrowly held my Manchester seat by a few thousand votes. But three-to-five-seat constituencies would have delivered UKIP no seats and Labour just shy of the mid-thirties.

Straw induced UKIP's birth as a party of consequence – and a delayed decade later provided Nick Griffin and the BNP a place in the *Sun*. He provided Farage with a platform and *Question Time* dutifully provided the audience. While the Referendum Party had shot its bolt in 1997, Jack's fragmented proportional representation birthed their successors. UKIP had a free media storm, TV time and floods of money. The underlying problems – and those yet to come – that drove emerging Euroscepticism would not have gone away absent PR for 1999. They were there and would inevitably manifest themselves. Nevertheless, when, how and on what scale would have been sharply different. Given more time, Labour and the left might have seen the danger. Yet it is not clear whether Jack, whose Europeanism was skin-deep, would have deeply regretted the unintended consequences.

Tribune tantrums

Left MPs in the House of Commons were more hindrance than help, as I've said earlier. My differences came to a head with a *Tribune* review of N. H. Twitchell's *The Tribune Group: Factional Conflict in the Labour Party*. Twitchell made the claim that in the 1960s the Tribune Group in the House of Commons was totally ineffective. I challenged his assessment, arguing that he and they were wrong on three counts: first, the organised opposition to Barbara Castle's 'In Place of Strife'; second, killing House of Lords reform; and third, firing the opening shots in Labour's civil war over Europe. Yet all these 'successes' were failures: 'The first acted as midwife to the birth of Thatcherism, the second put off reform of Britain's semi-feudal Parliament for two generations and the third helped to trigger the rift that kept Labour out of power for 18 years.'[16] I concluded, 'the Left's ineffectiveness in the sixties gives us much to be grateful for'.

My review was scarcely six hundred words. Some weeks later *Tribune* published a 750-word riposte from James Dickens, the Labour MP for West Lewisham and chair of the Tribune Group of MPs from 1968 to 1969. He was furious. The group's membership was exaggerated, with only twenty-five MPs active, yet 'had an influence out of all proportion to its numbers'.[17] They had provided cover for Harold Wilson's refusal to send British troops to Vietnam, had concerns that replacing hereditary peers with life peers would extend political patronage and were upholding Gaitskell's 1962 policy against British membership of the EEC. I replied in *Letters* (22 January 1999), saying he seemed to be arguing that most of the group's achievements were in support of party policy, thus the Tribune Group operated 'not as vanguard but rearguard – not quite the heroic "influence out of all proportion to its members"'. Dickens bit back with a letter of his own (12 February 1999), arguing the group was vindicated, noting that the Blair government was to set up a Royal Commission on the future composition of the Upper House: 'This will almost certainly include a directly elected element'. Looking back from a quarter of a century on, risible feudal remnant was repurposed for patronage and radical restraint.

Best liar

Graham Stringer was elected MP for Manchester Blackley in 1997 and two years later was made Parliamentary Secretary in the Cabinet Office. Part of his portfolio was 'better regulation' and he asked me if I could bring together a small group of MEPs to look at the issue from a European perspective. The main problem was avoiding 'better regulation' being simply a synonym for 'less regulation'. Nevertheless, the EU had some classic examples like the Waste from Electrical and Electronic Equipment Directive that cost more than it saved. I collected the usual suspects from the Socialist Group and ALDE, where the principal participant was Nick Clegg, who'd been elected an MEP in 1999. We had regular lunches during Strasbourg plenaries, which Graham would fly over from London to join. The theory was simple; implementation was the problem. Like with armed insurrection, one person's freedom fighter is another person's terrorist. Here it was protection versus bureaucratic creep. Sunset clauses looked to be one way forward.

Around 2003 the rumours began that Clegg was planning to head off to the UK to become a Liberal Democrat MP. I asked him straight out if it was true. His thrice denial convinced me. Of course, I wasn't surprised he didn't admit it, and it wasn't a hanging offence, but he was compellingly plausible. Like all politicians, I've been lied to by the best. But when six to nine months later Clegg's shift to Sheffield became public knowledge, I went out of my way to congratulate him on his ability to deceive. He didn't disappoint when he and the Liberals went into coalition with Cameron. My newfound faith was not misplaced.

Bending the rules

The EPs reputation in respect to abusing the expenses regime has never been a good one. Nowadays it's rather better, less because MEPs have improved – although after each exposé, rules have been tightened – but because Strasbourg has been challenged and overtaken by the boys (and it normally is boys) back home. The House of Commons expenses scandal of 2009 has the gold medal. The infamous 'sign in, sod off' is common to all legislatures paying a daily allowance, and the EP is one of them, the House of Lords another. It's against the spirit if not the letter of the law. In the EP, until the rules were changed, it could be particularly lucrative, as not only could you claim for the day but it brought with it a mileage allowance for travel from home to Brussels or Strasbourg. In one instance, an MEP who was away at an NUM Annual Conference was recorded present on the attendance list. When the anomaly was drawn to the attention of the parliament's services, the official explanation given was that someone had signed in the wrong place. Perfectly understandable, although it singularly failed to explain why they had also signed the wrong name. The chief suspect was the Eurosceptic MEP whose personal plan of action to destroy the EU's institutions was to phone home every morning and then leave his phone off the hook for the rest of the day. Quite how transferring European, including British, taxpayers' money to the bank accounts of France Telecom and Belgacom was supposed to bring the edifice crumbling down was never entirely clear. If nothing else, it stopped his constituents from bothering him and him from bothering them. For extra-EU travel, before boarding passes were made *de rigueur* and MEPs were downgraded from first to business class, some less scrupulous travel agents would 'sell' a used premium price ticket for 10 per cent of the list price. The MEP would then claim for the price of their executive ticket, despite having roughed it in economy.

It was an Italian Christian Democrat MEP who really took the *biscotti*. Salvatore 'Salvo' Lima had represented the Italian Islands in the EP since 1979 and was both a former mayor of Palermo and Italian cabinet minister. On the morning of 12 March 1992 Lima was in a chauffeur-driven car on his way to Palermo with two friends when the tyres were shot out; Lima, as he fled, was brought down by one shot and then executed 'Mafia style' with a bullet in the back of the head. His father had been a Mafia member and Salvo himself was a pillar of Mafia power in Palermo and Giulio Andreotti's 'proconsul' in Sicily. His death was ordered because of his failure to sabotage the confirmation of the sentences against Mafia leaders arising from the Maxi Trial. At the opening of the afternoon plenary session on the day of his death, a series of tributes were made by the parliament's president and the leaders and representatives of the EP's political groups, including the

Regionalist's Jaak Vandemeulebroucke who said, 'the Mafia still hold the reins in Palermo, and we can only express our deep respect for Mr Lima and his campaign against the Mafia.'[18] No one directly challenged Vandemeulebroucke's fable nor mentioned that, despite being shot at 9.30 a.m., Lima had heroically managed to sign that day's attendance register in Strasbourg that had opened for signature a bare thirty minutes before his death. The parliament services were required to orchestrate a hasty cover up.

I had my own set of allegations to answer. When I was moved by the Labour Party for the 1999 European elections from Greater Manchester to the South West with the change from first past the post to regional list elections, I had to take care of my existing staff. This was easier for the Brussels-based staff than those in the Mossley office. Nevertheless, for elected politicians there are no guarantees of re-election and staff contracts are terminated with the end of the mandate. My longest-serving staff member took umbrage. I offered, if elected, to relocate her to the South West. She declined. I then offered her a redundancy package that was double the statutory package, but she asked for five to six times the statutory amount. I felt it was impossible to acquiesce. Not only would it have crippled my ability to establish a serious constituency office in the South West, but I felt such generosity with taxpayers' money was impossible to justify.

The result was that she went off to the Tory tabloid the *Daily Express* with a collection of lurid claims of abuse of parliamentary expenses. I got front-page coverage and everyone believed she got the economic benefit. The only thing she was right about was the sin of omission. It took forensic accountants almost two years before I was fully exonerated. I'd actually spent marginally more money than allocated, the difference of which had come out of my pocket. It took so long because I'd trusted her beyond reasonable limits. The accounts were in a total mess and had to be reconstructed, and when they finally were we found she'd been paying her partner considerable sums. Tempted as I was to seek recompense, the advice was unequivocal: 'move on.'

Q.

Electoral liberties

Between 1977 and 2015 I fought thirteen elections for Labour: five local elections, winning two; seven European elections, winning five; and a lost general election. My success rate was just better than 50 per cent, although the general election and two of the local elections were fought with no prospect of victory. With by-elections I campaigned in more than a hundred seats. Out of all those I'm only aware of a single attempt of electoral fraud. That was in Droylsden in 1988.

Mark Hunter – who was subsequently to become the Liberal Democrat MP for Cheadle (2005–15) – had won the Tameside council seat for Droylsden in 1980 from Labour. He narrowly won for a second time four years later, before running against Ashton-under-Lyne's Labour MP, Robert Sheldon, in the 1987 general election. Some of the local activists were determined to remove him the following year. In 1984 he had benefited from a straight fight with Labour, so the first task was to fabricate more candidates.[19] Labour ended up effectively standing three of the four candidates: Labour, Conservative and Social Democratic. David Owen assisted: his Social Democratic Party (SDP) was disintegrating in front of his eyes after the bulk of its membership jumped ship to join the Social and Liberal Democrats. A letter from Labour's aspiring doppelgänger asking for Owen's endorsement as an SDP candidate swiftly received the latter's imprimatur. This is undeniable.

Unproven, however, was the boast by one couple that between the two of them they voted fifty-seven times. At one polling station she bottled it on a serial visit. It made absolutely no impact whatsoever. Hunter's majority soared to well over 1200 with the Conservative candidate on 175 and the SDP on a forlorn 38. Labour's loser to Hunter was ironically a former Liberal councillor. On the positive side, one unintended consequence of the laughable SDP result was it fast-tracked Owen's path to redundancy.

Redistribution: Tobin tax

Thatcher's financial deregulation had fed the casino economy. By the late 1990s, currency transactions had been captured by the speculators: across the year, less than 1 per cent of transactions were for the purchase of goods, services and raw materials, the other 99 per cent were for global gambling, with billions washing around the financial system as human parasites fed on and destroyed jobs, communities and countries. Speculation became a thing in itself driving commerce, trade and investment into the monetary margins.

A way of taxing, and hence curbing, the speculator was proposed by the economist and Nobel laureate James Tobin. A minute tax of say 0.05 per cent (€500 on €1 million) on all currency exchanges, totally insignificant to any real commercial transaction, would both calm the financial waters by driving the most assiduous of the gamblers out of the counting houses and in doing so raise serious money to be used to lift the world's poorest out of poverty on the backs of the casino economy. The tax would be too small to impact the cost of goods, services or investment, but large enough to put sand in the gears of the speculators bouncing money backwards and forwards around the globe in milliseconds.

Economic deregulation was a pup sold to the complicit (Thatcher) and the heedless (Brown) by speculators masquerading as financiers. Gordon Brown may have put out the financial inferno threatening to incinerate the global economy in 2008, yet he had earlier provided the matches to the putative arsonists. Almost a decade earlier I noted it was clear something needed to be done: 'The collapse of the "tiger economies" in the late 1990s brought the issue of currency speculation to the fore. The Southeast Asian economies are still recovering from the currency collapse that led to a corresponding collapse in investor confidence, small and large; a withdrawal of capital and investment; and closure of thousands of companies and massive job losses.'[20] After the 1999 European elections, with Harlem Désir as president, myself as secretary and Caroline Lucas as vice-president, we established in the EP an Intergroup on Taxation of Capital, Fiscal Systems and Globalisation. In 2000 we pushed for the introduction of a Tobin-type tax as a means by which to produce

funds to alleviate deep poverty in the world, specifically those living on less than €1/day.

Since the liberalisation of the currency markets, the volume of transactions had increased by 8300 per cent. More worryingly, the assets that global banks had available at that point equated to less than three days of trading. Yet foreign currency-exchange transactions remained untaxed. Governments were both losing out on a lucrative source of revenue and any ability to rein in the market. They were driving without brakes. The Tobin tax expert Professor Alex Michalos, chair of political science at the University of Northern Columbia, Canada, had stated: 'It is simply immoral and unacceptable that financial traders should be permitted to continue to take a free ride on the infrastructure of civil society without paying taxes to support their habit.'

The Tobin tax, we contended, could be considered a 'sin tax' akin to those on cigarettes, alcohol and gambling. A fag, a pint and a flutter feed the treasury. Venture capital feeds the Tories. I continued:

> *The Tobin tax could raise hundreds of billions for the fight against poverty – a real Robin Hood tax. In the mid-'90s, the United Nations Development Program estimated that the cost of eradicating the worst poverty, supplying water and energy, providing basic sanitary conditions and an education structure in the Third World would amount to between \$30 and \$40 billion per year. In 1995, the Bank for International Settlements estimated the annual foreign-exchange trading figure at \$312 trillion. Thus, the revenue obtainable from a Tobin tax of 0.25 percent, the highest rate suggested, is a staggering \$250 billion a year.*

The tax has its critics. Some bizarrely complain it would impair the efficiency of the foreign-exchange market, totally missing the point that that is exactly the objective: to curtail the financial feeding frenzies that destroy jobs and communities and threaten countries. Others argue that it would be evaded. Absolutely. Yet few would carry that argument's logic across to tobacco and liquor and argue to abandon taxes on cigarettes and alcohol. With the collaboration of the world's major foreign-exchange market countries, it could be possible to insist that the collection of such a transaction tax would be required from every member of the International Monetary Fund (IMF) as a condition of eligibility for credit from the fund. At the time, Europe, Japan and the United States would have constituted such a bloc.

Harlem and I also set up the Parliamentarian World Appeal for the Tobin Tax in April 2000, which campaigned to collect the signatures of 1000 politicians around the world in support of the measure, eventually listing 864 names from 33 countries.[21] With signatories ranging from small numbers from India and the US, to over a hundred each from the UK and France, the World Appeal jumped on board the growing awareness of a Tobin-type tax, as the World Bank and IMF were having meetings on it and the US Congress tabled a motion. Other national parliaments such as Canada and Brazil also took steps towards implementing the tax around 1999 and 2000. I attended major conferences in Dublin and Vancouver to promote the tax and gave evidence to the Italian Senate's Finance Committee. They were planning to pass the legislation to establish the tax with the rate set at zero to wait for the rest of the EU to catch up.

Part of the work of the intergroup included a conference, titled the First Inter-parliamentary Meeting on the Tobin Tax, which took place in the parliament on 28 June 2000.[22] Attendees included MEPs, representatives from SOLIDAR, a European network of NGOs working for social justice, MPs from Belgium, Canada, Finland, France, Ireland, Sweden and the UK, and members of ATTAC (a French activist organisation campaigning for the taxation of foreign-exchange transactions) and War on Want.

At the conference, Terry Provance of the Tobin Tax Initiative (USA) described demonstrations supporting the tax in the US as part of a wider push against the effects of globalisation. He argued that finding solutions to tackle corporate globalisation was difficult, but that Tobin-type taxes were one of the ways to do this. Describing the need to raise people's awareness of the tax, the international outreach group Organising for Tobin coordinated education and research programmes, as well as legislative lobbying initiatives. Provance

Q.

summarised a congressional resolution on transaction taxes that urged the US to get involved with a global Tobin-type tax, before warning of the reaction by the Republicans and the right wing of the Democratic party, who would paint it 'a United Nations Tax'.

Finnish Foreign Affairs Minister Erkki Tuomioja outlined his government's support for the introduction of international systems aimed at tackling the instability produced by globalisation, exhibited as speculative capital movements. He argued that more research was necessary to shape and promote a currency transaction tax.

I concluded the proceedings emphasising that the issue of speculation is global and so it must be tackled internationally. Globalisation cannot be stopped, but we can direct and channel it to a degree. I reiterated the importance of using the proceeds to eliminate global poverty, and stop it becoming just another revenue stream for the UK, EU or the US. I also argued that trade unions like UNISON should be involved, to widen the scope of the appeal. The progress seemed to be rapid at the time, but it was clear there was still a long way to go.

Although the resolution to produce a report on the Tobin tax was narrowly rejected in January 2000, my promotion of the tax continued in parliament and at conferences, events and workshops across Europe and beyond. In 2015 I was approached by John McDonnell following Corbyn's election as Labour leader, and asked to act for him as a possible incoming chancellor and help keep interest alive in the Commission. There is a provision in EU law, 'enhanced cooperation', under which nine countries can take a joint initiative without the involvement of the rest. The campaign was not long lived – after the 2016 referendum, things fell apart as the prospect of UK cavalry riding to the rescue disappeared. Financial speculation remains the cancer at the heart of the economy that needs to be cut out. Britain has been its victim of choice on several occasions and isolated outside the EU will be a tempting target again.

Single currency

It's the smaller weaker currencies that are prey to speculators, a reason - but not *the* reason - for endorsing the euro. As I've said above, the deep foundation of emerging political power is a solid industrial base, but immediately above that is a ground floor of economy and finance. This requires currency union. All the arguments about how a single currency was doomed to fail were stress tested in the shadow of the American Civil War (1861–65). All this is presented in easily digestible form in *Lincoln* (1984), the second volume of Gore Vidal's *Narratives of Empire* (also see Chapter 1). You'd be hard pressed to find anyone not prepared to concede that the US' single currency experiment with the 1863 introduction of the dollar turned out well.

There were only two brief periods before Brexit when British public opinion was in favour of joining the single currency. The first was in the immediate aftermath of Blair's 1997 landslide win in the general election and the second immediately after the euro's introduction on a 'cash basis' on 1 January 2002.[23] Blair could almost certainly have delivered a referendum in favour after either, although it would have been necessary to spend some serious political capital. At the time Blair had it, before he frittered it away on the brutal fiasco of Iraq. The main obstacle in the way was Gordon Brown and his mystical five economic tests to be answered before Britain could join the EU's Economic and Monetary Union that cast a spell over politics.

Gibraltar

In the early 1980s I made contact with the small Gibraltar Socialist Labour Party (GSLP), and its - then - only MP in the Gibraltar Assembly, Joe Bossano. I'd first visited the colony in the late 1960s as I hitch-hiked my way back from the Maghreb to the UK (see Chapter 2). I only returned a long decade later.

By then Whitehall was insistently and increasingly hostile to the wish for Gibraltar's greater integration with Britain and determined to tighten the financial screws. Gibraltar had gone from rock to block, threatening UK relations with post-Franco Spain. Consequently, I argued in the GSLP's *The People* that this could be as much opportunity as threat.[24] Integration could see Gibraltar a forgotten footnote of empire. Instead, rather than being pressed into an unwanted accommodation with Madrid, they should use their right of self-determination to opt for independence.

I furthered the discussion in *Tribune* with 'If Spain invades Gibraltar what would Labour do?'[25] The impending closure of the dockyard, which employed almost 20 per cent of the Gibraltarian workforce, and the resistance by the Transport and General Workers' Union led by Joe had seen Peter Blaker, the Tory Minister of State for the Armed Forces, effectively chased off the site when he attempted to tour the dockyard shortly after confirming the government's determination to sell it off. When I entered the EP, I joined the Gibraltar Friendship Group formed by a cross-party collection of Tory and Labour MEPs. It was led by Lord Bethel with Alf Lomas as his deputy. Its activities were limited, although I do recall that the Gibraltar Parliament rather solemnly made us all Freemen, allowing us apparently to march through the territory at will with fixed bayonets. It was not a privilege I ever actively considered exercising. In 1989 when Labour overtook the Tories as the largest delegation, Lord Bethel refused to serve under Alf and subsequently the number of friendship groups doubled.

Gibraltar's future was under continued threat. London was withdrawing financial and political support. Peter Hain became a hate figure in the territory because, despite hopes to the contrary, Labour's victory in 1997 made things worse rather than better. This provided the backdrop to the 1998 *Matthews v United Kingdom* court case. Gibraltar was the only part of the EU whose residents were denied a vote in European elections. When Denise Matthews, a resident, was denied the facility of registering to vote for the forthcoming 1999 EP elections, she took, via the Self-Determination for Gibraltar Group, the case to the European Court of Human Rights.[26] They won in February 1999, alas too late for the EP elections four months later.

The UK chose not to give Gibraltar its own seat. Denmark had, back in 1979, allocated a seat to Greenland, which had a population proportionally smaller. I had proposed to the parliament president that with our imminent 'Southern enlargement' Gibraltar should, like the Central and Eastern European enlargement countries, be offered an observer in the EP. Gibraltar did not receive the same treatment; instead, the UK wanted to tack it on as an appendage. The trick was to make sure it was not forgotten. The first choice for Whitehall was London, but I lobbied with the GSLP for the South West region, which I now represented. It was a better match both for Gibraltar and myself. The South West had the same problems of peripherality and exclusion facing Gibraltar, while Gibraltar's Labour vote – small as it was – was proportionally higher than any part of my South West constituency. Gibraltar joined the South West. Their votes never made that crucial difference, but it was fun campaigning there and producing targeted election material in Spanish. I tried to persuade the party to put a Gibraltarian on the list in both 2009 and 2014 to no avail, but I was listed in the EP's *vade mecum* as 'Labour and GSLP', much to the annoyance of Madrid and, I suspect, some in London.

Pedro Sanchez, who was later to become Spanish prime minister, with Joe Bossano, founder of the GSLP, at the PES Congress in Budapest 2015.

The GSLP has now lost its radical edge. When Joe Bossano stood down as leader, his replacement was Fabian Picardo, a lawyer, who moved the party to the right and into a formal coalition with the local Liberal Party, who receive a disproportionate share of the seats in the assembly. Nevertheless, I have to confess they do keep winning elections. Post-Brexit, the future for the territory looks uncertain, with Madrid holding the whip hand. In the referendum only 4 per cent of the territory's voters supported Leave, on an 84 per cent turnout, 19,322 to 823. The central issue is less tourism but the fourteen thousand cross-frontier workers.[27] Queues of over four hours would obviously affect the Gibraltarian economy hugely, as well as the lives of the nine thousand Spanish frontier workers living in the nearby La Linea, which already had 30 per cent unemployment compared to Gibraltar's fourteen people in the third quarter of 2020.[28] Gibraltar has its hidden-in-plain-sight own resource of location. Neither Madrid nor Brussels will want to see the territory forced to turn for succour to the Middle East or Beijing.

Dining tables

As EPLP leader I was Jean-Pierre Cot's de facto deputy. That came with its own set of obligations, which included entertaining important guests. Eminent and interesting was never a perfect match while it was arguable that there was often an inverse correlation between eminent and well mannered. The two extremes were Nelson Mandela and Edward Kennedy.

As a card-carrying atheist – I'm a paid-up member of Humanists UK – Mandela was a saint. I ate with him twice: once with Cot, and on a second occasion with the European Jewish Congress. I'd put the latter in contact with Mandela's office after my visit to South Africa on behalf of the Socialist Group to attend the first ANC conference and they were appreciative. Mandela's forgiving politics was enough in itself, but that was coupled with a personal engagement and interest in his interlocutors that was exceptional. He listened as well as spoke. I'd been tasked with escorting him around the parliament in Strasbourg for the two days of his visit. I even managed to introduce him to my future mother-in-law.

In contrast, Kennedy was a drunken boor the evening we dined with him in a Brussels restaurant in the Petite Sablon.

Arrogant, dismissive and self-absorbed, he liked the sound of his own voice more than we did. Cot and I barely restrained ourselves from walking out on him. Cot, egged on by some of the EPLP's 'tankies', may have learnt a lesson. When Boris Yeltsin came to the Socialist Group there were no dining privileges, but Cot refused to be intimidated. After a particularly brutal exchange when Yeltsin was refusing to respond to MEPs' questions, Cot pointed to the door and said he could always leave. He didn't take up the offer, but he might as well have done for what we got out of the rest of the meeting.

Escorting Nelson and Winnie Mandela around the European Parliament in Strasbourg in June 1990.

Tailends

It's always good to know when to stop. I could write about Marco Pannella, the Dadaist MEP from the Italian Radicals, and his attempts at turning the EP into a theatre of the absurd, despite furious competition from a set of Labour MEPs or his countryman Gianfranco Fini, who was quoted in 1995 as saying 'the MSI has taken on the task of preserving the memory of the fascist experience, which would otherwise be confined to the waste bin.'[29] Fini went on to be Deputy Prime Minister and Minister of Foreign Affairs in the Silvio Berlusconi government of 2001–06. I could also write about my unapologetic insults to Jonas Savimbi, apartheid South Africa's creature from the quisling National Union for the Total Independence of Angola, when he was perched in the EP VIP visitors' gallery.

Equally, there were my brief passages and interludes on the EP's Women's Rights (FEMM), Economic and Monetary Affairs (EMAC) and Fisheries committees. EMAC was a committee where I had little comprehension of what was going on, with its garnered herd of wearisome acronyms and esoteric language. Fisheries, in comparison, was a smooth sail. I failed, however, to appreciate its import. In 1999 more people had been made redundant from BAC than worked in the South West's fishing industry. My only practical contribution was to add a rider to the EU–Comoros Fisheries Agreement, demanding protection for West Indian Ocean coelacanths, a critically endangered species thought to have become extinct sixty-six million years ago until its discovery as a 'living fossil' in 1938. As a fish caught in time it had the evolutionary genius to survive four hundred million years after its Silurian origins. Would that mankind could prove as clever. The fish's survival can only have been helped by its clear 'don't eat me' messages, slimy with an unpleasant flavour, difficult to digest with resultant diarrhoea.

My other fossil was the Tory chair of the External Economic Relations Committee (REX, the precursor of INTA) in my first term, Dame Shelagh Roberts. The committee secretariat prepared 'chair's speaking notes' that I discovered by accident after one afternoon meeting. Leaving nothing to chance, they opened with 'Good afternoon, I will now start the meeting.' I never checked, but can only imagine that many pages on they concluded – as I do now – with 'Goodnight.'

Endnotes

[1] A review of the concert described his rant, published in *Sounds*, 14 August 1976. [2] Official Journal of the European Communities (1996), Written question by Glyn Ford to the Commission, 8 December 1995. [3] EP (1999), *Debates*, 23 July. [4] Official Journal of the European Communities (1995), Written question by Glyn Ford to the Commission, 19 September 1994. [5] Cour d'Appel, Liège (1995), Judgement of the Court: Case C-415/93 (The Bosman Ruling), 15 December. [6] An Interview with Glyn Ford, *King of the Kippax* 66, 1988. [7] EP (1993), *Debates*, 22 June. [8] 'Sport for a Change', *European Labour Forum*, Summer 1995. [9] See *Tameside Eye*, 16 November 1990. [10] EP (2003), 'Working Paper on Lobbying in the European Union: Current Rules and Practices', January, p. 37. [11] EP (1996), *Debates*, 16 January. [12] EP (1997), *Debates*, 12 May. [13] Blake Evans-Pritchard (2001), 'Calls for MEPs' interests to be published online', *EU Observer*, 22 January. [14] Ian Buruma (1996), 'Fear and loathing in Europe', *New York Review of Books*, 17 October. [15] Glyn Ford (1996), 'Today your love, tomorrow the world', *Tribune*, 1 November. [16] N. H. Twitchell (1999), *The Tribune Group: Factional Conflict in the Labour Party*, London: Rabbit Publications; Glyn Ford (1998), 'Tribune's Thatcherite legacy', *Tribune*, 23 October. [17] James Dickens (1999), 'Against the odds', *Tribune*, 1 January. [18] EP (1992), *Debates*, 12 March. [19] As was done in the Devon and East Plymouth seat in the 1994 European elections where a 'Literal Democrat' candidate polled 10,000 votes, allowing a 700-vote victory by Conservative Giles Chichester over the Liberal Democrat. [20] The quotes in this section are from my article 'Enlist currency speculators in poverty war', *Japan Times*, 30 July 2000. [21] The full list of politicians can be found on the website 'World parliamentarians call for Tobin Tax', http://tobintaxcall.free.fr/list.htm (accessed 4 November 2020). [22] The conference proceedings appeared as: Harlem Désir and Glyn Ford (eds) (2001), *Time for Tobin*, Strasbourg: Capital Tax, Fiscal Systems and Globalisation Intergroup. A French version was published simultaneously. [23] The euro was introduced as a 'virtual' currency three years earlier on 1 January 1999. [24] Glyn Ford (1982), 'Independence for Gib', *The People*, 25 August. (25) Glyn Ford (1982), 'If Spain invades Gibraltar what would Labour do?', *Tribune*, 1 October. [26] European Court of Human Rights (1999). Judgement on Case of *Matthews v. The United Kingdom*, 18 February. [27] HM Government of

Gibraltar (2020), Frontier Workers EMP.2: Frontier Workers by Nationality, 26 October, www.gibraltar.gov.gi/uploads/statistics/2020/employment/EMP.2.pdf (accessed 4 November 2020). [28] HM Government of Gibraltar (2020), EMP.16: Unemployment Quarterly Average, 26 October, www.gibraltar.gov.gi/uploads/statistics/2020/employment/EMP.16.pdf (accessed 4 November 2020). [29] Glyn Ford (1995), Fascist MEP calls for parliamentary third force, *Searchlight*, March.

10 Turbulent Resolution?

No man ever steps in the same river twice. For it's not the same river and he's not the same man.

Heraclitus

Lenin reputedly said, 'there are decades where nothing happens; and there are weeks where decades happen'. Maybe not quite at that pace, but the period since 2016 has seen the world turned upside down. The conjuncture and sequence of events starting in that tumultuous year have been as significant as the equivalent period spanning across the first and second world wars. The shot ringing out in Sarajevo sounded the death knell of London's empire and was the starting pistol for a second thirty years' war as Germany and Russia, Japan and the United States fought over the succession. The thunderclaps of Hiroshima and Nagasaki were the bells that rang Washington's victory and a new global order, save some skirmishing with communists. All catalysed and driven by that conjuncture of imperial war, the Bolshevik revolution and America's 'Spanish flu'.[1]

This time around the first act saw the election of Donald Trump – whose prologue was Brexit – the Covid pandemic and the imperial war of Vladimir Putin with Russia's invasion of the Ukraine in February 2022, with pestilence, war and famine's judgement on history. All in their impact symptomatic of deeper problems, and foreshocks of political earthquakes to follow. They stoked inflation, slashed living standards and

fed the rise of the demagogue. There is even the prospect of a born-again Trump as the forty-seventh president, which would make him the first since Grover Cleveland in 1892 to win a non-consecutive second term; biology appears more a threat than Joe Biden to his resurrection. At the same time, it is wise to be careful what you wish for: a younger Republican cast in the Trump mould would be worse, not better.

Thus, the world is now entering an interregnum of multipolar chaos with the opening skirmishes in a new struggle for global succession. Beijing may for the moment be deterred by a US–EU axis, but few outside of Washington see US hegemony celebrating its centenary in 2045. In this framing, as English and European, I look to where we stand now and the future of both the land of my birth and the place of my adoption. Of the first I am ever more despondent – my reasoning below. To me there is no passage to progress from the state we're in to the point of being free of turmoil, rupture and deep trauma. 'Business as usual' is incapable of even asking the right questions, let alone provide adequate answers. There is a perilous passage facing the English if they are to free themselves of the knots they have tied in the British body politic. Of the European Union I am more sanguine. Not necessarily because of any inherent virtue or wisdom of its leaders – although to be fair they did avoid the self-harming of Britain's Brexit – but the EU's heave and heft is such that it has the space to make and correct mistakes not available to medium-sized nation states like the disarticulating United Kingdom. The EU needs a programme and plan, underpinned by courage and political will, to create an equitable economy for a multicultural society backed by an independent capacity to defend itself and its values.

All of the above has put to the question the base assumptions the world rested on until 2008's global financial crisis. Brexit demonstrated in England that the alienation from the system was profound; that national populism had finally captured the last bastions of class politics. For those with eyes to see, it had been a long time coming, both in the UK and EU. Trump was the swallow whose transatlantic manifestation signalled Washington's economic retreat from globalisation to protectionism, more military adventurism and a new Cold War. Covid just stamped a heavy foot on the accelerators driving economic withdrawal, political reaction and military advance. Putin only gilded the lily.

While liberal democracy is not yet dead, it is on life support. The opening shots in the new Cold War between Washington and Beijing/Moscow threaten a global stand-off extending far beyond the political, social and military fronts of its first recital. There in the ashes of Washington's victory over the Soviet Union (1988-91) the seeds were planted whose fruit we are harvesting today. The ideological deterrence of existing 'socialism', flawed as it was, prior to 1989 constrained the levels of inequality and exploitation that it was wise for the West to visit upon its people. With the fall of the Soviet Empire, that restraint faded as wealth and inequality swelled and welfare states shrivelled. Meanwhile the settlement imposed on Moscow was every bit as vindictive and myopic as the Versailles Treaty imposed on Germany in 1919. Victors' justice was harsh. The promised restraints on NATO enlargement encroaching into the former Soviet Empire were still ringing as they were broken. It was this betrayal that sparked that zombie core of empire into revanchism in Ukraine.

When the Soviet Empire collapsed, the EU was walking the chalk line to superpower status, seen by some as potentially the only hegemonic power capable of challenging the US. Then the world's largest, richest and most powerful trading block, it had the potential to direct that weight to add a coherent, independent CFSP to protect and project European interests and values. With integrated defence procurement and policy, it could have held its own in the world. The crash of empire took Europe's eyes off the prize. It lost its way, distracted by greed over gumption, as it snatched at low-hanging fruit. Brussels really should have known better; the easy option is inevitably the wrong option. If it looks too good to be true, it is too good to be true.

Seduced by quantity over quality, led astray and misguided by Britain's anti-federalist saboteurs, Europe chose breadth over depth, explosive expansion over consolidation, and in a collective wedding married into the family manifestly unable and unfit countries of Central and Eastern Europe – immature democracies with needy economies and, in many cases, only a nodding acquaintance with the deep rule of law. This heedlessness threatened – and still does – to destroy the

Union's internal coherence, drive and ability to deliver. Viktor Orbán and Fidesz's fourth consecutive victory in Hungary's free, but not fair, elections in April 2022 is one prompt. To make a mistake once is unfortunate; to repeat it, insanity.

Serious and sustained help for the EU's 'near abroad' was and still is essential, but to acquiesce in railroading through new Union memberships to countries like Ukraine and Moldova – even Georgia – whose economies, democracies and acquaintance with the rule of law are even more remote from the minimum standards necessary than those undeserving states that crept in last time around, would be to compound a venial with a mortal sin. The debate over the limits to Europe has long been conducted in the shadows, for it has at its root bigotry and racism. On the right in Germany and Eastern Europe, geography is eclipsed by religion. For them, Europe is Christendom – the Protestants and Catholics with the Orthodox a late addition.

To support and aid the legitimate struggle of a population against brutal external intervention in a civil war and to welcome its refugees does not change the nature of the state. When in March 2022, at the Versailles Summit, European Council President Charles Michel, France's Emmanuel Macron and European Commission President Ursula von der Leyen stated that 'Ukraine belongs to the European family' because it 'fights for democracy and the values we hold dear', they were smuggling in special pleading for 'fast-tracking' membership for Ukraine and Moldova, while shunting into the enlargement sidings the long-standing and slow-moving applications of Turkey and the Balkans, whose majority and minority Muslim populations threaten to taint the right's Christian vision of Europe.[2] Transparency International had Russia and Ukraine in a virtual tie in 2021 in the corruption race, Moscow with a score of 29 – out of 100 – ranked 136th in the world, with Kyiv (whose oligarchs are as venial as Moscow's), on 32, coming in at 122nd. Ankara, meanwhile, scored 38 and was 96th. This is no argument for early Turkish membership, rather pointing to the Trojan horse that Europe's right wants to leapfrog into the Union under the cloak of solidarity. The European Council at the end of June confirmed Ukraine and Moldova's candidate status while acknowledging Georgia's 'European perspective'. Ukraine, like

Syria, Yemen and Libya, will require gigantic sums of money for post-war reconstruction, with talk of €750 billion for Kyiv – that is more than €20,000 for every man, woman and child in Ukraine. Their oligarchs will be laughing all the way to the bank. But that's only money. The more serious issue is protecting liberal democracy and Europe's values, and that means no or slow membership. Europe does not need another rotten state apple in the barrel; surely two – Hungary and Poland – are enough. Europe's eastern 'near abroad' should stay a long time a foreign country.

Those early prospects for global leadership passed Europe by as Brussels took its eyes off the prize in the wake of communist collapse. Following Brexit, Covid and the invasion of Ukraine, the EU, in unmapped political territory, has a second chance to get back on track to becoming a global player. Will doesn't operate independent of reality – Lukacs had that right. Nevertheless, the final destination is not set, as prevailing conditions offer passage to sundry futures. The best of these depend on the EU building strength, finding direction and insinuating itself as an organic part of the continent's national politics. Without prejudging the future, we are not without hope.

The only future that works for the majority is a strong, independent European Union capable of standing alone against the world and of protecting and nurturing its social democratic values. On the left, as argued in *Salvage*, we face a series of challenges.[3] The global financial crisis of 2008 saw battle won by capital in the class war that shackled the losers in the chains of austerity. The result was the acceleration of democratic decomposition with resurgent populism from right, left and centre – there were elements of populism in Emmanuel Macron's first coming – attracting subaltern groups with the linked spectacles of Trump and Brexit and the collapse of the geopolitical order. Trump's successor, Joe Biden, has neither agency nor Cnut's humility when he tries to arrest the tide of history. Whether in Britain or Europe, the fightback will continue to be under the rubric; the flag and the control of social democratic parties is far from settled. The centre cannot hold, as the ligaments tying together party, class and even constituencies tear, throwing up occasion for marginal forces to emerge from the virtual shadowlands

and take centre stage. The majority of these forces will be far from benign. The interregnum may be brutal, as pre-emptive counter-revolution is first mover. Meanwhile George Dangerfield's *The Strange Death of Liberal England* (1935) may yet find a sequel with a wider footprint.

What European Union?

The EU was ever a half-formed thing, but many preferred it that way, crippled and hobbled. The high priests of lean Europe, who wanted a mere single market and trading block bereft of politics and power, nestled in London, but they had their apostles, missionaries and agents embedded across the Union and with an outpost in Washington. With Britain's departure, the majority of Pharisees walked away from the temple. The EU is now at a crossroads. The required refurbishment of the institutional architecture has been well rehearsed in earlier chapters, but the new structures will need filling and feeding if Europe is to make its destiny. The war of position is easier won now one cohort of narrow nationalists have retired into isolation and events have ridden roughshod through their lines. Covid taught the need for health union, its costs to Europe's economies, fiscal union and Putin the necessity of common security and defence; even if at this juncture the road to strategic autonomy is diverted through NATO.

Brussels' challenges saw opportunity knock with British withdrawal. For many it was like being unchained from a mad dog. Health union might have been worn, but abandonment of EU austerity with neo-Keynesian European bonds and debt would have met stoic resistance from London, while strategic autonomy and Strategic Compass, re-energised in the repercussions of botched process and product of Afghan withdrawal and Moscow's later aggression, would have been filleted in reality, if not in name. The UK's lurch to 'poundstore provocateur' in the South China Sea might well have dragged Brussels with it.

Yet to seize the future needs leadership. Who will be in that vanguard? Looking across the continent, the EU's 'Big Five' quickly shrinks to a shortlist of two – Berlin and Paris. Neither domestic politics nor personality suggest any prospect of command for the moment slipping into the hands of Rome's broken politics or Madrid's, both at best more adjutants than generals; while Poland would be a prank as much because of Ukraine rather than despite it. Yet the situation in Germany and France is far from ideal. But worse than EU Franco-German leadership is no leadership at all.

Babylon Berlin

The traffic-light coalition in Germany that followed the September 2021 general election was Hobson's choice. With the combination of German electoral maths making Red-Red-Green impossible, the cordon sanitaire around the fascist-lite Alternative für Deutschland and the voters' clear repudiation of the centre-right's CDU/CSU Siamese twins there was no alternative. Yet the political bandwidth from the Greens' 'Fundis' to the neo-cons of the Freie Demokratische Partei (FDP) was a stretch that threatened incoherence. The good news was that Chancellor Olaf Scholz stitched together a coalition agreement steering Europe's path down the democratic road, with the commitment to a bloc of MEPs being elected in future on transnational lists (see below). Yet elsewhere tensions within the coalition were left unresolved. Ambition for action with a bold Green environmental agenda was countered by the FDP holding the coalition hostage with its fiscal red lines; its addiction to austerity is a habit even Merkel's conservatives kicked years ago. The challenges posed by Ukraine to German – and EU – energy supplies played all too easily into a delaying of the green transition. Yet the continuing rise of Green support in Lander elections, as that for the FDP falls, can strengthen their hand.

A second cause for hope is internal to the SPD and more accident than design. German governments are rarely threatened from within their parliamentary caucuses, but this time it just might be different because of the quirks of Germany's proportional representation system. More than half of both the SPD and Green MPs elected in 2021 were new. The left was strengthened, especially in the SPD, and these

new contingent members are less biddable. When the selections for constituencies and the lists took place, the SPD was down at 15 per cent in the polls, meaning they would lose half or more of their fifty-nine constituency seats but pick up seats on the list in partial compensation. The party insiders and factions organised accordingly. The late surge of SPD support confounded all expectations: they gained an additional sixty-two constituency seats with the list members shrinking from ninety-four to eighty-five. Many of these new constituency members, who had no expectation of election on selection, have little to lose when the shine comes off the coalition in rebelling.

The biggest danger was that Scholz, carrying the social democrat burden of the past, would find it all but impossible to lead on security and defence. That Scholz, at a special sitting of the Bundestag less than seventy-two hours after the invasion of the Ukraine, announced €100 billion in extra defence spending and future budgets conforming to NATO's 2 per cent of GDP target was a break with history. Yet this early, bold intervention was swiftly overtaken by events, with Germany slipping from vanguard to rearguard. Even the self-evident logic of common EU procurement did not survive engagement with geopolitics. Berlin havered between Paris and Washington, one moment re-energising the Franco-German Future Combat Air System and then immediately seduced and coerced into buying thirty Lockheed Martin F-35s rather than French Rafales on the grounds that US war planes are cheaper and better. Unless Europe envisages a war with America, France's aircraft are fully capable of doing all the business Europe needs. The necessary imperatives dictating what Europe needs to do to deliver strategic autonomy apparently does not stretch as far as the aircraft industry. The EU's capacity for independent action will never be found while member states' arms procurement prizes frugality over sovereignty and security.

The French connection

The second round of France's 2022 presidential elections – despite nerves brought on by Brexit and Trump – initially seemed to have, in the end, turned out for the best, as the threat of Marine Le Pen on the far right drove – albeit less vigorously than five years earlier – voters to Macron's side for a convincing 59–41 win, following which Le Pen all but indicated her political career was over. It quickly proved a pyrrhic victory. The subsequent National Assembly elections saw France vote Macron down. He lost his overall majority, squeezed between the extremes of left in the robust bloc around Jean-Luc Mélenchon's La France Insoumise, and Le Pen's Rassemblement National, formerly Front National (RN/FN). The gains for Mélenchon's Nouvelle Union Populaire Écologique et Sociale (NUPES) – in which he was joined by Greens, Socialists and Communists – were already factored in from the first round. The shock and awe were reserved for the performance of the RN/FN. For the first time, when the issue was not about the presidency, but rather curbing Macron's arrogance and threat to living standards, hundreds of thousands of left voters either stayed at home or held their noses in the second round and cast their votes for fascist 'lite' over the imperious centre.

This result left Le Pen as leader of the opposition with all the projection and privileges that goes with it. Her eighty-nine seats made the RN/FN the second-largest party after Macron's, with the NUPES bloc collapsing into its constituent parts immediately after the election, Mélenchon left with seventy-two seats, the Socialists twenty-six, Greens twenty-three and the Communists twelve. The quarantine isolating Le Pen – father and daughter – that had stubbornly held until then, was quickly broken by Macron when his party in the National Assembly colluded with the RN/FN to elect two of the latter's deputies among six vice-presidents. Despite the party having only eighty-nine seats, the two received 290 and 284 votes, respectively.

The consequence is the National Assembly and the streets will deliver Macron a rocky ride as he attempts to carry through on his threats to extend the retirement age to sixty-five and weaken social protection. Worse, Le Pen's

snatching victory from the jaws of defeat, along with the craven collaboration of the centre, tragically puts her in pole position for 2027, with the smell of Germany in the early 1930s in the air. For the moment, however, tomorrow is another day, and in the interim Macron's domestic disorder may be Europe and foreign policy's gain. Unable to run for a third term, and politically gridlocked in Paris, he may be forced to turn his undoubted ambitions to Brussels. Europe is the field of combat where he holds the high ground and his commitment to European integration can be given its head.

One opportunity will be in following up on the Conference on the Future of Europe, which symbolically delivered its recommendations in Strasbourg on Europe Day (9 May) 2022. Macron has the ability to shepherd this on to a Convention on the Future of the European Union, and then an intergovernmental conference (IGC). The first, like its predecessor in 2002, will, of course, recommend bold steps in the direction of ever-closer union, with the IGC then doctoring and diluting its adventure down to a draft palatable to the lowest common denominator of member states. Yet the exceptional times we live in will stay the IGC's ability to disavow the necessary for the status quo. Treaty change will likely be attempted, even if Lisbon still contains unused scope for innovation. The decision on Ukraine – and Moldova – makes it scarcely conceivable to contemplate enlargement without reform. Some changes will be smuggled through the treaties' back doors via the passerelle clauses, where specific minor changes can be made by unanimity without any messy need for ratification at member-state level. But few would see even audacious incrementalism carrying Europe far enough along the road less travelled. At minimum – over some resistance – European foreign and defence policy will receive a boost with elements under the command of QMV, while the precedent set with Eurobonds will be freshly exercised for Ukraine, turning 'unprecedented' into practice. The last Convention was chaired by former French president Valery Giscard D'Estaing. This time around, the obvious candidate would be Angela Merkel.

The Council will sign off on transnational lists for the EP elections, a move that does not require treaty change. Their parsimony in limiting the number of MEPs elected at large to twenty-eight will backfire. Making the European-wide list so exclusive can only cement the *Spitzenkandidat* system into the EU's political architecture, with the inevitability that the lead candidates on each European party list will be their standard bearers competing for the post of Commission President. Still a beauty contest, but now played out on a continental stage. If the 2019 European election results were replicated, the EPP would get six or seven seats, the S&D five or six and Renew Europe (Liberal) four. This means that these candidates, selected at European party congresses or even by primaries among party members, will need to cover the twenty-seven member states, and those in electable positions – at least – will inevitably be senior national and party figures. In the EP, these will be their political group's leadership cohort, while others will be their country's nominee for Commissioner. This will begin the process of transforming European elections from largely inconsequential mid-term referenda on unpopular governments into signposts to the future direction of Europe and the midwife at the birth of EU polity and civil society. The only question is whether artful member states postpone the inevitable until 2029.

Strategic Compass

Moscow's aggression in Ukraine at the start of 2022 unlocked a door that Josep Borrell – happily released from Britain's brake – pushed open to develop the ends and means of a serious security and defence policy en route to a European Defence Union. Borrell, taking the European Council with him, is filling the Lisbon Treaty's empty vessel, the Common Foreign, Security and Defence Policy. Alongside, its armed wing, the European Defence Agency (EDA), enabled by the swelling coffers of the European Peace Facility, are debuting in the world of war. The four key aspects of the Strategic Compass (the EU's plan of action for strengthening security and defence policy) are the Rapid Deployment Capacity (RDC), rising defence spending, the countering of hybrid threats, and the Transatlantic Partnership. The RDC will see an upgrading of battlegroups to remove the current limits

to their standby and deployment periods – six and three months, respectively – with accompanying revisions of cost sharing and deployment, and, in addition, an inventorying of member states' land, sea and air forces. The EU Military Committee plans live exercises for 2023 and a cost-sharing facility by 2025. All small beer in comparison to NATO's towering ambitions, but nevertheless an embryonic breakthrough in what can become a capacity for independent initiative.

EU member states will fill strategic gaps, and raise the collaborative military spend from a woeful 11 to a more acceptable 35 per cent. All underpinned by Commission proposals to integrate and strengthen the Union's defence industry, finally making the introduction of the single market to the defence sector that I urged thirty years ago (see Chapter 7). The result is that the previously echoing, empty hallways of barely known EU institutions are now bustling and thronging. The EU has long had the possibility for nine or more member states to engage in enhanced cooperation in areas of mutual interest in the absence of unanimity in Council. Here the EU has had like-minded nations working to consolidate divorce law, the property regimes for international couples and the creation of a financial transaction tax (see Chapter 9).[4] This more recently was extended to cover defence matters. Here within the European External Actions Service, the EU now has Permanent Structured Cooperation in Defence, administered by the European Union Military Staff and the EDA. Yet there is a prospect that enhanced cooperation may be almost over before it began, as Finland and Sweden sign up for NATO and even the circumspect Denmark sees its citizens overwhelmingly vote to end their opt-out from the EU's Common Foreign, Security and Defence Policy.

Beyond Europe

Washington won the Cold War in the West, but not the East. Military Keynesianism was the master stroke that drove economic growth in America and the collapse of the Soviet Empire in Eurasia. The Soviet Union was pushed into an arms race that simultaneously underpinned and strengthened the

US economy while it sucked the life out of the Soviet civilian sector, driving the population to drink, despair and indifference. This hollowing out ultimately proved fatal to Moscow as its colonies dropped like autumn leaves with the first breath of winter. But the US's win in the West saw it overlook the sleeping giant in the East.

Powers grow from the bottom up. Industry is the foundation for economic and financial strength that begets political domination and military hegemony, as they seamlessly cascade down from one to another. They rot the same way, collapsing like dominoes in order.

China not only survived the madness of Mao, but under Deng Xiaoping's dictum, 'hide your capabilities, bide your time', hid for a long quarter century in plain sight, avoiding becoming the shambling and stunted economic creature US policy created of the Soviet Union. Two generations on, Beijing's industrial muscle threatens to choke American global economic hegemony and begins to challenge its military muscle. The situation is made all the worse with the US a flawed and failing dysfunctional democracy in danger of foundering into authoritarianism, after billion-dollar elections produce mercenary Congresses in hock to foibled wealth and a legal system with law more partisan weapon than protection, all of this acted out to Republican loud and lying disavowals of reality. For the latter it is not truth that matters, only victory. This damaged colossus sees itself engaged in a life-and-death struggle to preserve the global mastery it has wielded for a short century. With wasting strength, it presses its friends into joint enterprise. Normally, such transitions are soaked in blood. The last alternation between 'Great Powers' – exceptionally – passed off peacefully as the British Empire was put down and American imperialism grew of age. Britain stepped to subaltern from sovereign. But this was the Anglo-Saxon clan in a court squabble. The US–China passage, on the other hand, is between civilisations. Here 'yellow' racism intermixed with an outdated 'better dead than red' ignorance and intolerance will colour the future pejorative 'orange'. Anyone with doubts should read Matt Pottinger, Trump's deputy national security adviser, in *Foreign Policy*.[5]

As written above, US domestic politics has seen a chasm open up between Republicans and Democrats; compromise and consensus have been abandoned in the collapse into internecine civil war with all bridges dismantled or burnt. The first are wallowing in bile, conspiracy and racism while the second are beset by ineptitude, irresolution and impotence. Yet, alone in battling Beijing – and now Moscow – the two march in lock-step. For the Republicans, China-bashing opens doors to the disgruntled white working class. While Biden has – sometimes mistakenly – stepped away from Trump on everything, China is the hapless exception. Here, the Trump game plan remains fully in play as Biden dances to his predecessors' tune.

Trump's defeat by Biden came as a blessed relief to Europe, but it's not clear whether Biden is pause or countermand, signal or noise. Biden's first voice confirming the death of austerity, with Keynesian infrastructure spending and a step-change to better levels of social spending, was cause for hope. Yet the realpolitik of Congress argues delivery will be long delayed on all save the first, and even here Washington is playing catch-up with the EU rather than forging ahead. The cuckoos – Joe Manchin and Kyrsten Sinema – in the Democratic nest have tossed out the core of Biden's proposals, leaving little behind. The mid-term elections in November 2022 will make that denial irrevocable and further relief inconceivable.

China was seen casting its lengthening shadow over the US economy under Obama with his consequent 'pivot to Asia.' This was the start of a full-spectrum redeployment of US economic, political and military assets to coerce, confront and confound Beijing. Under Trump, Pottinger and others persuaded the President to accelerate into the coming crash. Pacific Command became Indo-Pacific Command, while the Quad – a new alliance with an armed wing comprising the US, India, Japan and Australia – became the waiting-to-be-born NATO in Asia. Under Biden, from autumn 2021 there was an additional praetorian guard in AUKUS, the trilateral security pact between Australia, the UK and the US. In April 2021 the trio moved into joint research and acquisition of nuclear-capable hypersonic missiles that travel at five to fifteen times the speed of sound, representing a new phase in the nuclear arms race. Even Anthony Albanese's Labor Party's final victory in Australia, at the fourth time of asking, has offered no respite apart from a sideways swipe with an olive branch in the direction of Paris.

The Quad is en route to Quad+, while NATO in Asia was born in all but name at NATO's Madrid Summit in June 2022 by presence and policy. The prime ministers of Japan, Australia and New Zealand were in attendance along with the president of South Korea. NATO consummated the opening of a second front in Asia with a closing statement to contain and confront China, which also nodded malignly in the direction of Pyongyang. President Yoon Seok-youl, in bending the knee to NATO, has guaranteed China's total antipathy to Korean unification. NATO troops on the Yalu River will be as welcome to Beijing as the prospect of Ukrainian membership of NATO is to Moscow. Apparently, China is a challenge to NATO's 'interests and security'. It is always wise to get your retaliation in first; after all, Beijing might legitimately ask which of NATO's interests in the North Atlantic it is interfering with, while the organisation has clearly invaded the space where Beijing's interests and security lie.

Despite everything, Yoon, the conservative who took office in spring 2022, is eager both to take the Quad's shilling and consolidate cooperation with NATO with a new Republic of Korea Office in Brussels as an edge against over-dependence on Washington. Seoul continues to offer out-relief to the US military-industrial complex with a record 10 per cent increase in its defence budget, which has the South's military spending soaring up and above North Korea's total GDP. Yet Yoon is torn between pandering to Washington's desire for Seoul to add a blue water navy to its military assets, in the form of the aircraft carrier agreed by the previous administration, or maintaining full focus on Pyongyang as a precaution against America's next president collapsing extended deterrence and leaving Seoul to their own devices. All of this only forces forwards Pyongyang's nuclear and missile programmes. Having comprehensively lost the conventional arms by the nineties and currently outspent by a factor of sixty with the combined military budgets of Washington, Tokyo and Seoul, it was inevitable that the North's five-year self-inflicted moratorium on intercontinental ballistic missiles

(ICBM) and nuclear testing would draw to a close. The first ICBM launch was the month after Yoon's election. Few believe that renewed nuclear weapons testing will not follow.

The EU could have stood on the side lines, but Putin's desperate adventurism has pulled them part in/part out of NATO into the ruck. They had no dog in the fight with Beijing, but Moscow extended the field of battle. The EU has been pressed, not very reluctantly, to serve on the front line against Moscow and was quickly listed auxiliary in the Indo-Pacific encirclement of Beijing. The US led others into battle with no intention of diverting major resources to Eastern Europe, despite Washington escalation of the West's war aims in Ukraine from Russian withdrawal to retreat and then defeat. They will only find encouragement as Europe pays a heavy price and the cash registers of the US military-industrial complex chime with EU member states buying 'almost' state-of-the-art weaponry to arm and re-arm their national forces while they offload previous-generation equipment on Kyiv. Brussels will bear the brunt of the war's collateral damage along with the hungry in Africa and the Middle East. NATO's American leadership is there more to check than contribute. Europe is to do the heavy lifting under US command and control. At the same time, Brussels is under relentless pressure from Washington, as economic self-interest covered in a veneer of principle is brought into play to: change its terms of trade with Beijing; continue to subvert its 'One China' policy and court Taiwan; and sanction Beijing for its undoubted human rights abuses that go unremarked among the US's subordinate dictatorships in Saudi Arabia and elsewhere.

Progressing Europe

In a global world the battle for a progressive society requires the right level of full-spectrum integration to be winnable. The small and medium-sized nation state is not enough, if it ever was, and languishes as prey not player. Their leverage is too small to move the world. The necessary – but far from sufficient – condition is to be a global player in your own right, like the US and China, or be part of a wider whole like the EU. This is the only ground on which the battle can be fought and won. There is no guarantee of victory even here, but defeat is sure and certain for part players, even those that past history has washed up as permanent members of the UN Security Council.

During my tenure as an MEP, the EU went through one name change and three treaty changes with Maastricht, Amsterdam and Lisbon, augmenting power and responsibility. Of course, these changes were all ground through the mill of the parliament's plenary, a pillar of the Union dismissed by those hostile to the enterprise as mere talking shop. Back in 1984 – when I was first elected – this had a degree of truth. Yet even then the first battles to reshape and enhance the power of the parliament had been joined. This struggle has continued for forty years and more, making steady incremental progress absent the support and often with the active sabotage of those individuals most disparaging of the parliament. Consequently, by the time the electorate gave me my marching orders in 2009, the strength and influence of the EP within the Union was palpable and it has continued to grow.

As a practical demonstration, one consequence of the ratification of the Lisbon Treaty was to invest the EP's INTA with as much, if not more, power over trade policy than that exercised by the US Senate. Initially, many were unknowing and some unwilling. After dipping their toes in the water with the Anti-Counterfeiting Trade Agreement (ACTA; see below), they were swimming. By 2021 INTA had sunk both China's delayed gratification in the form of market economy status (MES) and the EU–China Comprehensive Agreement on Investment (CAI).

I was a member of REX – the precursor of INTA – in my first term as an MEP. At that time we produced opinions that scarcely troubled the Commission, let alone Council. When I returned twenty years on for what proved to be my last term, it was REX that was scarcely recognisable in INTA. In Autumn 2008 Cathy Ashton was parachuted into the Commission to replace Peter Mandelson as Trade Commissioner after Gordon Brown headhunted him in a last-ditch attempt to save the floundering government he was largely responsible for scuttling. Ashton got the call because she was a member of the House of Lords, with Gordon petrified he would

lose any by-election triggered by nominating a senior MP (see Chapter 7).

In autumn 2008 Ashton faced her confirmation hearing in INTA. In exchange for its endorsement, the self-confident committee forced her into anticipating the ratification of Lisbon by agreeing to withdraw any EU trade deal that INTA voted down, thus giving the EP a premature veto. As already noted, few outside - or even some inside - the parliament appreciated the gift that they had been given. Daniel Caspary, the EPP coordinator on INTA, was an exception. He was aware of exactly what new power the EP had acquired and worried it had fallen into unsafe hands. He initially shied away from fully exercising the new levers of power. When I proposed we take these 'out for a spin' using Rule 114 (4) to pre-empt the negotiations on future trade deals, he baulked.[6] His concern was that parliament would use its new power without responsibility. Yet there was no way back and Caspary learned to love it in the next and subsequent parliaments. Nevertheless, he had a point, as can be seen from the EP's China syndrome below. Nevertheless far better to make capricious decisions in open democratic debate than entrust them to behind-closed-door Council or Commission cabals.

Ashton was to go on - in December 2009, post-Lisbon - to become the EU's first Foreign Minister, formally the High Representative for CFSP. In a pre-meeting of Socialist prime ministers on the European Council, Brown offered them the pick of Peter Mandelson, Geoff Hoon or Ashton. She was unfairly criticised later as over-cautious and ineffectual. That was not her fault - she'd been chosen for exactly those qualities. Member state capitals, even Socialist ones, were as yet unpersuaded of foreign policy becoming the purview of Brussels. If it had to be done at all, 'twas best done badly. That attitude shifted in the last decade and has largely vanished with each new High Representative a step change better than the last. Ashton did play an important role in the negotiations with Iran that led to the signing of the Joint Comprehensive Plan of Action, even if it was her successor, Federica Mogherini, who carried the deal over the line.

The China syndrome

INTA's first scalp, when exercising of its new powers, was ACTA. When the agreement came into the public domain at the beginning of 2012, it was presented as establishing an international legal framework to protect copyright and generic medicines while allowing a clampdown on counterfeit goods. The interests of producers took pride of place over those of consumers in the text, with organisations like the Motion Picture Association of America having the ink stains to prove it. The first public protests were in Poland in January as civil society and NGOs protested the threat to freedom of expression. In February there were simultaneous protests across two hundred European cities. INTA had to follow the procedures, but in responding to Europe-wide rejection of ACTA and all it represented, there was the perfect opportunity for the EP to demonstrate its new power as the democratic pillar in the EU's political architecture. In July 2012 the rapporteur, David Martin, said of ACTA that its 'intended benefits are far outweighed by the potential threat to civil liberties'.[7] The EP saw ratification refused by 478 to 39 with 165 abstentions.

INTA waited for the next parliament before stretching its mandate to salt trade with geopolitics. In 2001 China had been carelessly promised MES fifteen years after its accession to the WTO by Western politicians who believed thinking past the next election was foresight, and beyond far-sight. In 2014 Beijing was just waiting for the second shoe to drop. Yet the granting of MES would disarm the EU. Its heavy trade defence weaponry in disputes and anti-dumping cases were unavailable to be deployed against countries with MES. Even so, Brussels' argument that China didn't meet the criteria was specious – there were no criteria laid down in 2001, only the smooth ticking of time's clock.

Yet Lisbon had changed the rules of Europe's trade game. I warned Chinese friends – including Yang Yanyi, then Chinese ambassador to the EU – of the consequences. Beijing huddled in disbelief, which was only broken when they were presented with Trade Commissioner Karel De Gucht's answer to a parliamentary question, confirming post-Lisbon that the EP would have the last word, and could break the 2001 promise. Of the EU's three institutions, the EP has perennially been

the most Sinosceptic when it hasn't been positively hostile. The reason is a conjuncture of different, but overlapping, constituencies. First, Taiwan has long assiduously courted MEPs with solace and sympathy, and for the more worldly largesse. Certainly, there was a standard offer while I was an MEP: first class air fare, five days in a five-star hotel and bringing a friend. Second, there was among Europe's Catholics a residual anti-communism collectivism that was resurrected and bolstered with EU membership for the countries of the former Soviet Empire, even if one suspects that if Karl Marx miraculously returned, he would see China more as ripe for revolution rather than its apotheosis. Third, there is the EP human rights lobby. Each of these separately lack the weight to shape policy, but in concert and collusion are capable of moving mountains.

Furious lobbying by those opposed to granting China MES soon made it clear to the Commission that they were on a road to nowhere. In May 2016, even before the issue was formally referred to the EP, the weight of industry, trade union and stakeholder pressure saw the parliament overwhelmingly carry an indicative vote against. The Commission read the writing on the wall, and in July sidestepped its commitment by essentially abandoning the very notion of MES in favour of a new set of 'country-neutral' measures that allowed Brussels to investigate State support and subsidies to domestic industry in the export sector. All were to be equal before the law. It was pure happenstance that China was to be the only country to face investigation. Few anticipated any early inquiry into Washington's ruse of using the military budget to subsidise the development of dual-use hi-tech products and processes favouring America's civil industry. Beijing took the EU to the WTO, but three years later quietly let the matter lapse.

If the resistance to granting MES was at its core a trade issue, the same was not true at the second time of asking when Beijing was in the dock again – it was more wanton with geopolitics riding trade. After seven years of negotiations, in the last days of December 2020 Brussels and Beijing signed off on their CAI. This would improve market access for EU companies and impose state-to-state dispute settlement where there were problems. As a trade deal, it was good news, giving the EU much, if not more, of what Washington already had. But the timing was all wrong. The transatlantic tendency joined the mobilisation. After an isolationist Trump had been swept aside in November's election by Atlanticist Biden, they spun the accord with Beijing as a serious snub to the incoming administration in Washington. China's human rights record in Xinjiang and Hong Kong was the icing on the cake.

Led by the EP's Taiwan Friendship Group and a hostile cabal of MEPs, an EP section of the Inter-Parliamentary Alliance on China was established. Some German MEPs acted more as if they were representatives of America's rust belt than of a country whose automobile workers' biggest customer is Beijing. Determined to cut off the branch they were sitting on, they successfully pressed the Council to impose sanctions on elected and high officials and organisations involved in the Xinjiang abuses. Beijing retaliated, sanctioning among others a group of these self-same MEPs. In an ironic twist, one of these was Reinhard Bütikofer, a German Green and former Maoist. Immediately after I lost my seat, he was involved with the German EPP MEP Elmer Brok and myself in forming and running what could be described as a China Friendship Group in the EP. In 2019 he was told by the Greens it would be his last term. Beijing sanctioning him was a gift that would keep on giving with a born-again political future rising phoenix-like from the ashes.

The EP has been spurred into not only demanding that China pre-fulfil its promises in the CAI on ratifying International Labour Organization conventions and ending forced labour, which as of May 2022 it is apparently doing, but in July the EP further qualified its position saying it would not ever consider the CAI before the sanctions against the MEPs be unilaterally lifted. Beijing is willing to talk, but it takes two to tango. There is movement on the first, but the second has killed any chance of the CAI being ratified by the EP before the 2024 elections. Even if in a fit of magnanimity Beijing lifted the sanctions, any chance of the EP endorsing the CAI is vanishingly small. In the current climate the prospect for movement even in the next parliament looks dubious.

With this, Washington wins twice. Its companies trade on more advantageous terms than the EU's with China, and Europe becomes camp followers if not yet combatants in the Second Cold War, undermining its single most important

trading relationship, which is worth well over €700 billion. Yet for all that I applaud INTA and the parliament using the tools and weapons Lisbon put at its disposal to impose democratic elements on EU decision-making, EU citizens must ask for more. I favour further strengthening of parliament's prerogatives. My choices would have been different and I would today echo Caspary's concerns (see above), reminding MEPs that with great power comes great responsibility.

History's trajectory

China is too big and too ugly to be ignored. The EU's 2019 China Strategy, labelling it as simultaneously partner, competitor and rival, pitched it right. A Second Cold War serves Europe badly. The European Union – and the United Kingdom – need an Indo-Pacific strategy, but one that is not cut and pasted from the Trump–Biden playbook. An independent EU security and defence policy is long overdue. But the EU needs that policy to be different, not the same – we need to fight our own battles, not Washington's, looking to our interests not theirs. Lean West, but don't fall into America's lap. As it is, Brussels's ostensive collusion in Washington's China crusade may provide the cause and cloak under which the EU finds the liberty and space to rearrange, repurpose and raise its military spending to achieve the very autonomy the US has guarded against. The delivery of its promises to Washington on enhanced military spending, and integrated European defence production and procurement will, over time, give the EU the wherewithal, the structures and the ability to stand alone in a manner impossible today. Neither will it harm Europe's economy to get its own boost from military Keynesianism; this will be especially potent if 'Buy European' forms part of the package.

Back in London there has been a creeping Tory collaboration with Washington's Asian ambitions back to Trump and earlier. This collusion has gone unnoticed, or at least unremarked, by Labour. In November 2016, Operation Invincible saw a squadron of RAF Typhoons form part of a US–South Korean 'decapitation' exercise on the Korean

peninsula, followed by US, UK and Japanese special forces joining together in Operation Vambrace Warrior, which saw a seaboard raid launched to 'capture' the moribund Trawsfynydd nuclear power station, which coincidentally is of the same design as North Korea's Yongbyon plant. Where Theresa May walked, Boris Johnson ran. The maiden deployment of the UK's new aircraft carrier, HMS *Queen Elizabeth*, saw a traverse of the disputed South China Sea and sequential joint exercises with India, the US and South Korea, and Japan. China, meanwhile, is chided for its failures to adhere to a Law of the Sea treaty that Washington has obdurately refused to sign. Britain's Asian adventurism and provocations looked all the more misdirected in the wake of Ukraine.

While Johnson joyfully embraced Washington's confrontation with China, Brussels is more circumspect and steps with caution. They have seen where blindly following Washington can lead, whether it's the killing fields of Iraq or the flight from Afghanistan. That ability to stand aside requires autonomy with Brussels looking to its own capabilities rather than capacities – collectively EU member states are the world's number-two military spender; they just spend the funds criminally badly. During Yugoslavia's interlocking civil wars we lacked the ability to independently intervene in our near abroad. Bush the Younger put Brussels on notice when he said that if he had been president at the time, the US would not have intervened. It was criminal back then, but now after Ukraine it would be unconscionable.

For the US, every problem is a nail, and it brings its own hammer. In the Trump era it was only common sense to avoid relying on American muscle memory and thus develop the capacity for independent action. If this is best done initially under the umbrella of an increasingly EU-flavoured NATO, so be it. Washington wants Europe on tap, not on top. The very idea that the EU might at some point slip its leash is an American anathema. Eastern Europe is not there yet, while the West is prepared to take some risks before its time comes. Nevertheless the studiously unremarked absence of the promised

EU–NATO Joint Statement at the Madrid Summit showed Brussels' willingness not to allow itself to be cowed entirely in taking the lead from a belligerent Washington.

Europe's job is to manage and balance its relationship between a diminished US and a rising China. There is little question that history, language and links see Brussels closer to Washington than Beijing. That makes perfect sense. But the danger is that elective affinities become effective subordination. This is both wrong in general and particular. While EU interests are similar, they are far from identical to those of the US. Washington must not be allowed control of the agenda.

The pandemic provided the best reasons for the EU to look mitigating its dependency on Beijing - and others - by increasing its own autonomy. But as Seoul discovered the optimum way is a smooth passage of seperation that does not tear the fabric of the relationship. The heavy cost to Britain of its brutal Brexit is all too obvious for those that have eyes to see. Brussels must learn the right lessons from the experience. A precipitate exit from the world's biggest trading relationship between Beijing and Brussels will also have a high cost that combined with the nexus of inflation, Covid recovery and Ukraine's arming and rehabilitation threaten to, unnecessarily, push the EU and the world into recession or worse depression.

For decades while I served in the EP, whenever the EU talked trade with Japan, we beat Tokyo up about the closed nature of its rice market – important for Washington, yet of vanishing insignificance for Europe. Loud protestations of unity do serve to mask the sounds of cracking behind the scenes. The EU is split between old and new, West and East. The former countries of the Soviet Empire are wary of Moscow and on the rebound look to Washington as minder and mentor. For them the EU is prized for prosperity, not security. Old Europe has the self-assurance to imagine it could stand alone.

Wither Britain – Remain was right

Where is Britain now? Having no sense of direction, we've ended up driving ourselves into a cul-de-sac. There is no way forward, yet little or no space to turn around. Covid and Ukraine were timely strokes of good fortune for Johnson. All of the dire downsides of Brexit, with the consequent impediments to the free movement of goods, shortages in the labour market and rising prices, found convenient excuses as the products of pathology and pugnaciousness. Yet Johnson was all too well aware that at some point some would declare he had no clothes, but that did not stop him preparing the ground for his party with a Procrustean approach to cut the people to fit Tory politics, winnowing and sifting the electorate by gerrymandering boundaries and impeding both voter registration and the ability to vote. Here the Conservatives have form. Dame Shirley Porter was the Tory trailblazer of sustained and extensive electoral manipulation in the Borough of Westminster in the late 1980s and early 1990s. In 1991, almost on the eve of her conviction by the District Auditor for electoral fraud, she was made a dame by John Major for 'services to local government'. You could not make it up. She escaped prison by fleeing to seek sanctuary in Israel. Yet what Porter did behind closed doors is now hidden in plain sight in the Commons and Lords.

The purported imperative to act on now, as with America's Republicans, is to combat a wave of electoral fraud. In half a century in politics I know of only one case (see Chapter 3). In 2019, out of 595 cases of alleged electoral fraud, there were four convictions, a rate on par with the annual death toll from lightning strikes, on which there is a strangely conspicuous absence of government intervention despite the fatalities. To stop this ostensible 'crime wave', voters will need to produce photographic proof of identity. Of course, every Muslim woman of eighteen has a passport or driving licence in their name!

The language of politics is the language of priorities. I don't disagree with the demands for a higher minimum wage, better and more humane treatment for those who desperately wash up on our shores seeking life and hope, nor with a real levelling up of society by region, race, class and gender. The

same is true of policy towards the EU, climate change and development, where we should be going further and faster. Yet if we allow the Tories to subvert the democratic process, these are all less – much less – achievable. Labour's priority should be the fight to stop democratic decay, but the party's future ability to achieve power will be compromised if the Tories are allowed to stack the electoral deck. Such a campaign, however, is only conspicuous in its absence.

In faith, Remain was right. Leaving the EU will continue to be a blight on Britain as we slip back to being a dank, offshore island bypassed by the future, overshadowed by a growing likelihood of an independent Scotland and united Ireland as the most enduring products of our self-harming, all foreshadowed in recent elections in Scotland and Northern Ireland with the SNP continuing its advance and Sinn Fein surpassing the Democratic Unionists for the first time. Ideally, we would apply again to join the Union, but living in the real world I am disquieted that it might just come to that. For that would require the Brexit settlement to be disastrous rather than merely disadvantageous, calamitous not just costly. It is difficult to wish that on anyone outside of the Tory European Research Group. While there is a lot worse to fear than a slow slide into maudlin mediocrity and the margins, even that comes with cruel consequences and political dangers.

England's political class, including Labour, must escape its myopic obsession with Westminster. There was palpable disappointment among Europe's political mainstream with the outcome of the 2016 referendum. During the whole subsequent painful and protracted amputation, hope remained that the limb might be saved – a moment of madness that time would cure. That hope died when Johnson's political assassins murdered May. They got Brexit done, storming out bad winners, on a false prospectus that continues to unravel in the north of Ireland and Britain's peripheries as Johnson is exiled to the lucrative pages of the *Daily Telegraph* and itinerant dining. Every bad deed has its own rewards.

Join the European Union

The passive acceptance of the result of the deeply flawed 2016 referendum was craven and disquieting. Only a small minority are prepared to fight the lie, yet they harbour their own delusions having lost the plot with glib talk of rejoining. They are in denial, misdirected by wish as father to the thought. Rejoining is not an option. There is no 'back to the future' with a seamless slipping back into our seat at the table, kept warm for us by a Union that had pressed pause, waiting and desperate for reconciliation after Great Britain saw the error of its ways. You don't join the same European Union twice; exit and entry are separate portals. Our Chance card is 'Go to Jail, do not pass Go, do not collect £200' – to be followed, if we apply, with tough, prolonged, full-blown accession negotiations with no prospect of opt-out, rebate or free pass anywhere in sight. For Britain, gradualism died with Brexit. The way of return passes through deep-seated structural transformation.

Yet with misbelief as the price of victory, Keir Starmer has no intention of allowing 'rejoin', or barely even 're-engage', to be words found in the next Labour Party manifesto. He has determined to never enter the promised land. During the Black Death there emerged a Roman Catholic cult, the Flagellants, who flogged themselves with a whip – the discipline – to mortify the flesh. The Inquisition, after the cult were eventually labelled heretics, helped their masochism by burning them at the stake. Post-Covid they have been reborn, but this time within the broad church of the Labour Party, who are now to discipline themselves to the chant of 'Make Brexit Work.' Yet that love that shall not speak its name is endemic within the PLP. In private, among consenting Party members, MPs confess, 'I'm personally in favour of rejoining, but ...' It's all painfully reminiscent of that grisly scene in Mark Twain's incomplete masterpiece *The Mysterious Stranger*, where after the mob has stoned a woman to death, the Devil betrays to the narrator that 90 per cent of the throng were appalled by what they did but were too spineless to do anything. I do make an exception for one voice in Labour's silence, Stella Creasy MP, who as the chair of LME has been loudly proclaiming that nothing should be off the table.

Boris Johnson was for months a dead man walking, as his lies, nepotism and little corruptions were exposed to the full gaze of public and party, with the public seeing him for what he was long before his party followed suit. At the end, few had a good word to say for the personality and conduct, manners and comportment of Britain's worst prime minister since Neville Chamberlain. Johnson proved a truly shabby and shameful human being, who had to be hounded from office. Despite that, there is still a refusal to make the link between policy and personality. The Brexit prospectus was every bit as shoddy and cheapjack as Johnson, its initial victory founded on fraud, and its delivery built on a tissue of lies, fabrications and misdirection. With the Eton mess long gone, I only wish that half the effort that went into playing the man not the ball will be directed at undoing the damage the charlatan con man and his cult perpetrated against our country with their Ponzi politics.

Nevertheless, the only way is forward, for if by some miracle or manoeuvre 'Rejoin' ended up a manifesto pledge, Brussels would be darkly sceptical, incredulous and horrified. They would see vanity Britain imagining itself as the sun in a heliocentric universe around which the EU solar system orbits, unaware of the trust destroyed and the antipathy created by the decade's run of Whitehall farces. For Europe's federalists, Brexit was a blessing. For Britain to return, likely the voters of France, Ireland and other member states would need to hold referenda, and it would be unwise to pre-judge the results. The very prospect of even getting close to that point is far-fetched. In Brussels the UK is already a foreign country as the two career off in very different directions.

Some in Britain see a halfway house and argue the UK should rejoin the single market and customs union. Economically, a serious and sensible move, yet politically impossible for the Tory party as it is presently constituted, even if the odd one, like Bournemouth's Tobias Ellwood, breaks ranks and is prepared to put their head above the parapet with the endorsement of the *Financial Times*. It would be a public acknowledgement of Brexit's failure as that raft of measures passed to deliberately and gratuitously distance ourselves would need to be undone in the face of querulous Leavers and ungrateful Remainers. Even for Labour it would be a hard sell, with Britain forced to follow other people's rules that it would have no part in making; a painful stopover between a rock and a hard place. No return to the top table, only a spectator at the back of the room with responsibility and no power.

The EU we would apply to join would be the Europe that is, not the Europe that was. The rattle of events since the 2016 referendum has made it a different place, and each passing year's changes by design, chance and necessity transfigure it still further. The very idea that bespoke rules would be available for Britain is fantasy. London will be the supplicants, not the sought, in a bull market. After all, if the EU was in such a state of dissolution that it actually needed the UK, the advice would be 'keep well away'. Thus, there will be no question over the requirement to join Schengen, the euro and the Defence Union. Some argue this won't be immediate. That is absolutely right, for first there will be the long process of realigning our laws with the *acquis communautaire*, Brussels' accumulated legislation, as part of the domestic economic and political restructuring required for all new member states. Nevertheless, there will be no hiding the fact this is execution postponed, not pardon. From the off, we will be on an unyielding timetable based on hard promises. This is only the part of the levy Brussels will impose.

Should Britain decide it wanted to rejoin, the EU would not take 'yes' for an answer. To even open negotiations Brussels would likely require an absolute majority of the electorate – or some equivalent measure of support – to demonstrate full-blown citizen consent, as proof this is no temporary electoral swing but instead the consequence of an irreversible transformation of politics, society and the economy. It would be magical if that conversion could be born of hope, but in truth it is far more likely a product of fear and despair with all the social turmoil entailed. Yet, counterintuitively, in some senses it may be easier in the latter case than the former, because we will need political leadership ready to wipe the slate clean; to wash away, dismantle and destroy the accumulated weight of history and start anew. The problem will be the damage and destruction required to get us to that point.

Brussels will almost certainly force us to remodel and renovate our anachronistic political architecture. When we joined the EU in 1973 it was a buyer's market and the Cold

War was in full swing. There was a casualness and indulgence about conditions that didn't survive the Soviet collapse in 1989. The 'Copenhagen criteria' subsequently laid down by the European Council in 1993 had first 'stable institutions guaranteeing democracy'. No member state since the UK voted to join has been allowed into membership other than as a full democracy. Ukraine's fast-track, if Brussels is reckless enough, will not be available to London. After the EU's experience of Hungary and Poland, they will be even less willing to compromise. A House of Lords founded on peers, patronage and purchase has less legitimacy than the pre-2004 Indonesian parliament's topping up its ranks with a military draft. Current utility and historical origins are different subjects.

Across the Atlantic, the game is afoot to rightly label the US – with the Republican minority capture of State legislatures, Senate and Supreme Court – a failed democracy. London's case is different. After all, you can't lose what you never had. The House of Lords has kept radicalism on a perpetual short lead. Nevertheless, under the Tories the bad is becoming worse – far worse. The pathways to change in the UK are being closed off, civil society is being coerced and what's left of the non-house-trained media is cowed. For those that doubt the problem of minority capture here, let them look to the newly constituted immiscible politics of the UK in the post-Blair era. There are redoubts in Scotland and Wales where the Tory writ barely runs, and in England's cities Tory councillors are an endangered species. Yet in all, it is the edicts of Westminster that rule. Brussels is unlikely to buy that.

Decomposition and disintegration

Despite everything, since Labour's crushing defeat in 2019 in England – particularly the north – Tory gains among the disaffected poor have proved distressingly hardy and far from balanced by Labour's metropolitan advances among the educated young. When Hartlepool has a Tory MP and Canterbury a Labour one, politics is doing a headstand. Meanwhile, the twentieth-century political architecture is being destroyed from within. The Tories, under Johnson, seeded the grounds for illiberalism and the peremptory State as they destroyed all remaining respect for politics and politicians of all ilks with their orgies of self-serving greed and amorality, indifference and carelessness. The stench of decomposition and decay pervades Westminster and is not entirely limited to one part of the chamber.

Johnson became a caricature of himself. Yet his defenestration was no solution in itself, for he shaped the party so that the path to fresh leadership untainted by preferment and largesse is choked off.[8] The Tories are exposed as the servants and stewards of oligarchs and the minions of hedge-fund owners, all accompanied by the arrogance of self-entitlement and small corruption. Misconduct tips over into venality and jobbery begets sleaze. Conservative scorched-earth policy is premised on the same ill-begotten assumptions that Labour made about its own heartland votes – that they had nowhere else to go. Nature abhors a vacuum, and so it turned out in Labour's case there was an emergency exit. Red Wall voters did the unimaginable by voting against self-interest as an inchoate cry of rage and despair. They are not wedded to the Tories, but neither are they just visiting, and easily homesick. Many are settlers, and even the sojourners are not returners. Today, increasingly for the electorate it is 'none of the above', while others, having broken the habit, are open to new, uncharted destinations. 'Apres moi, le deluge' is a melody future politics can play.

People – angry, forlorn and ready to lash out – want at best to find hope and at worst explanations. Those destinations are, as yet, not on the departure board. Labour can make an offer of inspiration and expectation. But the elements underpinning such a programme are not to be found in Labour's present policy pronouncements. This will not be a war of position, but a war of manoeuvre. Incremental change is not the currency of future politics in Britain. It will not be building policy like Lego with bricks for all the disparate groups in identity politics, but changing minds by an emotional appeal; not painting by numbers but selling a vision. Economic interests will star centre stage, with identity and culture playing supporting roles. Labour has to offer to rebuild anew from the bottom up, to reconstruct our country on new foundations.

We need to look back beyond Corbyn, Blair and even Wilson, to Attlee to see the task in front of us with the scale and intensity of the transformation required. We are not looking to the past to find policies. They grow from where we are today, rather than deep dives into history. The inescapable is that the push for equality has worked its successes with larger State apparatus, not smaller – strength not weakness. Outside the ranks of the far right and Tory libertarians, can anyone seriously claim that taking on, controlling and house-training the wild global behemoths, like Amazon and Facebook, Google and Uber, is possible in the absence of a strong, large State? There is no surer recipe for decline than isolation or unilateralism in the face of technology and climate, pathogens and migration as these non-State forces sweep over medium-sized nation states.

There is a great deal of talk about the rise of the precariat, a growing section of the working class whose employment and income are insecure. There are real prospects of being out of work, but even in work it's the fiction and fantasy of self-employment and zero-hours contracts that workers live in. Many would support the TUC's push for a four-day week, but not with four days' pay. This precariat class is portrayed as new and unfamiliar, but that's a myth: they represent the historic norm rather than the exception. We just don't connect the inequities and the unfairnesses of the gig economy, driven by smart phones and weak trade unions, with yesterday's hooters from Forest of Dean collieries sounding whether there was work today, and casual dock labourers waiting at the wharfs in London and Liverpool for the daily beauty contests that determined who worked and who didn't. The exception came in the West with that long two-generation period after the Second World War when social democracy at home, communism abroad and technology-driven leaps in productivity allowed the cake to both grow and those cutting it to need and be willing to give labour an unprecedented slice of the spoils. Here is one point of return.

We have to ask questions not written to fit the answers that have already been found wanting, to develop an inventory and hierarchy of needs. A rematch of the Corbyn wars would be a dysfunctional diversion from the task ahead. Yet there are lessons to be learnt. The three elements we need are a new institutional architecture that harvests the rich growth from below, that allows the searchers to find the messages that resonate with both reality and requirement, and an elect to deliver for the many. We need a modern party that has an activist role in policy and not a fan club where loyal masses service the leader – a PLP that is the party in microcosm and not a detached professional honour guard. The first requirement for change that works is understanding. That means bursting the Westminster bubble and looking afresh at the state of the union.

I wouldn't start from here

Attlee's advantage was that Britain had just come out of a long, brutal, bloody war that had touched every family. This had created a broad fellow feeling and willingness to sacrifice that is absent today. This has to be built and directed and it will be far from easy. Thatcher's 'there is no such thing as society' was no throwaway comment, but a manifesto pledge, a forecast of where she was to take Britain. There will be ingrained, die-hard opposition to the reconstruction of social solidarity from the few who have much to lose. The Tory financiers will be the hidden hand of reaction behind the scenes, not fighting on the frontline but utilising mercenaries in their power and employ. As we saw with Jeremy Corbyn, many of these hard guns infest the media and will weaponise any weakness.

Britain can only get to that point with a rolling revolution that sweeps away the social and political anachronisms that have trapped our people for so long. Britain's success in hosting the first industrial revolution allowed us to keep that baggage that others were forced to jettison in the forced march needed to catch up. We never had to make that choice as we long continued to collect the tithes of primacy. That period has ended and a choice lies before us. This new offer has two elements: first, a dynamic renegotiation of our place in Europe, with a second concurrent transformation at home to enable that to be achieved. It will not be quick, however, to sweep away little nationalism in favour of progressive federalism. People are looking for leadership, but that leadership has

to be created, not found. The task is not a headhunt among the PLP and wider to identify the unacknowledged messiah, but rather to create that political hothouse that grows her or him as one of a team of rivals.

There is a real danger in the absence of such a vision that those alienated from society will grasp at straws. If hope fails, hate takes the stage. The disaffected will be shown a mirage and walk towards it. They will accept the claims of the mad, the bad and the sad, whose explanations for their predicament cast the blame on the folk devils, the poor, the strangers and the different. They will march to the beat of authoritarian protectionism and the rhetoric of 'us against them.' Britain saw race riots in Oldham, Bradford and Burnley in the early 2000s. These were signs of what was to come. There is no reason why Britain is immune from its own Trumps and Orbáns, let alone Le Pens and Salvinis and the fascists in lounge suits. It has already seen their pale likeness in Nick Griffin, Nigel Farage and Boris Johnson. Authoritarian populism answers too many of the wrong questions for it not to be part of the agenda. Yet there may be one trauma that could make England arise: the breakup of Britain.

Requiem for the English Empire?

The empire, especially the white Commonwealth, still brings a lump to the throat of the stale, pale and male, but that alternative reality died long ago. Yet there was a hiatus to its decomposition that held the process short of completion. Like Russian dolls, within a greater empire there was a smaller one hiding. The post-war collapse of the British Empire was the first act of a drama whose second seriously kicked off with the Brexit vote and was only spurred by its sullied unreeling. The play was far from finished despite the protracted interval. Act 2 begins: the English Empire that for so long lived in the shadowlands of history is now back in plain sight as the consequent political, economic and cultural strains tear it apart.

Now Brexit presages the last decolonisation. Scotland, Northern Ireland and the Welsh all voted Remain (the narrow majority for Leave in Wales was the arithmetic of England's colonists). Front of house lies Scotland, long resentful of Westminster rule, a country still with a sense of community lost generations ago in London and the South East. Its Scottish National Party has gone from the home of contingent protest votes to the foundation of government, and from nativist traditionalism to social democracy. The 2014 referendum saw 55–45 opt for the status quo as Britain's political establishment wrapped themselves in the Union Jack.

Backward to Europe

Labour sacrificed party for nation, hammering the last nail in its coffin in Scotland; it is unconscionable they could ever challenge the Tories as the party of union. There was a strong left case for remaining in the UK and Europe, but Labour never made it – a class case that pitched the interests of employees against employers, labour versus capital, which would conclude that the best interests of the labour movement were served by staying in both. For Labour supporters, opting for independence from the EU in 2016 would have left Scotland adrift in the North Atlantic with no guarantee Madrid would not abort any attempted rescue.

Four years on, coffled to Britain's other nations, Caledonia has been cruelly dragged from a continental union in the interests of a middling nation state. The very idea that circumstances have not changed sufficiently to warrant a second independence referendum would be farcical if it wasn't so consequential. When the referendum comes, the money will be on leave – and it should be. From an economic and political standpoint, the choice of being an integral part of the EU – one of the world's three largest economic powers – or marooned as a peripheral appendage of 'Singapore on Thames' is not difficult to answer. Apart from the single-currency issue – which should not be understated – negotiations with Brussels for Edinburgh would be simple and quick.

As for Northern Ireland, May and Johnson between them welded the economies of North and South together while simultaneously pulling those across the Irish Sea apart. The surge in North–South trade in many sectors far exceeds any

losses across the Irish sea. Northern unionism was politically sacrificed to 'Get Brexit Done', all at a time when Dublin has demonstrated over abortion, equal marriage and the rest that it is streets ahead of democratic unionism's reactionary instincts. 'Rome rule' holds few fears for the young and progressive today in the North. Now the economic benefits of a united Ireland add their voice. With Sinn Fein in 2022 the largest party in North and South, a Scottish vote for independence would see Dublin trigger the proviso in the Good Friday Agreement for a referendum on a united Ireland and the end of partition. Dublin would have to be very stupid to lose. The preparation of a comprehensive plan for unification with high levels of autonomy for education, policing and local government in the Six Counties would smooth an end to partition. Even better placed than Scotland – as German unification demonstrated – with the Northern Ireland protocol Belfast can slip smoothly back into the EU without negotiations. Wales has always been the laggard; Cardiff will never lead, but it may follow. With Scotland and Northern Ireland gone, England's last settlement may increasingly lack appeal, and there are seven EU member states with smaller populations.

Where do I stand? I accept Scotland, Northern Ireland and Wales have the right to self-determination. In 2014 the progressive vote in Scotland should have unquestionably been cast in favour of union and Union. The 2016 Leave vote changed the balance of benefit. It was both self-harming for the English – and Welsh – and injurious to Scotland and Northern Ireland. Now it's impossible not to counsel progressives in the colonies of the English Empire that their interests will be better served by Brussels than London. Some may self-servingly argue Labour can't win without Scotland. For me it's unclear whether there is any prospect of hearing the distant bugles of the Scottish cavalry coming to rescue English Labour's circled wagons any time soon. Even were it true, do we really expect the periphery to immolate itself for a centre that bears responsibility for their plight? That's seeking self-sacrifice of a heroic order.

It may in fact be the case that the best or only route back to the EU lies through the backroads of Scottish independence and the unfinished business of Irish unification – a broken UK glued back together within the curtilage of the EU; unity through community. Like the Panda's thumb, the proof of evolution after all lies in those adaptations that arise from improbable foundations.[9] As Tom Nairn argued in *The Break-Up of Britain* (1977, revised 1982), it would be the very process of disintegration that would offer respair by finally destroying Britain's feudal state institutions and allowing a new politics and polity to be born from the ashes. The wisest choice might be to embrace the prospect and work to ensure Nairn is proved right.

Endnotes

[1] The 1918 influenza pandemic is known by the misnomer 'Spanish flu' – the first case was in Kansas in March 1918, with outbreaks in France, Germany and the UK before it reached Spain. There were between seventeen and one hundred million deaths among a global population less than 30 per cent of today's. [2] Charles Michel (2022), Speech at the European Council's Versailles Summit, 10 March. [3] Principally Jonas Marvin, 'Brexit from below: nation, race and class', and Gary Howe, 'Brexit from above: British capital and the tensions in global capital accumulation', both *Salvage* 10 (Spring/Summer 2021); alongside *Salvage* 9: 'That hideous strength' (Autumn/Winter 2020). [4] For a period up until the Brexit vote I was charged by John McDonnell, Labour's then Shadow Chancellor, with keeping contact with the teams in the European Commission dealing with these negotiations to enable an incoming Labour government to readily slip in alongside the rest after the general election. It was not to be. [5] Matt Pottinger (2021), 'Beijing's American hustle: how Chinese grand strategy exploits US power', *Foreign Policy*, September/October. [6] Rule 114 (4): At any stage of the negotiations and from the end of the negotiations to the conclusion of the international agreement, Parliament may, on the basis of a report from the committee responsible, drawn up by that committee on its own initiative or after considering any relevant proposal tabled by a political group or Members reaching at least the low threshold, adopt recommendations to the Council, the Commission or the Vice President of the Commission/High Representative of the Union for Foreign Affairs and Security Policy and require them to be taken into account before the conclusion of that agreement. [7] European Parliament (2012), Steps to rejection, 4 July, www.europarl.europa.eu/news/en/press-room/20120217BKG38488/acta-before-the-european-parliament/4/steps-to-rejection (accessed 20 May 2022). [8] The scale of the change from 2019 was revealed by the fate of the reluctant leaver Jeremy Hunt, who was in the final run off against Johnson in the previous Tory leadership contest with the support of 25% of MPs, but in 2022 eliminated in the first ballot with 18 votes and less than 5% of MPs. [9] Stephen Gould (1980), *The Panda's Thumb: More Reflections in Natural History*, New York and London: Norton.

Appendix

Soundtrack

The Clash – Spanish Bombs
The Cream – Politician
Bob Dylan – I Pity the Poor Immigrant[1]
Kina Shoukichi and Champloose – Hana
Laibach – The Sound of Music
Les Rallizes Desnudés – Yodo-Go-A-Go-Go
Reverend and the Makers – The State of Things
Rolling Stones – Sympathy for the Devil
Sex Pistols – God Save the Queen
The Stranglers – No More Heroes
Velvet Underground and Nico – European Son
Frank Zappa (vocals from Captain Beefheart) – Willie the Pimp

Library

The Arabian Nights - Richard Burton version (1880s)
R. G. Collingwood (1946), The Idea of History
Alexander Dumas (1846), The Count of Monte Cristo
Paul Feyerabend (1975), Against Method
Michael Foot (1975), Aneurin Bevan
Stephen J Gould (1989), Wonderful Life
Ismail Kadare (1981), The Palace of Dreams
Thomas Kuhn (1962), The Structure of Scientific Revolutions
Naguib Mahfouz (1956), Palace Walk
George Orwell (1938), Homage to Catalonia
Pramoedya Ananta Toer (1988), The Mute's Soliloquy
Emile Zola (1903), Truth

---

1 Dylan played this as part of his set at the Isle of White Festival on 31 August 1969 which I was trying to listen to while in quarantine on the Afghan/Iran border.

Almost all of my articles are available at: www.glynford.eu

Select bibliography

I made extensive use of European Parliament *Debates* and *Minutes* which are available from the European Parliament's Historical Archives.

Ackroyd, Carol et al (1977), *The Technology of Political Control*, London: Penguin.

Agee, Philip (1987), *On the Run*, New York: Lyle Stuart.

Allison, Graham (2017), *Destined for War: Can America and China Escape Thucydides's Trap*, New York: Houghton Mifflin Harcourt.

Anderson, Paul and Nyta Mann (1997), *Safety First; The Making of New Labour,* London: Granta.

Bell, Andrew (1986), *Against Racism and Fascism in Europe,* Socialist Group in the European Parliament.

Buruma, Ian (1996), 'Fear and loathing in Europe', *New York Review of Books*, 17 October.

Castellina, Luciana (2014), *Discovery of the World; A Political Awakening in the Shadow of Mussolini,* London: Verso.

Clark, Stephen and Julian Priestley (2012), *Europe's Parliament; People, Places, Politics,* London: John Harper.

Desir, Harlem (1985), *Touche Pas a Mon Pote,* Paris: Bernard Grasset.

Desir, Harlem and Glyn Ford (eds.) (2001), *Time for Tobin,* Capital Tax, Fiscal Systems and Globalisation Intergroup.

Foot, Michael (1962), *Aneurin Bevan,* (vol. 1) (vol. 2:1973) London: Faber.

Ford, Glyn (1991), *Fascist Europe: The Rise of Racism and Xenophobia,* London: Pluto Press.

Ford, Glyn (2000), 'The European Parliament and Human Rights on the Internet' in Stephen Hick, Edward F. Halpin and Eric Hoskins (eds), *Human Rights and the Internet,* Stuttgart: MacMillan.

Ford, Glyn (2018), *Talking to North Korea,* London: Pluto Press.

Ford, Glyn, Glenys Kinnock and Arlene McCarthy (eds), (1996), *Changing States; A Labour Agenda for Europe*, London: Mandarin.

Frazier, Robeson Taj (2015), *The East is Black: Cold War China in the Black Radical Imagination*, Duke University Press.

Fumimura, Sho and Ryoichi Ikegami (1990-1995), *Sanctuary*, Tokyo: Shogakukan Inc.

Garcia, Nereo Penalver and Julian Priestley (2015), *The Making of a European President*, London: Palgrave.

Givens, Terri E. and Rhonda Evans Case (2014), *Legislating Equality; The Politics of Antidiscrimination in Europe*, Oxford University Press.

Green, Kenneth, Rod Coombs and Keith Holroyd (1980), *The Effects of Microelectronic Technologies on Employment Prospects: A Case Study of Tameside*, Aldershot: Gower.

Haerlin, Benedikt (1988), 'Biotechnology in Europe', *Science and Public Policy*, December.

Hann, Dave and Steve Tilzey (2003), *No Retreat: The Secret War Between Britain's Anti-Fascists and the Far Right*, Lancashire: Milo Books.

Harris, Geoffrey (1990), *The Dark Side of Europe; The Extreme Right Today*, Edinburgh University Press.

Huntington, Samuel P. (1996), *The Clash of Civilizations and the Remaking of World Order*, New York: Simon & Schuster.

Ichiro, Ozawa (1994), *Blueprint for a New Japan*, Tokyo: Kodansha International.

Jenkins, Robert with Jim Frederick (2008), *The Reluctant Communist: My Desertion, Court Martial, and Forty-Year Imprisonment in North Korea*, Berkeley: University of California Press.

Jones, Hazel J. (1980), *Live Machines: Hired Foreigners and Meiji Japan*, Vancouver: University of British Columbia Press.

Langrish, John et al (1972), *Wealth from Knowledge; A Study of Innovation in Industry*, Stuttgart: Macmillan.

Lawley, Jonathan (2020), *A Road to Extinction: Can Paleolithic Africans Survive in the Andaman Islands?*, London: EnvelopeBooks.

Li, Yuk-sa (ed.) (1972), *The Speeches and Writings of Kim Il Sung*, with a Foreword by Eldridge Cleaver, New York: Grossman.

Lowles Nick and Steve Silver (eds.) (1998), *White Noise: Inside the International Nazi Skinhead Scene*, London: Searchlight.

Mackay, RWG (1940), *Federal Europe: The Case for European Federation*, London: M Joseph.

Maclean, John (1919), *The Coming War with America.*

MacShane, Denis (2015), *Brexit; How Britain will Leave Europe*, London: I.B. Tauris.

MacShane, Denis (2021), *Must Labour Always Lose?*, London: Claret Press.

Makin-Waite, Mike (2021), *On Burnley Road: Class, Race and Politics in a Northern English Town,* London: Lawrence and Wishart.

Nairn, Tom (1972), 'The Left Against Europe', *New Left Review* 75, September/October.

Newens, Arthur Stanley (2013), *In Quest of a Fairer Society; My Life and Politics,* Durham: The Memoir Club.

Ohmae, Kenichi (1985), *Triad Power; The Coming Shape of Global Competition,* New York: The Free Press.

Orwell, George (1941), *The Lion and the Unicorn: Socialism and the English Genius,* London: Secker & Warburg.

Piening, Christopher (1997), *Global Europe; European Union in World Affairs,* Boulder: Lynne Rienner.

Pollack, Anita (2009), *Wreckers or Builders; A History of Labour MEPs 1979-99,* London: John Harper.

Pollack, Anita (2016), *New Labour in Europe: Leadership and Lost Opportunities,* London: John Harper.

Priestley, Julian (2008), *Six Battles that Shaped the European Parliament,* London: John Harper

Priestley, Julian (2010), *European Political Parties: the Missing Link,* Paris: Notre Europe.

Priestley, Julian and Glyn Ford, (2016), *Our Europe, Not Theirs,* London: Lawrence and Wishart.

Remnick, David (2010), *The Bridge: The Life and Rise of Barack Obama,* London: Picador.

Ridley, F.A. and Bob Edwards (1943), *The United Socialist States of Europe,* National Labour Press.

Rose, Hilary, Steven Rose (eds.) (1979), *Ideology Of/In the Natural Sciences* (2 volumes), Massachusetts: Schenkman.

Rovelli, Carlo (2020), *Helgoland,* London: Allen Lane.

Ryutaro, Hashimoto (1994), *Vision of Japan; A Realistic Direction for the 21st Century,* Tokyo: Bestsellers.

Siebenschuh, William R. and Tashi Tsering (2003), *The Struggle for Education in Modern Tibet,* Lampeter: The Edwin Mellen Press.

Thompson, E. P. (ed.) (1987), *Star Wars,* London: Penguin.

Thwaites, Peter (2020), *Waiting for the Workers; A History of the Independent Labour Party 1938-1950,* Gloucester: The Choir Press.

Twitchell, N.H (1999), *The Tribune Group: Factional Conflict in the Labour Party,* Rabbit Publications.

Van Middelaar, Luuk (2013), *The Passage to Europe: How a Continent Became a Union*, Yale University Press.

Van Middelaar, Luke (2019), *Alarums and Excursions: Improvising Politics on the European Stage*, Newcastle upon Tyne: Agenda Publishing.

Vine, David (2009), *Island of Shame: The Secret History of the U.S. Military Base on Diego Garcia*, New Jersey: Princeton University Press.

Woodward, Bob (2018), *Fear: Trump in the White House*, New York: Simon & Schuster.

Wright, Ian (2017), *Coal on the One Hand, Men on the Other: The Forest of Dean Miners' Association and the First World War 1910–1922* (2nd edn), Bristol Radical History Group.

Wright, Ian (2020), *God's Beautiful Sunshine; The 1921 Miners' Lockout in the Forest of Dean*, Bristol Radical History Group.

Wright, Peter with Paul Greengrass, (1987), *Spycatcher; The Candid Autobiography of a Senior Intelligence Officer*, Australia: Heinemann.

Zhang, Lijia (2008), *Socialism is Great!: A Worker's Memoir of the New China*, Atlas & Co.

Index

A

Abe Shinzo *173–175*
academia *65, 80, 93–101, 106, 191*. *See also* education
Afghanistan *217*
Agee, Philip *209*
Albania *135*
Algeria *121*
Almirante, Giorgio *256–257, 274*
Andaman and Nicobar Islands *96*
Anderson, Paul *124, 151*
Anderton, James *90–91*
animal welfare *181–182*
anti-Semitism *256, 259, 262, 278, 284–285, 293, 295*
    IPCAA (Inter-Parliamentary Council Against Antisemitism) *295*
Armed Forces Parliamentary Scheme *217, 229*
arms race. *See* defence
Arndt, Rudi *107, 107–108, 108, 151, 258*
Asahi Shimbun *204–205*
ASEAN (Association of Southeast Asian Nations) *249*
Ashton, Baroness Cathy *250–251, 252, 358–359*
Ashton-under-Lyne *75–77, 80–83, 85, 87, 92, 116–117, 283*
Aung San Suu Kyi *157–158*
austerity *31, 37, 39, 41*
Australia *208, 355*
Austria *280*
Axis of Evil *219*

B

BAC (British Aircraft Corporation) *58–59, 65*
Balfe, Richard *113–114, 130, 139, 152*
Baltic States *136*
Banotti, Mary *91*
Beckett, Margaret *142*
Bella, Ahmed Ben *121–122*
Benn, Tony *32, 122, 125, 292*
Bevan, Aneurin *127, 129*
Bindman, Geoffrey *139, 321*
Blair, Tony *33, 35, 39, 96, 114, 118, 127, 137, 139, 140, 142–147, 151, 160, 218–219, 228, 323, 325, 334*
BLG (British Labour Group). *See* EPLP (European Parliamentary Labour Party)
BNP (British National Party) *275, 288, 289, 290, 297, 298, 323*
Bowe, David *130, 145*

Brown, Gordon *21–22, 26, 33–35, 143, 147–148, 228, 250, 253, 292, 330, 334, 359*
Brussels Labour Group *xv*
Buchan, Janey *107, 112–113, 130*

C

Callaghan, Jim *76*
Cambodia *244–245*
Cameron, David *21, 23, 35, 38, 40, 43, 108*
Canada *208*
Carter, Jimmy *238*
Caspary, Daniel *359*
Castellina, Luciana *131, 152, 286*
Castle, Barbara *105, 107, 110, 137–138, 284, 325*
Catholic Church *30*
censorship *78–81*
centralisation *37*
Chagos Islands *252*
China *ix, 17,* 37, *43, 180–184, 187, 343, 354, 360–366, 381–384. See also* Tibet; *See also* Chapter 10
  Aksai Chin *182*
  cuisine *181*
  Taiwan *357, 361*
Chun Doo-hwan *155*
Churchill, Winston *26, 30, 54, 65*
class *xiii, 16–17, 20, 26, 31, 35–38, 41, 44, 149, 189, 296–297, 373, 376*
Christendom *345*
CLASS (Centre for Labour and Social Studies) *296–297*
Clegg, Nick *326*
Clinton, Hillary *35*
Clynes, J. R. *27*
coal mining *48–49, 52, 54–55, 74*
  1983-84 miners' strike *103, 106, 109–110, 134*
  NCB (National Coal Board) *49*
  NUM (National Union of Mineworkers) *103, 106, 109–110, 127, 194–195*
  pneumoconiosis *49*
Coates, Ken *32, 120–122, 124. See also* Federalist Four
Cockfield, Lord Arthur *115*
Collins, Ken *110, 113, 124, 139*
comfort women *163*
communism *16, 26, 29, 43, 63, 76, 98, 107, 113, 131, 138, 151, 161, 166, 170, 174, 180, 198, 234, 342, 346, 361, 382*
Conservative Party *23, 26, 28, 30–31, 34–39, 41, 44, 46, 49, 70, 75–78, 82–89, 92, 103, 108–109, 112, 114–119, 130, 134, 146, 149, 189, 199, 202, 268, 331, 339, 363, 366–367, 371*
  democratic subversion *366–367*
  European Research Group *xiv, 367*
Corbett, Richard *149–150*
Corbyn, Jeremy *41, 44, 150, 333, 373–374*

Corfu *134*
Cot, Jean-Pierre *124*
Council of the Socialist International *141*
COVID-19 *342–347, 366, 368*
CPGB (Communist Party of Great Britain) *26, 31, 70, 72, 107, 113, 194*
Crawley, Christine *110–112, 135, 151*
Cryer, Bob *108, 113, 127, 204*
currency speculation *330–333*

D

D'Alema, Massimo *132–133, 145*
De Angelis, Marialaura *307, 309*
defence *216–230, 352–353. See also* arms race; *See also* nuclear weapons
- arms conversion *226*
- arms race *202, 353*
- neutrality *222*

defence union *123, 220. See also* Wallerstein, Immanuel
Delors, Jacques *116, 118, 133, 140, 274, 278–279, 285, 301*
democracy *xiii, 19, 21–25, 31, 38–40*
Denmark *42, 184, 222, 321, 335, 353*
Désir, Harlem *257–258, 272, 281, 285–286, 301, 330–333*
Dhillon, Keir *150, 306*
DMZ (demilitarised zone) *162*
Dokdo/Takeshima Islands *157*
DPJ (Democratic Party of Japan) *173, 176–177*
DPRK (Democratic People's Republic of Korea) *142, 159–165, 168, 219, 248, 305, 356–357*
- abductions *162, 170, 173–175*
- American 'defectors' *161–162*
- Juche *160*
- Kim Il Sung University *165*
- prisoners abroad *162–163*
- Rason Special Economic Zone *179*

Dresnok, James *161*

E

East-West Center (Hawai'i) *179*
economics *17, 31, 35–40*
- SPES (Stimulation Plan for Economic Science) *211–212*

education *53, 77, 83–90. See also* academia
- Marling School *53–55*
- university *64–71*

election observation. *See* EU (European Union): EUEOM (European Union Election Observation Mission)
electoral fraud *329, 366*
Emmerson, Stuart *306*
empire *17, 26, 30, 33, 45, 100, 108, 187, 342, 354*

EPLP (European Parliamentary Labour Party) *32, 34, 204, 217, 323*. *See* Chapter 4
  factions *106–114, 137–138*
    Broad Left *108, 110*
    Campaign Group *108, 112–113, 120, 123, 129, 137– 138, 140, 144*
    Federalist Four *120, 122, 124*
    Tribune Group *108, 112, 120, 122, 325*
  influence *138, 141, 150*
  involvement with PLP *125–128*. *See also* Labour Party: Clause IV
  leadership *119, 122–125, 137–142*
  name change *124*
EPP (European People's Party) *108, 133, 182, 201, 208, 352, 359, 362*
EU (European Union) *110, 123, 168, 216, 347–348*. *See also* defence union
  elections
    1984 *32, 199*
    1989 *115, 118–120, 199, 265*
    1994 *132, 142, 144*
    1999 *145, 279, 328, 330, 335*
    2004 *220*
    2009 *148*
      defeat *148*
    2014 *21, 150*
    2019 *21, 24, 352*
    2024 *25, 362*
  Article 7 *280*
  British opt-outs *140, 143, 146, 274, 347*
  CFSP (Common Foreign and Security Policy) *17, 123, 141, 227–228, 344, 359*
  Commission *19–24, 43–44, 116, 120–122, 129, 140, 160, 196–197, 201–211, 225, 234, 254, 259, 264, 269, 274, 276–277, 279, 300–301, 333, 352*
  Council *19, 21, 24–25, 122, 129–130, 140–141, 143, 168, 217, 232, 254, 259, 264, 268, 270, 274, 276–278, 280–281, 286, 295, 300–301, 351, 362*
  EEC (European Economic Community) *18, 32*
    trans-European lists *25*
  EP (European Parliament) *20–25, 29, 43*. *See also* EPLP (European Parliamentary Labour Party); *See also* Socialist Group
    AFET (Foreign Affairs Committee) *217, 217–220*
    Anti-Racism Intergroup *281, 287*
    atmosphere *266*
    Communist Group *29*
    ERT (Energy, Research and Technology Committee) *159, 195–200, 204, 206, 211*
    Group of the European Right *258*
    influence within EU *358*
    INTA (International Trade Committee) *358–360*. *See also* trade
    LIBE (Civil Liberties and Internal Affairs Committee) *279, 323*
    REX (External Economic Relations Committee) *195*

Rules of Procedure Committee *318*
Sinoscepticism *360–363*
STOA (Science and Technology Options Assessment). *See* science: Echelon
EUEOM (European Union Election Observation Mission) *230–247*
EUMC (European Monitoring Centre on Racism and Xenophobia) *277–281*
European political parties *20–21*
ALDE *21–24*
EPP *21–24*
PES *20–24, 33*
European Technological Community *205*
global standing *346*
institutional reform *20*
involvement in Indo-Pacific *357*
president *19*
campaign *23–25*
Spitzenkandidat *21–22, 25, 352*
single currency *34, 123, 140, 146, 334*
single market *17–18, 28, 31–32,* 72–*73, 76, 108, 110–111, 118–120, 123, 143, 146, 220, 369*
Social Charter *See* social union
treaties
1957 Rome *30, 222*
1992 Maastricht 35, *277*
1999 Amsterdam *278*
2007 Lisbon *19, 21, 23, 33, 37, 251, 268, 352*
ratification *23*
widening *136, 344–345*
Eurasia *45*
Europäische Union (resistance group) *27–28*
Europe
community *120*
United States of Europe *26, 29, 43*
European Coal and Steel Community *30*
European Migrants' Forum *274, 277*
Euroscepticism *23, 34, 36, 37, 73, 116–117, 125–126, 129, 132, 137–140, 144, 149, 324, 327*
Evans, Robert *128, 149, 244*
Evrigenis, Dimitrios *262–263, 264*

F

Falconer, Alex *109, 113, 145, 204*
Falklands War *221*
fascism *29, 45, 91, 98, 108–109, 117, 132, 138, 151, 189, 193, 198, 258, 260–266, 282–288, 305, 323, 338, 350. See also* racism; *See* Chapter 8
ANL (Anti Nazi League) *258, 282, 284, 288, 290*
Anti-Fascist Action *293*
federalism *27, 146*
feudalism *31*

financial crisis 2007/8 *148–149, 343, 346*
Fini, Gianfranco *132, 256, 271, 388*
fiscal dumping *23*
Fleet, Ken *121*
Flynn, Padraig *279*
football *50, 118–119, 133, 170–171, 289–293, 303–313*
  French Football Federation *309–313*
Foot, Michael *32, 66, 76, 103, 127*
Fordism *35*
foreign policy *19, 37, 40*
Forest of Dean *xiii, 16, 37, 44, 47, 51, 74, 307, 373*
Fortress Europe *273*
France *22, 27, 29, 40–42, 347, 350–352, 356*
Freemasons *75, 316–317*
free movement *41, 273*
Front National/ Rassemblement National (France) *198, 255–257, 264–265, 267, 272–276*
fugu *181*
Fujita Yukihisa *xii, 173, 178*

G

Gaitskell, Hugh *31, 147*
geology *65*
Germany *23, 25, 28–29, 36, 40, 45, 107, 123, 201, 342, 347, 348–349*
  CDU (Christian Democratic Union of Germany) *25*
  Paris Congress (1949) *32*
  SPD (Social Democratic Party of Germany) *x, 20, 23, 25, 28*
Gibraltar *57, 133–337*
gig economy *36*
Gill, Neena *127, 149–150*
Giscard d'Estaing, Valery *198, 267–269, 275–276*
Glezos, Manolis *197–198*
global united left *167*
Goldsmith, James *321*
Gollnisch, Bruno *256, 268, 271*
Greater Manchester East. *See* MEP (Member of European Parliament)
Greece *42, 133, 135, 198, 264*
  junta *255*
Green, Ken *93, 106*
Green, Pauline *137–138, 142–143*
Greens *113, 131, 199*
Group of the European Right *255–258, 266*
Gulf Wars *216–220, 224*

H

Haensch, Klaus *20, 158*
Haider, Jorg *280–281, 286, 301*
Haiti *246–247*
Härlin, Benedikt *198–200, 214*

Hata Tsutomu *167–168*
Hatoyama Yukio *176–178*
Hazel Grove *114*
Helgoland *194, 214*
Heseltine, Michael *122, 130*
hijackers. *See* Japanese Red Army Faction
Hindley, Michael *112, 130, 137, 145*
Hodgson, Geoff *71, 72*
Holland, Stuart *121*
Hoxha, Enver *134–136*
Huckfield, Les *108–110, 113, 118, 127, 140, 317*
Hughes, Stephen *122, 124, 145*
Hungary *23, 25, 42, 113, 136, 259, 270, 281, 298, 345*
Hwang Jang Yop *160*

I

igognat *139*
ILP (Independent Labour Party) *28, 30, 32, 44, 50, 70–73*
  publications *70–73*
India *182, 185–186. See also* Oldham: Muslim community
  Andaman and Nicobar Islands *185*
Indonesia *230–243*
  2004 tsunami *240*
  Aceh *240–243*
industry *viii, 17, 153, 382. See also* Wallerstein, Immanuel
intergovernmentalism *19*
Iraq *216–220, 223*
  Iraq War *147, 171*
ISK (International Socialist Struggle League) *viii, 28*
Islamophobia *158, 295*
Israel *122, 282*
Italy *26–27, 29, 40, 42, 131–133*
IWC (Institute for Workers' Control) *72, 120*

J

Japan *43–46, 64, 84, 96–102, 105, 120, 123, 151, 153, 157, 159, 162, 164, 166–178, 180–181, 187–188, 195–196, 248, 251, 342. See also* science: HFSP (Human Frontier Science Programme)
  cultural similarities *166*
  electoral system *168–169*
  normalisation *171–173*
  Okinawa *176, 177, 178*
  relations with DPRK *173. See also* DPRK (Democratic People's Republic of Korea): abductions
  Ryukyu Islands *177*
  US marine bases *176–177*
  Yaeyama Islands *178*
Japanese Red Army Faction *162, 168, 170–171*
JCP (Japanese Communist Party) *174*

Jepson, Peter *116*
Johnson, Boris *36, 128–129, 364–369*
Jordan *295*
Joseph, Sir Keith *87*
JSP (Japan Socialist Party) *viii, 98, 105, 159, 166–169, 178*
Juncker, Jean-Claude *22, 43*

K

Kaldor, Mary *201*
Kang Suk Ju *165*
KEDO (Korean Peninsula Energy Development Organization) *159–160*
Kenya *244*
Kim Dae-jung *153–154, 162*
Kim Il Sung *160–161, 165*
Kim Jong Il *156, 160, 173*
Kim Jong Un *164, 308. See also* DPRK (Democratic People's Republic of Korea)
Kina Shoukichi *176*
King, Oona *131, 152*
Kinnock, Glenys *124, 158*
Kinnock, Neil *32–33, 103, 111, 124–126, 127, 132, 137, 142–143, 147, 152, 158, 191, 216, 243, 253*
Kishida Fumio *175*
Klöckner, Michael *198–199*
Kuhn, Thomas *65, 193*

L

Labour Party *i, v–xv, 20–59, 68, 70, 74–77, 80–113, 124–127, 141–143, 150, 289, 323–326, 363, 368, 376, 381, 382–383*
  Ashton-under-Lyne Constituency *75-76, 81*
  Clause IV *144–147, 323*
  Manifesto 1983 *191*
  party conferences *34–35, 53*
    1979 *92*
    1982 *191*
    1991 *124*
    1992 *284*
    1992 European Conference *125*
    1994 *143*
    2007 *148*
  position on Europe *105-108*
  science policy *190*
  Special Conference 1971 *32*
  Stroud Constituency *68, 76*
  Tameside District *81*
LDP (Liberal Democratic Party), Japan *viii, 98, 159, 167–169, 171–177*
Lee-Jay Cho *178–179*
Left Book Club *28*

Lenin, Vladimir *26, 31, 112, 151, 342*
Le Pen, Jean-Marie *27, 198, 255–258, 265–269, 274, 300*
Le Pen, Marine *256, 350–352*
Liberal Democrats *38, 76, 114, 116, 128, 145, 159, 326, 329*
Liverpool *129, 151, 170*
Livingstone, Ken *139, 319*
LME (Labour Movement for Europe) *37–38*
lobbying *201, 317–320, 361*
Lomas, Alf *107, 110–112, 130, 335*
Lucas, Caroline *230, 330*

M

Mackay, Kim *27, 29*
Macron, Emmanuel *25, 345–346, 350–351*
Major, John *130, 133, 146, 147, 229, 274, 366*
Mandela, Nelson *337*
Mandelson, Peter *250*
manga *169, 187*
Maoism *32*
Martin, David *111–113, 124, 128, 138, 140, 142, 151, 228, 360*
Marxism *68, 72, 93, 190*
McDonnell, John *333*
McMahon, Hugh *113, 145*
MEP (Member of European Parliament) *See* Chapter 4
  campaigns *104–106, 114, 119, 149–150, 329*
  eyes on Westminster *126–127*
  reselection *116–118, 145*
Merkel, Angela *22*
migrant labour *85, 185*
Miliband, Ed *33, 38*
Miliband, Ralph *26*
Mitterrand, François *123*
monarchy *31, 77, 107, 133, 134*
Monday Dining Club *131*
Moon Jae-in *156*
Morgan, Eluned *124, 144, 149*
Moriyama Mayumi *169, 170*
Morris, David *111*
Morris, William *194*
Murayama Tomiichi *159, 173*
Mussolini, Benito *29, 381*
Myanmar *158*

N

Nairn, Tom *32, 44, 73, 378*
Nakayama Taro *171*
Napolitano, Giorgio *132*
National Front *91, 283*
nationalism *xv, 26, 27*

NATO (North Atlantic Treaty Organization) *222, 227–230, 344, 347–349, 353–357, 364–365*
NEAEF (North East Asia Economic Forum) *178–179*
The Netherlands *123, 131, 194, 209, 212*
Newens, Stan *108, 110, 112, 145, 180*
Newman, Eddie *106, 108, 145*
New Zealand *208*
NHS *47*
NLP (National Labour Press) *71*
Non-Inscrits *263, 266–267*
Nordmann, Jean-Thomas *266–268, 275–276*
North Korea. *See* DPRK (Democratic People's Republic of Korea)
nuclear power *96, 195, 197, 364*
nuclear weapons *80, 89–90, 108, 117, 159, 164, 173, 218, 226–230, 355–357*
    AWRE (Atomic Weapons Research Establishment) *67–68*
    END (European Nuclear Disarmament) *32*
    SDI (Strategic Defense Initiative) *112, 130, 195, 200–205, 214*
    Trident *228–229*

O

Oddy, Christine *134, 145*
Ohmae Kenichi *123, 173, 205*
Oldham
    Muslim community *85–89, 185–186, 289–293*
    Riots *289–293*
Oldham, Roy *82*
oligarchs *19, 24*
Olympics *313–316*
Orwell, George *29, 32, 44, 46, 70, 189, 380*

P

Paisley, Reverend Ian *218, 271*
Pakistan *185*
Palmer, 'Buzz' and Alice *See* racism: Congressional Black Caucus
Palmer, John *128*
Pandolfi, Filippo *211–212*
Papandreou, Andreas *134*
Park Guen-hye *156*
Patten, Chris *231*
PCI (Partito Comunista Italiano) *113, 131–132*
Pflimlin, Pierre *109, 258, 264*
Piening,Chris *119*
Plumb, Sir Henry *112*
Poland *25, 42*
Pollack, Anita *118, 124, 137, 151–152*
Poniatowski, Michel *198*
Pope John Paul II *198*
POUM (Partido Obrero de Unificación Marxista) *32, 70–71*

Powell, Jonathan *142, 150*
Prescott, John *125, 142, 145*
preventing nuclear apocalypse *163–164*
Priestley, Julian *xi, 19, 43, 118–122, 134, 142, 151, 179, 195, 381–382*
PR (proportional representation) *127, 145*
Purcell, Albert *48*

Q

QMV (qualified majority voting) *ix, 21, 25*

R

racism *89, 117, 140, 150, 172, 192, 193, 208, 245, 354. See* Chapter 8
  1984-85 CoI *258–264*
  1989–90 CoI *264–276*
  1994–95 Kahn committee *276–279*
  Congressional Black Caucus *293–295*
  extra-parliamentary anti-racism *282–288*
  institutional *298*
  Rock Against Racism *292*
RD&D (research, development and demonstration) *123, 192, 204*
R&D (research and development) *120, 140. See also* science
Reagan, Ronald *130, 200, 204*
Reformism *26*
regional list *323*
reports *216*
  1989 European arms exports *222–224*
  1990 racism and xenophobia *266–276*
  1992 supervision of arms exports and industry *224–226*
  1994 disarmament, arms export and non-proliferation *226–228*
  1996 lobbying *319–320*
  2004 Indonesian EOM *239*
  2008 iEPA (interim economic partnership agreement) *251*
Republic of Korea *154–157, 187, 250, 356–357*
Ri Su Yong *164*
Ri Ung Gil *161*
Rose, Steven *190, 260, 284*
Russia *30, 342, 352, 357*

S

Saddam Hussein *218*
Scargill, Arthur *xv, 103–104, 110, 130, 151*
Schmidt, Helmut *29*
Schulz, Martin *22–24*
science *80, 83–85, 94, 100–101, 106, 180–181. See also* technology; *See* Chapter 6; *See also* nuclear weapons
  decision making *190*
  Echelon *206–209*

ESPRIT (European Strategic Programme on Research in Information Technology) *196, 212*
EUREKA *204–206*
Framework Programme *195, 205, 211, 215*
genetic modification *209–211*
HFSP (Human Frontier Science Programme) *195, 204–206*
Islamic science *194, 214*
Ispra (Joint Research Centre) *197*
pure vs applied *191–192*
technology gap *204*
Seal, Barry *112, 114, 130, 139*
Searchlight *270, 277, 288, 301*
sectarianism *138*
Seddon, Mark *xi, 180*
Selmayr, Martin *22*
Shigeru, Nakayama *97, 100*
Simpson, Brian *119, 145*
Sinn Fein *134, 271, 367, 377*
Six-Party Talks *173–175*
skinheads *270*
Skinner, Dennis *125*
Smith, C. A. *28*
Smith, John *33, 137, 147*
Smith, Llew *109, 127, 211*
Snowden, Edward *209*
socialism *xiii, 16, 26–31, 40, 43, 44, 106, 108, 111, 123, 132, 138, 145, 151, 190, 344, 383–384*
Socialist Group *ii, x, xv, 20–21, 29, 91, 107–108, 112, 124, 129–130, 132–137, 139–142, 200, 204, 212, 220, 250, 258–259, 263–268, 272, 280, 287, 300, 318, 352, 381*
1994 PES manifesto *140*
deputy leader *124, 337–338*
travels *184*
Socialist International *141, 167*
Socialist Movement for the United States of Europe *29*
social union *122–128, 146, 273. See also* Europe: community; *See also* Wallerstein, Immanuel
soft power *120. See* Chapter 7
SOS Racisme *258, 272, 284–285, 293, 301*
South Africa *243–244*
South Korea. *See* Republic of Korea
South West *328. See also* Gibraltar
sovereignty *19, 31, 36*
Soviet Union *26, 29, 48, 68, 98, 113, 122, 136, 180, 193, 198, 200, 203, 284, 353*
collapse *226*
Comecon *122*
Red Army *27*
Spain
Ceuta and Melilla *287*
El Ejido *287*

speculation *37*
Spycatcher *291–292*
Stalin, Joseph *26, 30, 31*
Starmer, Keir *368*
Star Wars. *See* nuclear weapons: SDI (Strategic Defense Initiative)
Stephenson, George *139*
Stewart, Ken *108, 110, 129–130, 134, 152*
Straw, Jack *145, 209, 219, 322–324*
Suga Yoshihide *175*
surveillance. *See* science: Echelon
Sylla, Fode *285*

T

Tameside *94, 262–263; See* Chapter 3.
  1979 power shift *78*
  bikers *90*
  Droylsden *329*
  Education Committee *77, 82–83*
    corporal punishment *90*
    free milk *89*
    school closures *86–87*
  Environmental Health and Control Committee *78. See also* censorship
  Hurst East *76, 92*
tangogi *181*
technology *16, 18, 31, 36, 117, 140, 190, 203. See also* science
Teller, Edward *201*
Thae Yong Ho *307–309*
Thatcher, Margaret *31–36, 76–78, 84, 89–93, 103–104, 115–122, 133, 291, 325, 330*
The Sun. *See* Livingstone, Ken
Tibet *182–184*
Timmermans, Frans *24*
Titley, Gary *219–220*
Tobin tax. *See* currency speculation
Tokyo University. *See* academia
Tomlinson, John *110, 112, 137*
Tongue, Carole *120–125, 131–132, 151*
trade *248–252, 358–363*
  countertrade *223, 248*
  negotiations *23*
trade unions *30, 32, 36, 108, 155, 190, 194, 260, 265, 270, 296*
  Amalgamated Union of Engineering Workers *50*
  National Society of Brushmakers *53*
  Rengo (Japanese Trade Union Confederation) *166*
  Transport and General Workers' Union *335*
  TUC (Trades Union Congress) *48–49, 116, 118, 130, 146–147, 284, 373*
  Unite the Union *27, 227*
transparency *23, 316*

Tribune *30, 38, 43–44, 73, 106, 108, 110–112, 127, 144, 148, 151–152, 155, 166, 176, 180, 188, 195, 214, 320, 324, 335*
Trotsky, Leon *26, 31, 43*

U

UK *ii, vi, 17, 19, 26–31, 34, 36–44, 196, 201, 208, 263, 347, 355, 382*
  1974 general election *76*
  1975 European Referendum *35, 76*
  1982 local elections *91–92*
  1983 general election *32, 92*
  1987 general election *114*
  1992 general election *33*
  1997 general election *143*
  2016 referendum *19, 37*
  2019 general election *41*
  breakup *375*
  Brexit *35–42, 342, 365*
    beginnings *322–324*
  England
    electoral nihilism *371–374*
    English exceptionalism *27, 40, 106, 288, 298, 369–370*
    global standing *46*
    little Englandism *118, 123, 147*
  Falklands War *92, 104*
  FCO (Foreign and Commonwealth Office) *219, 306*
  foreign policy *19*
  House of Commons *111, 120, 124–128, 137, 324, 366*
    anti-racism *284*
    expenses scandal *149, 326*
  House of Lords *38, 46, 73, 114, 127, 134, 232, 251, 326, 358, 366, 371*
  Northern Ireland *41, 98, 271, 375–376*
  rejoining the EU *368–371*
  Scotland *39, 41, 128, 131, 367, 375–376*
    2014 referendum *38*
  Socialist Party of Great Britain *109*
  social solidarity *374*
  Union Jack *17*
  Wales *21, 41, 127, 375*
  Westminster *49*
UKIP (United Kingdom Independence Party) *34, 149, 230, 288, 296, 323–324*
Ukraine *246, 342–357, 364–366, 371*
UNCLOS (UN Conference on the Law of the Sea) *96–97*
Unit 731 *180*
University College London *See* education
University of Manchester *See* academia
University of Reading *See* education
USA *17–20, 26–45, 59, 96, 98, 123, 139, 159–220, 282, 342, 354, 362, 381–384. See also* nuclear weapons: SDI (Strategic Defense Initiative); *See* Gulf Wars; *See also* racism: Congressional Black Caucus

Atlanticism *123*
Challenger disaster *201*
coercion *171, 202–203, 357*
Congress *355*
domestic politics *355*
Electoral College *21, 23*
OTA (Office of Technology Assessment). *See* science: Echelon

V

Van Hemeldonck, Marijke *131, 263, 268*
van Middelaar, Luuk *19, 43*
Van Rompuy, Herman *22*
Vanunu, Mordechai *121–122*
VAT *115–116*
von der Leyen, Ursula *25, 345*
von Habsburg, Otto *109, 259*
von Stauffenberg, Frank-Ludwig *259–260*

W

Wallerstein, Immanuel *18, 41, 354*
waterwheels *99–100*
Weber, Manfred *24*
West, Norman *110, 113, 130, 195, 200*
White, Ian *119*
Wilson, Harold *31, 53, 67, 74, 103, 190*
Workers' Party of Korea *See* DPRK (Democratic People's Republic of Korea)
workers' rights *34, 117, 373. See also* Labour Party: Clause IV
WWII *27, 45, 50, 64, 96, 159, 178, 189*
Wynn, Terry *118, 141*

X

xenophobia *See* racism
Xi Jinping *184*

Z

Zhang Lijia *184*
Zhang Zhijun *180, 250*